# THE DAILY NEEDS AND INTERESTS OF OLDER PEOPLE

# THE DAILY NEEDS AND INTERESTS OF OLDER PEOPLE

*Second Printing*

*Compiled and Edited by*

**ADELINE M. HOFFMAN, Ph.D.**

*Professor, Department of Home Economics*
*and*
*Affiliate Staff Member*
*Institute of Gerontology*
*The University of Iowa*
*Iowa City, Iowa*

*With a Foreword by*

**William D. Bechill**

*Commissioner, Administration on Aging*
*United States Department of Health, Education and Welfare*
*Washington, D.C.*

CHARLES C THOMAS · PUBLISHER
***Springfield • Illinois • U.S.A.***

*Published and Distributed Throughout the World by*

CHARLES C THOMAS • PUBLISHER
Bannerstone House
301-327 East Lawrence Avenue, Springfield, Illinois, U.S.A.



ISBN 0-398-00852-3

Library of Congress Catalog Card Number: 75-83836

First Printing, 1970
Second Printing, 1976

*With* THOMAS BOOKS *careful attention is given to all details of manufacturing and design. It is the Publisher's desire to present books that are satisfactory as to their physical qualities and artistic possibilities and appropriate for their particular use.* THOMAS BOOKS *will be true to those laws of quality that assure a good name and good will.*

*Printed in the United States of America*
*R-1*

# CONTRIBUTORS

PATRICIA S. AUGHENBAUGH, B.A.

Research Associate, National Institutes of Health,
Public Health Service, Department of Health, Education,
and Welfare, Washington, D.C.

LEONARD Z. BREEN, Ph.D.

Professor and Chairman, Department of Sociology,
Purdue University, Lafayette, Indiana.

AUSTIN B. CHINN, M.D.

Director, University of Southern California Rehabilitation
and Research Training Center, Los Angeles, California.

DONALD O. COWGILL, Ph.D.

Professor, Department of Sociology,
University of Missouri, Columbia, Missouri.

CARL EISDORFER, M.D., Ph.D.

Associate Professor, Medical Psychology and Psychiatry;
Director of Training, Research Coordinator, Center for
the Study of Aging and Human Development, Duke University,
Durham, North Carolina.

HELEN M. FLINT, Ed.D.

Director, Training and Educational Developments
Division, U. S. Navy Personnel Research
Laboratory, Washington, D. C.

JOE BALES GRABER, M.P.H.

Special Assistant to the Director,
Bureau of Disease Prevention and Environmental Control,
Public Health Service, Department of Health, Education,
and Welfare, Washington, D.C.

ROBERT J. HAVIGHURST, Ph.D.

Professor of Education and Human Development,
Department of Education,
University of Chicago,
Chicago, Illinois.

ADELINE M. HOFFMAN, Ph.D.

Professor, Department of Home Economics;
Affiliate Staff Member, Institute of Gerontology,
University of Iowa, Iowa City, Iowa.

FRANK ITZIN, M.A.

Professor, Jane Addams Graduate School of Social Work,
University of Illinois, Urbana, Illinois.

H. LEE JACOBS, Ph.D.

Associate Professor, Institute of Gerontology,
University of Iowa, Iowa City, Iowa.

JEROME KAPLAN, Ph.D.

Executive Director, Mansfield Memorial Homes, Inc.;
Senior Member and Resident Sociologist,
Department of Sociology, Mansfield Campus,
Ohio State University, Mansfield, Ohio.

DAVID O. MOBERG, Ph.D.

Professor and Chairman, Department of Sociology,
Marquette University, Milwaukee, Wisconsin.

WOODROW W. MORRIS, Ph.D.

Director, Institute of Gerontology;
Associate Dean, College of Medicine,
University of Iowa, Iowa City, Iowa.

WILLIAM E. ORIOL, B.A.

Staff Director, Special Committee on Aging,
United States Senate,
Washington, D.C.

Margaret O. Osborn, Ph.D.

Associate Professor, Department of Home Economics,
University of Iowa, Iowa City, Iowa.

Edith G. Robins, B.A.

Information Officer,
Division of Medical Care Administration,
Public Health Service, Department of Health, Education
and Welfare, Washington, D.C.

Arnold M. Rose, Ph.D.*

Professor, Department of Sociology,
University of Minnesota, Minneapolis, Minnesota.

John R. Schmidhauser, Ph.D.

Professor, Department of Political Science,
University of Iowa, Iowa City, Iowa.

Nathan W. Shock, Ph.D.

Chief, Gerontology Branch, National Heart Intitute
National Institutes of Health, Department of Health,
Education and Welfare, Bethesda, Maryland, and Baltimore
City Hospitals, Baltimore, Maryland.

Anthony V. Sinicropi, Ph.D.

Associate Professor and Associate Director,
Center for Labor and Management, College of Business
Administration, University of Iowa, Iowa City, Iowa.

Neill Solomon, M.D., Ph.D.

Assistant Chief of Medicine, Baltimore City Hospitals;
Associate Professor of Physiology, Assistant Professor of
Medicine, School of Medicine, University of Maryland,
Baltimore, Maryland.

---

* Deceased

Ada Barnett Stough

Program Policy Staff, Administration on Aging,
Social and Rehabilitation Service, Department of Health,
Education and Welfare, Washington, D.C.

Marvin B. Sussman, Ph.D.

Professor and Chairman, Department of Sociology,
Case Western Reserve University, Cleveland, Ohio.

Walter K. Vivrett, M.A.

Professor of Architecture and Planning, School of Architecture;
Project Director, Minnesota Experimental City;
Director of Graduate Studies in Architecture and Planning,
University of Minnesota, Minneapolis, Minnesota.

Frances L. Wilkie, M.A.

Research Associate in Medical Psychology,
Duke University Medical Center, Center for the Study of
Aging and Human Development, Durham, North Carolina.

**To**
**Dorothy Emerson**

# FOREWORD

THIS BOOK can be important for older people because it is designed to encourage increased attention and concern of home economists for various needs of the older individual.

It opens to the home economist the broad field of aging. The authors of individual chapters are all highly dedicated and informed persons in the field with a rich scope of experience. Many of the points of view raised by the individual contributors to this work are provocative and challenging and should help many students to decide upon a specialty in aging within their field.

Dr. Hoffman, a researcher and innovator, has covered in this volume the needs and interests of older people as related to their daily living. For all their diversity and individuality, older people as a group find their calendar years bring certain natural and many man-made restrictions and special problems. Some of the obstacles older people face are based on myth and stereotype; others are very real—increased need for safety measures in the home; hostility or lack of awareness in the marketplace; less money with which to budget; problems of mobility and transportation.

Just finding suitable clothing to buy, or the physical act of getting dressed can be a problem for older people. Preparing a meal safely and adequately can become a marathon of difficulty from shop to stove—often felt not worth the struggle when one lives alone.

Even for the vigorous, healthy, able and independent older person—the great majority, incidentally—age brings complications and restrictions and the need for new knowledge and expert help in finding ways to maintain independence and to cope with daily life. For the frail and the ill, and for those old people who are also poor, the maintaining of a home—even a single room—becomes a battle to be fought daily—a battle in which they need allies.

May I say here to practicing or potential home economists—you could find no more rewarding use of your skills and your insights than in the field of aging. We are grateful to Dr. Hoffman for carrying our message so skillfully and completely to a discipline we look to as an expanding resource now, and in the future.

William D. Bechill

# PREFACE

SOME TEN YEARS AGO, the Inter-university Council on Social Gerontology, comprising sixteen major American Universities, conducted two summer institutes, published three volumes* and a set of five syllabi† covering the field of social gerontology. Through the institutes, about seventy-five college and university teachers in the social sciences were given a thorough grounding in the essentials of social gerontology. The design of the project was concerned primarily with preparing teachers to teach, i.e. to develop and offer new courses in social gerontology at their schools or to include appropriate aspects of social gerontology in already existing courses. Through the books, additional thousands have been informed and social gerontology has been launched on its collegiate course.

It was the hope of some of us who were involved in the planning and implementation of the Inter-university project that the next step would be a similar effort, extending the knowledge of social gerontology to those who would teach and use it in its many *applications* to individuals and groups of aging and aged persons. Thus, it seemed to us, *applied* social gerontology would have been launched so that practitioners could bring their knowledge to bear in their work in social welfare, clinical settings of all kinds, recreational programing, in counseling individuals and families, and in the design

* Three volumes published by the University of Chicago Press in 1959 include *Handbook of Social Gerontology* edited by Clark Tibbitts, *Handbook of Aging and the Individual* edited by James E. Birren, and *Aging in Western Societies* edited by Ernest W. Burgess.

† Copies of these syllabi may be obtained from the Institute for Social Gerontology, University of Michigan, Ann Arbor, Michigan. The set includes No. 1: *A Syllabus and Annotated Bibliography on the Economics of an Aging Population* by Walter H. Franke and Richard C. Wilcock; No. 2: *A Syllabus and Annotated Bibliography on the Psychological Aspects of Aging* by Raymond G. Kuhlen and Woodrow W. Morris; No. 3: *A Syllabus and Annotated Bibliography on the Sociology of Aging and the Aged* by Irving L. Webber and Gordon F. Streib; No. 4: *A Syllabus and Annotated Bibliography on Social Welfare and the Aged* by Gordon J. Aldridge and Fedele F. Fauri; and No. 5: *A Syllabus and Annotated Bibliography on an Interdisciplinary Course in Social Gerontology* by Bernice L. Neugarten, Robert J. Havighurst and Claire F. Ryder.

of meaningful programs in multi-purpose centers and in congregate living arrangements of all types. This hope was never realized and, therefore, the same stimulation to develop and expand the applications of what is known of social gerontology was not given the same boost that was afforded to the social science teachers.

The needs of society in the care and general welfare of the older American have not yet reached their peak. Predictions are that increases in demands on services to the elderly will have a truly phenomenal growth in the next ten to fifteen years. An example from the area of nursing and personal care homes may serve to illustrate this.

With increased *quality* of care there has been and will continue to be an increased demand for care. This, in turn, will mean an ever-increasing number of nursing and personal care homes and, since such institutions will tend to be larger, there will be an increasing number of nursing home beds.

As a consequence of this, there will be a demand for more trained administrators and supporting personnel of all types. One estimate suggests that this demand for administrators and managerial staff will be in the range of between one hundred thousand and almost four hundred thousand by 1980, depending on the staff to dwelling unit ratio used in making the estimate.

Again, if we project the rate of growth in expenditures (they have increased at about 12% per year since 1950) or the growth in bed capacity (11% per year from 1963 to 1967), the resultant estimate is three million beds in 1980 contrasted with some 385,000 in 1967.

The major response to information and projections such as these must be to tool up educational and training programs for all of those professional and other persons who will be needed to supply these demands for services. In Chapter 21, current needs and training programs are presented in some detail.

The present volume will help since it covers very adequately our current knowledge of gerontology and, in addition, provides information concerning most of the applied aspects. Although Dr. Hoffman's original purpose in editing this volume was to provide Home Economists with a source of information for their use, most of what is presented would be equally useful to those many others who come into daily contact with the aging and aged. Thus, I believe nurses of all types, nursing and retirement home staff personnel, health and allied health professions, social workers, counsellors, recreational leaders, community planners, and others would all find the knowledge as useful and practical as will home economists themselves.

Finally, improved services depend on new knowledge, insights, and understanding. These, in turn, depend on research which is, basically, the search for knowledge. The reader's attention is directed especially to Chapter 20 and also to the many other references to the contributions of research and innovation in other chapters. By using the references, the reader may inform himself even further with respect not only to research findings, but also to the methods of research. This is noted here because the clinician and other applied workers can, by their careful, perceptive observations and recording of human behavior make valuable research contributions—just as surely as the laboratory scientist.

WOODROW W. MORRIS, Ph.D.
*Director Institute of Gerontology*
*Associate Dean, College of Medicine*
*University of Iowa, Iowa City, Iowa*

# INTRODUCTION

THIS BOOK is an outgrowth of some years of cooperative work conducted by the Department of Home Economics and the Institute of Gerontology at the University of Iowa. The initial effort, concerned with clothing problems and clothing behavior of older women, resulted in the publication of a comprehensive bibliography in 1962 entitled "The Social Science Aspects of Clothing with Implications for Older Women" and an annotated bibliography in 1964 entitled "Social Science Aspects of Clothing for Older Women." Also in 1964, a workshop was conducted on "Social Gerontology for Home Economists," of which the proceedings were published the following year. The demand for both bibliographies and the workshop proceedings was so much greater than was anticipated, that the supply was exhausted very soon after publication. This suggested the need for literature in the field directed to home economists.

The purpose of this book, then, is to provide for home economists a source of information on the needs and interests of older people which will have application in many home economics courses at both the college and university level and secondary level, also in extension service programs and in the field of social work.

Heretofore, attention has been focused mainly on younger members of the family and on the family at earlier stages in the life cycle, thus disregarding the later years for both individuals and families. However, since the National Workshop on Aging, sponsored by the American Home Economics Association at Purdue University in April, 1962, there has been increased interest and activity among home economists in the field of aging, through committees on aging in the state home economics associations, workshops and seminars conducted by schools of home economics, and research done in a number of aspects of aging. The following statement from the Philosophy of Aging, adopted by the American Home Economics Association, following the workshop, defines the new responsibility which must be assumed by all society concerning aging:

> The current phenomenon of extended later life places new responsibilities upon the individual, the family and all those organizations and agencies that make up the community, to work toward the goal of assuring a satisfying and contributing participation of all individuals in society throughout their lifetime. This requires understanding, and appreciation of the total life span—as well as active support—by all society.

Although this book is directed primarily to home economists, it will be of interest to other professional groups concerned with older people, and to anyone who has a family member, a relative or friend in the category generally referred to as the older people, meaning specifically age 65 and over.

Because gerontology is concerned with so many facets of the lives of older people, this book is multi-authored in order to bring to the reader the knowledge, experience and points of view on aging of distinguished leaders from the social sciences, biological sciences, home economics, and government. Each contributor to the book is well known in his particular field and is a recognized authority. Biographical sketches, which appear at the end of the book, highlight the leadership and special achievement of each contributor.

The first chapter in the book, entitled "The Discipline of Gerontology," provides an excellent introduction for the reader who is unfamiliar with the field of aging and with the term "gerontology," which is of fairly recent origin in the vocabulary of the social sciences. In a number of the chapters, there are references to the increase in the proportion and actual number of older people in the population which has given rise to greater interest in the study of aging and to conducting research. The increase in interest is reflected in the growth of the literature concerned with the subject. In the first bibliography compiled by Nathan W. Shock, for the years from 1900 to 1949, there were 589 pages. In his second bibliography reporting the literature from 1949 to the end of 1955, there were 525 pages, and in his third bibliography from 1956 to 1961, there were 624 pages. The growth in the literature of gerontology is readily seen also in the bibliographies published each month in the *Journal of Gerontology.*

Home economists and others interested in undertaking research in particular aspects of aging may find it advantageous to become familiar with more of the literature of gerontology as suggested at the end of each of the chapters in the book and also in the publications of the Gerontological Society, particularly the *Journal of Gerontology* and the *Gerontologist.*

ADELINE M. HOFFMAN

# ACKNOWLEDGMENTS

THERE ARE MANY SCIENTISTS, educators and government officials who are recognized for their high level of specialization and authority in one or more areas of gerontology, but there are probably none who are sufficiently knowledgeable in all of them to author a volume alone which covers as many areas as *The Daily Needs and Interests of Older People.* Thus, I am greatly indebted to all who have contributed chapters.

I am greatly indebted also to the members of the staff of the Institute of Gerontology at The University of Iowa for their many kinds of assistance during the planning stages and the later work on the manuscript. To Dr. W. W. Morris, Director of the Institute of Gerontology, I am particularly grateful for his initial interest in this undertaking and his counsel, encouragement and suggestions; and to Dr. H. Lee Jacobs, Assistant Professor, Institute of Gerontology, for his suggestions concerning the arrangement and coverage of the book. To Mabel Edwards, editor of *Adding Life to Years,* I am most appreciative for directing me to the literature resources of the Institute.

Also, I acknowledge with thanks the scholarly work of Iva M. Bader as research assistant and later as co-author, which had much to do with establishing the need for this volume.

A.M.H.

# CONTENTS

## Part IV

## Biological Aspects of Aging



## Part V

## Basic Needs of People



## Part VI

## Citizen Responsibility in Social Gerontology

# THE DAILY NEEDS AND INTERESTS OF OLDER PEOPLE

# PART I

# HISTORY AND DEVELOPMENT OF GERONTOLOGY

*Chapter 1*

# THE DISCIPLINE OF GERONTOLOGY

LEONARD Z. BREEN

IN THE RECORDED MEMORY of mankind and in tomorrow morning's newspaper, one finds concerns expressed for the elders of the Society. Such continuing interest is today producing a new area of science, art and practice. This new and growing discipline of gerontology is, in fact, an ancient field of concern, one approached by science, philosophy, art and ideology. Through the ages, moralists, philosophers, and scientists may not have agreed as to the nature of the aging process, or its consequences for the individual, or even the time of its onset, but they all sought to learn something of what old age meant both to the older person and to the society of which he was a part. Throughout the records of history, we find statements of what it means to grow old and what one should do about it. These comments were never intended to be organized, systematic statements of the character and scope of the discipline of gerontology; they were, rather, attempts to bring together custom, belief, and rudimentary knowledge in such a way as to make explicable the nature of the process with which we are here concerned.

## EXPLICATION: ON THE NATURE OF GERONTOLOGY

Gerontology, as an emerging scientific discipline, is certainly no more than three decades old when thought of as a systematic examination of data and logical sets of conclusions concerning the aging process. But, first to set straight a common misunderstanding: gerontology is not geriatrics. In the year 1909, Dr. Ignatz L. Nascher, one of the physicians who early began to work in the field of social medicine, first coined the term "geriatrics." [1] Nascher constructed this word out of the two Greek roots *geronto* (or *geron*) meaning "the old man," and *iatrike,* meaning "surgery, medicine, or the treatment of." Thus we have geriatrics, "the treatment of the old man" (and we presume Nascher meant to include the "old lady" as well). Somewhat later, the word *gerontology* came into use based upon the same root *geronto,* and this time adding *ology* (also Greek), "the study of." Therefore, geriatrics is the medical treatment of older persons while gerontology is the study of older persons and the aging process.

More recently, Clark Tibbitts has brought into use and popularized the term "social gerontology," [2] that aspect of gerontology having a major component of social factors and forces. Within this framework, the sociology of aging has come to take on a significant aspect of gerontology: the study of the social basis of aging. Sociology thus becomes concerned with the social definition of who is thought to be old and how they know that they are old; a matter of age grading of social behavior. Expectations of behavior of older persons, held by the rest of the society, are communicated in a great many ways. Normative aspects of aging then determine much of one's behavior. Social gerontology and the sociology of aging are, as a consequence, closely interrelated.

## ELABORATION: THE FIELD OF GERONTOLOGY

Sociology is not the only discipline which makes contributions to our understandings of social gerontology. Economics, psychology, anthropology, demography, medicine, philosophy, and other fields all have made significant additions to our knowledge about older persons and the aging process. Many have promoted social action programs in attempts to improve the lot of the older person. More recently, social work, political science (voting behavior and political organization), social psychology, adult education, law and home economics (particularly in nutrition, family housing and family economics) have begun to make themselves felt in this area.

It should be noted immediately that the aged are not a monolith; the only significant similarity among persons defined by the society as old or aged has to do with a minimum number of chronological years passed. But differences between individuals do exist, and this is true even between collections of individuals. Social history, personal experiences, nationality, education, work and occupation, residential location, all provide those forces that produce the differences that we find among the older persons. This, of course, is no different than it is for younger persons, but there is in our society a prevailing mode of interpretation which makes all older persons seem alike and somehow part of the "geriatric cohort."

In one of the early discussions of the nature of aging, a group of scientists met and each attempted his own definition.[3] A physiologist, Dr. A. V. Albertini, thought that there were three periods in the curve of life: (a) growing up, (b) full life after maturity, and (c) going down. The problem he saw was one of the balance between loss and regeneration, and he felt that in period (c) the loss was greater than regeneration and hence was the measure of physiological aging.

Dr. A. I. Lansing, a physician, defined the aging process as one in which there is a series of unfavorable progressive changes, usually correlated with the passage of time, becoming apparent after maturity and terminating invariably in death of the individual. Another physician, Dr. J. Jensen, argued that if adaptability is assumed to be the most important single fundamental process in life, then the loss of adaptability would be an essential measure of the process of aging and the study of this one of the most promising fields in gerontology. Another physiologist, Dr. Nathan W. Shock (who has produced the significant and continuing bibliography on aging[4]), thought that the only logical definition of aging was the simple study of changes that take place in time, and that the complexity of the process defied specific definition. Finally, a social scientist, Dr. H. S. Simms, thought of aging as a group of processes characterized by various manifestations, particularly loss of physical and mental abilities and the progressive increase in mortality rate.

More recently the field of gerontology has come to be defined in a variety of ways depending upon one's own particular discipline. The aged have been seen as a cause for concern and receivers of help, as objects of study and sympathy, as instruments of politics, as marginal members of the society, as participants in the culture and life of the society which in some fashion was not complete.[5] The first scientific concerns with the aging process were attempts to learn how to change it. Such concerns gave way to efforts of amelioration, and many persons working in the field sought to make the life of the older person an easier one. Then older persons themselves became objects of investigation and this finally led to social and political activity and organization. An overview of the history of the field should help to make clear the stages through which we have come and the direction we are likely to take.

## SIGNIFICANT STAGES IN THE GROWTH OF GERONTOLOGY

There may be discerned five separate stages in the developing discipline of gerontology. While not mutually exclusive, their individual significance as well as their interrelationship is worth noting.

### Philosophical Stage

Without question, the first historical stage in the investigation of gerontology must be that having to do with the philosophical consideration of old age. Philosophers sought to describe the satisfactions of old age and the wisdom that came in one's later years. It was in this conception of aging that early writers spoke about the lessening of passion and the control by the intellect of one's behavior. It was thus that one began to see long-term importance in the process of aging rather than short-term desirability in the affairs of man.

> I am wise in that I follow that good guide nature; it is not likely, when she has written the rest of the play well, that she should, like a lazy playwright, skimp the last act. There had to be an ending, just as fruits and crops come in the course of time to a period of fall and decay.

And while Cicero finds a need to accept the end of life, he also later notes the following:

> I find that the reasons why old age is regarded as unhappy are four: one, it withdraws us from active employments; another, it impairs physical vigor; the third, it deprives us of nearly all sensual pleasures; and four, it is the verge of death.

The similarity of this argument with that of Burgess as discussed in the next section below should not go unnoticed.

The five desires of the aged in the preliterate societies as noted by Simmons earlier, would also fall into the general category of the philosophical stage, since the expectations of the aged are so clearly reflected there. Not only the preliterate have contemplated the nature and consequences of aging for the individual, however.

Shakespeare's classic statement in his "The Seven Ages of Man" reflects on the last two ages with some dismay.

> The sixth age shifts
> Into the lean and slipper'd pantaloon,
> With spectacles on nose and pouch on side,
> His youthful hose, well sav'd, a world too wide
> For his shrunk shank; and his big manly voice
> Turning again toward childish treble, pipes
> And whistles in his sound. Last scene of all,
> That ends this strange eventful history,
> Is second childishness and mere oblivion,
> Sans teeth, sans eyes, sans taste, sans everything.

Horace (65-8 B.C.), in his essay "To Venus," says the following:

> Oh Venus, having so long left me in quiet, do you begin again to raise war against me? Spare, goddess, I pray you, spare; I am no more what I was under the reign of beautiful Cynara. Cruel mother of amorous desires, cease attempting to bring under your yoke a man now arrived at his fiftieth year, and therefore stubborn to submit to your voluptious commands. Go wither you are called by the pressing entreaties and flatteries of our youth.

Aristotle (384-322 B.C.) had a jaundiced view of older persons. He notes, with respect to older men:

> They are small minded, because they have been humbled by life; their desires are set upon nothing more exalted or unusual than what will help them to keep alive. They are not generous, because money is one of the things they must have, and at the same time their experience has taught them how hard it is to get and how easy to lose.

And later he says, "They live by memory rather than by hope; for what is left to them of life is but little as compared with the long past; and hope is of the future, memory of the past."

In *De Senectute,* Cicero (106-43 B.C.) is more positively oriented. He asks, "Does old age steal upon youth more quickly than youth upon boyhood? Would old age be less irksome if they were in their eight hundredth rather than in their eightieth year?" One must accept nature and life as he finds it.

## Biologic Stage

Having gone through the several thousand years of philosophical concern with aging, researchers and scholars became concerned with the causes of aging in a biological sense. Many sought to find a reversal of the aging process. The search for the fountain of youth or an elixar of youth was carried on throughout the world. The scientific age and technological developments accompanying the industrial revolution raised hopes for a "cure." The industrial revolution, it was widely thought, could produce change of a fundamental sort in the biological nature of man. It only remained for the technologist to implement this change. Volumes were written as descriptions of ways of producing the desired changes. Special foods to be eaten, special relationships to be cultivated, surgery which might be undertaken, special waters or other liquids to be ingested, all were thought to be solutions by some. The industrial revolution came and interest in the biology of aging persisted. People kept returning to philosophical considerations and though there seemed to be no way out, as Cicero said about this fact, "No reasonable man would resent it."

## Psychologic Stage

As time progressed interest began to focus upon the older person as an individual. If we could not reverse the inexorable physiological changes which seemed to take place for all, we had to find some way for the individual to adjust psychologically to that process. One had to learn to accept the cosmetic changes that occur with age and the "physical insults" which attack men in their later years. The person as a worker came to be of some consequence, and considerable discussion took place in regard to the productivity potentials of older workers. Psychological changes and psychological adjustments were noted.

Concern was expressed for the mental health of the elderly and institutional facilities began to be developed. Therapy centers emerged, and long-term care centers for the aged came into vogue. Experimentally oriented psychologists became interested in senility, and sought to investigate it to discover whether in fact it might be a reversable syndrome. Through this entire period, interest lay in the older individual himself and only peripherally with his relationship to others.

## Social Stage

More recently we have come to examine the situation of older persons as collectivities. This older group has come into focus largely because of the increasing numbers (both relatively and absolutely) of such persons since the beginning of the present century and our increasing awareness of them. The dynamics of population change impress themselves upon and effect our social concerns. The aged have come to be seen as collective objects of social action for political reasons as well as social organization. Now writers interpret society's behavior in sociological terms: the impact of segregated housing facilities, the development of a social security program, the withdrawal of older persons from social participation, the discovery of meaningful opportunities for older persons to take part in the larger society, the development of employment opportunities, the consideration of housing for the aged as a proper public function, etc. All of these activities see the aged as a significant, distinguishable social group in interaction with other groups as a consequence of which the behavior patterns of individuals become manifest.

## Political Stage

Since the mid-forties, the aged in our society have come to be seen as both an object of and source for political action. Older persons have been organized into a great variety of social and political groups and have themselves begun to exert political pressure in their own behalf. The first White House Conference on Aging was held in 1961 to express public concern for the aged through political mechanisms. In the 1960 Presidential election Senior Citizens For Kennedy as well as a similar group working in behalf of Richard Nixon were established as formal political direct-action groups. The American Association of Retired Persons, the National Retired Teachers Association, the National Council on the Aging, the Association of Emeriti, all have come into being. Federal programs in virtually every major governmental agency have been directed toward the elderly and their problems. An Administration on Aging has been established in the Department of Health, Education, and Welfare (see the section on Other Federal Efforts below). Senior Citizen

Centers have emerged in many locations in the United States sponsored by cities, churches, unions, fraternal groups, service clubs, etc. In all, we now seem to be living in a period of growing political concern and involvement by and on behalf of the aged.

Although these five stages developed in approximately the order indicated, the onset of each is lost in time. We do not mean to indicate that there has been a termination of any single stage. In fact, while the activity of each prestaged the development of the next, all have continued to exist to some extent, overlapping with each other. It is certainly true that the psychological and social stages are more clearly related to the political one, and that the political one is now the most apparent. While the political stage will remain most obvious, all provide opportunities for the examination of the process of aging and the elaboration of the field of gerontology.

## THE TEMPORAL HISTORY OF MODERN GERONTOLOGY

The beginning of man's concern with the nature and process of aging is lost in antiquity. Many writers have discussed this matter and there are as many disagreements. Tibbitts, in a work cited earlier, would begin the history of scientific social gerontology at a rather recent date in the present century. Streib and Orbach, however, date that beginning much earlier.[7] Their argument is as follows:

> Scientific concern with gerontology—that is, the study of the nature and process of aging—may be dated as Comfort does with Francis Bacon's *History of Life and Death* (1645), but it was not until the twentieth century that systematic study of aging commenced, although there were many attempts in the nineteenth century.[8]

Other writers have argued other times and other ways of understanding the periods in which the first concern with aging occurred.

Ernest W. Burgess, one of the giants of the field, argued that the changes that gave rise to the field of gerontology were those which developed during the period of the latter part of the industrial revolution. In particular he noted that four significant changes occurred during that period that gave rise to the field of gerontology: (1) the change from self-employed person to an employee working for another, (2) the change from gradual to compulsory retirement and its present manifestation in industry, (3) the shift from economic independence of the individual to dependence on the government and an employer for economic security, and (4) the significant change from a recognized status enjoyed by the older person and by adults generally to an uncertain and undefined social role.[9] This latter change came to be discussed by Burgess and by others as the "roleless role." As such, it has influenced thinking to a large extent about the situation of the older person as an isolated individual.

In another attempt to examine the stages of development, Robert J. Havighurst sought to distinguish between medical gerontology and social gerontology, and has described what he believes to be the significant three sequential stages in the development of each.[10]

He sees the following three stages in medical gerontology. (1) The treatment of the elderly patient which is as old as the profession of medicine itself. (2) The twentieth century development of the prevention of disease and disability. Multiple screening is a significant aspect of this change, and accompanying it the idea of rehabilitation developed and was promoted. (3) More recently there has been developed a positive approach to physical aging. This is the attempt to help adults preserve their full vigor as long as possible. Concern with diet, hormone and vitamin therapy, for instance, are designed to add life to years.

Three stages of social gerontology are also observed by Havighurst. (1) Beginning about 1900, old age pension schemes began to provide some basis for the financial support of older persons. This was a consequence of the recognition of the economic needs of the elderly and of attempts to meet those needs. Havighurst thinks that this is still a frontier stage in which major changes must and will occur. (2) As homes and families have grown smaller, the general stage of development came to be one concerned with housing and living arrangements. Because of many changes, older people cannot live with their children any longer and a variety of public and private solutions have been developed for low-cost decent housing for these persons. This is a product of the last thirty years. (3) The third stage is that of the development of a recognition of the need for ego support. One needs to be needed—to have a function in the society. We may note the similarity of this stage with Burgess's idea of the roleless role. Havighurst argues a need for companionship. Many social institutions respond to this need by developing educational and other programs for the elderly.

All three of these stages are seen by Havighurst as a function of urbanization and industrialization which have a positive correlation with the last two stages in the development of social gerontology.

To review certain significant dates in the field of gerontology, we should begin by taking note of the significant volume published in 1922 by G. Stanley Hall on senescence which he designed to accompany an earlier volume that he had done on adolescence. His view of the course of human life, both ends of which were explicable, seems to be the first serious work in the new field of gerontology.[11] During the 1930's, Stanford University began its Later Maturity Research Project under the directorship of W. R. Miles.[12]

During the last part of the 1930's, Leo Simmons carried on his significant research on aging from the Yale cross-cultural files In that volume, Simmons studied material from seventy-one preliterate cultures and concluded that there were five universal desires held by these cultures for older people: (1) to prolong life, (2) through the conservation of energy to find some rest and release from one's occupation, (3) to remain socially active, (4) to maintain control over one's property, one's authority, and one's prestige in the society, and (5) eventually to seek an honorable death with reasonable expectation of a new and better existence in the hereafter.[13]

In 1935, researchers in Britain formed an International Club for Research on Aging. Toward the end of that year they sent Dr. Korenchevsky to promote the development of this international club in America. Because of this interest, the American Research Club on Aging was founded in 1939 by the Josiah Macy, Jr. Foundation. That research club published a series of monographs entitled *Ageing.*

In the 1940's gerontology began to come into its own. In 1945, the Gerontological Society was organized. The next year, 1946, saw the beginning of the *Journal of Gerontology* which has continued to be published since that date.

In 1947, the well-established American Psychological Association formed its Division 20, the Division of Later Maturity and Old Age. This division has since been a fundamental group in the discipline of psychology promoting an interest in research on aging. In 1948, the Social Science Research Council undertook a major effort to examine the field of gerontology and this was culminated by a significant volume on social adjustment by Otto Pollak.[14] That same summer of 1948 saw the first annual University of Michigan Conference on Aging held. Clark Tibbitts was the prime mover in this effort, and an annual conference has been held at Michigan since that time sponsored by the University's Institute of Gerontology directed by Dr. Wilma T. Donahue. In 1950, the first National Conference on Aging (more of which later) was held.

In 1952, the Gerontological Society, Inc., then seven years old, established its Division of Psychology and Social Science and thus began to develop the special interest areas that now come to dominate the activities of the Society. In 1956, two significant events took place: (1) the establishment of the Inter-university Training Institute in Social Gerontology and the Pan-American Congress of Gerontology held in Mexico City.

During the early and middle 1950's, a group of researchers from the University of Chicago, in cooperation with Community Studies, Inc. of Kansas City, undertook what came to be known as the Kansas City Study of Adult Life. One of these researchers, David Riesman,[15] proposed a threefold typology of the aging process in which he sought to characterize the kinds of persons and various dimensions of successful aging. There were the *autonomous* types who are adaptive and creative individuals developing despite changes occurring about them. There are also the *adjusted* types, who do not have the same personal resources as the autonomous, but are supported by the society around them and are sustained by their occupations and by the social positions which they occupy. As long as there is stability in the society these types will continue to adjust well. The third group he calls the *anomic,* who have neither the internal personal strength nor the social supports that might assist in their adjustment to the aging process.[16]

Toward the end of the 1950's things began to quicken in the field of gerontology. This quickening may be better discussed under the more general heading of Conferences and Education and Training in Gerontology, discussed below.

## THE NATIONAL CONFERENCES UNDER FEDERAL AUSPICES

Four significant national conferences called by government agencies have been especially significant in the last two decades. The first National Conference on Aging took place in August of 1950 after having been initiated by the then Federal Security Administration. President Truman, at that time, had become aware of the rising problems of older people and thus directed the Federal Security Administrator to examine this problem through a national conference. This conference brought together 816 participants to discuss the ways in which government should utilize its resources to meet the needs of older people. A volume entitled *Man and His Years* summarizes the conference and presents a report of their hopes for change.

Two years later representatives of thirty states were called to a national Conference of State Commissions on Aging and Federal Agencies. This meeting was designed to discuss questions of organization, function, and services to be provided by state agencies as well as on the federal level. Some fifteen states at that time had already established committees or commissions on aging. They came together to exchange experiences and explore the possibilities of resolution of problems in a joint effort.

In June, 1956, the Council of State Governments and the then existing Federal Council on Aging called together a second federal-state conference on aging. This time, forty-one states and two territories sent official delegates to the conference entitled "Mobilizing Resources for Older People." There were 240 delegates and official participants in that conference providing a significant opportunity for state and federal agencies to share their knowledge and experience and to design programs in the field of gerontology.

The last, and probably most significant national conference was the White House Conference on Aging held in January, 1961. More than three thousand delegates attended that conference representing all of the states and territories. Twenty subject matter areas were established and pre-conference reports were prepared for each by special task groups. A variety of materials, including guidelines for community action, suggested school curricula, and other publications, were prepared to explore activities in the United States and abroad with regard to aging. A set of recommendations was prepared by and voted on by the conferees. A report was then sent to the President for his action,[17] and has been widely distributed.

At the time of writing of this volume, another White House conference is being discussed in Congress, and it is likely that one will take place quite soon. One date being considered is early in 1970.

Not all national conferences are or have been convened by federal agencies. Each year in the summer, the University of Michigan has a conference on aging to which come several hundred persons from the entire country representing fields which are professional, educational, service and governmental. The Gerontological Society, Inc., has its national membership meeting each fall. The National Council on Aging usually holds one meeting in New York in the winter and another meeting elsewhere in the spring for its membership and other interested persons. In addition, there are many other national conferences called by state agencies, educational institutions, pharmaceutical companies, church groups and organizations of older persons such as the American Association of Retired Persons, the National Retired Teachers Association, the American Association of Homes for the Aged, the Senior Citizens Association, the National Association of State Units on Aging, and many others.

## OTHER FEDERAL EFFORTS

In 1956, the Department of Health, Education and Welfare established a Special Staff on Aging. This special staff, reporting directly to the secretary, was assigned the responsibility of marshaling federal forces with regard to programs in aging. A federal council on aging was formally organized to bring together policy-making representatives from each of the federal agencies concerned with such programs. That federal council was, in 1962, reorganized as the President's Council on Aging. It had as its members the Secretary of Health, Education and Welfare as chairman, the Secretary of the Treasury, Secretary of Agriculture, Secretary of Commerce, Secretary of Labor, Chairman of the U. S. Civil Service Commission, Administrator of the Housing and Home Finance Agency (later the Secretary of Housing and Urban Development) and the Administrator of Veterans Affairs. In 1963, in an attempt to upgrade the activities at the federal level, an office of aging was established in the Department of Health, Education and Welfare, and it subsumed all of the activities of the special staff on aging.

The Older Americans Act of 1965, introduced in the House of Representatives by John Fogarty of Rhode Island and in the Senate by Pat McNamara of Michigan, established a new framework for the expression of federal responsibility in the field of aging. This law, passed in July of 1965, established an Administration on Aging within the Department of Health, Education and Welfare. It provided grants to the states to develop services in home communities, for public and nonprofit agencies for demonstration and research, and for training grants in the field of aging all to be administered by this newly created office. A commissioner on aging was appointed by the President to administer these functions. (William Bechill of California was named the first commissioner, Dr. Marvin Taves was made responsible for research activities and Dr. Clark Tibbitts heads the section on training.) The act also established a fifteen-member advisory committee chaired by the commissioner and reporting to the Secretary of Health, Education and Welfare. For the first time, there was established a congressionally sanctioned bill of objectives for older persons as title I of the act. These ten objectives for our older citizens were directed toward the following: (1) an adequate income, (2) a concern for the best possible physical and mental health, (3) suitable housing, (4) full restorative services for those requiring institutional care, (5) opportunity for employment, (6) retirement in health, honor and dignity, (7) pursuit of meaningful activity, (8) efficient community services, (9) immediate benefit from proven research, and (10) freedom and independence with individual initiative. The Administration on Aging in an attempt to implement this general statement of expectations has moved vigorously to develop a variety of programs that are necessary and meaningful.

## EDUCATION AND TRAINING IN GERONTOLOGY

It was noted earlier that in 1956 an Inter-university Training Institute in Social Gerontology was established. That institute determined that a great need existed for the development of programs of education in gerontology, and that the only way that this could be resolved was to provide for additional teachers. As a consequence, that group initiated an Inter-university Summer Training Institute to be held in 1958 at Storrs, Connecticut. A nine-man executive committee chaired by Dr. Wilma T. Donahue worked with representatives of sixteen sponsoring universities to develop this program. In the summer of 1958, thirty-six selected persons attended the one-month seminar. The next summer (1959), an additional forty persons attended the second month-long seminar.[18]

In 1961, the Division of Gerontology (now the Institute of Gerontology established jointly at the University of Michigan, Ann Arbor, and Wayne State University, Detroit) of the Institute for Human Adjustment at the University of Michigan, under the directorship of Dr. Wilma T. Donahue, reported on a national survey of educational activities in gerontology. During the preceding three years (1958 to 1961), an average of thirty-four fellowships, traineeships and assistantships in gerontology per year were awarded at fifteen institutions. From 112 institutions, 161 departments reported 221 research projects in aging and 137 theses and dissertations in gerontology during the same period. Forty-five institutions reported that theses or dissertations were, in 1961, then being carried out in gerontology, and thirty-one of these institutions had ongoing researches in the field. Sociology, psychology, and human development were the fields producing ten or more Ph.D. dissertations in gerontology. Social work was then the major contributor of master's degrees in gerontology.[19]

Many universities had earlier developed programs of their own, and many more have since then instituted new programs. The Cornell University Study of Occupational Retirement, operating out of the Department of Sociology during the 1950's made a very significant contribution to the development of educational and training programs in gerontology, in educational institutions and in industrial and business organizations. The University of Chicago, with its already cited Kansas City Study of Adult Life begun in the early 1950's, also was an innovator in this field. Its Industrial Relations Center, working with Dr. Ernest W. Burgess, developed and extensively tested a major program in Preparation for Retirement operated as a ten-session (once a week) seminar activity. Duke University brought together the school of medicine and its Department of Psychiatry with the Department of Sociology and the Department of Economics to examine at a very early stage problems of older persons. The University of California at Berkeley developed a program of research through its Institute of Labor and Industrial Relations. The University of Michigan with its already cited Institute of Gerontology has for twenty years been a leader in this field. The University of Iowa at Iowa City developed one of the early institutes of gerontology. The University of Florida began its program in gerontology during the 1950's and annually published a series of monographs based upon their conference papers.

Many educators have raised questions about how to approach the discipline of gerontology. A main question is whether one can have a separate intellectual scholarly discipline of this kind and train specialists in gerontology. Many argue that one may only be trained as a generalist in gerontology having their scholarly training and specializing in a traditional field such as psychology, economics, biology or sociology. While the discussion goes on as to whether the gerontologist is a generalist or specialist, the overriding question has to do with whether the traditional disciplines could contribute most in the development of the field, or whether it is necessary to create a new discipline.

Gerontology, as a field of community activity, has often recruited persons from those fields of work which traditionally were concerned with children and youth. This has particularly been the case with operators of homes for the aged and similar protective facilities. This is likely true because such persons are those who have worked with dependents, even though young. The aged are seen by many as a similarly dependent group; and those who work with them have frequently been recruited from fields reflecting experience in this area. Professional persons from the field of social work have been most significantly involved in the emerging new institutions which have developed, and in new counseling procedures which have evolved. New educational programs are constantly being developed at many universities in the United States.

In March, 1964, the Gerontological Society, Inc., undertook to produce a report on training needs and mechanisms in gerontology, especially with respect to a projection of training goals, manpower requirements and modes of training in the field. To carry this out, a survey was undertaken to discover the nature and extent of existing training programs in the United States as well as an analysis of the current modes of training. In March of 1968, the final report on this project was completed by the Gerontological Society and submitted to the Adult Development and Aging Branch of the National Institute of Child Health and Human Development. While not yet published at the time of this writing, certain findings of this survey may now be reported.

The entire project was organized to discover programs in six areas: biological sciences, molecular and cellular biology, human and comparative biology, psychology and social sciences, behavioral sciences, and social gerontology. Mail questionnaires as well as focused interviews were carried out. Twenty-six institutions were chosen for specific visits and depth interviews. In all, 159 institutions reported some training in gerontology. Of these, eighty were academic institutions, forty were medical and professional schools, and the balance were foundations, government agencies and applied settings.

It was estimated in this survey that at the time of completion of the report, 199 students were either then enrolled or had recently completed a program in research training in gerontology, and 1,089 were in the same situation in applied programs. This report, when published, will make proposals for increased funding for research and training over the next five-year period by the National Institute of Child Health and Human Development. Other recommendations such as the development of other facilities and resources, the establishment of university chairs in gerontology, the development of career awards, and a visiting scientist program are all included. Suggestions are made for developing inter-disciplinary mechanisms and inter-university cooperation. The implementation of this final report holds great promise for the future of gerontology.

## A FINAL NOTE

As has been already noted by Simmons,[20] "Everywhere the human cycle begins with the dependency of the young on those who are older, and ends with the dependency of the old on those who are younger." Throughout history man has sought to justify and seek meaning in his life, protect and immortalize his soul, and rejuvenate his body to remain young. The defeat of old age and of death have been major preoccupations of man, since the former is interpreted as the permanent conquest of the latter.

Although people of all ages die, the probabilities of death increase with age. For the individual to have lived long, and especially to have lived well, is a measure of social and biological advance for the society. The definition of what it means to live long, or more obviously, what it means to live well, are matters of social definition that change in time and place. While an individual death is an unhappy event, the fact that today more people are dying at an older age is for the society a positive gain to be viewed with satisfaction. Clearly, the Society must produce persons who can and will work effectively on the problems of the increasing number of older persons, and it must train them to do these things usefully. Gerontology, while a relatively new discipline, takes for itself a significant task. It has a long history, and an even longer future.

## REFERENCES

1. FREEMAN, JOSEPH T.: The first fifty years of geriatrics (1909-1959). *Geriatrics,* 1960, Vol. XV.
2. TIBBITTS, CLARK (Ed.): Origin, Scope, and fields of social gerontology. In *Societal Aspects of Aging, Handbook of Social Gerontology.* Chicago, U. of Chicago, 1960, chap. 1.
3. LANSING, A.I. (Ed.): Panel discussion. *J Geront, 7*:452-463, 1952.
4. SHOCK, N.W.: *A Classified Bibliography of Gerontology and Geriatrics: 1900-1948.* Stanford, Stanford U. P., 1951, and *ibid.,* Supplement One, Stanford, Stanford U. P., 1956. (This bibliography was later continued as a regular series in *J Geront*).
5. TIBBITTS, *op. cit.,* (also see BREEN, L.: Aging and its social aspects. *J Home Econ,* Oct. 1962, vol. 54, No. 8).
6. TIBBITTS, CLARK, AND DONAHUE, WILMA (Eds.): An interesting examination of statements by early philosophers, as well as philosophical statements made by persons more recently. In *Aging in Today's Society.* Englewood Cliffs, Prentice-Hall, 1960.
7. STREIB, GORDON F., AND ORBACH, HAROLD L.: Aging. In Lazarsfeld, P.F.; Sewell, W.H., and Wilensky, H.L. (Eds.): *The Uses of Sociology.* New York, Basic Books, 1967, chap. 22.
8. *Ibid.,* p. 615. See in particular the excellent set of references listed at the end of the chapter referred to.
9. *The States and Their Older Citizens,* Chicago, The Council of State Governments, 1955. (This report for the 1955 annual Governers Conference

was prepared by Ernest W. Burgess and Sidney Spector. See pp. 6-8 for a discussion of the four points made by Burgess.)
10. Havighurst, R.J.: *J Geront* (Suppl. 1) Volume 13, Oct. 31, 1957, vol. 13.
11. Hall, G.S.: *Senescence: The Last Half of Life.* New York, Appleton, 1922.
12. Cowdry, E.V.: Psychological aspects of aging. In Cowdry, E.V. (Ed.): *Problems of Aging.* Baltimore, William & Wilkins, 1939.
13. Simmons, L.W.: *The Role of the Aged in Primitive Society.* New Haven, Yale, 1945.
14. Pollak, Otto: *Social Adjustment in Old Age.* New York, The Social Science Research Council, Bulletin 59, 1948.
15. Riesman, D.: Some clinical and cultural aspects of Aging. *Amer J Sociol, 59*:379-383, 1954.
16. Williams, Richard H.: Changing status, roles, and relationships. In Tibbitts, *op. cit.* (For a more complete discussion of types of persons and their personal and social responses to the aging process. chap. IX).
17. *The Nation and Its Older People.* U.S. Department of Health, Education and Welfare, The Special Staff on Aging, Washington, D.C., U.S. Government Printing Office, April 1961.
18. Donahue, Wilma T.: Training in social gerontology. *Geriatrics,* Nov. 1960, vol. 15. (A complete preview of the Institute in Social Gerontology and all of the materials developed for it, as well as a complete examination of the persons involved in the summer institute as fellows. The 16 cooperating universities were California, Chicago, Connecticut, Cornell, Duke, Florida, Illinois, Iowa, Michigan, Minnesota, Pennsylvania State, Pittsburgh, Purdue, Syracuse, Washington (St. Louis), and Wisconsin.)
19. For a more complete report, see *ibid.*
20. Simmons, *op. cit.*

## ADDITIONAL READINGS

Birren, J.E. (Ed.): *Handbook of Aging and the Individual.* Chicago, U. of Chicago, 1959.

Birren, J.E.; Butler, R.N.; Greenhouse, S.W.; Sokoloff, L., and Yarrow, M.R. (Eds.): *Human Aging,* Washington, U.S. Government Printing Office, Public Health Service Publication Number 986, undated.

Burgess, E.W. (Ed.): *Aging In Western Societies,* Chicago, U. of Chicago, 1960.

Cumming, E., and Henry, W.E.: *Growing Old: The Process of Disengagement.* New York, Basic Books, 1961.

Hansen, P.F. (Ed.): *Age With a Future.* Copenhagen, Munksgaard Press, 1964.

Koller, M.R.: *Social Gerontology.* New York, Random, 1968.

Loether, H.J.: *Problems of Aging.* Belmont, California, Dickenson, 1967.

McKinney, John C., and de Vyver, F.T.: *Aging and Social Policy.* New York, Appleton, 1966.

Niebanck, P.L.: *The Elderly In Older Urban Areas.* Philadelphia, U. of Pa., 1965.

Rose, A.M., and Peterson, W.A.: *Older People and Their Social World.* Philadelphia, Davis, 1965.

Shock, N.W.: *Trends In Gerontology.* 2nd ed., Stanford, Stanford, 1957.

Vedder, C.B.: *Gerontology: A Book of Readings.* Springfield, Thomas, 1963.

# PART II

# DEMOGRAPHIC, POLITICAL AND ECONOMIC ASPECTS OF AGING

*Chapter 2*

# THE DEMOGRAPHY OF AGING

DONALD O. COWGILL

THE AVERAGE READER may have a fairly clear idea about what is meant when he is told that our population is aging, but he may be puzzled when told that at the same time the population is "younging." In this chapter, we shall try to clarify such terms and provide perspective on the phenomena to which they refer. We shall address ourselves to such questions as the following: What does a demographer mean when he talks about "an aging population" or "an aged population?" When does old age begin? How long do people live? How does this compare with earlier populations? What is the age structure of our population and how does this compare with people in other parts of the world and at other periods in history? How can we classify populations in terms of their "agedness?" Are there any general trends in the aging of populations? Are these predictable? What factors produce aging of a population? What are the characteristics of an aged population? Where are most old people to be found? Are there definite patterns of distribution of the aged within the nation, within our cities and in different sizes of communities?

## THE MEANING OF "AN AGING POPULATION"

When a demographer speaks of "an aging population," he is not merely acknowledging the fact that with the passage of time any specific group of individuals must perforce grow older; he is more probably referring to an increase of numbers or proportions of old people in a population resulting from the combined effects of births, deaths and migrations when added to or subtracted from a given population as it passes through time.

For some purposes, there is significance in the mere increase of numbers of old people in the population. It is largely numbers which determine the volume of need for services, such as medical care or Social Security. But an increase in numbers does not necessarily mean an increase in the proportion within the total population. If the total population is growing, some increase in the number of the aged will be required just to maintain the same proportion. In order for the proportion of aged to increase, the number of aged must be increasing faster than the rest of the population.

This is the condition which is usually referred to when we speak of "an aging population." Such a process may be indicated by increases in any one of a number of conventional measures of relative age of a population. One of the crudest of such measures is the *median age* of the total population. This is defined as that age which divides the total population into two equal groups, 50 per cent older than the median and 50 per cent younger. In 1960, the median age of the population of the United States was 29.5 years. The fact that this median age was lower in 1960 than it had been in 1950 when the median as 30.2 merely reflects the fact that the "younging" tendency resulting from the "baby boom" following World War II was slightly stronger than the aging trend during this period. That the median age of the population could actually decrease during a period when other indicators showed a continued aging of the population confirms the observation that median age is a poor measure of aging, if our interest is primarily in the proportion of old people in the population.

A second and more definitive measure of aging is the *per cent 65 and over*. In 1960, the per cent 65 and over in the United States population was 9.2 and this was significantly more than it had been in 1950 when it was 8.2. By this measure, then, the proportion of aged in the population had increased 1 per cent even though during the same period the median age of the total population had decreased. Of course, such a development was possible only because this aging trend was more than counterbalanced by a simultaneous "younging" trend, i.e. during the same period the percent of the population which was under 18 also increased, from 31.0 per cent to 35.8 per cent. Numerically this was a far greater increase than the increase of the aged and this had the consequence of pulling the median age downward. Another consequence of the fact that such decisive increases took place at both ends of the age scale, both among the very young and among the old, was that the proportion in the middle ages decreased. As a matter of fact, the per cent in the ages 18 through 64 dropped from 60.8 to 55.0.

Another measure of the relative age of a population is Valaoris' *index of aging*.[1] This is a ratio between the extremes of age in a population, i.e. between the old and the young. More specifically, it is the number of persons 60 years of age and over, per one hundred persons under 15. The United States is a relatively old population, as we shall see later; it has almost half as many old people in its population as it has young and its index of aging in 1960 was 42.5. This index is quite high when compared with Thailand, for example, where the index in the same year was only 10.7. However, again because of the "younging" trend which was taking place in the United States during the 1950's, the index was lower in 1960 than it was in 1950 when it stood at 45.3.[2]

Still another measure of relative age which is sometimes used is the *old age dependency ratio*. This is the ratio between the number of people 65 and over and the number 20 through 64. Of course, the rationale for this ratio and for calling it a "dependency" ratio is the assumption that for the most part, the population over 65 is non-productive and dependent for its economic support upon the productive or working population most of which will be between the ages of 20 and 65. In 1960, the old age dependency ratio for the United States was 17.7, i.e. there were 17.7 persons 65 and over for each one hundred persons 20 to 64. This was a marked increase over 1950 when the ratio was only 13.8.[3]

Thus it is evident that the different measures of relative age measure different things and that they must be employed with discernment and discrimination. For most purposes, the per cent of the total population which is 65 and over will be adequate and it is this index which will be employed throughout the remainder of this chapter.

## WHEN DOES OLD AGE BEGIN?

There is no universally accepted criterion as to when old age begins. Within given cultures, we may find somewhat standardized conceptions, but certainly definitions of old age have varied widely from time to time and place to place.

Early Chinese scholars used to refer to the period from 60 to

70 years of age as "the longed-for age," and "old age" began at 70.[4] Pythagoras likened the stages of life to the seasons of the year; each season comprised a twenty-year period and the last season, winter, or old age, began at 60.[5] However, the great Greek physician, Hippocrates, had a more complex system of ages; for him, the life span consisted of ten 7-year cycles, with the ninth cycle, 56 to 63, apparently marking the onset of old age.[6] A more optimistic and modern view is that of the French nineteenth century physiologist, Flourens, who divided life into eight periods of variable length, the first two comprising childhood and extending to 20 years of age, the second two described as youth and lasting until 40, the first period of maturity stretching from 40 to 54, and a period of later maturity including the ages 55 to 69, and finally old age beginning at 70 and again consisting of two periods with the last one starting at age 85.[7]

The Polish anatomist, Bochenek, divided old age into three decades; the first degree of aging was between 60 and 70, the second between 70 and 80, and the final degree from 80 to 90.[8] He apparently assumed that no one would live beyond 90. The Soviet gerontologist, Frenkel, after surveying a number of age classifications, concludes the following "Most nations, in various periods of history, have employed 60 as the beginning of old age." [9] However, a few pages later, he contradicts himself and asserts that for hundreds and thousands of years, old age has meant an age of 70 and over.[10]

The British physician-demographer, William Farr, provides a euphoric flourish when he refers to the period from 60 to 80 as the "Laureate age." In other words, this was the age when a person having earned his laurels, rested on them.[11]

A final illustration of an age classification is one proposed by the American Public Health Association: [12]

(1) Infancy; up to 1 year
(2) Preschool period; 1 to 4 years
(3) School years: 5 to 14 years
(4) Adolescence: 14 to 24 years
(5) Years of greatest activity: 25 to 44 years
(6) Middle age: 45 to 64 years
(7) Early period of old age: 65 to 74 years
(8) Old age: 75 years and over

The most notable features of this classification are the fact that adolescence is extended up to the age of 24 and old age proper does not begin until age 75. This classification appears to be based more upon the modern pattern of work than upon physiological development.

On the basis of these and other classifications, the following generalizations appear to be justified as to the beginning of old age:

1. Various people have defined the beginning of old age all the way from 45 years to 70 years of age.
2. There is a strong predilection toward the use of multiples of five in stating the age at which old age begins.
3. The most commonly designated years appear to be 60 and 70.
4. Obviously there is no single, natural, or universally valid age for the beginning of old age.
5. The age which is designated as the beginning of old age varies with the culture and is relative to the state of general health and the functional roles which people perform at different ages.
6. More recent definitions tend to set somewhat higher ages for the onset of old age.

Leo Simmons has stated the following: "The farther back we go in human society the earlier people become 'old.' "[13]

In many primitive societies, a person is defined as old by the age of 45 or 50, whereas in most modern societies old age is thought not to begin until 65 or 70 years. Elsewhere this author has stated the following: "[T]he concept of old age itself appears to be relative to the degree of modernization."[14]

As the average expectation of life increases, as the health of older people improves, there is a tendency to specify a later age as the beginning of old age. Presently in America, we still exaggerate the significance of the work role in life and hence we identify old age with the age of retirement, but with retirement taking place at earlier and earlier ages, there is increasing incongruity between physiological aging and occupational aging. We may soon be forced to differentiate the two and to acknowledge that retirement has no relevance to old age. When this point is reached, we may move back in the direction of using physiological aging as the primary criterion for the onset of old age and this may lead us to adopt a somewhat higher age to mark the beginning of the period of old age.

For purposes of the present chapter, however, we will conform to the most prevalent convention in American society at the present time and assume that old age begins at 65. With this in mind when we refer to the aged population, we will mean all of the people 65 and over.

## HUMAN LONGEVITY IN HISTORICAL PERSPECTIVE

An increasing expectation of life is a necessary prelude to the aging of a population. The reduction of the death rate which leads to increased life expectancy and this in turn to increased numbers of older people in a population, does not necessarily lead to an increased proportion of aged in the population. That depends on whether the numbers in younger age groups continue to increase as rapidly as the numbers of aged. Nevertheless, since the prolongation of life is one of the necessary ingredients in the aging of populations, it may be helpful to obtain some historical perspective on this phenomenon.

It is obvious that the systematic registration of deaths is a very recent, modern practice. Our knowledge of life expectancy of populations at earlier times must therefore rest on other kinds of evidence. For preliterate populations, the only evidence we have is the apparent stage of growth and development of the individuals whose skeletons have been excavated. The approximate age at death of these individuals may be estimated and when we have a sufficient sample of any population we may therefore estimate the average age at death in such a population and impute the mortality conditions which would have had to prevail in such a population.

> According to Vallois (1937), none of the known Neanderthal individuals passed the age of fifty; of 102 skeletons of the Upper Paleolithic only one (Oberkassel) did so, possibly passing sixty; and of sixty-five Mesolithic individuals, largely European, only two passed fifty. Of forty-eight Mesolithic skeletons of Northwest Africa none was older than forty-five—no woman older than thirty-five; ninety-four Silesian Neolithic skeletons furnished only four over fifty years of age . . . [15]

Thus, for Neanderthal man, living 150,000 to 100,000 years ago, only half reached adulthood, 95 per cent died before the age of 40, and, as far as present evidence tells us, none lived to be 50.[16] This would indicate an average expectation of life of less than 20 years, and a usual death rate of about fifty per thousand per year. For the Paleolithic period in the Near East, 35,000 to eight thousand years ago, about 10 per cent of the population appears to have reached 40 and 1 per cent passed 50.[17] An extensive excavation at Indian Knoll, Kentucky, dating from about 500 B.C. to 500 A.D., yielded 1,132 skeletons of which 57 per cent were thought to be of individuals under 21 years of age.[18] The distribution of the ages of the remnants of this population led Howells to construct a life table which indicated that only 48.6 per cent survived to the age of 20, 3.0 per cent reached 40, and a mere 0.3 per cent lived to be 50.[19] This also would suggest an average life expectancy of less than 20 and a death rate of more than fifty per thousand per year.

Apparently life expectancy increased somewhat during the Greek and Roman period; inscriptions on stelae in Greece around 400 B.C. indicate that life expectancy may have been as high as 30. In the later Greek and Roman periods, while only 46 per cent reached 20 years of age, judging by epitaphs, greater proportions lived to older ages—18 per cent to 40, 9 per cent to 60, and 2 per cent even to 80.[20] However, estimates based on epitaphs are very likely to overestimate life expectancy, since infants are rarely memorialized in this way and hence their deaths are not averaged in with the total.

Durand estimated that the urban population during the Roman Empire had a life expectancy of somewhere between 15 and 25 years, but the rural population lived longer, and thus the expectation for the whole empire may have ranged up to 30. He suggested that the death rate during this period was probably thirty-five or forty deaths per thousand.[21] It is probable that average life expectancy dropped after the fall of Rome and remained at a near primitive level through the Middle Ages. Peller found in using genealogical records for the nobility in Europe from 1480 to 1579, that even these favored classes had an average length of life of only about 30 years.[22] Near the end of the seventeenth century, Halley constructed the first life table based on the city of Breslau and found an average expectation of life of 35.5 years.[23] However, most of the estimates for eighteenth century Europe still place the average between 25 and 30 and indicate a crude death rate of about thirty-five per thousand per year.

Thus, it appears that in prehistoric times, average life expectancy was probably less than 20, and, while there were modest gains during the height of ancient civilizations, these gains were lost during the so-called Dark Ages and were certainly wiped out entirely during the periods of the Black Plague. By the opening of the nineteenth century in Europe and America, we had only managed to retrieve such modest gains as had been achieved by the Romans two millenia earlier and the average person still lived only about 30 years.

In the next century and a half, longevity more than doubled and now most modern areas of the world, including most of Europe and America have average life expectancies of 70 years or more. Such is the measure of the Revolution of Aging which modern populations are experiencing.

## HISTORICAL PERSPECTIVE ON POPULATION STRUCTURE

However, the increase in longevity is only one aspect of this revolution. Another aspect with which we are chiefly concerned in this chapter is the proportion of older people present in the population at any given time.

Given no change in fertility, as the death rate goes down and as the expectation of life increases, we may expect slight increases in the proportions of a population which will be over 50 or over 65. We cannot know actual percentages of older people in prehistoric or even early historic populations; we can only guess on the basis of the scanty knowledge concerning the age of death, reviewed above. Table I contains such guesses.

Thus, through most of human history, old people have been

TABLE I

ESTIMATED PER CENT OF SPECIFIED POPULATIONS 50 YEARS OF AGE AND OVER AND 65 YEARS OF AGE AND OVER

| | *Per Cent 50 and Over* | *Per Cent 65 and Over* |
|---|---|---|
| Neanderthal Man | none | none |
| Paleolithic, Near East | 1 | none |
| Pre-Columbian Indians | 1 | none |
| Early Greek | 3 | 1 |
| Later Greek and Roman | 4 | 1 |
| Medieval Europe | 3 | 1 |
| 17th century Europe | 4 | 1 |
| 19th century Europe | 8 | 4 |

exceedingly rare. Up to the opening of the nineteenth century, persons 65 and over rarely constituted more than 1 per cent of the population. Since that time, the dramatic increase in longevity coupled with reduced fertility have produced the revolution in age structure which has eventuated in some modern populations with more than 12 per cent 65 and over.

## AGEDNESS OF CONTEMPORARY POPULATIONS

Because contemporary populations run the gamut from those which are very primitive in technology and standard of living to those which have been in the forefront of scientific and technological development, we also find populations which range from the most primitive age structure to the most modern form, i.e. from populations comprised mostly of children (because the death rate is so high that most people die before reaching maturity) to populations reflecting the maximum application of that science and technology to the most vital business of life, the prolongation of life. Too often we concentrate on the problems attendant upon the aging of populations; forgetting that this very aging is one of the truest and most meaningful measures of progress. It probably reflects man's greatest achievement. It could certainly be used to differentiate between underdeveloped and developed nations.

Data are not available for the most primitive contemporary populations, because such countries do not have censuses which permit the classification of the population by age. But Table II illustrates the range of variation in agedness of some forty nations.

The classification used in this table differs from that formerly employed by the United Nations (UN).[24] The UN proposed that all populations with less than 4 per cent 65 and over be classified as "young"; the present classification agrees with that designation. However, the second class, from 4.0 to 6.9 per cent, was labeled "mature" by the UN and the present author believes that designation overstates the case since such populations are merely in the early stages of the aging process; therefore, he prefers to retain the category but to rename it with the more accurate title, "youthful." The UN classification contained only three classes, the final one being called "aged" and including all populations with more than 7 per cent 65 and over.

TABLE II
PER CENT OF POPULATION 65 AND OVER
FOR SELECTED COUNTRIES, 1965*

| *Country by Degree of Agedness* | *Per Cent 65 and Over* |
|---|---|
| "Young" Populations | (Less than 4) |
| French Somaliland | 0.8 |
| Honduras | 1.9 |
| Ceylon | 1.9 |
| Philippines | 2.6 |
| Haiti | 2.9 |
| Nepal | 2.9 |
| Thailand | 3.0 |
| India | 3.1 |
| Ecuador | 3.7 |
| Mexico | 3.7 |
| Turkey | 3.7 |
| Peru | 3.7 |
| "Youthful" Populations | (4.0 to 6.9) |
| Algeria | 4.1 |
| Chile | 4.3 |
| Jordan | 4.5 |
| Syria | 4.8 |
| Paraguay | 4.9 |
| Iraq | 5.3 |
| Israel | 5.5 |
| Japan | 6.2 |
| Yugoslavia | 6.3 |
| Argentina | 6.4 |
| Poland | 6.5 |
| Ukrainian S.S.R. | 6.9 |
| "Mature" Populations | (7.0 to 9.9) |
| Byelorussian S.S.R. | 7.3 |
| Canada | 7.6 |
| Uruguay | 8.4 |
| Australia | 8.4 |
| United States | 9.3 |
| Czechoslovakia | 9.3 |
| "Aged" Populations | (10.0 and over) |
| Switzerland | 10.6 |
| Denmark | 11.1 |
| Ireland | 11.2 |
| United Kingdom | 12.2 |
| Sweden | 12.3 |
| Belgium | 12.4 |
| France | 12.4 |
| Austria | 13.0 |
| E. Germany | 14.4 |
| Monaco | 19.9 |

*Percentages have been computed from data in the *Demographic Yearbook,* published by the United Nations, 1965.

The present author contends that the range of variation above 7 per cent is too great to include in one such open-ended class; to call Romania and Finland (7.6%) "aged" along with France and Belgium (12.4%) appears to conceal significant differences. Furthermore, it will be noted that there is more difference between Canada (7.6%) and France (12.4%), both of which would be classed as "aged" by the UN, than between Canada and Mexico (3.7%) and yet Mexico would fall in the lowest class and be labeled "young." Not only is there too great disparity within the class called "aged" by the UN, there is even some trace of bimodality, with one cluster around 8 and 9 per cent and a second cluster around 12 per cent. For these reasons, the author prefers to divide the UN "aged" class into two classes, with 10 per cent as the breaking point between them and to call the class from 7.0 per cent to 9.9 per cent "mature" and to reserve the designation of "aged" for those with more than 10 per cent 65 and over.

This appears to result in a symmetrical and meaningful classification which fits the real range of aging in contemporary populations. In populations unaffected by selective migration, it appears that the effective range in the percentage of aging today is from about 1 per cent 65 and over to about 13 per cent, i.e. a range of about twelve percentage points. The classification which is proposed here divides that range into four classes of three percentage points each, leaving the lower and upper classes open-ended in order to include any which fall outside of that range.

Utilizing this classification in Table II, we note that the youngest among the "young" populations is French Somaliland with less than 1 per cent and that several Latin American countries, such as, Honduras, Ecuador and Peru, are classed along with such Asian countries as Ceylon, Nepal, Thailand and India as "young" populations. All of these, of course, are nations in the early stages of economic development.

In addition to other Latin American and Asian countries with slightly greater proportions of aged, the "youthful" populations include such eastern European countries as Yugoslavia and Poland. The countries which are here classified as "mature" appear to include the more youthful of the highly developed nations. These include

Canada, Australia and the United States. It will be noted in passing that the new classification employed here converts the United States from being designated "aged" (under the UN classification) to merely one of the "mature" populations. For a nation which is still trying to absorb the products of a "baby boom" the latter classification appears more apt.

All of the "aged" populations are in Europe. They range from Switzerland with 10.6 per cent 65 and over to Monaco with 19.9 per cent. The latter case is obviously an abnormal population in which the high proportion of the aged appears to be brought about by inmigration of the older population, many of whom are retired.

Thus, the "young" populations are to be found in underdeveloped countries of Asia and Latin America, and all of the "aged" populations are found in Europe. The latter consist entirely of the countries which were earliest to feel the effects of industrialization and the applications of modern science and technology.

## AGING AND THE DEMOGRAPHIC TRANSITION

Except for the cases which are distorted by migration, the above classification results largely from the fact that these countries are presently in different stages of what is known as "the Demographic Transition." Some understanding of this phenomenon is necessary in order to fully understand the aging process.

The demographic transition is strictly a modern phenomenon; it has never happened previously in human history. This is not to say that we have never had cycles of population growth comparable to the modern "population explosion"; on the contrary, there have been many periods of fairly rapid population increase and likewise many periods of decrease. However, in the past, such cycles have been produced almost entirely by fluctuations in the death rate with no particular change in the birth rate.[25] Under those conditions, a cycle of growth was set off by a falling death rate due to good crops, plenteous rainfall, peaceful conditions, or a lack of epidemics, and, by the same token, the cycle was ended, i.e. the growth of population ceased when drouth recurred, crops failed, war broke out, or epidemics set in which brought an increase in the death rate.

By contrast, in the modern cycle or the demographic transition, it appears that there is a permanent reduction of the death rate. It appears to drop from about thirty-five or forty deaths per thousand to about eight to twelve and remains at this lower level. Of course, such a condition is only possible if the birth rate is also reduced; otherwise, any area would soon be grossly overpopulated.

It is the permanence of this transition from high death rates to low death rates, plus a subsequent similar transition in the birth rate which distinguishes the modern population cycle from previous ones and leads us to call this one "the demographic transition." Its major feature is the transition from high death rates and high birth rates to low death rates and low birth rates. Its general nature is depicted in Figure 2-1.

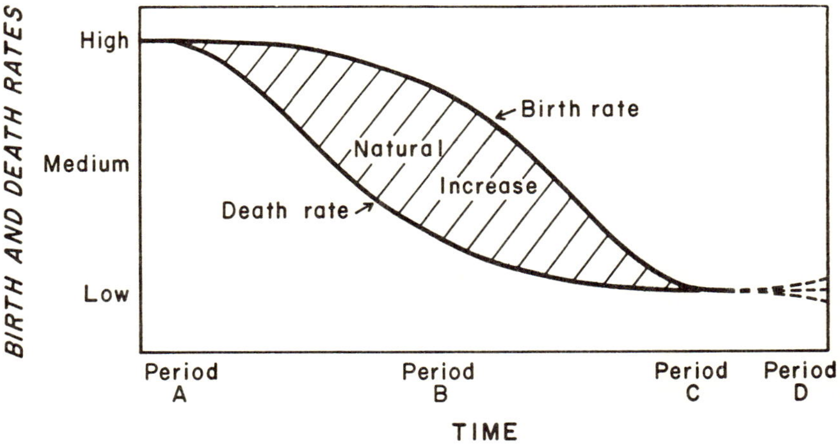


Figure 2-1. The demographic transition. (*From* Thomlinson, Ralph, *Population Dynamics,* New York, Random House, 1965, p. 18.)

It will be noted that at the outset both rates are high and that the cycle begins with a falling death rate. Eventually, as the death rate reaches a quite low level, it begins to level off. Some time after the death rate starts falling—often a generation or more—the birth rate begins its descent and eventually it may fall to a level of unity with the death rate. During this transition, since the birth rate is higher than the death rate, there is extensive population increase. If the death rate falls very quickly, as it has in many places in recent decades, this increase can become so massive as to warrant the sobriquet, "population explosion." However, our interest in the transition in the present context is not focused on the increase in size, but rather upon the change in the age composition which accompanies it.[26]

There are increases both in numbers and in proportions of the aged, but both effects are most in evidence in the late phases of the transition. The early reduction of the death rate is more likely to decrease the proportion of the aged in the population than to increase it. This is true because most of the reduction is in infant and child mortality; there is only minor improvement in mortality of older persons. The immediate effect therefore of a major reduction in the death rate is to increase the number of children who are kept alive and who are permitted to grow up. This therefore tends to increase the proportion of children in such populations and, at the same time, to decrease the proportion of the aged; only as these babies grow old, some 65 years later, do the numbers of the aged begin to increase.

Many people find it hard to understand that changes in the birth rate are far more important for the aging of the population than are changes in the death rate. It is true that with a lag of some 65 years, a drop in the death rate will begin to manifest itself in an increase in the *numbers* of older people, but unless some reduction has also occurred in the birth rate, by then the numbers of children will also have increased with the result that the *proportion* of the aged will have changed very little. It is doubtful if the percentage of the aged in the population would ever exceed 4 per cent as a result of the reduction of the death rate alone. Such a population, in other words, would always remain "young."

A reduction of the birth rate has an almost immediate impact on the *proportions* in all age groups. Within ten years, for example, a reduction of the birth rate will reduce the proportion of the population under 10 years of age, and increase the proportions in all other age groups, including the proportion 65 and over. It is for this reason that demographers maintain that most of the aging of populations is the result of lowered birth rates.[27]

However, it is really the interaction of these two factors which has produced the dramatic Aging Revolution which has eventuated in "Aged" populations such as those in Europe today. At the same time that we have increasing *numbers* of people reaching their sixty-fifth birthdays due to improved infant and child mortality 65 years ago, we also have relatively fewer babies being added to the populations in consequence of record low birth rates. The United States would now be among the aged populations had it not been for the "younging" trend that partially counteracted the "aging" trend for more than a decade after World War II. Now, however, the birth rate has been falling for a decade and the population is again aging apace. In 1967, the birth rate was only 17.9 which is the lowest the United States birth rate has ever been.[28] In numbers, this meant that in 1967, there were only about 3.5 million births added to the youthful base of our population, as compared with several post-war years when there were more than four million such births. At the same time, then, that we have decreasing numbers of births, we have increasing numbers of people reaching their sixty-fifth birthdays. This is the essence and the fact of the aging of populations.

## MIGRATION AND AGING

Migration is not taken into account in the theory of the demographic transition, but wherever extensive migration occurs it always has effects on the age structures of both the populations of origin and the populations of destination. While this is too complicated a subject to attempt to treat fully in this chapter, we may briefly indicate some of the major ways in which migration usually affects the age structure of populations, with particular emphasis upon the aged population.

One overriding principle in this connection is: Most migrants are young adults. We may deduce from this principle that at the time of migration, immigration tends to have a "younging" effect on the population which is receiving these young people, and conversely, emigration tends to have an "aging" effect upon the population which is losing them. This must be kept in mind as an added factor which has contributed to the aging of most of the European populations which are now classified as "aged" in Table II. Almost all of them have experienced extensive outmigration for many decades and the continuous effect of this has been to decrease the proportion of young adults in their populations.

Furthermore, there is a secondary and cumulative effect of such migrations. Since most of the migrants are at the ages of maximum reproductivity, their emigration tends not only to deplete the numbers of young adults in the population, but also to decrease the fertility of such populations, hence to reduce the proportions of babies and children. Thus, emigration tends to have a double effect in the direction of aging of a population.

Immigration, of course, tends to have the opposite compound effect. Not only do the young adult migrants themselves produce a "younging" effect on the host population; very shortly they start reproducing and thus contribute babies and children to an already "younging" population. This epitomizes the situation in the United States at the opening of the twentieth century. In fact, the "younging" effect was augmented at that time by the fact that the immigrants maintained higher fertility patterns than our native population of the same age. However, there is little evidence to support the contention that immigrants are always more fertile than native populations. The experience of the United States at that particular point in its history may have been unique.

However, these generalizations pertain mainly to international migrations or, at least, to long distance migrations. Detailed knowledge of the nature and consequences of internal and short-distance migration in reference to age structure is not yet available. We do know that in the main, the westward migration of population within the United States continues to subtract young people out of the east and to add them to the west, thus contributing to the "aging" of the population in the east and the "younging" of the population in the west. This selective migration contributes to the finding, as we shall note presently, that the population of Alaska is a "young" population.

We will also find that there are pockets in certain rural areas of America with high proportions of aged, areas from which the younger population continues to migrate leaving the more sedentary older population behind. Such areas may be found in New England, Appallachia and in the Midwest. On the other hand, we must not assume that old people never migrate. On the contrary, it is evident that there is some increase of rate of migration between 65 and 70 years of age. This rate of migration is by no means as high as the rate for people in their 20's, but it is higher than for those in their 50's and early 60's. Such migration appears to be associated with two events in the life cycle—retirement and widowhood.

Many farmers upon retirement move into nearby towns. This largely accounts for the fact that the towns between one thousand and 2500 in population have 12.2 per cent 65 and over. Widowhood appears to produce different patterns of migration for males than for females. Elderly widowers are more likely to remain on farms and ranches, whereas farm widows most frequently move to towns and cities after the death of their husbands. This contributes to a low ratio of males among the elderly people in the urban population.

There is also some tendency for older men to move to areas where outdoor sports such as hunting and fishing may be enjoyed. Such areas not only provide recreational possibilities, they also afford business opportunities in what may be viewed as semiretirement through the operation of hunting lodges, tourist courts, and the like. This leads to high proportions of elderly males in such areas as the Ozarks and the Minnesota lakes.

## FACTORS IN THE AGING OF THE AMERICAN POPULATION

Earlier we have noted that the decline of the birth rate is the most significant and immediate factor in the aging of populations, and that compared with the birth rate, the declining death rate and immigration play minor roles. It may be well for us to examine these factors in more detail with reference to the American population.

Sheldon made such an analysis for the period from 1900 to 1950. In regard to the increase in the *numbers* of people between the ages of 60 and 89, he said the following:

> [O]f the increase in the total population 60 to 89 between 1900 and 1950 (13.3 million), about 6.6 million, or about 50 per cent can be attributed to the difference in the numbers of births; about 1.4 million, or about 11 per cent to the decline in mortality per se; about 2.8 million, or 21 per cent, to declining mortality among excess births; and about 2.5 million, or nearly 20 per cent, to immigration.[29]

By this, Sheldon means that 50 per cent of the increase in the aged population in 1950 over 1900 was due to the fact that there were more births between 1860 and 1890 (the aged in 1950) than there were between 1810 and 1840 (the aged in 1900). This was not an increase in the birth rate; it was chiefly due to an increase in the base population. Secondly, Sheldon says, if there had been only the same number of births from 1860 to 1890 that there were from 18.0 to 1840, 1.4 million more of them would have survived to old age and this accounts for 11 per cent of the increased aged in 1950. However, thirdly, the number of births during the latter period was actually much greater, and of these, 2.8 million more were surviving in 1950 than would have under the earlier death rates; thus the lower mortality among the excess births accounts for 21 per cent of the increased aged population in 1950. And, finally, in 1950, 2.5 million of the aged were survivors from earlier immigration, i.e. they were foreign-born, and this contributed another 20 per cent to the increase of the aged during the half-century.

Sheldon's calculations have two deficiencies for our present purposes. First, they are rather old, being based on the census of 1950, and, second, it is unfortunate that he defines the aged population to include persons aged 60 to 89, instead of the more conventional definition of 65 and over. Nevertheless, his calculations make the significant points that as far as increased *numbers* of the aged are concerned: the greatest contribution is from increased numbers of births, lowered death rates account for only one-third of the increase, and immigration contributes the remainder.

On the question of increasing *proportions* of the aged in our population, Sheldon makes the following comments:

> Although the decline in mortality has made an appreciable contribution to the increase in the *number* of older persons between 1900 and 1950, the data suggests that this decline has made but a small contribution to the increase in the *proportion* of older persons.
>
> [T]he contribution of immigration to the increase in the proportion of older persons in the total population between 1900 and 1950 would have been considerably less than that implied by the data on the foreign born alone.
>
> It seems reasonably clear, then that the increase in the proportion of older persons between 1900 and 1950 was for the most part a matter of declining fertility.[30]

Thus, Sheldon reaches the conclusion that the decline in the birth rate has been a preponderant margin: the most significant factor in the increased proportion of the aged in the population. The declining death rate was a small factor during the period of his study and, while most of the immigrants are now in or are approaching old age, if account were taken of the children and grandchildren of these immigrants who are now indistinguishable from the rest of the younger population, much, if not all, of this apparent "aging" influence of the earlier immigration would be canceled.

However, it is probable that Sheldon's data exaggerate the effects of declining fertility and minimize the effects of declining mortality, because of the particular period which he studied, 1900 to 1950. This was a period of rapid decline in fertility. The birth rate was about twenty-eight per thousand population in 1900, declined to 16.6 in 1933, remained relatively low until after the war when the "baby boom" brought a brief increase just prior to the 1950 census. On the other hand, most of the decrease in the death rate had already taken place before 1900; it was already down to seventeen by the beginning of the century and fell to eleven by 1921. For the remaining thirty years from 1920 to 1950, there was only slight reduction in general mortality, and much of this continued to be in the realm of infant and child mortality. Thus, the period which Sheldon studied represents a relatively short segment in the latter part of the demographic transition, a period during which there was a major change in the birth rate but relatively little change in the death rate.

It can also be argued that the United States is not a very representative case to study in order to discern the relative effects of the various dynamic factors on aging during the transition for two reasons: (1) Being a new country with a high ratio of resources to people, it has never had a really primitive death rate; at the highest it appears to have been only about thirty-five. (2) Immigration has been a highly significant, but quite variable factor, and the effects of immigration are not only difficult to sort out, as noted above, but they also confuse the issue with reference to both fertility and mortality.

However, on the basis of our general knowledge and the examination of this particular case, we may make the following generalizations:

1. A lowering of the death rate will eventuate in a greater number of older people in a population after a lag of 65 years.

2. If this is coupled with a lower fertility, such as has been the case in the demographic transition in Europe and the United States, there will be a significant increase in the proportion of older people.

3. It is the interaction of these two variables which has produced the "aged" populations shown in Table II.

4. The effects of changes in fertility on aging of populations are more immediate, dramatic and more easily perceived and measured, while the effects of changing mortality on aging are more diffuse, longer delayed and harder to perceive.

## GROWTH OF THE AGED POPULATION IN AMERICA

As of the time of this writing, there are about nineteen million persons 65 and over in America.[31] This is more than sixteen times the number a century ago, 1870, when our census first became sufficiently detailed and definitive to permit of a separate enumeration of this age group. At that time, there were only 1.2 million persons 65 and over in the population. As will be seen in Figure 2-2 and Table III, the number of aged doubled from 1870 to 1890 and by 1900 there were more than three million. This number was tripled by 1940 when there were more than nine millions and this number in turn was doubled by 1966 when the number of aged was estimated

TABLE III

NUMBER AND PER CENT OF POPULATION 65 AND OVER, UNITED STATES, 1870-1966*

| *Year* | *Number 65 and Over (Thousands)* | *Per Cent of Total Population* |
|---|---|---|
| 1870 | 1,154 | 2.9 |
| 1880 | 1,723 | 3.4 |
| 1890 | 2,417 | 3.8 |
| 1900 | 3,080 | 4.1 |
| 1910 | 3,950 | 4.3 |
| 1920 | 4,933 | 4.7 |
| 1930 | 6,634 | 5.4 |
| 1940 | 9,019 | 6.8 |
| 1950 | 12,295 | 8.1 |
| 1960 | 16,560 | 9.2 |
| 1966 | 18,457 | 9.4 |

*Data from 1870 to 1960 are from the U.S. census as summarized in "Population Trends, National, 1790-1960," *Facts on Aging,* No. 1, Jan., 1963, published by Special Staff on Aging, U.S. Department of Health, Education and Welfare. 1966 estimates from Herman B. Brotman: "National Population Trends as of July 1, 1966." *Useful Facts,* No. 15, Administration on Aging, Jan. 6, 1967.

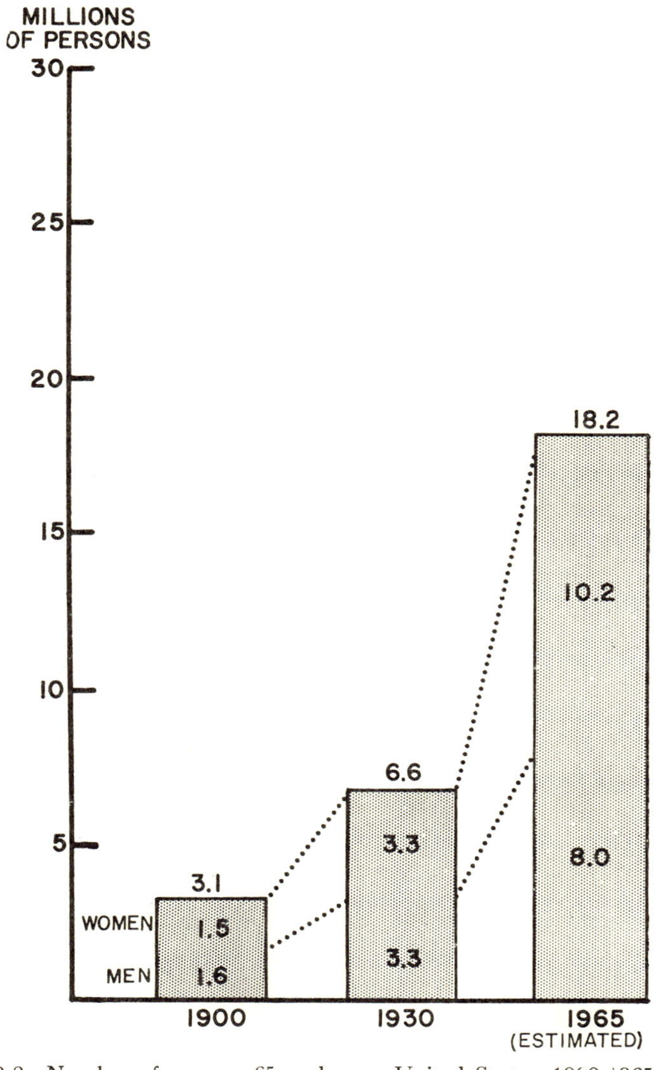


Figure 2-2. Number of persons 65 and over, United States, 1900-1965. (*From* Brotman, Herman B.: Charts of population trends, marital status, and income. *Useful Facts.* Administration of Aging, Memorandum No. 12, Dec. 7, 1966.

to be 18.5 millions. Presently, about 1.4 million pass their sixty-fifth birthday each year, but since almost 1.1 persons 65 and over die each year, we may expect an increase in the numbers of aged each year to net about 300,000.[32] At this rate of increase, there were about nineteen million as of January 1, 1968 and we should reach twenty millions early in 1971.

The past century, then, has been a period of exceedingly rapid growth of the aged population of the United States. Furthermore, the increase of the aged population has far outstripped that of the total population. During the century, the total population multiplied five times, while the aged population multiplied to sixteen times its size in 1870.

This faster rate of growth of the aged population, of course, led to a major increase in the percentage of aged in the total population, i.e. to significant aging of the population. In 1870, the aged comprised less than 3 per cent of the total. In other words, a century ago, the United States population would still have been classified as a "young" population by our classification of Table II. By 1900, it had increased to more than 4 per cent and would have been classified as a "youthful" population from 1900 to 1940, but by 1950 we had moved into the stage of "maturity," and with 9.4 per cent aged, we are now close to becoming an "aged" population. Just when we will cross that line depends on the level of the birth rate. If it continues the downward trend of the last ten years, we will become an "aged" population within the very near future, probably within the next decade.

## LIFE EXPECTANCY OF THE AMERICAN POPULATION

In terms of recent mortality rates, the average infant at birth may expect to live about 70 years. Compared with primitive populations in which, as we have seen, a child has only about a 50-50 chance of even reaching maturity, this extension of life to three score and ten years is a dramatic and revolutionary achievement.

While the trend has been under way from the very beginning of our national life, much of it has occurred during the twentieth century, as indicated in Table IV. In 1900, the life expectancy at birth for both sexes was only 47.3 years. By 1910, it had increased to 50 years and by 1930 it had almost reached 60 years. So, in two-thirds of a century, the average length of time a baby may expect to live has been extended by nearly 23 years. This is almost a 50 per cent increase.

TABLE IV
AVERAGE EXPECTATION OF LIFE AT BIRTH, BY SEX, UNITED STATES 1900-1962*

| *Year* | *Both Sexes* | *Male* | *Female* |
|---|---|---|---|
| 1900 | 47.3 | 46.3 | 48.3 |
| 1910 | 50.0 | 48.4 | 51.8 |
| 1920 | 54.1 | 53.6 | 54.6 |
| 1930 | 59.7 | 58.1 | 61.6 |
| 1940 | 62.9 | 60.8 | 65.2 |
| 1950 | 68.2 | 65.6 | 71.1 |
| 1960 | 69.7 | 66.6 | 73.1 |
| 1963 | 69.9 | 66.6 | 73.4 |

*Figures from 1900 to 1960 extracted from Herman B. Brotman: *Useful Data on Older People,* Office of Aging, Memorandum No. VII, Nov. 2/, 1964. 1963 figures from Memorandum No. 27, March 10, 1966.

Throughout our history, the average length of life of females has been greater than that of males, but the difference has tended to increase in recent decades. Table IV shows that for males in 1900, future life expectancy at birth was 46.3 years and by 1962, it had increased to 66.8, but, on the other hand, female life expectancy during the same period rose from 48.3 years to 73.4 years. In other words, while female life expectancy was only 2 years longer than male expectancy in 1900, the female advantage had widened to 6.6 years in 1962. While 20 years were being added to the life of the average male, 25 years were gained for the average female. Much of the greater margin of increase for females was due to the drastic reduction, almost the elimination, of the risk of death in childbirth.

## UNBALANCED SEX RATIOS AMONG THE AGED

The greater life expectancy of females of course results in a greater number of females in the older population. Whereas the sex ratio of the total population, including all ages, is only 103.1 females per one hundred males, an excess of only three females per one hundred males, for the population 65 and over, the ratio increases to 130.6, or an excess of thirty-one females per 100 males.[33] Stated in another way, this means that in the aged population, there are about four females for each three males.

Since the death rate for males is higher at all ages than it is for the females, the proportion of females increases steadily with age. At ages 65 to 69, the sex ratio is 119.8 females per one hundred males; but it increases to 129.5 at ages 70 to 74; to 135.8 at ages 75 to 79; to 145.2 at ages 80 to 84; and to 161.4 at ages 85 and over.[34] Thus, by the age of 85, we find that the ratio has increased to about five females for each three males.

Of course, these unbalanced sex ratios among the aged have very significant impact upon the marital status and living arrangements of the aged, as we shall see presently.

## AGED DISTRIBUTION OF THE AGED

Of the population 65 and over, half are under 73 and the other half are over 73, i.e. the median age of the aged population is 73 years. This is obviously a very skewed distribution, with most of the individuals at the lower end of the range. The details of this distribution are shown in Table V.

TABLE V

NUMBER AND PER CENT OF PEOPLE 65 AND OVER IN THE UNITED STATES POPULATION, JULY 1, 1966*

| | *Number (Thousands)* | *Per Cent of Total Population* | *Per Cent of Aged Population* |
|---|---|---|---|
| *Total* | 18,457 | 9.4 | 100.0 |
| 65-69 | 6,378 | 3.2 | 34.6 |
| 70-74 | 5,190 | 2.6 | 28.1 |
| 75-79 | 3,688 | 1.9 | 20.0 |
| 80-84 | 2,076 | 1.0 | 11.2 |
| 85 and Over | 1,124 | 0.6 | 6.1 |

*Data from Herman B. Brotman: "National Population Trends as of July 1, 1966." *Useful Facts,* No. 15, Administration on Aging, Jan. 6, 1967, Table 1, Part A & C.

Here we see that more than one-third of the aged population is to be found in the lowest 5-year age-group, 65 to 69. Another one-fourth of the aged are found in the age-group, 70 to 74, with the result that fully five-eighths of the aged population is under 75 years of age. However, this is to be expected, and what should be emphasized is not the high proportions in the younger ages, but the unprecedentedly high proportions in the upper ages. What is really important and dramatic about these statistics is that as many as 3.5 per cent of the total population is over 75 years of age, and that this comprises about three out of eight of all of the population 65 years of age and over. Futhermore, one out of six of the aged, 17.3 per cent, is 80 years of age and older, and 6.1 per cent is 85 years of age or older.

It may be more important to see these individuals as numbers rather than as percentages. In the United States, we now have nearly seven million persons who are 75 years of age or older, more than one million who are 85 years of age and older, and about thirteen thousand centenarians.

## MARITAL STATUS OF THE AGED

Because of the greater life expectancy of females and the fact that husbands are usually two to three years older than their wives, we find a great excess of widows among the aged population. Among the total population 65 and over in 1965, less than one-fifth of the men were widowers, while more than one-half of the women were widows. This accounts for the fact that among the aged population, we find 5.5 million widows as compared with only 1.5 million widowers. (See Fig. 2-3.)

The counterpart of these figures is the fact that two-thirds of the males 65 and over are married and living with their spouses (67.9 per cent) while only one-third of the women 65 and over are married and living with their husbands (34.1 per cent). Many of the

TABLE VI

MARITAL STATUS OF PERSONS 65 AND OVER BY SEX, UNITED STATES, MARCH, 1965

(number in thousands)

| *Marital Status* | *Both Sexes* | *Male* | *Female* |
|---|---|---|---|
| Total | 18,077 | 7,910 | 10,167 |
| Single | 1,310 | 526 | 784 |
| Married | 9,300 | 5,641 | 3,659 |
| Spouse present | 8,840 | 5,373 | 3,467 |
| Spouse absent | 460 | 268 | 192 |
| Widowed | 7,068 | 1,540 | 5,528 |
| Divorced | 401 | 203 | 198 |

Data from Herman B. Brotman: "Marital Status of Older Persons," Administration on Aging, *Useful Data on Older People,* Memorandum No. 18, Jan. 27, 1966.

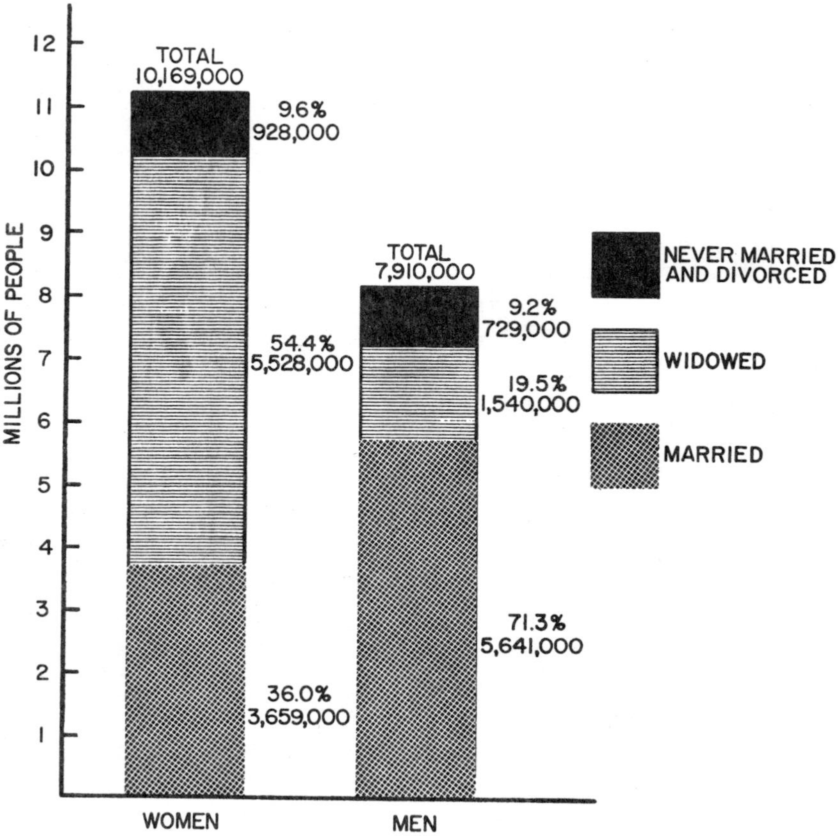


Figure 2-3. Marital status of persons 65 and over, by sex, United States, 1965. (*From* Brotman, Herman B., Charts of population trends, marital status, and income, *Useful Facts,* Administration on Aging, Memorandum No. 12, Dec. 7, 1966.

husbands 65 and over have wives who are under 65; this is the main explanation for the fact that there are about 5.4 million males married with wives present while there are only about 3.5 million women 65 and over who are married and living with their husbands as shown in Table VI. Very few of either sex are single and have never been married and likewise the proportions who are currently divorced are very small.

Of course, marital status changes with increasing age and this applies to people over 65 as well as those who are younger. (See

TABLE VII

MARITAL STATUS OF PERSONS 65 AND OVER BY AGE AND SEX, UNITED STATES, MARCH, 1965*

(*Per Cent*)

| *Marital Status* | Male Total | Male 65-74 | Male 75+ | Female Total | Female 65-74 | Female 75+ |
|---|---|---|---|---|---|---|
| Total | 100.0 | 100.0 | 100.0 | 100.0 | 100.0 | 100.0 |
| Single | 6.6 | 6.1 | 7.6 | 7.7 | 7.5 | 8.0 |
| Married | 71.3 | 78.9 | 57.1 | 36.0 | 45.7 | 20.2 |
| Spouse present | 67.9 | 75.3 | 54.0 | 34.1 | 43.3 | 19.0 |
| Spouse absent | 3.4 | 3.6 | 3.1 | 1.9 | 2.3 | 1.2 |
| Widowed | 19.5 | 11.8 | 34.0 | 54.4 | 44.4 | 70.6 |
| Divorced | 2.6 | 3.3 | 1.3 | 1.9 | 2.4 | 1.2 |

Data from Herman B Brotman: "Marital Status of Older persons," *Useful Data on Older People,* Administration on Aging, Memorandum No. 18, Jan. 27, 1966.

Table VII.) With increasing age, beyond 65, the proportion of persons widowed continues to rise and the proportion currently married declines. For example, whereas only 12 per cent of the males 65 to 74 years of age are widowed, the percentage rises to 34 for those 75 and over. For females, both percentages are much higher, but the change is in the same direction and is greater in degree; 44 per cent of those 65 to 74 are widowed and the percentage rises to 71 for those 75 and over. Thus we find that one out of three of the males 75 and over are widowers while seven out of ten females of this advanced age are widows. The numbers behind these percentages may be impressive; there are less than a million widowers aged 75 and over, but there are about three times as many widows of this age, 2.7 million.

Three-fourths of the men 65 to 74 years of age are married and living with their wives, but the proportion drops to 54 per cent for those 75 and over. Of course, both proportions are much lower for women; only 43 per cent of those 65 to 74 are still married and living with their husbands and the percentage drops to only nineteen for those 75 and over. Thus, slightly more than half of the males 75 and over are still married and living with their wives, but only one out of five women 75 and over is married and living with her husband.

Marital status is one of the primary factors which determines living arrangements and family status, but it does not tell the entire story. Considering both sexes together, we find that seven out of ten persons 65 and over live in families, half of them including an elderly couple. Three out of ten do not live in families, but only 4 per cent live in institutions. The actual number in institutions is quite small, 717,000.

However, as we would expect in terms of the sex ratio and marital status, the family statuses of males and of females are quite different. As Figure 2-4 indicates, a much greater proportion of the older men are living in a family setting than of the older women. Eight out of ten older men are in families, while only six out of ten older women are so situated. For two-thirds of the men this family includes their wives, but the proportion is reversed for the women, only one-third of them are living in families which include their

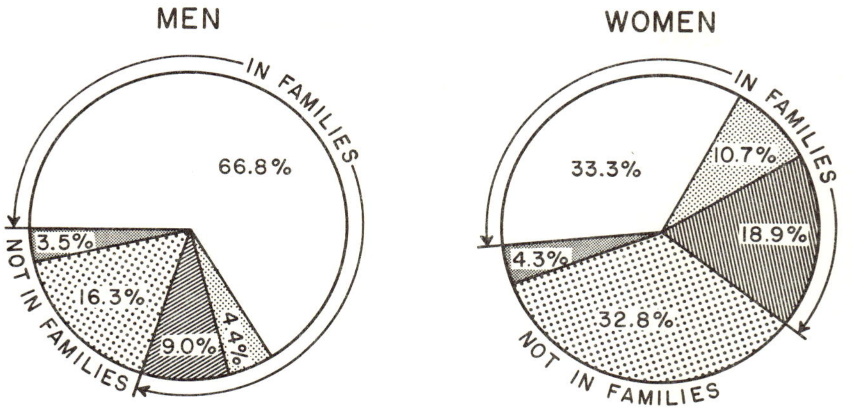


| | NUMBER MEN | NUMBER WOMEN |
|---|---|---|
| In husband-wife family | 5,287,000 | 3,389,000 |
| Family head, no spouse present | 351,000 | 1,091,000 |
| Family member related to head | 712,000 | 1,918,000 |
| Living alone or with no relatives | 1,283,000 | 3,329,000 |
| Living in an institution | 277,000 | 440,000 |

Figure 2-4. Family status of persons 65 and over, by sex, United States, 1965. (*From* Facts about Older Americans, U. S. Department of Health, Education, and Welfare, Administration on Aging. Publication No. 410, May, 1966.

husbands. About one-tenth of the women are heads of households containing other relatives and another two-tenths are living in the households of relatives.

One-third of the women live alone or with nonrelatives, while only one-sixth of the men live in such surroundings. However, these two categories total more than 4.6 million older people who are living by themselves or with nonrelatives and these added to the institutional population, comprise 5.3 million individuals who are living apart from their own families.

However, what is most impressive about these figures, is the fact that many older people manage to maintain themselves in a family setting in spite of widowhood. About 1.4 million maintain their own households with other relatives living with them, and an additional 2.6 million live in the households of relatives. This amounts to more than four million older persons (22.5%) who are living with relatives other than their spouses. This bespeaks a greater viability and adaptability of the American family than has usually been thought. In spite of the attenuation of kinship relationships and the extended form of the family in Western society, in old age we find many older people being incorporated into various extensions and compromise versions of the extended family. Apparently blood is not only thicker than water; it is thicker than freeway traffic.

## RACE AND NATIVITY OF THE AGED

We noted earlier that immigration was one of the factors which has had an influence on the aging of our population. This observation is confirmed by an analysis of the origins and nativity of our contemporary aged population as shown in Table VIII. Whereas only 5 per cent of the total population is now made up of persons who were born in other countries, 20 per cent of the aged are foreign-born. This, of course, is a function of the fact that the peak of the immigration into this country took place sixty years ago and while most of the immigrants were young adults when they arrived, they are now becoming aged. In fact, the median age of the foreign-born in 1960 was 58 years.[35]

TABLE VIII
NATIVITY AND PARENTAGE OF THE POPULATION, BY AGE, UNITED STATES, 1960

| | *All Ages* | *Under 65* | *65+* |
|---|---|---|---|
| *Total* | *100.0* | *100.0* | *100.0* |
| Native born | 94.6 | 96.0 | 80.4 |
| Native parentage | 81.0 | 82.9 | 61.7 |
| Foreign or mixed parentage | 13.6 | 13.0 | 18.7 |
| Foreign born | 5.4 | 4.0 | 19.6 |
| Foreign ancestry | 19.0 | 17.0 | 38.3 |

Data from Herman B. Brotman: "Highlights," *Useful Data on Older People,* Administration on Aging, Memorandum No. 27, March 10, 1966.

It is also significant to note that an almost equal proportion of the aged population is second generation, i.e. of foreign or mixed parentage. In other words, almost two out of five (38.3%) of our elderly population either were born abroad themselves or one or both of their parents were.

This means that many of our aged derive from divergent cultural backgrounds, for many their mother tongue was not English, many have experienced the conflict of cultures attendant upon immigration, and many have had only a limited amount of formal education, as we shall see later.

While the older population contains more than its share of those of foreign extraction, it contains less than the expected proportions of nonwhites. Only 1.4 million of the aged are nonwhites and these comprise only 7.7 per cent of the aged whereas nonwhites make up nearly 12 per cent of the total population of the country.[36] The counterpart of these statistics is the fact that only 6.1 per cent of the nonwhite population is 65 and over, as compared with 9.3 per cent of the total population and 9.8 per cent of the white population.

This lower proportion of nonwhites among the aged and the lower proportion of aged in the nonwhite population reflects chiefly the higher death rate among the nonwhites, although a somewhat higher birth rate tends in the same direction.

## EDUCATIONAL ATTAINMENT OF THE AGED

America's aged grew up in a period when the principle of universal education was just becoming established and before education had become acknowledged everywhere as a state function which must be enforced by compulsory attendance laws. In view of this, it is not surprising that for the population which is 65 years of age and over today, the median years of school completed is only 8.4 years. This indicates that the standard level of education in that era, even if not universally compulsory, was an elementary school education. Since that time, of course, the standard has increased and for the succeeding generation a high school education became the mode, with the result that the median for the entire population 25 years of age and over is now almost twelve years (11.7).

These figures are shown in Table IX, which also indicates the percentages of the two age groups which are classified as functionally illiterate, i.e. those with less than five years of formal schooling. For the population 65 and over, one out of five is so classified, com-

TABLE IX

MEDIAN YEARS OF SCHOOL COMPLETED AND PERCENT FUNCTIONALLY ILLITERATE, BY AGE, SEX AND COLOR, UNITED STATES, MARCH, 1964

| | *Median Years Completed* | | *Per Cent Functionally Illiterate** | |
|---|---|---|---|---|
| | *25+* | *65+* | *25+* | *65+* |
| Both sexes | 11.7 | 8.4 | 7.1 | 19.4 |
| Male | 11.5 | 8.3 | 8.1 | 21.9 |
| Female | 11.8 | 8.5 | 6.3 | 17.3 |
| Nonwhite | 8.9 | 5.0 | 18.6 | 50.3 |

Data from Herman B. Brotman: "Highlights," *Useful Data on Older People,* Administration on Aging, Memorandum No. 27, March 10, 1966.
*None or less than 5 years of schooling.

pared with only one out of fourteen for the entire adult population. Both measures indicate that females in our population have received more education than males.

However, Table IX also reveals that the nonwhites, both old and young, are under a great educational handicap. Nonwhites 65 and over have a median of only five years of education and fully half of them are rated as functionally illiterate.

## THE AGED IN THE LABOR FORCE

Retirement from full-time employment is becoming a more widespread practice in old age and the age at which retirement takes place is tending downward. These trends explain the relatively low proportion of the aged who are now either employed or seeking employment in the United States.

In 1965, only one out of four males (27.8 per cent) 65 and over was in the labor force, and for females the proportion was only one out of ten, as shown in Table X. However, the trends are in the opposite directions for the two sexes. Since 1890, when more than two-thirds (68.3 per cent) of the aged males were in the labor force, the trend has been steadily and decisively downward. By 1930 only about one-half were still in the labor force, by 1960 less than one-third were working or seeking work, and the trend is continuing downward. On the other hand, there has been a slight increase in the proportion of elderly females in the labor force, but this has been quite recent (since 1950) and appears to be just a spill-over effect from a very dramatic increase in the proportion of middle-aged women (45 to 64) in the labor force. From only 12.1 per cent of the women 45 to 64 in the labor force in 1890, we have witnessed a rapid increase to almost half (46.6%) in 1965. A few of these women apparently are continuing to work beyond the age of 65 and thus are contributing to a slight rise in that percentage.

TABLE X

PERCENT OF POPULATION IN LABOR FORCE, BY AGE AND SEX, UNITED STATES, 1890-1965

| | *Males* | | | *Females* | | |
|---|---|---|---|---|---|---|
| *Year* | 14+ | 45-64 | 65+ | 14+ | 45-64 | 65+ |
| 1890 | 84.3 | 92.0 | 68.3 | 18.2 | 12.1 | 7.6 |
| 1900 | 85.7 | 90.3 | 63.1 | 20.0 | .3.6 | 8.3 |
| 1920 | 84.6 | 90.7 | 55.6 | 22.7 | 16.5 | 7.3 |
| 1930 | 82.1 | 91.0 | 54.0 | 23.6 | 18.0 | 7.3 |
| 1940 | 79.7 | 89.4 | 42.2 | 25.7 | 20.0 | 6.0 |
| 1950 | 79.0 | 88.2 | 41.4 | 29.0 | 28.8 | 7.8 |
| 1960 | 77.4 | 89.0 | 30.5 | 34.5 | 41.6 | 10.3 |
| 1965 | 78.3 | 90.9 | 27.8 | 38.0 | 46.6 | 10.0 |

Data from Herman B. Brotman: "The Older Worker in 1965," *Useful Facts,* Administration on Aging, Memorandum No. 5, Nov. 16, 1966.

However, the numbers of older people who are currently employed are relatively small; slightly more than three million, with a little more than two million males and slightly less than one million females. Together these comprise less than 4 per cent of the total labor force.

## GEOGRAPHIC DISTRIBUTION OF THE AGED

If we were to apply the classification of populations in terms of the degree of agedness which was proposed earlier to the various states of the United States, we would find that twenty of the fifty states are now "aged." That is, twenty of the states have populations in which 10 per cent or more of the people are 65 and over. However, since the United States as a whole is one of the more "mature" populations and since there is considerable variation among the states, it is necessary in developing a map of these variations to increase the lower limits of the classes. In Figure 2-5, the class of states with the most aged, including nine of the fifty states, includes those with 11 per cent or more 65 and over.

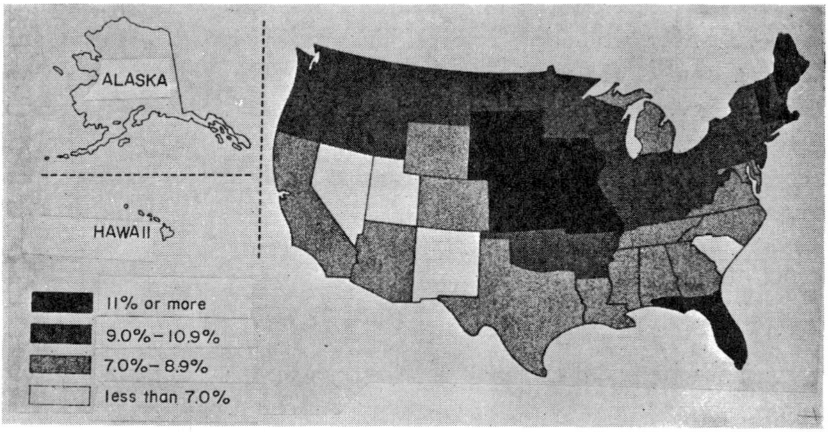


Figure 2-5. Per cent of the population 65 and over, by state, United States, 1965. (*From* Facts About Older Americans. U.S. Department of Health, Education, and Welfare, Administration on Aging, Publication No. 410, May 1966.

As will be seen, the most aged states are to be found in three separate sections of the country. The largest and most compact group of aged states include five in the heart of the nation—Iowa, Nebraska, Missouri, Kansas and South Dakota. Iowa ranks number 1 among all of the states in the proportion of the aged with 12.5 per cent, Nebraska ranks third, Missouri fourth, Kansas fifth and South Dakota ninth. A second concentration of the aged is to be found in the New England States of Maine, Vermont and Massachusetts, the third area of concentration is the single state of Florida which ranks second among all of the states.

Other states that are relatively high in the proportion include all of the northern tier of states from New Hampshire to Washington with the single exception of Michigan. This band of states extends southward enough to include West Virginia, Kentucky, Arkansas, Oklahoma and Oregon.

At the opposite extreme with a very young population is Alaska with only 2.4 per cent of its population 65 and over. Close behind are Hawaii and three southwestern states—Nevada, Utah and New Mexico—and South Carolina. However, we may note that with the exception of Florida, all of the southern and southwestern states, including California, have less than 9 per cent of their populations 65 and over.

Several different factors lie behind these varying proportions, but in the main they boil down to variations in fertility, mortality and migration. High fertility rates coupled with high mortality in the south and southwest militate in the direction of relatively young populations. In the Far West, however, including Alaska, Hawaii and California, there is the added factor of continued inmigration of young from the Midwest, South and East. On the other hand, Florida, Oregon and Washington appear to be recipients of greater numbers of older migrants, enough to increase the proportion of the aged.

As usual, the areas from which the bulk of the migration flows are drained of their youthful populations to a sufficient degree that the more sedentary aged population constitutes a higher proportion of the remainder. This, chiefly, accounts for the high proportions of the aged in the Midwest and in New England. These areas have relatively low fertility and low mortality rates also, but outmigration of the young population is undoubtedly the major factor contributing to their agedness.

In the main, there appears to be a tendency for these variations to be abated, since, with the exception of Florida, the states which have shown the greatest increases in their aged populations since 1960 have been Arizona, Nevada, Hawaii, and New Mexico, all of which are states with relatively low proportions of the aged. In all of these states, the numbers of aged increased by more than 20 per cent from 1960 to 1966.[37] Likewise, some of the states with the highest proportions of the aged emerge among those with the least increase during this period. Vermont had no increase at all, and Montana, Maine, North Dakota, Missouri, Iowa, Indiana, and West Virginia had increases of less than 6 per cent, as compared with an average increase in the aged population for the United States as a whole of 11.4 per cent and an increase of 9.2 per cent in the total population.

In spite of these varying and changing patterns of distribution in terms of proportions of the total population, we must not assume that the highest percentages necessarily indicate the points of concentration of the greatest numbers of the aged. For the most part, the pattern of distribution of the aged in terms of numbers resembles that of the general population, except that it is slightly more concentrated, with fewer in the wide open spaces of the Southwest, and more in the cities and small towns of the Midwest and East. While California is now larger than New York in terms of total population, New York still has the greater number of aged, and these two states plus Pennsylvania and Illinois contain nearly one-third of all of the aged in the country. In planning services and markets, numbers mean more than percentages.

## LOCAL VARIATIONS IN THE AGED POPULATION

The analysis of the distribution of the aged population on an interstate basis reveals some of the gross variations and differences, but it does not get at the details of local residential preference and migration which begin to emerge when analysis is reduced from the interstate level to a county-by-county basis. Such an analysis on a nationwide basis would be desirable and revealing, but it is also quite massive in scale, since it involves calculations for more than three thousand separate territorial units. Such an analysis has not yet been carried out, but this type of analysis has been conducted for the midwestern region including nine states which as we have already seen contain that pocket of the United States in which there is the highest proportion of the aged in the country.[38] The region contains six of the top ten states in the proportion of the aged, and seven out of the nine states have more than 10 per cent of their populations 65 and over.

Earlier in our history, cities were the haven of the young, and rural areas, the sources of young migrants to the cities, were left with high proportions of older people. This pattern is rapidly disappearing and, in 1960, for the country as a whole, rural areas had only the slightest margin over the urban in the proportion of persons 65 and over: 9.3 per cent compared with 9.2 per cent in the urban population. However, this obscures more than it reveals about residential patterns of the aged. In the first place, the rural population includes people both on farms and in small towns, places up to 2500 population, and while old people have been increasingly moving off of farms at retirement, there are significant numbers who move into small towns and make these communities their retirement homes. This accounts for the fact that 12.2 per cent of the population of towns one thousand to 2500 in population was 65 and over in 1960. In the second place, this pattern appears to be a much more prevalent pattern in the Midwest than it is in other parts of the country. When old people migrate to Florida or Arizona they settle in cities, but when they move from the farm in Iowa to the nearest town, they most commonly are found in villages and small towns. This accounts for the fact that whereas in Florida and California "retirement communities" are artificially planned, built and promoted, in the Midwest they are "home grown" and natural, i.e. nobody plans them, they just grow. But there are far more old people in the thousands of such natural small towns in the Midwest and other parts of the country than in the "hothouse" retirement communities of the South and West.

Figure 2-6 shows that in one of the centers of concentration of the aged in the United States, the highest proportions are to be found in rural pockets in northern Missouri, southwestern Missouri and eastern Kansas, and in northern Kansas and southern Nebraska. Some of the counties in these areas have more than one out of five of their inhabitants 65 and over, and in certain towns, such as Howard, Kansas, almost one-third of the people are elderly.

The areas in which these concentrations occur are predominantly rural, with much of the population, particularly the aged population, living in small towns and villages. They are areas which are removed some distance from major metropolitan centers, but not so far away as to be completely inaccessible to the services and facilities of such centers, as are sparsely settled sections of western North and South Dakota, for example.

The areas of relatively high concentration of the aged are areas of declining population, due to outmigration of the young and areas of low income and stagnant economies. Thus, again we find that the relative concentration of the aged is not due to the migration of the aged but to the migration of the young, the young moving out and leaving the aged behind.

However, there are local exceptions to this and even in the Midwest there are areas which are sufficiently attractive as retirement havens to draw retirees from greater distances than the adjacent farm areas and thus to produce local concentrations of the aged which are

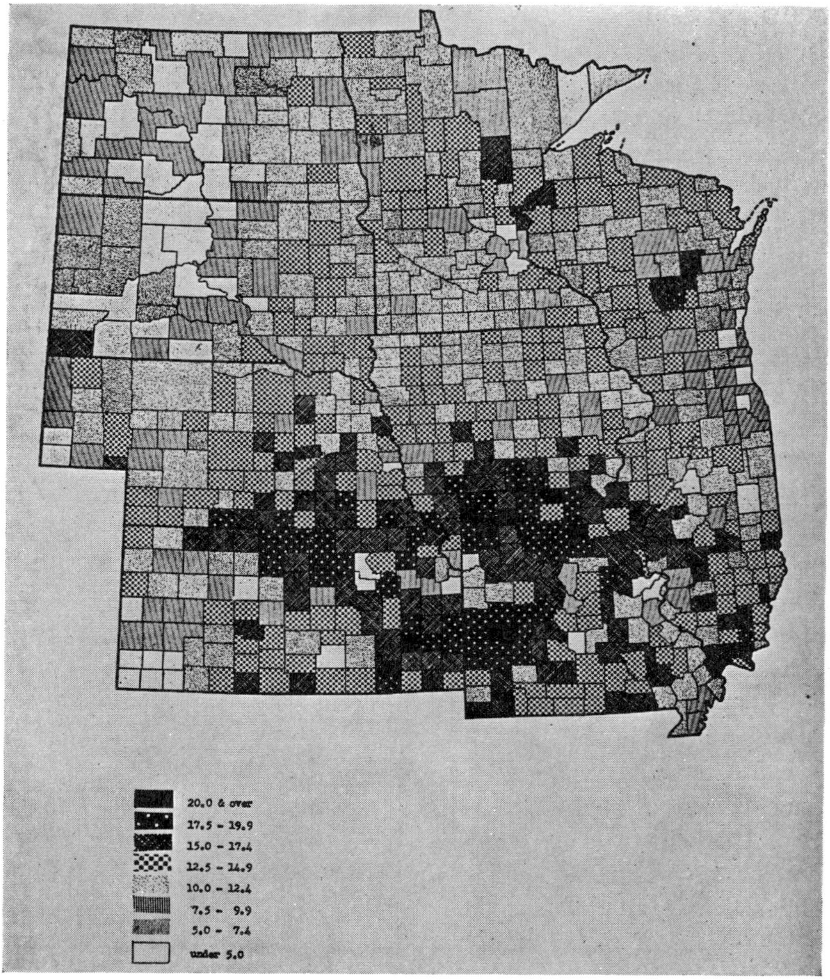


Figure 2-6. Per cent of population 65 and over, by county in nine midwestern states, 1960. (*From* Rose, A. H. and Peterson, W. A.: *Older People and Their Social World,* Philadelphia, F. A. Davis Company, 1965. p. 280.

not due to outmigration of the young, but to inmigration of the old. Some of the local concentrations in Minnesota, Wisconsin, and the Ozarks region of Missouri appear to be of this order. Furthermore, we may observe that these areas are most attractive to older men both for business and recreational purposes.[39] It may also be remarked that older people, like their younger counterparts, continue to migrate out of the Great Plains areas of the western Dakotas, and that in all parts of the region, older women have a tendency to gravitate to the cities while older men have a greater tendency either to remain in the rural areas or to migrate to resort areas.[40]

## THE ECOLOGY OF AGING IN AMERICAN CITIES

In general, the aged are more concentrated in the central cities of our metropolitan area than the general population and they even have a tendency to be concentrated toward the center of the inner cities.

This pattern is clearly illustrated in Figure 2-7 which shows the per cent of the population 65 and over by census tract for Wichita, Kansas.[41] From one-fourth to one-fifth of the population in the central areas of the city, in and adjacent to the central business district, are 65 and over, and the proportion of the aged declines steadily to the city limits and beyond into the suburbs.

While there are local variations in this pattern from city to city and

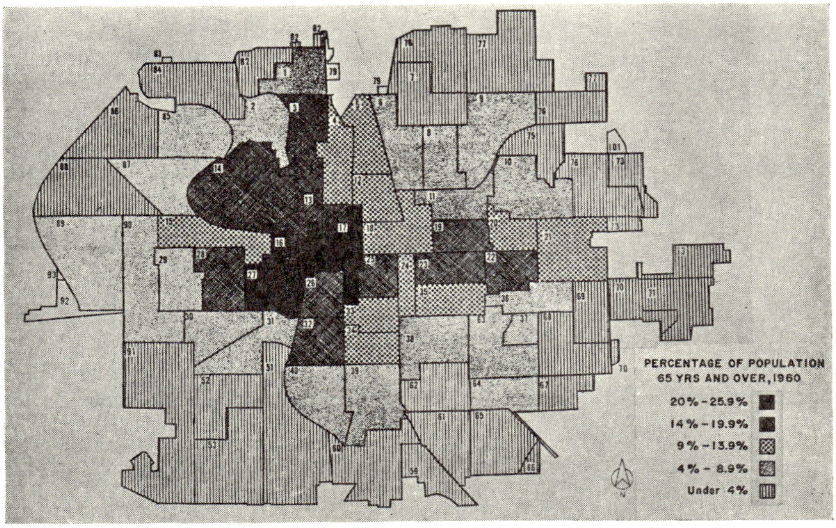


Figue 2-7. Per cent of the population 65 and over, by census tract, Wichita, Kansas, 1960. (*From* Cowgill, Donald O. and Ostertag, F. Samuel, Jr.: *The People of Wichita, 1960,* Wichita: Urban Studies Center, 1962, p. 22.

not all cities have such distinctive patterns as Wichita, all appear to manifest a considerable degree of concentration of the aged near the center.[42] Furthermore, this pattern appears to persist through time.[43]

## SUMMARY

Modern populations are undergoing a Revolution of Aging. As they pass through the Demographic Transition, they accumulate greater numbers and proportions of older people. Pre-industrial populations are "young"; rarely do they have as many as 4 per cent of their population 65 and over. By contrast, populations in highly industrialized portions of the world which for the most part are in the late phases of the Transition are "aged" populations, i.e. they usually have 10 per cent or more of their population aged 65 and over.

The United States now has a "mature" but not "aged" population. It is aging for the same reasons that populations of other modern and industrialized nations have aged, namely, a decline in mortality coupled with a subsequent decline in fertility. The decline in mortality permits greater numbers of people to live to old age, while a decline in fertility ultimately reduces the proportion of the population in the younger years. Presently 9.4 per cent of the population is 65 and over and average life expectancy at birth is 70 years.

As is generally true, our older population has a very high proportion of females and, of course, a high proportion of widows. More than half of the women 65 and over are widowed, but only one out of five older men is a widower. This is the chief reason that a much higher proportion of the older men are living in normal family settings and that fully one-third of the older women either live alone or with nonrelatives. A high proportion of America's aged at the present time are either foreign-born or second generation, but a low proportion of them are nonwhite. The average older person in the population has completed only eight years of formal schooling and one out of five has less than five years. About one out of four males and one out of ten females is in the labor force, and the proportion of males in the labor force continues to decline.

The highest proportions of the aged are found in the Midwest, New England and Florida, but the greatest numbers, of course, are still found in the most populous states which, by and large, are the most highly urbanized. However, local variations within the Midwest indicate that the highest proportions are found neither in sparsely settled rural areas nor in metropolitan centers, but in small towns in diversified farming areas of Iowa, Missouri, Kansas and Nebraska. These concentrations are produced chiefly by outmigration of the younger population. Within the cities themselves the aged tend to be concentrated in the central areas where housing is older and often in a deteriorated or dilapidated condition.

## REFERENCES

1. Valaoris, V.G.: Patterns of aging of human populations. In *The Social and Biological Challenge of Our Aging Population,* Proceedings of the the Eastern States Health Education Conference, March 31-April 1, 1949. New York, Columbia, 1950, pp. 67-85.
2. Sheldon, Henry D.: 1950 figures in The changing demographic profile. In Tibbitts, Clark: *Handbook of Social Gerontology.* Chicago, U. of Chicago, 1960, p. 29. (The index for 1960 was computed by Cowgill from Census figures.)
3. *Ibid.,* p. 50. (Again the 1960 ratio was computed by Cowgill from Census figures.)
4. Rosset, Edward: *Aging Process of Population.* New York, Macmillan, 1964, p. 89.
5. *Ibid.,* p. 90.
6. *Ibid.*
7. *Ibid.,* pp. 91-92.
8. *Ibid.,* p. 95.
9. *Ibid.*
10. *Ibid.,* p. 96.
11. *Ibid.,* p. 98.
12. *Ibid.,* p. 98.
13. Simmons, Leo: *The Role of the Aged in Primitive Society.* London, Oxford U. P., 1945, p. 6.
14. Cowgill, Donald O.: Toward a Sociological Theory of Aging Based on Cross-Cultural Observations. A paper prepared for the annual meeting of the Gerontological Society, St. Petersburg, Florida, November 9-12, 1967.
15. Howells, W.W.: Estimating population numbers through archeological and skeletal remains. In Heizer, Robert F., and Cook, Sherburne F.: *The Application of Quantitative Methods in Archeology.* Chicago, Quadrangle, 1960, p. 171.
16. Thomlinson, Ralph: *Population Dynamics.* New York, Random, 1965, p. 75.

17. *Ibid.*
18. Howells, W.W., *op. cit.,* p. 169.
19. *Ibid.,* p. 170.
20. Thomlinson, *op. cit.,* p. 76.
21. *Ibid.*
22. *Ibid.*
23. *Ibid.*
24. United Nations: *The Aging of Populations and Its Economic and Social Implications.* New York, United Nations, Population Studies, 1956.
25. Cowgill, Donald O.: The theory of population growth cycles. *Amer J Sociol, LV*:163-170, Sept. 1949.
26 Cowgill, Donald O.: Transition theory as general population theory. *Social Forces, XLI*:270-274, 1963. (Statement of other concomitant changes of composition.)
27. Sheldon, Henry D., *op. cit.,* chap. 2; also Coale, Ansley J.: How a population ages or grows younger. In Freedman, Ronald (Ed.): *Population: The Vital Revolution.* Chicago, Aldine, 1964, chap. 3.
28. U.S. Department of Health, Education and Welfare, National Center for Health Statistics: *Monthly Vital Statistics Report.* February 26, 1968, Vol. 16.
29. Sheldon, Henry D.: *The Older Population of the United States.* New York, Wiley, 1958, p. 18.
30. *Ibid.,* p. 19.
31. Brotman, Herman B.: A profile of the older American. *Useful Facts,* Administration on Aging, Memorandum No. 31, Nov. 20, 1967.
32. Brotman, Herman B.: Highlights. *Useful Data on Older People.* Administration on Aging, Memorandum No. 27, March 10, 1966.
33. Brotman, Herman B.: National population trends as of July 1, 1966. *Useful Facts.* Administration on Aging, Memorandum No. 15, Jan. 6, 1967.
34. *Ibid.*
35. Thompson, Warren S., and Lewis, David T.: *Population Problems,* 5th ed., New York, McGraw, 1965, p. 89.
36. Brotman, Herman B.: Recent national trends, mid-1964. *Facts on Aging.* Office of Aging, Memorandum No. 9, June 1965.
37. Brotman, Herman B.: Older population, 1966, by state. *Useful Facts.* Administration on Aging, Memorandum No. 3, Oct. 28, 1966.
38. Cowgill, Donald O.: The demography of aging in the midwest. In Rose, Arnold M. and Peterson, Warren A.: *Older People and Their Social World.* Philadelphia, Davis, 1965, chap. 18.
39. *Ibid.,* p. 288.
40. Cleland, Courtney B.: Shifting population in North Dakota and its relation to the aged. (An address to the Action for the Aging Conference at the University of North Dakota, September 6, 1962) and Smith, T. Lynn, and Marshall, Douglas G.: *Our Aging Population: The United*

*States and Wisconsin.* Madison, U. Wis., Department of Rural Sociology, Wisconsin Population Series, April 1963, p. 15.

41. Cowgill, Donald O., and Ostertag, Samuel F., Jr.: *The People of Wichita, 1960.* Wichita, Wichita State University, The Center for Urban Studies, 1962, p. 22.
42. Cowgill, Donald O.: Ecological patterns of the aged in American cities. *Midwest Sociol. XX*:78-83. 1958.
43. Cowgill, Donald O.: Trends in the ecology of the aged in American cities, 1940-1950. *J Geront, XII*:75-80, Jan. 1957.

*Chapter 3*

# THE ELDERLY AND POLITICS

JOHN R. SCHMIDHAUSER

## INTRODUCTION

IN TWENTIETH CENTURY America, the political role of elderly persons remains one of the least understood aspects of our political and social life. Clearly the elderly have not been the subject of so complete an analysis as Gunnar Myrdal's *An American Dilemma* or the wide ranging explorations of juvenile delinquency. Yet it is evident that the elderly comprise a significantly large segment of our population. Indeed as early as 1948, Otto Pollak estimated that the elderly made up a larger proportion of our population than did either Negroes or juveniles.[1]

A striking example of the kind of sweeping assertion occasionally made about the political behavior of the elderly appeared in an article entitled "Old Age Turns Explosive." This widely disseminated piece illustrates the broad kind of generalization, often devoid of supporting evidence, which is made, on occasion, about older persons.

> [C]onsider the rapidity with which the aging of the population is creating a problem for the politicians. They have known that this change in our age level was loaded with political dynamite ever since Dr. Francis E. Townsend flashed over the national horizon. In such states as California, Florida and Arizona the "retired" vote may soon come as close to holding a balance of political power as has the Jewish vote in New York. . . . The effect on national as well as state politics may, in a couple of decades, turn out to be spectacular. And since these "elder citizens" tend to think in patterns laid down in these formative years, they constitute a ticklish factor for the politician—conservatism on large questions of national policy coupled with desires for radical gains in their own social benefits.[2]

How valid are these assertions? Are movements like the Townsend

---

*Note:* Some of the materials for this chapter were taken from the author's works that appeared in the *Western Political Quarterly,* March 1958, and *The Gerontologist,* Spring 1968, and are used here with permission of the Editors.

movement apt to recur? Do the elderly engage in bloc voting? Does the adoption of old-age programs by the national Congress or some of the state legislatures reflect the fruits of a cohesive drive by the elderly or a more broadly based support from all age groups? The first such analysis by this author was published in 1958. There is increasing evidence that the political behavior of the elderly is much more complex than the foregoing generalization would suggest.

Age differences and the variation in cultural definitions of age differences have been recognized as among the most important factors in the study of human behavior. The concept of generational differences stressed by sociologists such as Eisenstadt has challenging implications for the study of political behavior.[3] Two recent articles in the *Public Opinion Quarterly* by Elmo Roper and Stuart Chase represent tentative beginnings of such exploration.[4] The role of the elderly as members of interest groups received early treatment by journalists Richard Neuberger and Kelley Loe and social scientist Hadley Cantril.[5] Since the 1940's, the development of accurate survey research sampling has contributed significant material on the political behavior of older persons, although much additional investigation is needed.

Through utilization of the studies of the Columbia University Bureau of Applied Social Research and the University of Michigan Survey Research Center, several aspects of senior citizen political behavior could be identified.

## The Problem of Definition

As was pointed out in an earlier analysis,

> Criteria for defining the precise age at which individuals are termed "old" or "aged" vary. Age 65 is perhaps most frequently used because it represents a terminal year in many private retirement and annuity programs and because it has been accepted as the age of eligibility for social security benefits. There is, however, evidence of a downward trend in retirement programs.
>
> When social attitudes toward older persons are taken into consideration, age 60 or younger has been suggested as more appropriate. In this account, a person whose age is 55 or over will be classified as old for the practical reason that the political behavior studies utilized for much of what follows generally accept this classification. When material from investigations employing different standards for distinguishing older persons from members of other age groups is utilized, the variation in standards will be noted in parentheses in the text.[6]

## THE SIGNIFICANT CONCENTRATION OF THE ELDERLY

The political importance of the elderly is impressively portrayed in a variety of population statistics. Cowgill's recent analysis of midwestern demographic data, for example, contains information which dramatizes a most significant factor in political analysis. The location or more dense concentration of elderly persons in certain states and in the counties of certain states suggests that the voting behavior of elderly persons is particularly significant in certain regions or states. On the basis of the 1960 Census data, three states in the Midwest, Iowa (11.9%), Missouri (11.7%) and Nebraska (11.6%)[7] ranked as the top three among all states in the percentage of population aged 65 years and over.

While the greatest numbers of elderly persons are living in the cities, the heaviest proportion of elderly persons live in the rural areas of these states. To the extent that some Congressional and state legislative districts reflect vestiges of the malapportionment which was widespread before "one man, one vote," the geographic distribution of elderly persons has an important impact on the relative importance of voting by the aged.

Prior to recent legislative apportionment of the state legislature, the situation in Iowa highlighted this situation. A study in the 1950's indicated the following: [8]

> The twelve Iowa counties having the highest concentrations of older persons (percentagewise) are rural and located in the southern portion of the state which has the poorest soil. The high concentration of older people is largely the result of steady population losses. The young adults migrate to nearby or out-of-state urban centers; the elders remain, tending to settle in small towns in these rural counties.[9]
>
> The political significance of the twelve Iowa counties which contain a heavy proportion of older people rested on the fact that they make up a large portion of the region in Iowa (the southern tiers of counties) which was heavily overrepresented in the Iowa General Assembly.
>
> Over 50 per cent of Iowa's state legislators then represented slightly less than one-third of the people of the state. Because they constitute so great a proportion of the population of the overrepresented rural areas, the aged had the strategic political advantage of being concentrated where their numbers are most effective in state legislative elections.
>
> Since demographic evidence indicates that there is a long-range national trend toward the settlement of older people in rural non-farm areas,[10]

it is probable that the aged enjoyed similar strategic advantages in other states that had failed to reapportion state legislative seats in accordance with population.

One may conclude that in certain regions the voting power of the elderly is strategically located where capable of maximizing its influence.

Evidence in several of the major voting behavior studies shows that the political influence of the aged may be much greater than the general population statistics would indicate. For a greater proportion of the aged actually vote in presidential elections than do adults in two of the other three age groupings which were classified. Persons 55 and over voted more heavily than those in either age group 21 to 34 or 35 to 44. Only the middle-aged group, 45 to 54, surpassed them.[11]

---

* Edwards, Mabel I. Unpublished manuscript on the Ecological Distribution of the Aged in Iowa, University of Iowa, Institute of Gerontology, Iowa City, Iowa. *Editorial Note:* The fifteen Iowa counties listed below remained consistently as those counties having the highest proportion of persons aged 65 and over in their total population for the three 5-year periods. Variation in their rank order is to be observed as due to the population changes in each county in total number and in age grouping. All fifteen counties showed a decrease, both in total population and number of persons aged 65 and over as indicated below.

PERCENTAGE OF POPULATION AGED 65 AND OVER IN FIFTEEN IOWA COUNTIES WITH HIGHEST PERCENTAGES OF OLDER PERSONS

| *County* | *1960*[a] | *1970*[b] | *1975*[b] |
|---|---|---|---|
| Appanoose | 19.3 | 21.0 | 22.2 |
| Wayne | 19.1 | 21.1 | 22.4 |
| Taylor | 18.6 | 20.0 | 20.5 |
| Lucas | 17.8 | 18.2 | 19.0 |
| Union | 17.8 | 18.9 | 20.0 |
| Van Buren | 16.9 | 17.7 | 17.3 |
| Clarke | 16.8 | 17.9 | 18.6 |
| Decatur | 16.8 | 18.0 | 19.3 |
| Page | 16.6 | 18.0 | 18.8 |
| Montgomery | 16.5 | 17.6 | 18.6 |
| Henry | 16.4 | 16.8 | 16.9 |
| Keokuk | 16.3 | 16.7 | 16.4 |
| Monroe | 16.3 | 17.4 | 18.1 |
| Guthrie | 15.8 | 17.0 | 18.0 |
| Ringgold | 15.8 | 17.3 | 18.4 |

[a] *U.S. Cenus of Population, 1960: Iowa, Number of Inhabitants,* PC (1), 17A Table 6, pp. 10-11.

[b] Based on population estimates given in *Iowa's Population: Recent Trends, Future Prospects* by Jon Doerflinger and Ronald Klimek, Special Report No. 47, Cooperative Extension Service, Iowa State University, Ames, Iowa, May, 1966.

## SENSE OF POLITICAL EFFICACY

### Low Political Efficacy

In spite of the fact "that older persons participate in voting more than any group except the 45 to 54 age category, persons 55 years old or over rank lowest in sense of political efficacy (defined as "the feeling that individual political action does have, or can have, an impact upon the political process"). Generally, this low sense of political efficacy was matched by a low index of political participation, but in the case of older people, this correlation was not consistently established. This suggests that older people have a more pessimistic view of their possibilities for political effectiveness, but are determined, nevertheless, to participate politically.

Since persons 55 and over had tended to vote more heavily Republican than Democratic in the elections studied prior to that of 1952 (the election in which the test of political efficacy was first made), the pessimism of older people could in part reflect past electoral disappointments during the long period of Democratic presidential victories, 1932 through 1948. In addition, differences in participation records appear among adults in general which may partially explain this behavior of the aged—men participate more frequently than women, Republicans more frequently than Democrats.

### High Political Participation

A special aspect of the political behavior of older persons analyzed in the Michigan study of the 1952 election provides an additional explanation of the low sense of political efficacy but high political participation ratio of the aged.

A measurement of the sense of citizen duty (defined as "the feeling that oneself and others ought to participate in the political process, regardless of whether such political activity is seen as worthwhile or efficacious") indicated that older persons ranked both first in the category of high sense of citizen duty, and at the opposite extreme—first in low sense of citizen duty.

This tendency toward extremes suggests that oldsters having a sense of citizen duty are frequently highly motivated, perhaps more highly motivated than those in other age groups, while oldsters who have a low sense of citizen duty gravitate toward virtually complete political indifference.[12]

It should be noted that one's sense of political efficacy may be determined, at least in part, by one's expectations for the fulfillment of needs via the political process. Professor Merlin Taber and his associates have stressed the fact that an enormous gap exists between the professionally recognized needs of the elderly and the processes by which these needs are fulfilled or even initially recognized as public policy.

What then can be expected concerning informed leadership? To what extent does the dedicated "idea man" either in Congress on a committee staff or in an administrative agency play a meaningful role? Perhaps the most significant modern example of an individual contribution of this kind is the work of Wilbur Cohen whose work over several decades significantly shaped the legislative proposals which became the measure known as Medicare.

Another is the late Congressman John Fogarty whose legislative work was outstanding. But for every Wilbur Cohen, or John Fogarty, the forces opposed to constructive change often frustrate or delay the public policy proposals aiding the elderly. The American Medical Association's ability to defeat medical assistance for the elderly for many decades is a striking example.[13]

Yet with this and numerous additional evidences of the power of private interest groups to block constructive change, there often are more prosaic reasons, such as economics, for the continued existence of major problem areas.

## THE RURAL ELDERLY

We may take the current situation of the elderly agricultural producer in the midwest as an important example.[14] The average age of the midwestern farm operator has been steadily increasing. In Iowa it has risen from an average of 47.7 years in 1959 to 48.5 years in 1964. Historically, the pattern of retirement and of ideological outlook of farm retirees comprised three major facets: (a) gradual reduction of physical activity rather than abrupt withdrawal, (b) a traditional belief that retirement problems were primarily an urban problem, and (c) the belief that close knit family ties guaranteed the basic economic needs and the emotional security of elderly farm producers.

A number of studies indicated that the 1930's represented a turning point. The impact of the great depression and the decline of the family farm because of increased opportunities in nonagricultural pursuits and the mechanization and commercialization of farming has seriously weakened the three historic concepts influencing rural retirees.

What are some of the basic problems which have developed for the rural elderly as a result of the shift of economic and ideological outlook? Despite the fact that a high proportion of farmers participate in the social security program, a high percentage (nearly 60%) depend upon rentals from land as a portion of their retirement income. Significantly only 20 per cent of the land released by the retirement of farm operators was made available to beginning farm operators. This finding, documented by Christensen, is related to two additional problems.

Because land rental is an important economic factor for the retired farmer, it can be assumed that accessibility is, in part, denied to beginners. In addition, the evidence is strong that the quality of land possessed by retirees is higher than that of others. The economic factors play a significant part in contradicting several basic personal aspirations of the rural elderly.

A number of studies have stressed the strong desire of the rural elderly to remain in the country or to move to small communities in the region in which they lived most of their lives. Christensen's data, concerned with retiring Iowa farm operators in the period 1959 to 1961, indicated that well over 90 per cent expressed such a preference.

This aspiration is closely related to the desire of rural elderly persons to live in proximity to their children and grandchildren. Older farmers generally prefer to live in their own homes rather than with someone else. These farm residences are generally older frame dwellings (in Christensen's study 87 per cent were constructed before 1920, 30 per cent before 1900). In short, the economic circumstances attendant to the retirement of farm producers generally tend to create conditions *least conducive* to one of the primary aspirations of the rural retirees by making it difficult for the beginning farmer or potential beginners to get a start in the region in which his parents live.

It is pertinent to ask our colleagues in the natural sciences the extent to whch this growing tension between personal aspiration and economic necessity may help create difficult problems of adjustment for rural retirees. Do such tensions contribute to the following pessimistic attitudes as reported by Christensen? Individuals over 60 in Iowa open country rated their own health lower than their urban counterparts. Retired farmers born before 1920 found it difficult to develop new interests. Economic and health factors "tend to produce a negative attitude toward all aspects of life."

Further study of these motivational differences among older persons stressing such factors as sex, party, education, and social and economic status is necessary before anything except rather tentative hypotheses can be made. But it is clear that delay and frustration may contribute to a low sense of political efficacy among some elderly persons.

## OLDER VOTER BEHAVIOR

Voting in presidential elections, the level at which particiation is greatest, is only one manifestation of voting behavior. Congressional and state elections held in years in which there is no presidential election uniformly attract less voter attention. And primary elections for the purpose of selecting party candidates for congressional and state offices generally stimulate the least voter participation. To date, with a few exceptions, the survey research approach has not been applied to non-presidential elections, either general or primary. For the study of older people, several questions may be raised. What proportion of participants in off-presidential-year general elections are older persons? What proportion of the select group of voters who participate in primary elections are aged? If participation by the aged is heavy, perhaps the previous estimates of the political importance of older people need further revision.

The Campbell and Cooper national survey of the election of members of the House of Representatives in 1954, the most extensive non-presidential election study available, indicated that persons 55 and over maintained the same relatively high participation ratio established in the presidential elections of 1948 and 1952.[15] They participated more heavily than persons in age groups 21 to 34 and 35 to 44, but less heavily than members of age group 45 to 54. Insofar as one election can be taken as indicative, the relationship of the ratio of participation of older persons to that of other age groups did show some changes. All age groups participated less heavily in 1954 than in 1948 or 1952. The drop-off among the youngest voters (21 to 34) was most marked, however, while the decline in participation among persons 35 to 44 paralleled but was heavier than that of the oldest group.

Consequently, in a comparison of the oldest (55 and over) with the two youngest age groupings, older persons definitely did gain in political influence in this nonpresidential election. It should be noted, however, that older persons did show a much heavier decline in participation than the middle-aged group (45 to 54), but even when this was taken into account, older persons clearly made up a larger percentage of those participating than they had in the 1948 and 1952 presidential elections.

In addition to the graduations of participation that exist in a comparison of presidential, congressional, and state elections, it is recognized that a very small minority of the adult population participates in the specialized political activities such as attending political rallies, fund-raising or money-giving, and actual work for or management of political parties or voluntary political organizations.

A vital but presently unanswered question is what percentage of the adults who are really politically active are older persons? Here popular political mythology, with its frequent references to "the old guard" suggests that a large number are older persons. Yet this has never been investigated systematically on a regional or national basis.

The Elmira study indicated that the local leadership of the minority political party (which by 1948 had not tasted the spoils of local office for nearly two decades) was held by six men all of whom were over seventy years of age.[16] Yet the same study showed that the precinct workers of the same party (Democratic) were younger than their Republican counterparts. Both political parties in Elmira drew over 10 per cent of their workers from retired or widowed persons.

The participation of the aged in the more specialized political activities could be studied through survey research methods utilizing a national sample. An investigation of the ample biographical literature on old-time and modern political bosses could turn up interesting evidence at this level. Community studies of the pertinent biographical data of county party chairmen, members of state and county central committees, and precinct workers could supplement the broader studies suggested above. The many sociological studies of community power structures probably contain untapped data for such an inquiry.

Public affairs leadership may be treated as a function which is much broader in its scope of community influence than that of specialized political participation. The Katz and Lazarsfeld study of Decatur, Illinois, concluded that "public affairs leadership declines steadily, though very undramatically, with advancing age." [17] This study probably cannot be used as a basis for generalization about older persons because the findings related to women only.

The study conducted by Floyd Hunter, in which the community leaders analyzed were all men, suggests that older men retain community influence rather tenaciously, but the prospect of gradual loss of influence in old age was also recognized.[18] A thorough study of the literature on community social structures could throw more light on this aspect ot the behavior of older people.

Virtually all of the foregoing discussions of the growing population proportions of older people—their strategic location for state legislative politics in certain states, their high voting record in presidential elections and probable high participation record in nonpresidential general and prmary elections, their higher motivation toward political participation, their possible roles as public affairs leaders—all these underscore the real as well as potential influence oldsters have in American politics. Therefore a crucial question is, how do older persons exercise their influence? Are older people as a group in American society any more self-seeking than other social groupings? Do they constitute a cohesive group in any sense? Do they vote as a bloc?

## POLITICAL INFLUENCE OF THE ELDERLY

The answers that may be ventured are again necessarily tentative. The study of voter behavior in the city of Elmira, New York, in the 1948 election by Berelson, Lazarsfeld, and McPhee represents the most extensive effort to date which gives attention to age differences. The Michigan national sample surveys of the 1948 and 1952 elections also add pertinent information. Both the Elmira study and the second Michigan study indicated that a large proportion of oldsters who had identified themselves with a political party the first time they voted still adhered to that party. This tendency to retain the political allegiance of one's formative political years does not lend support to the concept of an elder citizens' voting bloc.

People did tend to discuss politics with persons in their own age group, although younger adults tended to show respect for the political opinions of their elders (an attitude which was not reciprocated by oldsters). This apparent age cohesiveness was not based primarily upon age per se, however, but upon social factors such as family ties, occupational and economic status, and the political climate in the community. For example, the Elmira study showed that 90 per cent of adult family members living together in the same house made the same voting decision in late October of the 1948 presidential campaign. Furthermore, insofar as political discussion was engaged in, people tended generally to discuss politics with members of their own party.

A noteworthy finding of the Elmira study concerned the influence of the community political climate. Where the political cohesiveness of primary social groups such as the family was weakened or destroyed, the prevailing political traditions of the community had a significant bearing on voting dispositions. This community influence worked to the disadvantage of the minority party. In heavily Republican Elmira, advancing age brought an increasing proportion of conversions of former Democrats to the Republican party, perhaps explaining in part the rather heavy proportion of Republican votes among the aged in that city.

The heavy influence of social factors such as those discussed above probably seriously qualifies the popular conception that the aged are a cohesive voting bloc primarily interested in economic panaceas for themselves. However, the experiences of the depression years suggest that if our society fails to meet the vital economic and social needs of the aged, older persons, like the members of any other social group, might well develop such political cohesiveness on the basis of mutual disillusionment and insecurity.

Perhaps one of the most difficult of the problems relating to the study of the political behavior of the aged is that of analysis of their alleged conservatism. In part, the problem is a serious one of definition of the word conservatism; in large part, the problem is one of insufficient social scientific data. As a result of their pioneering study of presidential voting in Erie County, Pennsylvania, in 1940, Lazarsfeld, Berelson, and Gaudet concluded that older persons demonstrated not so much political, but rather social conservatism.[19]

The major voting behavior studies, the Erie County (1940), the Elmira (1948), and the two Michigan-sponsored ones (1948, 1952), indicate that Republicans comprise a majority among older voters. Does this mean that the aged are more "conservative" than other persons? The image created by a political party in different social settings has a bearing on this. Could one argue that an aged Southern Democrat in Mississippi is more "liberal" than an aged Northern Republican in New Jersey or vice versa? The difficulty of using party labels as criteria for distinguishing liberal or conservative positions on contemporary social and economic questions. But from the point of view of a Fabian Socialist, the fact that older Americans vote overwhelmingly for the two major parties might be interpreted as conclusive evidence of the general conservatism of the American aged.

The Elmira study concluded that "age generations" did exist in American politics, but that party affiliation was less important than the social factors basic to party allegiance. The generation which came of age in the 1920's tended to be more Republican, but the underlying split in this generation was religion. The political generation which came of age in the 1930's tended to be more Democratic and here the basis for political division was socioeconomic. Although the formation of relatively stable political attitudes may come early in Europe, most young American adults do not make that adjustment until age 35. This in part was attributed to the apolitical nature of young Americans. The whole area concerning the early formulation and conditioning of the political attitudes and values of older persons still remains virtually unexplored.

## SUMMARY

As was discussed previously, the aged tend to retain their affiliation with the party for which they first cast a ballot. If conservatism is defined as rigid adherence to outdated ideas, would retention of party affiliation in old age brand the aged as conservative? Here again, exceeding caution is required. The contents of party programs change, sometimes radically, over the passage of years, and insofar as our scanty data permits generalization, the aged may accept such changes along with other age groups.[20] This is another area for investigation.

Several modern studies in sociology and psychology lend support to the view that older persons are capable of broad social adjustment and seriously challenge the assumption that there is a necessary relationship between conservatism and old age. For example, the Lorge and Helfant study of the sociopolitical verbal attitudes of a group of adolescents and their parents concluded that "for the age range of adults tested (36 to 64), there is not evidence of increasing conservatism in the older years . . ." Yet several of the sociological studies of American communities present a different picture of older persons.

In Plainville, U.S.A., for example, there are references to "a few old people" who have a "strange hold" on much of "the money and land in the county," and are usually "no longer interested in the schools except to try to keep taxes down."[21] The latter view represents the observation of inhabitants, but similar views occur with frequency in other community studies.

Persons 55 and over tend to be rather steadfast in their voting preferences, ranking the lowest of all age groups as split-voters and as independents. Older persons also indicate greater consistency in expressed pre-election intention and actual voting preference than persons in other age groups. Although all of these behavior patterns reflect the greater political consistency of the aged, it cannot be implied that older persons are necessarily inflexible.

Sociologists have pointed out that the aged can learn and that such learning can facilitate the acceptance of new ideas. Psychological testing provides evidence that older people are frequently more careful and deliberate than younger ones. Consequently, it has been argued that what is commonly referred to as the conservatism of the aged may be related to their tendency to be more deliberate rather than to inherent inflexibility. The social environment may determine the political stability of an older person rather than age itself.

The information about the social and political attitudes of older persons often seems contradictory. Thorough investigation of the question of the alleged conservatism of older persons could include (a) all of the sociological community studies, (b) all of the major public opinion polls in which age differences were noted, and (c) more extensive psychological testing.

## REFERENCES


1. Pollak, Otto: *Social Adjustment in Old Age.* New York, Social Science Research Council, 1948, p. 17.
2. *Christian Century,* March 18, 1953, p. 309.
3. Eisenstadt, Samuel N.: *From Generation to Generation: Age Groups and Social Structure.* Glencoe, Free Press, 1956, pp. 21-55.
4. Roper, Elmo: The politics of three decades. *Public Opinion Quarterly,* Fall, 1965, pp. 368-376; and Chase, Stuart: American values: a generation of change. *Public Opinion Quarterly,* Fall, 1965, pp. 356-376.
5. Neuberger, Richard L., and Loe, Kelley: *Army of the Aged.* Caldwell, Caxton, 1936; and Cantril, Hadley: *The Psychology of Social Movements.* New York, Wiley, 1941.

6. SCHMIDHAUSER, JOHN R.: The political behavior of older persons: a discussion of some frontiers in research. XI. *Western Political Quarterly,* March 1958, pp. 114-115.
7. COWGILL, DONALD O.: The demography of aging in the midwest. In Rose, Arnold M., and Peterson, Warren A.: *Older People and Their Social World.* Philadelphia, Davis, 1965, pp. 275-310.
8. SCHMIDHAUSER, JOHN R., *op cit.,* pp. 114-115.
9. EDWARDS, MABEL I.: Ecological Distribution of the Aged in Iowa. Iowa City, U. of Iowa, Institute of Gerontology (unpublished manuscript).
10. *Man and His Years, An Account of the First National Conference on Aging.* Raleigh, Health Publications Institute, 1951, p. 20.
11. CAMPBELL, ANGUS, and KAHN, ROBERT L.: *The People Elect A President.* Ann Arbor, Institute for Social Research, 1952, p. 34.; Campbell, Angus; Gurin, Gerald; and Miller, Warren: *The Voter Decides.* Evanston, Row, Peterson, 1954, p. 70. (The Woodward and Roper study also supports this, although the age categories utilized are not precisely the same; see Research on political parties and leadership. *American Political Science Review, XLIV*:877, XLIV, 1950.)
12. SCHMIDHAUSER, JOHN R., *op. cit.,* pp. 114-115.
13. See HARRIS, RICHARD: *A Sacred Trust.* New York, New Am. Lib., 1966 (for an excellent account of the positive role of contributors such as Wilbur Cohen and for a detailed summary of the American Medical Association's forty-five year opposition campaign).
14. CHRISTENSEN, LEE: Characteristics and Experiences of Operators Retiring from Iowa Farms, 1959-1961. Ames, 1966, pp. 5-6, Unpublished doctoral dissertation.
15. CAMPBELL, ANGUS, and COOPER, HOMER C.: *Group Differences in Attitudes and Votes.* Ann Arbor, Institute for Social Research, 1956.
16. BERELSON, BERNARD; LAZARFELD, PAUL, and MCPHEE, HALSEY: *Voting.* Chicago, University of Chicago Press, 1954.
17. KATZ, ELIHU, and LAZARFELD, PAUL: *Personal Influence.* Glencoe, Free Press, 1955.
18. HUNTER, FLOYD: *Community Power Structure.* Chapel Hill, University of North Carolina Press, 1953.
19. LAZARFELD, PAUL; BERELSON, BERNARD, and GAUDET, GEORGE: *The People's Choice.* New York, Snell, Sloan and Pearce, 1944, pp. 24-25.
20. LORGE, IRVING, and BELFANT, KENNETH: The Independence of Chronological Age and Sociological Attitudes. *Journal of Abnormal and Normal Psychology,* 1953, pp. 598.
21. WEST, JAMES: *Plainville, U.S.A.* New York, Columbia University Press, 1945.

*Chapter 4*

# EMPLOYMENT, RETIREMENT, AND INCOME MAINTENANCE

ANTHONY V. SINICROPI

TODAY THE AMERICAN economy has achieved an advanced state which has been unparalleled in the history of civilization. This complex and forward looking economic society is predicated upon an industrial base rather than the agricultural foundations common to so many other nations. Additionally, the 1960 American economic structure reflects a new occupational and industrial framework as the result of post World War II developments.

Prior to World War II, Americans were primarily blue collar workers employed in manufacturing industries. In the middle of the decade following World War II, white collar employees exceeded those blue collar workers. Shortly thereafter service workers became more numerous than those employed in manufacturing.

The industrial economy, with all of the benefits it has created for society, poses special problems for the aged. In the agricultural society, old people were more secure since they were cared for by their families—the basic economic unit. In the advanced industrial economy, the family loses its position as the basic economic unit; consequently, older peoples' problems come to the fore as their ability to produce diminishes.

Economists tell us that one of the measures of a strong economy is the health and vigor of its workers. Experience demonstrates that employers seek young workers not only because they are healthy and vigorous but also because they usually are better educated and more flexible in their ability to meet the everchanging demands of the world of work than the older worker.

In recent years, the spread of technology, the increasing coverage of public and private retirement programs, the current social thought, and the resultant legislation emphasize that the older worker should be absented from the work environment. However, the picture becomes clouded by such changes as the increasing life expectancy made possible by advances in the medical sciences and health care fields, and the changing work environment itself which has occurred as a result of increased technology and changes in the managerial sciences. With these few concepts in mind, the next step will be to examine the employment characteristics and the unemployment characteristics of America's older workers.

## EMPLOYMENT OF THE OLDER WORKER

There are more older workers in our nation today than ever before in our history. In 1900, there were three million people over 65 years of age out of a population of seventy-six million or less than 4 per cent. In 1950, twelve million of the 151 million people in the United States were in this age group (8.1%) and by 1963, there were eighteen million or 9.3 per cent in this age group.[1] Thus, the proportion of people in our times in this age group is six times as great as in 1900. Table XI gives the absolute numbers and percentages in this age group for three periods in this century.

TABLE XI
ABSOLUTE NUMBERS AND PERCENTAGES OF MALES AND FEMALES 65 AND OLDER IN 1910, 1960, AND 1980

| | *Male* | | *Female* | |
|---|---|---|---|---|
| *Year* | No. in Millions | % of Total Male Pop. | No. in Millions | % of Total Female Pop. |
| 1910 | 1.986 | 4.2 | 1.963 | 4.4 |
| 1960 | 7.501 | 8.5 | 9.057 | 10.0 |
| 1980 (projected) | 10.267 | 8.5 | 14.259 | 11.5 |

From Turnbull, John G., *The Changing Faces of Economic Insecurity,* Minneapolis, The University of Minnesota Press, 1966, p. 45.

While the numbers of people in the over 65 age group have increased greatly since 1900 and the indications are that the increases will continue at least until 1980, it is interesting to note that the employment of these older people has not kept pace. Table XII shows the labor force participation rates for the 65 and older group from 1900 to 1980. The rates for males and females are given for every decade since 1900. It also includes data from 1965 and projects participation rates every five years thereafter until 1980.

TABLE XII
LABOR FORCE PARTICIPATION RATES
FOR PERSONS OVER 65
1900-1980

| *Year* | *Male* | *Female* |
|---|---|---|
| 1900 | 63.1 | 8.3 |
| 1910 | N.D. | N.D. |
| 1920 | 55.6 | 7.3 |
| 1930 | 54.0 | 7.3 |
| 1940 | 42.2 | 6.0 |
| 1950 | 41.4 | 7.8 |
| 1960 | 32.2 | 10.5 |
| 1965 | 26.9 | 9.5 |
| 1967* | 25.6* | 9.6* |
| 1970 (projected) | 25.1 | 9.8 |
| 1975 (projected) | 23.4 | 9.8 |
| 1980 (projected) | 21.8 | 9.9 |

N.D.—No data

*1967 figures were secured from the Bureau of Labor Statistics publication, *Employment and Earnings* and *Monthly Report on the Labor Force,* Vol. No. 18, April, 1968, pp. 18-19.

From *Historical Statistics of the United States Bureau of Census,* Washington, D.C., 1960, p. 71 and *Statistical Abstract of the United States,* U.S. Bureau of Census (87th Edition) Washington, D.C., p. 219.

It may be noted that the male participation rate dropped almost 50 per cent in the sixty years since 1900 and the expectation is that the rate will continue to decrease. The female rates have risen slightly and this is due primarily to the status of women in our working society.

From Table XI and Table XII it is appropriate to conclude that although the absolute numbers of people over 65 attached to the labor force has increased, a smaller proportion of them are actually working.

Another way to consider the plight of the older worker is to view his situation in the following example developed by Seymour Wolfbein:[2]

> *Under 1900 conditions* a man of twenty had a life expectancy of *42.2* years and a work life expectancy of *39.4* years. Thus his outlook was for a period of retirement of *2.8* years. *Under 1960 conditions* a man of twenty had a life expectancy of *49.6* years and a work life expectancy of *42.6* years. Thus his outlook was for a period of retirement of *7.0* years.

Therefore, a man of 20 in 1960 would have more than two and one-half times the retirement years as his counterpart did in 1900.

The older worker of today and most certainly tomorrow is confronted with living with the difficulties of the nonemployment life.

He should not be considered unemployed since his propensity to work is decreasing and his opportunities for work are likewise decreasing. The factors contributing to this change have been touched on in the introduction to this section and will be discussed more fully in the following pages.

## INDUSTRIAL AND OCCUPATIONAL ATTACHMENT

Tables XIII and XIV show the proportion of aged persons employed in the industrial and occupational groups. The highest proportion of aged males is represented in the railroad and railway express; finance, real estate, and insurance; and entertainment industries. The rate of participation in the former two industries are quite understandable since railroad seniority clauses found in labor agreements and the tradition of working one's way up the ladder in the financial institutions are common knowledge. There seems to be no plausible explanation, however, for their high proportion in the entertainment

TABLE XIII

PER CENT OF PERSONS EMPLOYED IN INDUSTRIAL GROUPS WHO ARE 65 AND OLDER 1965

| *Industrial Group* | *Persons 65 and Older* | | |
|---|---|---|---|
| | *Male* | *Female* | *Total* |
| Forestry, fisheries and mining | 2.5 | — | 2.5 |
| Construction | 2.8 | .1 | 2.9 |
| Manufacturing | 1.4 | .4 | 2.8 |
| Durable goods | 1.3 | .1 | 1.4 |
| Non-durable goods | 1.4 | .7 | 2.1 |
| Transportation and public utilities | 2.0 | .2 | 2.2 |
| Railroad and Railway express | 4.0 | .5 | 4.5 |
| Other transportation | 2.0 | .2 | 2.2 |
| Communication and other public utilities | 1.3 | .1 | 1.4 |
| Wholesale and retail trade | 2.8 | 1.3 | 4.1 |
| Wholesale | 3.6 | .6 | 4.2 |
| Retail | 2.7 | 1.5 | 4.2 |
| Service and finance | 3.0 | 2.8 | 5.8 |
| Finance, insurance and real estate | 4.4 | 1.7 | 6.1 |
| Business and repair | 4.2 | .4 | 4.6 |
| Private household | 1.6 | 7.3 | 8.9 |
| Personal services except private household | 3.6 | 3.7 | 7.3 |
| Entertainment | 4.3 | 1.0 | 5.3 |
| Educational services | 1.1 | 2.4 | 3.5 |
| Other professional services | 3.4 | 2.4 | 5.8 |
| Public administration | 2.8 | 1.0 | 3.8 |

From *Labor Force & Employment in 1965*, U. S. Department of Labor, Bureau of Labor Statistics (Reprint no. 2494) Special Labor Force Report No. 69, Washington, D.C. page A 24.

field. On the other hand, it logically follows that females over 65 make up a high proportion of the workers in private household occupations and personal services.

The implications here should be related to the stability of employment and the wages paid in these industries. For example, railroad work is declining and in most instances "silent firing" or the nonreplacement of deceased, retired, or otherwise severed old-age employees gives ample reason to expect lesser opportunities to exist in that industry in the future. The financial institutions are fast changing their hiring and promotion policies as well as their retirement policies; in addition, they are highly automating and computerizing their operations. Therefore, it can be expected that employment opportunities for the aged should diminish there also. As for the females, the wages are extremely low in the industries and occupations where the largest number of women are employed, and although employment opportunities may remain relatively high, the economic benefits are quite limited.

Table XIV shows that older male workers are found to be by far in the highest proportion in farm occupations. This occupation is rapidly disappearing, and as farms grow larger and become more mechanized with a corporate structure predominant over the family unit, the employment opportunities for the older male workers dimin-

TABLE XIV

PER CENT OF PERSONS 65 AND OLDER EMPLOYED IN OCCUPATIONAL GROUPS 1965

| *Major Occupational Groups* | *Male* | *Female* | *Total* |
|---|---|---|---|
| All occupational groups | 2.8 | 1.3 | 4.1 |
| Professional, technical and kindred | 2.3 | 1.5 | 3.8 |
| Farmers and farm managers | 15.8 | 1.4 | 17.2 |
| Managers, officials and proprietors except farm | 5.3 | 1.3 | 6.6 |
| Clerical and kindred workers | 1.2 | 1.2 | 2.4 |
| Sales workers | 3.3 | 1.8 | 5.1 |
| Craftsmen, foremen and kindred workers | 2.7 | .1 | 2.8 |
| Operatives and kindred workers | 1.2 | .7 | 1.9 |
| Private household | .3 | 8.0 | 8.3 |
| Service workers except private household | 3.1 | 2.2 | 5.3 |
| Farm laborer and foreman | 3.5 | 1.3 | 4.8 |
| Laborers except farm and mine | 2.8 | .1 | 2.9 |

From *Labor Force & Employment in 1965,* U. S. Department of Labor, Bureau of Labor Statistics (Reprint No. 2494) Special Labor Force Report No. 69, Washington, D.C., p. A 23.

ish. For females, the situation is somewhat similar with their high proportion in private household occupations, and although these may not disappear rapidly, they do offer a low wage with little security and fringe benefit protection.

It is obvious that older workers are not found in what may be considered growth industries and occupations. With little exception, where they are found in some numbers, their remuneration is poor.

## Factors Affecting Changes in Employment

The older workers' participation rate in the labor force is, indeed, dropping and the probability that these rates will increase or stabilize is quite remote. Corson and McConnell indicate that one-third of the older men who leave the labor force do so for health reasons and Sawyer points out that physical disabilities are more prevalent among older workers than younger workers.[3]

Still another factor in the diminishing participation rate is the obsolescence of skill in our changing automated society. The changing character of industries and jobs are often too frequent and too rapid for the older worker to keep pace.[4] The educational level of the older worker is somewhat less than the younger person and, of course, the toll mounts on this count.

Other important factors accounting for the declining participation rate are plant relocations and corporate compulsory retirement programs and discrimination against older workers. Loether describes a study conducted in 1960 among three hundred of the largest firms in the United States.[5] The results of this study indicated that only 6 per cent of the firms responding did not regard age as a relevant factor in their hiring practices. Some of this discrimination may be alleviated by the Age Discrimination Employment Act which went into effect June 12, 1968.

## Unemployment and the Older Worker

Unemployment has been a problem plaguing our economic system since its inception. The great concern for this problem is reflected in the Employment Act of 1946. While the alleviation of unemployment has always been an objective of our nation as a result of the 1946 law, it is now part of the public policy of our government.

In the past ten years, however, the unemployment problem has taken on a new dimension. Rather than being a condition which indiscriminately displaced workers on a temporary basis as had previously been assumed, the spectre of unemployment singles out the youngster, the uneducated, the unskilled, the negro, and the *older worker.* It brands them as unfit for employment for prolonged periods of time. Legislation such as the Social Security Act with its unemployment insurance provisions and privately negotiated "cushioning clauses" such as supplemental unemployment benefit plans were not designed to aid individuals caught in prolonged seiges of unemployment.

For several years, there was an inverse ratio between employment and unemployment. But starting in the mid-1950's, employment and unemployment began to show that they could and did increase together. Economists studying this phenomenon split into two camps—one group explaining the unemployment rise as the result of a structural change in our industrial and occupational makeup and the other group using the conventional argument that aggregate demand was inadequate to keep the economy at a level where unemployment could be held within reasonable limits. Whatever course one follows, the problem of unemployed persons in the older category is significant.[6] It must be borne in mind that most people 65 and older do not actively seek work for a variety of reasons. Rated high among these reasons are personal beliefs that they cannot perform the jobs which are open or that few jobs are available.[7] Others would rather not work and elect not to do so. For these reasons, it is apparent that the figures themselves are not true indicators of the number of unemployed older people.

Figure 4-1, indicating the unemployment rates by age in 1962, shows that employment rates for young people from 14 to 24 are particularly high. But it must be remembered that workers in this group can be expected to be out of work since they are beginning their careers, have the least job seniority, engage in considerable moving around and job changing, and generally lack any considerable background of work experience and skill development.[8] It is interesting to note, however, that unemployment rates begin to climb after age 64.

Figure 4-2 shows the duration of unemployment which is particu-

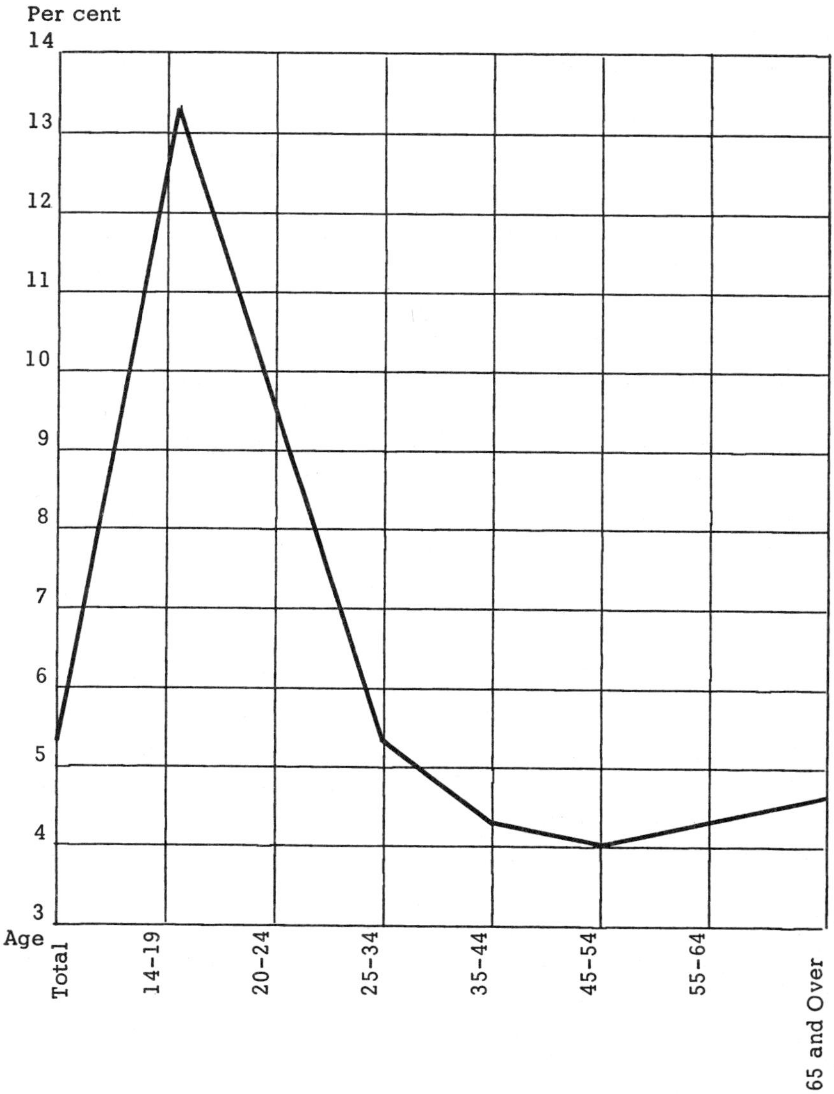


Figure 4-1. Unemployment rates in the U.S.A. by age, 1962. (*From* Wolfbein, Seymour: *Employment & Unemployment in the United States,* Chicago, Science Research Associates, Inc., 1964, p. 301.)

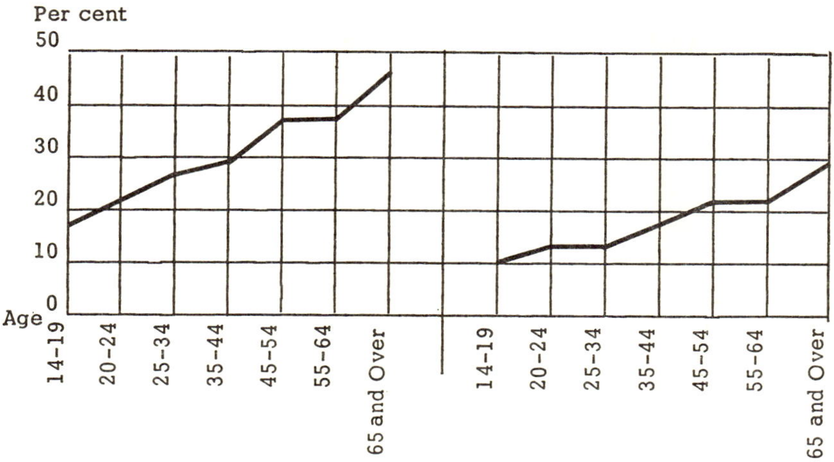


Figure 4-2. Long-term unemployment in the U.S.A. by age (as per cent of unemployed in age group). (*From* Wolfbein, *Employment and Unemployment in the United States,* Chicago, Science Research Associates, Inc., 1964, p. 302.)

larly meaningful since it deals with the question of unprotected unemployment or that condition where benefits are exhausted. Here the older workers have a much higher incidence than do younger workers. It is apparent that those persons at the upper end of the age scale have a higher level of unemployment than those in their middle years and the persistence of such unemployment (long-term unemployment) exceeds every other age group. There is no question that once the over 65 person loses a job, he has great difficulty finding employment again and even if he does, it is only after a long period of unemployment, i.e. in excess of fifteen weeks.

## INCOME MAINTENANCE AND RETIREMENT

The annual money income of persons 65 and older is substantially less than those under 65.[9] Data collected by the U.S. Bureau of Census shows that in 1962 the median money income for the older group was less than $3000. Table XV vividly points out the differences in the income distribution between the older and younger groups in our society.

Comparison of the income of the older worker with the under 65 group may be made on an individual, family unit, head of household

TABLE XV
MONEY INCOME OF FAMILIES WITH THE HEAD OF FAMILY OVER 65 AND UNDER 65 IN 1960
(noninstitutional population of the United States)

| *Money Income by Class* | *Per cent of All Families* *Head 65 and over* | *Head under 65* |
|---|---|---|
| Less than $2000 | 31.4 | 10.2 |
| $ 2000 - $3900 | 32.4 | 16.5 |
| $ 4000 - $6999 | 36.1 | 73.3 |
| $ 7000 - $9999 | 8.5 | 21.8 |
| $10,000 and over | 7.9 | 15.3 |
| Median income | $2,897 | $5,905 |

From "Income of Families and Persons in the United States: 1960" *Current Population Report Consumer Income,* U.S. Bureau of Census, Series P-60 No. 37 (Jan. 17, 1962).

or other basis. However, each of these comparisons reveal the same general disparities which appear on Table XV.* What is particularly significant in viewing Table XV is that one out of three older persons earn $4000 to $6999 per year whereas the younger group has three out of four of their number earning this amount. The $7000 to $9999 income bracket includes about one out of twelve of the older group and nearly one out of six of the younger group. The overwhelming body of statistics points out that older citizens have a difficult time maintaining an income level consistent with the minimal demands of present day societal living patterns.

Many critics offer the argument that the persons over 65 have met their major economic obligations; therefore, this low income level is adequate for their needs. In addition, it is often heard that income for the older worker is not as important as might be expected since they often have accumulated savings and investments of considerable size to secure the future. On the contrary, Cohen points out that 42 per cent of the spending units headed by persons 65 or over had a net worth of $5000 and 27 per cent had less than $1000.[10]

A logical question to be asked regarding older workers' income relates to the source or sources of his income. Contrary to popular belief that public and private retirement and pension programs are the

*For a detailed and comprehensive analysis of such data, see Lenore A. Epstein, "The Income Position of the Aged," *Aging and the Economy,* Harold L. Orbach and Clark Tibbetts (eds.), The University of Michigan Press, Ann Arbor, 1963, p. 91.

principal sources of income, it is employment of the aged which is, in fact, the largest single source for their earnings.

## Retirement and the Older Worker

The largest single source of *retirement income* for the person over 65 is the old age and survivors' insurance program under the Social Security Act. This is contrasted to total earnings—it relates only to retirement income. The number of persons drawing benefits under this program in 1964 was 13.6 million, and included in that number were 75 per cent of those persons 65 and over.[11] The Social Security Administration estimates that 21.5 million persons will be drawing Old Age Survivors and Disability Insurance (OASDI) benefits in 1980, and this number will constitute over 85 per cent of those in the older category.[12]

Private pension and retirement programs have grown with the public programs, and their rapid advance has been due in part to the significant social change which the Social Security law provided. In 1964, about twenty-five million workers were covered by private pension plans and 2.6 million beneficiaries were 65 and older.[13] These 2.6 million recipients made up 14 per cent of those in the older category.

While the experience and growth of these plans in recent years is indeed admirable, it is well to bear in mind that many persons are employed in those industries and occupations where such plans are not practicable. Moreover, many of the present older people are employed or were formerly employed in just such jobs and industries. A survey of 17,600 beneficiaries of OASDI in 1951 and 1952 indicated they received a total money income of less than $1200 per year.[14] In 1965, the monthly benefit payment to retired workers was about $84.00 and annual payments were $1,183.[15] Obviously these amounts will not buy economic security at today's price level and as it was indicated above, aged citizens most often cannot depend upon their past earnings to sustain them since these are also meager.

The second largest source of retirement income for persons over 65 is employer pension plans.[16] Alvin M. David indicates that 25 per cent of couples and 15 per cent of nonmarried retired workers receive pensions from their former employers. The median annual retirement income for this group of beneficiaries in 1957 was $2,440 for couples and $1,690 for nonmarried persons.[17]

In addition to the OASDI program and company retirement programs, there are those persons who have retired on retirement plans purchased through private annuity contracts with private insurance companies. In 1952, about 645,000 persons were receiving payments under private annuity contracts and insurance policies while 807,000 such annuities and supplementary agreements were providing benefits in 1961. David states that the best estimates are that about 75 per cent of these annuity income plans were going to people 65 and older.[18]

If one were to total the income realized by persons 65 and older from any single source listed above or any combination of sources, the annual income would be substantially less than $3000 per year.[19]

Many economists have described income adequacy by the measure of family income under $3000 per year. While the definition of income adequacy is admittedly a complex one, it nevertheless is quite meaningful to use the $3000 measure since money income is perhaps the best measure which our society has been able to devise at the present time. The Joint Council on Economic Education recently reported on family income under $3000 per year. Among the eight million families in 1965 which realized incomes under that amount, 36.2 per cent consisted of households where the head of the family was 65 years of age or over.[20] This was more than twice the amount for the 55 to 64 age group and about three times the number for all other age groups.

The American economy is in an expansion stage where productivity has resulted in a sevenfold increase in the Gross National Product (GNP) since 1940. This growth necessarily involves some inflation particularly in the last few years; consequently, most retirement programs by and large are not flexible enough to allow for such change. Arnold Paulsen of Iowa State University said that "productivity increases make older people relatively worse off compared to working people and inflation makes them absolutely worse off." [21] The gist of Paulsen's statement is that older people have fared poorly in our economy and in effect they "can't afford to retire."

## PUBLIC POLICY AND THE OLDER WORKER

On June 12, 1968, the Age Discrimination in Employment Act of

1967 (P.L. 90-202) went into effect. In this statute, the Federal Government passed a law which provides for the employment protection of those persons between the ages of 40 and 65. While it is indeed a step in the right direction, it still falls short of those protections which are needed for the persons who are 65 and older in our society.*

The President's Council on Aging was created in 1962, and its main task has been to "explore in detail the existing procedures for exchange of information about older people, including statistical data essential for the evaluation of existing programs, and for identifying gaps in these programs for the aged." [22] In addition, both the Senate and the House of Representatives have special subcommittees which have been examining and studying the problems of older people. However, none of these groups have moved forward to espouse a particular position regarding the employment or retirement of older workers excepting such niceties which promote adequate wages, retirement schedules, and freedom to work or not to work.

Some increased appropriations ($2.5 million) to the Bureau of Employment Security have been added to Public Law 89-787 to assist older persons in their efforts to secure employment and amendments to the Manpower Development and Training Act (Public Law 89-792) which provides for more testing, counseling, selection, and referral for persons 45 years of age and older. Many other proposals have been offered by congressmen and senators. Those considered recently include the following: increased deductions of medical and drug expenses from income tax; increased dependency allowances for

---

* The Age Discrimination in Employment Act of 1967 makes it unlawful for an employer (1) to refuse to hire or discharge or to discriminate against a person because of age; (2) to limit, segregate, or classify an employee which would deprive him or adversely effect him as compared to other employees; and (3) to reduce the wage rate of an employee because of age. The same acts apply to employment agencies and to labor unions as it relates to membership therein. In addition, employment advertisements cannot contain statements with reference to age. Of course, the law protects employers, unions, and employment agencies where their actions are predicated on job requirements and not upon age discrimination.

The law is administered by the Secretary of Labor and criminal penalties may be imposed up to $500 or 1 year imprisonment or both.

The law provides that the Secretary of Labor undertake studies to provide information to labor unions, management, and the public regarding the needs and abilities of the older workers. To do this, the Secretary shall carry on a continuous education program through (1) research (2) publications (3) promotion. He shall also recommend to Congress changes in the legislation.

relatives supporting older persons; and liberalization of private pension programs for self-employed and their employees.

The uncertainty of a government position until the passage of the new law is reflected in the testimony of a number of experts who appeared before the House Subcommittee in 1965. Garth L. Mangum, Executive Secretary of the National Commission on Technology Automation and Economic Progress indicated that the push by labor unions to seek early retirement for workers was a mistake.[23] Otto Eckstein, a member of the President's Council of Economic Advisors said there was no social purpose in hastening the retirement of experienced workers who have the skills the economy needs.[24] He went on to say that the public policy should "at least be neutral" on early retirement and that freedom of choice should be left to the individual.[25]

On the other hand, Woodrow Ginsburg, Director of Research for the Industrial Union Department of the AFL-CIO and John Dunlop, Harvard economics professor, both favor retirement provided public and private programs benefits be increased to provide an adequate retirement income.

## SUMMARY

This nation's social conscience has been awakened in the last year or so, and it now appears that concern for all types of minorities, including the older persons (65 or above), is becoming a reality. The real question to be tested is to change this concern to action programs.

Wilbur Cohen, Secretary of Health, Education and Welfare is optimistic about the nation's ability to meet the needs of our elderly citizens.*

America can be proud of the public-private framework that has been constructed in the last three decades. Improvements have been made throughout this period because Americans have never lost sight of their goal to provide economic security for those among them who suffer income loss due to unemployment, age, disability or sickness. While some gaps remain in the framework, the goal is being ap-

---

* For the most comprehensive and current account on the economic security program for the aged, the author refers the reader to the Cohen article which was published just as this writing went to press. See Wilbur J. Cohen, "Economic Security for the Aged Sick and Disabled—Some Issues and Implications," *Towards Freedom from Want.* Sar A. Levitan, Wilbur J. Cohen, Robert J. Lampman (eds.), Industrial Relations Research Association, Madison, 1968.

proached and Americans show no sign of wavering in their resolve. For this very reason, economic security for the aged, sick and disabled will continue to be improved in the years to come.[26]

## REFERENCES


1. Carter, Allan M., and Marshall, F. Ray: *Labor Economics: Wages, Employment and Trade Unionism.* Homewood, Irwin, 1967, p. 466.
2. Wolfbein, Seymour: *Employment and Unemployment in the United States.* Chicago, Sci. Res. Assoc., 1964, p. 122.
3. Corson, John J., and McConnell, John W.: *Economic Needs of Older People.* New York. Twentieth Century, 1956, p. 50.
4. Sawyer, William A.: Health considerations. In Donahue, Wilma (Ed.): *Earning Opportunities for Older Workers.* Ann Arbor, U. of Mich., 1955, p. 77.
5. Loether, Herman J.: *Problems of Aging.* Belmont, Dickenson, 1967, p. 54.
6. Loether, *op. cit.*, p. 58.
7. Ball, Robert: Retirement programs and the changing participation of the aged in labor force. *Proceedings of the Fourth Annual Social Security Conference.* W.E. Upjohn Institute for Employment and Research, July 1962.
8. Ball, *op. cit.*
9. Epstein, Lenore A.: The income position of the aged. Orbach, Harold L., and Tibbetts, Clark (Eds.): *Aging and the Economy.* Ann Arbor, U. of Mich., 1963, p. 91.
10. Cohen, Sanford: *Labor in the United States.* Columbus, Merrill, 1960, p. 588.
11. *Ibid.*
12. President's Committee on Corporate Pension Funds and other private retirement and welfare programs. *Public Policy and Private Pension Programs.* Washington, D.C., U.S. Government Printing Office, Jan. 1965, Appendix A, p. 2.
13. *Ibid.*
14. *Ibid.*
15. Corson, John J., and McConnell, John W., *op. cit.*, p. 219.
16. U.S., Bureau of Census: *Statistical Abstract of the United States,* 87th ed., p. 289.
17. David, Alvin M.: Trends and probabilities in sources of retirement income. Orbach, Harold L., and Tibbetts, Clark (Eds.): *Aging and the Economy.* Ann Arbor, U. of Mich., 1963, p. 120.
18. *Ibid.*
19. *Ibid.*, p. 118.
20. *Ibid.*, p. 119.
21. Hains, Ed: The plight of retired on pensions. *Des Moines Sunday Register,* *118*(341):L-1, June 4, 1967.

22. Bechill, William D. (Commissioner Administration on Aging): The President's Council on Aging. *The Older American.* Washington, D.C., U.S. Government Printing Office, 1963, p. 73.
23. *Labor Relations Reference Manual.* Washington, D.C., Bureau of National Affairs. September 1, 1965, LRRM91-60-LRRM92, vol. 60, p. 60.
24. *Ibid.*
25. *Ibid.*
26. Cohen, Wilbur J.: Economic Security for the Aged Sick and Disabled. In Levitan, Sar A.; Cohen, Wilbur J., and Lampman, Robert J. (Eds.): *Towards Freedom from Want.* Madison, Industrial Relations Research Association, 1968, p. 87.

## ADDITIONAL READINGS

Levitan, S.A., *et al.*: *Towards Freedom from Want.* Madison, Industrial Relations Research Association, 1968.

Orbach, Harold L., and Tibbetts, Clark: *Aging and the Economy.* Ann Arbor, U. of Mich., 1963.

Turnbull, John G.: *The Changing Faces of Economic Insecurity.* Minneapolis, U. of Minn., 1966.

Albrecht, Ruth E. (Ed.): *Aging in a Changing Society.* Eleventh Annual Southern Conference on Gerontology. Gainesville, U. of Florida, 1962.

Culley, Jack F., and Slavick, Fred: *Employment Problems of Older Workers.* Iowa City, U. of Iowa, 1959.

Ferguson, Robert H.: *Unemployment: Its Scope Measurement and Effect on Poverty.* Ithaca, New York State School of Industrial and Labor Relations, Cornell University, 1965. Bulletin 53-2.

Foote, George H., and McLaughlin, David J.: The President's stake in pension planning. *Harvard Business Review, 43*(5):91-106, Sept.-Oct. 1965, pp. 91-106.

Jacobs, H. Lee (Ed.): *The Older Person in the Family Challenges and Conflicts.* Iowa City, The Institute of Gerontology, U. of Iowa, 1965.

U.S. Bureau of Labor Statistics: *Labor Force and Employment in 1965.* Washington, D.C., Government Printing Office, Special Labor Force Report No. 69 (Reprint No. 2494).

U.S. Bureau of Labor Statistics: *Private Pension Plan Benefits.* Washington, D.C.: Government Printing Office, Bulletin No. 1485, 1966.

U.S. Congress, Senate, Special Committee on Aging: *Report on The Special Committee on Aging.* 89th Cong., 1st Sess., 1967.

U.S. Department of Labor: *Manpower Report of the President.* April 1967.

U.S. Federal Council on Aging: *White House Conference on Aging, Chart Book.* 1961.

U.S. President's Council on Aging: *The Older American.* 1963.

U.S. President's Council on Aging: *On Growing Older.* 1964.

Bankers Trust Co.: *1965 Study of Industrial Retirement Plans.* New York, Bankers Trust Co., p. 263.

*Chapter 5*

# FEDERAL ROLE IN CONSUMER PROTECTION

William E. Oriol

The increasing responsibility of Government to help consumers make informed choices in the national market place was made clear by President Johnson when he said in his 1967 Special Message on Consumers:

> [T]he march of technology that has brought unparalleled abundance and opportunity to the consumer has also exposed him to new complexities and hazards. It has made many of our laws obsolete and has created the need for new legal remedies and safeguards. In short, we are faced with new problems of prosperity.

To older Americans, such problems have added urgency. Reasons for that urgency were given by knowledgeable witnesses at a Senate hearing[1] early in 1967 before Senator Harrison A. Williams, Jr., of New Jersey.[2] To summarize the major points made at that time:

> The average income of the nineteen million persons past 65 years of age in the United States is about half that of younger people.

In 1965, the average median income of 4.7 million aged living alone was $1,348, while that for younger people was $3,320; the median income for the 6.9 million older families with heads aged 65 and over was $3,460 in 1965, while for younger families that amount was $7,352.

> Heterogenous and highly individualistic as the elderly may be, they share common needs. Health care is the most obvoius. Four out of five people past 65 have one or more chronic illnesses or conditions; they pay about three times as much for medicine as younger people do. The elderly also pay proportionately more of their incomes on food, shelter, and fuel than younger people do.
>
> [T]he complexity of the modern market-place offers increasing opportunities for distortion or omission of facts. This, together with immobility, illness, loneliness, and other factors affecting many older people, makes them susceptible to fraudulent schemes or at least places them

at a disadvantage in finding the best buys for their limited funds. (Testimony by The Honorable William D. Bechill, Commissioner, U.S. Administration on Aging.)

What can government do to be of assistance to the elders of the society it serves? The Senate Special Committee on Aging has been exploring that question since 1963, when it turned its attention primarily to frauds and misrepresentations affecting older Americans.

## INQUIRY INTO FRAUDS AND DECEPTIONS

Testimony was taken from a large number of expert witnesses by the full Committee in 1963.[3] Impressed by testimony clearly indicating that the elderly are major victims of many questionable sales promotions, the Committee members established a subcommittee to investigate problem areas more intensively. In a report drawn from hearings conducted in 1964, the subcommittee concentrated on two major subject areas, quackery and mail-order land sales.[4, 5] The following excerpts from that report give some idea of the magnitude of the problems encountered.

### Quackery and Health

Americans are now paying the greatest price they have ever paid for worthless nostrums, ineffectual and potentially dangerous devices, treatments given by unqualified practitioners, food fads and diet supplements that are not needed, and other alluring products or services that make misleading promises of cure or end to pain.

It is incredible that a wealthy nation, priding itself on its enlightenment and its thirst for progress, should pay such a heavy penalty for ignorance or lack of adequate enforcement.

And it is shameful that the elderly of the United States are now clearly the major victims of the highly organized, high-pressure techniques of the modern day medicine man. But this is clearly the case, and it was verified as woeful fact by witnesses who addressed the subcommittee.

### Caliornia—Major Programs, Major Concern

To begin its survey of health frauds and quackery, the subcommittee heard its first witnesses in California. This state was chosen, not only because of its relatively large number of retired persons, but also because the state agencies are waging a comprehensive counterattack on the cheaters.

Even though the dangers are recognized, however, witnesses readily testified that they foresaw even greater enforcement difficulties ahead. Dr. Hamlet C. Pulley, Assistant Director of the California State Department of Health stated the following:

> We are convinced that quackery exists in California to a degree substantially detrimental to the health and welfare of its citizens.
>
> A greater than usual number of referrals and complaints were received last year from consumers, civic organizations, voluntary health organizations, and other interested persons. These, coupled with our own observations, lead us to conclude that quackery is extensive in California and appears to be increasing.

The same witness gave a poignant statistical picture of the vulnerability of the aged to salesmen of false hope:

> Eight per cent of California's seventeen million people are 65 years of age or older. In southern California this percentage may be higher, approximately 10 per cent.
>
> Three-quarters of these have some type of chronic condition, cancer, rheumatoid arthritis, heart disease or other chronic disability.
>
> It is this senior citizen with chronic ailments, approximately one-half million, who is the most severely affected by the activities of the medical confidence man.
>
> It is this class that becomes the main target for extensive exploitation.

An assistant district attorney for Los Angeles County, confirmed this conclusion. He said his records of quack prosecutions showed that seven out of ten victims are over the age of 60.

Example after example was given in California to prove, in the words of a spokesman for the attorney general of California, that:

> [T]he snake oil medicine man has exchanged his stock for food supplements, and has rephrased his pitch in twentieth century language. He has added to his stock, electronic devices with curious dials. He can cure and prevent cancer, cardiac conditions, chronic disturbances of the gastrointestinal tract, dermatoses, rheumatism, improper blood pressure, nervousness, and anemia.

Similar conclusions were reached during three days of hearings in

Washington, D.C., by witnesses describing quackery as a national problem.

## The National Scene: Fraudulent Schemes On The Increase

Asked whether fraudulent schemes are on the increase, the Chief Postal Inspector of the United States gave a definite affirmative. He also gave reasons for the increasing complexity of medical fraud cases:

> Although postal inspectors still occasionally encounter medical quackery items involving electric belts, buzzers, bell ringing, and even black magic potions guaranteed to cure all manner of disease, today's frauds are generally more sophisticated. Promoters do not so often promise outright cures for serious diseases but offer preparations to "aid in curing" various conditions which the American consumer finds undesirable, such as baldness, obesity, and such.
>
> Treatments are offered by mail for every conceivable condition, including cancer, diabetes, prostate trouble, asthma, arthritis, heart diseases and impotency, to name but a few. Such schemes continue to be a source of great concern since the victims are frequently induced to attempt self-diagnosis and treatment, meanwhile deferring proper attention.

Mrs. Esther Peterson, who served as the first chairman of the President's Committee on Consumer Interests, described the vulnerability of the elderly, not as sheer gullibility, but as the result of several causes:

> In my capacity as Special Assistant to the President for Consumer Affairs, I am concerned, of course, with the myriad problems facing consumers of all ages and conditions.
>
> Yet, I confess willingly to a special concern for our aged, whose capacity to resolve many of their problems independently is considerably less than that of our younger citizen-consumers.
>
> The aging men and women in our society are becoming increasingly a more significant percentage of our total population. As their numbers increase, so also will the incidence of fraud and quackery increase. For these people, removed—as many of them are—from the mainstream of daily business activity, cut off from the stimulation of regular "back fence" exchanges with neighbors, become in their loneliness evermore susceptible to the blandishments of facile hucksters.
>
> I receive daily in my office scores of letters from older people all over the country. The range of subject matter with which these people are concerned is broad and varied, but there has been a heavy emphasis on health frauds and quackery.

Many of the writers have dispaired long since of any redress of their grievances; they want simply to share their disappointment, their sense of loss, with someone, with anyone who will offer a bit of understanding. I am tremendously impressed with this dread of loneliness that seems to run through so many of the letters and interviews with people as I run around the country.

Others of them, confident still that frauds and quacks will somehow be searched out and restrained, plead with the eloquence of age for the Government to take some kind of action against those who would victimize the weak and the innocent.

## Mail Order Retirement Sites

Until recent years, comparatively few Americans dreamed of retiring in distant States on land they had never seen. Approximately a decade ago, however, a mail-order land sale boom began. Buyers were urged to make small payments—usually $10 down and $10 a month—for sites hundreds and even thousands of miles away. To many individuals near or past retirement age, the bright advertising brochures seemed to offer solid reason to believe that security, good climate, and a new way of life could be found on faraway sites in communities not yet built.

As 1962 neared its end, however, some purchasers, many enforcement officials, and a number of journalists began to find flaws in the boom. They tried to alert would-be purchasers to be on the watch for overly optimistic promoters and for outright fraud. Complaints and confusion increased and Federal agencies stepped up their surveillance.

### *Magnitude Of The Industry*

Even at an early stage of growth, the mail-order land sales industry has already attracted many hundreds of millions of dollars from investors; it has great potential for increased service to the public as the demand for new homesites continues to mount.

One of the major goals of the subcommittee was to arrive at some estimate of the magnitude of the industry. Difficulties in arriving at that estimate were summed up at the hearing by Gerald J. McBride, president of the National Association of License Law Officials:

A total estimate, for the entire United States, will take some time to compile, for there is no accurate source at the present time. This is a

> difficult project, since the great bulk of these transactions are as yet unrecorded except in the records of the subdividers. The cumulative total of contracts on which purchasers are still paying must be enormous.

In spite of the difficulties in arriving at a total, there is good reason to believe that many hundreds of millions of dollars have already been invested.

## *Many Reputable Firms At Work*

Although the subcommittee was primarily concerned with promoters who deliberately cheat their victims, it recognizes that mail-order land sales industry already has performed major service for many individual buyers. One developer, for example, told the subcommittee that his corporation devoted five years of research and approximately $16 million in the planning and construction of its first retirement community. Substantial, reputable developers are making comprehensive efforts to provide livable retirement environment for the elderly and others who buy through the mail.

The subcommittee also recognizes that increasing population pressures, and the ever-growing mobility of all citizens, will increase the demand for the opening of new, and sometimes marginal, land for development. Well-managed mail sales can make a considerable contribution to such development.

## *Tricks Of The Trade*

Notwithstanding the salutary effect of the mail-fraud statute and new state laws, the subcommittee has become concerned about other practices that do not fall within the strictly defined jurisdiction of mail-fraud investigators. Slippery language and omission of important facts can, in the opinion of the subcommittee, cause almost total misunderstanding and confusion.

A concise summary of present techniques was given by Alton W. Van Horn, then commissioner and now president of the New Jersey Real Estate Commission. Mr. Van Horn, who has conducted on-site investigations for the commission in many states to compare advertising copy with on-the-spot realities, told the subcommittee:

> The difference between the impression created by the promotional material and the true fact is of the greatest concern.

Artists' conceptions not labeled as such and alleged or suggestedly nearby—but actually quite distant—scenes are routinely used, instead of on-site or accurately labeled photos.

What pass to the uninformed as maps are too frequently prepared with shocking disregard to scale and proportion. Recreational areas, bodies of water, and places where shopping, schools, and other facilities might be available, are pictured much closer than they are.

Distances tend to be indicated as "minutes away" instead of hours (at legal speeds) or in miles over travelable roads. There was one illustration where you would have had to drive sixty-eight miles in forty-five minutes which is a little beyond the driving capability of most people.

The fact that flash floods, windstorms, sandstorms, temperature extremes and other weather phenomena affect some areas is not usually revealed, nor are such things as water depth (and cost to reach it), and the absence of vital services.

Another factor is the contract often used. The small down payment makes it easy to take. The long terms postpone the day of discovery (of just what one has purchased). This is like a long-delayed fuse on a potentially explosive situation.

Quite general is the nonacceleration clause which prevents taking title and delivery of deed before it meshes with the developer's convnience or his ability to release his mortgage or get subdivision approval. Some would take the money and give a certificate of ownership because they can't deliver a recordable deed.

The matter of a firm declaration of exactly what improvements will be installed—and when—is omitted more often than not and seems a very painful area even for discussion.

The usual money refund and transfer guarantee are far more useful to the promoter than to the investor or the retiree. They lull one into thinking it must be safe but, on close scrutiny, the money is returnable only on inspection and often only at the property, rather than at the point of sale. The exercise of the switch privilege—in order to reduce by many miles the distance between your lot and the nearest human abode, a water source or powerline—may add to or multiply your cost.

The guarantees are sometimes amusing. One even makes the generous guarantee that the "full one-acre rancho" embraces 43,560 square feet, a little like guaranteeing the foot to be twelve inches.

A fairly new trend in mail-order land sales was described at the hearing by Mr. McBride:

Now we find that stress is being placed either on holding the land as an investment for resale later at a profit or buying it now, so that when retirement age is reached the land will be paid for and ready for occupation.

Unlike those who claim that their subdivisions are idyllic and well endowed with modern conveniences, the investment acreage merchandiser usually specifically says that the land is undeveloped without any public facilities at all. He may also suggest, however, that the value of the land is almost certain to go up, perhaps to two or three times the original investment. He will also probably point out that Miami Beach and Los Angeles once were regarded as poor investment risks, but that fortunes have been made from wise real estate purchases on land once regarded as absolutely unpromising.

The subcommittee agrees that astute, or even lucky, buyers can make substantial profits by speculating in real estate. The subcommittee believes that nothing should interfere with the right of a buyer to make a purchase, no matter how risky it may seem at the time of purchase. But the subcommittee also believes that omission or distortion of facts, even under these circumstances, can lead a purchaser to make a transaction far more unfavorable than he may realize.

This attitude was expressed emphatically by Mr. John R. Hoffman, vice president of the National Better Business Bureau. He said the following:

> We tell the public inquiring on "investment offers" that the purchase of undeveloped acreage is a highly speculative proposition depending for success on many factors that are difficult to estimate even when one is completely familiar with a given area. We urge a thorough personal investigation and a decision based on facts, after personal inspection.

## Health Insurance

The subcommittee also conducted hearings and issued findings and recommendations on deceptive or misleading practices used to sell health insurance to older Americans. The subcommittee studies, however, were made before the advent of Medicare and are out-of-date. Under subcommittee study at this writing is an entirely new subject: health insurance policies offered to "supplement" medicare benefits.

## MAJOR RECOMMENDATIONS: 1965 REPORT

Congress will only add to buyers' confusion if it enacts unwieldly or unnecessarily harsh regulations in today's market-place. Instead, every attempt should be made to help provide the purchaser with the facts he needs to make wise choices. "Let the buyer beware" should be superseded by a new motto: "Let the buyer be informed."

The subcommittee attempted to follow that philosophy in its major recommendations. It encouraged educational efforts on the part of federal departments and agencies, greater federal and state cooperation in exchange of information, and research on buyer attitudes. When legislation was called for it was intended to be constructive.

To deal with mail-order land sales abuses, for example, the subcommittee called for full disclosure of all the facts needed by the buyer *before* the purchase was to be made. The legislation, introduced in 1966 and again in 1967[6] by Senator Williams, was endorsed by President Johnson in his message on American Consumer Protection on February 16, 1967.

The subcommittee also attempted to prevent abuses before they can occur. Worthless medical devices, as we have already seen, take a heavy toll in dollars and anguish. Legislation proposed by the subcommittee would require pre-market testing of such devices *before* they can reach the market-place. Similarly, the subcommittee also asked for changes in the administrative fraud statute to enable authorities to act promptly when confronted with clearly questionable promotional activity.

## BROADENED SUBCOMMITTEE ROLE

Recognizing its responsibility to inform as well as recommend new legislation, the subcommittee took on a new name and new responsibilities. The Subcommittee on Consumer Interests of the Elderly, as it is now called, added to its jurisdiction such new areas of study as buying habits of the elderly, products needed by the elderly but not offered to them, and marketing practices that affect the elderly.

The magnitude of that assignment became clear at the survey hearing conducted in January, 1967. Among the major themes were three of particular importance:

### *I. Responsibilities of the Administration on Aging*

The AOA, established by the Older Americans Act of 1965, is intended to provide a strong central focal point within the Federal Government on all matters of concern to older people. AOA Commissioner Bechill described a four-point plan of action to meet that agency's responsibility to elderly consumers. The following excerpts from his statement gives some idea of the work still to be done in this area:

> *One.* We intend to contract with appropriate research groups who are qualified to gather badly needed data concerning older people in the consumer field.
>
> During our first year in operation, it has become strikingly evident to the Administration on Aging that there is a crucial need for such information concerning the older person as a consumer. For example, we have no recent data on the expenditure and consumption patterns of the elderly.
>
> We do not know enough about their eating habits and consequent nutritional problems; we know nothing of their understanding of today's market-place and all of its complexities; we do not know what their demand for new products, specifically designed for them, may be; we do not know how many participate in federal, state and local programs aimed at meeting their specific needs.
>
> In other words, what we do not know, but realize increasingly that we need to know, is how efficiently older people are performing as consumers. Such data will provide us and others with this understanding.
>
> *Two.* We will prepare informational materials specifically designed for use by professional and lay leaders who intend to conduct consumer education programs for older people and, similarly, special materials to be read by the elderly themselves.
>
> We recognize the severe handicap of attempting to conduct effective consumer information programs without effective supportive materials. Again, we invite all agencies—government or private—to join us in this effort.
>
> *Three.* We will support pilot demonstrations in the consumer education field. We have pinpointed ten areas of great concern to older consumers toward which these demonstrations will be directed. They are as follows:
>
> 1. Sound nutrition,
> 2. Economy food purchasing,
> 3. The careful purchase of credit,
> 4. Avoidance of quackery,
> 5. Avoidance of fraudulent products and practices,
> 6. Safe and effective use of drugs,
> 7. Accident prevention,
> 8. Management of retirement income,
> 9. Medicare and supplementary health insurance plans, and
> 10. Care of clothing and household equipment.

We will expand this basic ten as additional needs become apparent. We believe that this program will bring much needed, long overdue information to older people.

*Four.* In our consumer education plan, we intend to push more vigorously for cooperative programs with other Government agencies, and with private, nonprofit organizations which in one way or another, serve older Americans. AOA has taken significant steps to establish coordinated activities with these groups.

## 2. *The Elderly as a New Market*

Individual incomes of most older Americans may be inadequate, but their aggregate buying power is now estimated to be between $40 and $45 billion dollars.[7] To several witnesses, it seemed clear that such a market should be an attractive lure to merchandisers with specially designed products for that age group. Mrs. Geneva Mathiasen, Executive Director of the National Council on the Aging, put the argument succinctly:

> For many years, NCOA has directed attention to a number of areas where the inventiveness which characterizes modern industrial design and engineering might be utilized to help create a living environment conducive to the well-being of individuals as they grow older, to help them retain independence and perform their daily tasks with less effort, and to enjoy with greater zest their leisure time. Whether a dress has a zipper up the back or up the front may make the difference between a woman's being able to dress herself or not. The simple act of rising from a chair, or getting in and out of a taxicab, can add or subtract years to a man's apparent age, depending on how the chair or taxicab is designed.
>
> Four years ago NCOA conducted a consumer institute in furniture requirements and furniture design for older people. The institute was held at the request of a man who, having supervised the planning and building of a large housing development for older people, was having great difficulty in finding furniture appropriate to the needs of the residents.
>
> The report of the institute also contains many practical and specific suggestions relating to furniture construction and design essential to the requirements of people as they grow older. It is not appropriate to this hearing to dwell on these in detail. I only want to point out that even those elderly people who are financially able to buy consumer goods are often unable to find products suited to their needs—from clothing, to furniture, to automobiles, to bathtubs.

A Professor of Marketing from Columbia University told the subcommittee that the elderly are far from conservative in acceptance of new products:

> It is widely held axiom in marketing practice that senior citizens are less inclined to try new products. This is generally believed. It may be true for some new products, but our evidence from the project at Columbia University would suggest it is certainly not true for all new products. We find that oldsters, which we have arbitrarily defined as over 64, are even more inclined than the middle-aged, and those are 55 to 64, to have favorable ideas to innovation.

## 3. *Income Still the Basic Problem*

This brief report has already pointed out that the average retirement income is half that enjoyed by members of the work force. Approximately five million elderly are still below official poverty levels, and the average 13 per cent Social Security increase voted by Congress late in 1967 will not alter the situation significantly. The great unresolved problem of all elderly Americans is still inadequate income in the face of rising productivity and increased earnings of those still at work.

Until that basic problem is solved, however, every attempt should be made to help the elderly make the most of the income they do have.

### TWO PROMISING EXPERIMENTS

Federal agencies and private organizations have been active in providing information and other forms of help to elderly consumers. The Food and Drug Administration and the Administration on Aging, for example, have sponsored conferences for community leaders. The FDA has issued several helpful publications, including a large-size edition of an antiquackery publication called, "Your Money and Your Life." The District of Columbia Home Economics Association Committee on Aging—working in conjunction with the American Association of Retired Persons—has prepared a list of "Selected Consumer Publications for Older Persons." Mention has already been made of the institutes on consumer needs sponsored by the National Council on the Aging. Many of the consumer education programs sponsored through the Office of Economic Opportunity are of great help to the elderly.

In addition, two experimental programs began in 1967, using governmental and private resources to inform the public. This chapter will conclude with a brief description of each in anticipation of similar efforts elsewhere.

## Project Moneywise—Senior

The Federal Bureau of Credit Unions, with funds provided through the Office of Economic Opportunity, developed training courses in six cities during 1966 in order to give limited-income persons information intended to make best use of their money. Among the subjects discussed were: family financial counseling, preparing a family budget, and group effort to combat financial ills.

That basic program was adapted for older participants in Boston, Massachusetts, from September 18 through October 13 in a pilot program called Project Moneywise—Senior. Enrollees ranged in age from 40 to 79. The trainees were expected to return to their local communities and help both older citizens and younger persons to help themselves. The trainees were also taught credit union operations and management in order to develop a job skill for income supplementation.

## Consumer Education Project, Hudson Guild, New York City

Older Americans Act Funds were provided through the New York State Office for the Aging to initiate this project, which is conducted through the Hudson Guild. The Guild, one of the most prominent of the settlement houses operated in Manhattan, services individuals who reside in a public housing project on the West Side. Working directly with elderly individuals in a high density population area in Manhattan, the director of this project has encountered a multitude of problems faced in the market-place. The project also demonstrates the value of a sustained consumer education effort, as indicated by this description of activities within the first year of operation:

> Our program has (1) demonstrated a need for adequate food programs, (2) cooperated in a Medicare Alert, (3) developed a drug plan, (4) attempted to involve older people in social action, (5) initiated an information program with welfare, (6) held a citywide conference on consumer problems of older people, and (7) began testing various educa-

tional techniques. Our next year will be focused on social action and the development of a family security program.[8]

## CONCLUSION

The Senate Special Committee on Aging, working with other congressional units and federal agencies, will continue to study consumer problems of the elderly; but it is not likely to find easy answers for many of these problems. Legislation may be needed to deal with some abuses; indeed, 1968 has already become a year of significant progress in terms of new laws intended to protect the consumer. But more and more the Committee is offering suggestions for information programs that will help prevent abuses from occurring.

There is much to do just in that area alone, and the elderly could well become the major beneficiaries from educational programs that —with some ingenuity and deep understanding of the unique problems of aging—could well become a force for similar efforts on behalf of all age groups.

## REFERENCES

1. Consumer Interests of the Elderly, Hearings before the Subcommittee on Consumer Interests of the Elderly, of the U.S. Senate Special Committee on Aging, Washington, D.C., Jan. 17-18, 1967.
2. Chairman, U.S. Senate Special Committee on Aging, and Chairman, Subcommittee on Consumer Interests of the Elderly.
3. Frauds and Quackery Affecting the Older Citizen. Hearings before the U.S. Senate Special Committee on Aging, Washington, D.C., Jan. 15, 16, 17, 1963.
4. Frauds and Deceptions Affecting the Elderly, Investigations, Findings and Recommendations. 1964, a report of the Subcommittee on Frauds and Misrepresentations Affecting the Elderly to the U.S. Senate Special Committee on Aging, Washington, D.C., Jan. 31, 1965.
5. Hearings held by the Subcommittee on Frauds and Misrepresentations Af-
   Health Frauds and Quackery:
   fecting the Elderly in 1964.
   Part 1. San Francisco, California, January 13, 1964
   Part 2. Washington, D.C., March 9, 1964.
   Part 3. Washington, D.C., March 10, 1964.
   Part 4a. Eye Care, Washington, D.C., April 6, 1964
   Part 4b. Eye Care, Washington, D.C., April 6, 1964
   Interstate Mail Order Land Sales:
   Part 1. Washington, D.C., May 18, 1964

Part 2. Washington, D.C., May 19, 1964
Part 3. Washington, D.C., May 20, 1964
Preneed Burial Service:
Washington, D.C., May 19, 1964
Deceptive or Misleading Methods in Health Insurance Sales:
Washington, D.C., May 4, 1964.

6. Hearings on the Interstate Land Sales Full Disclosure Act of 1967 were conducted on February 28 and March 1, 1967, before the Subcommittee on Securities, U.S. Senate Committee on Banking and Currency, Washington, D.C.
7. BROTMAN, HERMAN B. (Chief): *A Profile of the Older American.* Reports and Analysis. Administration on Aging, Department of Health, Education and Welfare, Oct. 16, 1967.
8. CARTER, PATRICIA G. (Director, Consumer Education and Income Maintenance, of the Hudson Guild): Statement submitted to the Subcommittee on Health of the Elderly. U.S. Senate Special Committee on Aging, New York City, Oct. 19, 1967.

# PART III

# PSYCHOLOGICAL AND SOCIOLOGICAL ASPECTS OF AGING

*Chapter 6*

# UNDERSTANDING THE AGING PROCESS: PSYCHOLOGICAL ASPECTS AND THEIR IMPLICATIONS FOR ECONOMIC NEED

Woodrow W. Morris

## INTRODUCTION

A process is an on-going, constantly changing, predictable set of events; it is both growing and deteriorating but is always lawful and consistent. Nothing is true of nature if this basic premise is not true.

And so it is with life and so it is with individual human lives in all their many aspects. The significant thing about the process of living can be summed up in the word "integrity." As one studies biology and its kindred natural sciences and as one studies psychology as it relates to the developing and declining life processes, it is striking how well the whole hangs together. In this instance, then, the whole is not equal to the sum of the parts plus all of the important integrating relationships between and among the parts. Just as there are no two fingerprints in the universe which are identical, neither are there two human lives, viewed as wholes, which are identical. It is this great diversity among people, this great plethora of individual differences which makes life among people so exciting, challenging, stimulating, perplexing, and difficult of predictability. This, then, is the nature of the subject with which we are dealing and this discussion will be restricted to only two or three aspects of human psychology as it pertains to the aging process.

## A CONCEPT OF ADJUSTMENT

We will begin with a frame of reference, within which adjustment might be regarded as a dynamic, complex, living, continually changing aspect of human behavior.

Freud has had much to say about this; some of which has been misstated and misunderstood with unhappy consequences. Some of these consequences have become more and more apparent recently through a reappraisal of some of the tenets of the progressive education movement and so-called "modern child psychology." For example, the following paradigm has been attributed to Freud: "Frustration of wishes and needs produces conflict and stress, and conflict and stress are the basic elements of neurosis." This is an entirely sensible, logical statement; one with which one might not want to argue. But consider what follows from such a concept. If frustration produces conflict and conflict leads to neurosis, then the most obvious way to handle child behavior in order to produce good adjustment would be to avoid the danger of producing conflicts and stresses by not frustrating the child in his needs and wishes. Too often this is exactly the course which has been followed—and with dire results.

How different the entire frame of reference becomes when the clause which was omitted from what Freud *really* said is added to the statement: "Frustration of wishes and needs produces conflict and stress, which are the basic elements of neurosis; but *the successful resolution of conflict is the basis of growth and development.*" With this addition all the sequelae change. It not only becomes all right to frustrate the child and to put him in conflict and in stress situations, but it would appear that this is the healthy thing to do, providing parents, teachers, psychologists, truant officers and other parent-figures do everything possible to help the child resolve these conflicts successfully and to master the stress situations as they arise. This is what makes being a parent so trying at times. The mother or father must on the one hand attempt to assist in the socialization of a child by frustrating him; thus producing conflict and stress; and on the other hand they must somehow point this experience in a positive direction by the manner in which they administer discipline. This probably led to the development of the expression, "As the twig is bent, the parents are bushed."

The central position of frustration and stress in this system has much to do with the fact that in most of the discussion of adjustment, one encounters a great deal of emphasis on the importance of mastering the stresses and strains of living. Such stresses take many forms such as the frustration of personal needs and goals, the presses emanating from the environment, demands put on the individual by his friends, relatives and co-workers, and changing physiological conditions within the person himself in relation to previously learned and expected demands. Here stress is conceived as a momentary, acute, emergency situation and also as a system which operates through time. Not nearly enough is known about the relationships between the "mastery of stress" and adjustment but some research has been reported and more should be undertaken as time goes on. Already it seems quite closely related to such factors as early training and development, available personal resources, and previous experiences.

One of the most recent and interesting reports of studies of stress is that of Funkenstein and his colleagues entitled *Mastery of Stress*.[1] In it, Funkenstein makes a very thorough and ingenious series of controlled laboratory explorations of psychological and physiological correlates of both acute emergency reactions to stress and the ability to master stress as time passed. In the former he posits a parallelism between psychological and physiological mechanisms of behavior, *and concludes that the habitual emergency reaction of a man during acute stress is seen as a deeply laid down feature of personality, its roots extending backward into the biological and evolutionary development of men and upward into his childhood experience, and forming his basic disposition throughout life.* The personality correlates of acute emergency reactions to stress *included the person's perceptions of his parents, his internal self-concept, his fantasy life, and his social attitudes.*

On the other hand, Funkenstein reports that mastery or failure of mastery of stress over time were independent of the emotion reported during acute reactions. Mastery or failure of mastery of stress were related to different aspects of the personality from those related to reactions during acute stress. The important personality correlates of the ability to handle stress as time passed were the following: *interpersonal relationships, the ability to assess reality,* and *general personality integration.* In other words, this aspect of stress is related to ego strength, especially as seen in its "adaptive" function.

Funkenstein's methods were applied to college age students. The methods would be equally applicable to other age groups and the potentialities for developing important new information along the age continuum are exciting to contemplate. As can be seen from the foregoing, attitudes play an important role, especially in relation to one's own attitude toward aging and those of other people toward the aging person.

In the *Way of All Flesh,* Samuel Butler has stated the problem concisely and clearly:

> All our lives, every day and every hour, we are engaged in the process of accommodating our changed and unchanged selves to changed and unchanged surroundings; living, in fact, is nothing else than this process of accommodation; when we fail in it a little we are stupid, when we fail flagrantly we are mad; when we suspend it temporarily we sleep; when we give up the attempt altogether we die. In quiet, uneventful lives the changes internal and external are so small that there is little or no strain in the process of fusion and accommodation; in other lives there is great strain, but there is also great fusing and accommodating power. A life will be successful or not, according as the power of accommodation is equal to or unequal to the strain of fusing and adjusting internal and external change.[2]

## THE GROWTH AND CHANGE OF INTELLIGENCE

What most of us have been taught about changes in adult intelligence has been pretty consistent from textbook to textbook and coincides rather well with what the man in the street usually believes about what happens to intellectual behavior with increasing age. To illustrate this let me quote from a standard text on the measurement of adult intelligence:

> Senility, or extreme mental deterioration, is merely terminal state of certain processes which begin relatively early in life and continue progressively with age. The net result of the accompanying changes is to *impair all original endowment.* [3]

And again the following is said:

> We have put forth the hypothesis that the decline of mental ability with age is part of the general organic process which constitutes the universal phenomenon of senescence, and have insisted upon the fact that phenomenon begins relatively early in life.[4]

The growth and changes in intelligence, then, are depicted as showing the well-known rapid growth and development in children; beginning at an age varying from 15 to 22, the curve begins to fall off; and after age 35, it falls off rapidly. This, then, is the common curve

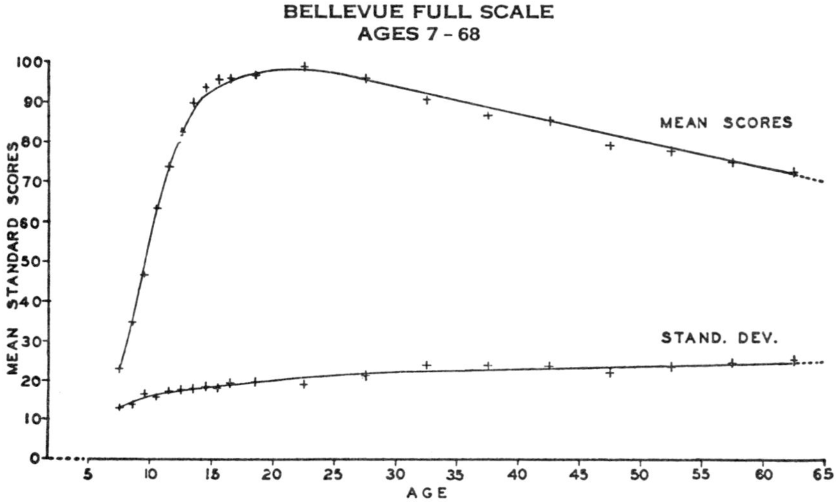


Figure 6-1. Curve of mental growth and decline.

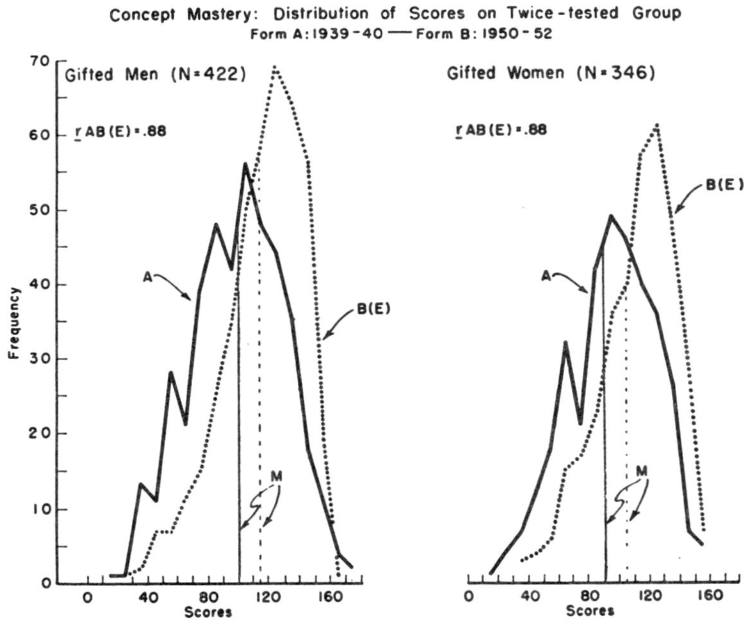


Figure 6-2. Frequency distributions of Form A and Form B (E) scores on the Concept Mastery Test: Gifted Study Men and Women.

of mental growth and decline as described in the quotation above. (See Figure 6-1.) In science nothing is sacred, and a few psychologists have carried on research with somewhat different results.

The first of these is by Bayley and Oden.[5] This was a study of the adult intelligence of the original subjects of the Terman Study of Gifted Children. In this study, over a thousand subjects comprising adults who were formerly subjects in the gifted children studies and their spouses were located and given the difficult Concept Mastery Test. After a twelve-year period they were reexamined. At the first testing these subjects averaged 30 years of age; at the second, 42 years of age; the range in age was from about 20 to 50 years. According to the curve of mental decline, a decline would have been predicted during this critical period of life. The results, however, showed the reverse; there was an increase on the retest. (See Fig. 6-2.) This was just as true, furthermore, for the men as for the women subjects. (See Fig. 6-3.) There was a similar increase in the instances of spouses of the Gifted Study subjects, suggesting again the selectivity that takes place in marriage choices.

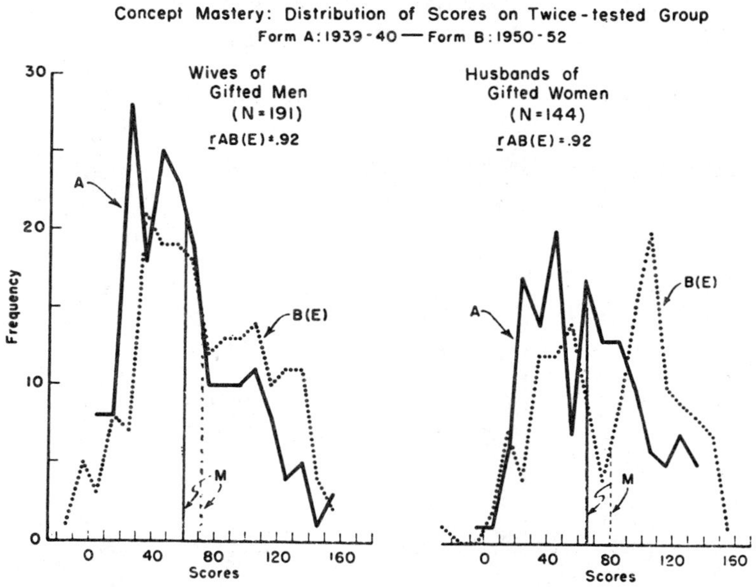


Figure 6-3. Frequency distributions of Form A and Form B (E) scores on the Concept Mastery Test: Husbands and Wives of Gifted Study subjects.

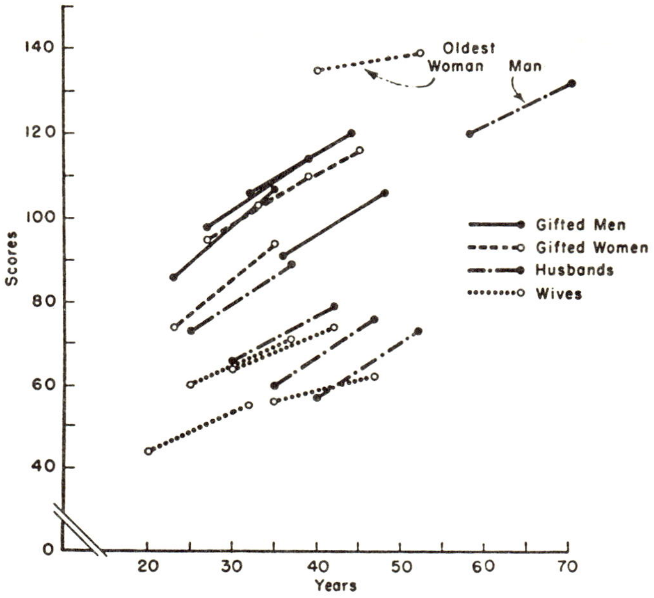


Figure 6-4. Series of average scores grouped by age.

Concerned lest some of this increase might be reflected by the different ages of the subjects, Bayley and Oden grouped them into five-year intervals, which showed that the test-retest scores of *all* age groups increased. (See Fig. 6-4.) Now educational attainment and professional and vocational pursuits of these subjects were regarded as of some interest in this connection, since these factors could be related to the changes in scores. (See Table XVI.) The tendency was clear that the scores improved with age, the lower scoring ones improving most, although this trend may in part be due to ceilings on the second test which limited the gains of those who originally scored very high.

Gains in score occurred at all educational levels; again there seemed to be the tendency for those scoring low at the first testing to gain the most on retest. (See Table XVII.)

A second study is that reported by Owens at Iowa State University.[6] In this instance, Owens located 127 former Iowa State students, to all of whom had been administered the Army Alpha Test in 1918 to 1919 when they were entering freshmen at the school. His retesting took place some thirty years later in 1949 to 1950. In brief, Owens'

TABLE XVI

COMPARISON OF CONCEPT MASTERY SCORES OF MEN IN OCCUPATIONAL CLASS I ACCORDING TO PROFESSION.

| | | *Form A* | | | *Form B(E)* | | |
|---|---|---|---|---|---|---|---|
| *Profession** | *N* | *Mean* | *S.D.* | *N* | *Mean* | *S.D.* | *Difference B(E)-A* |
| 1. University teacher or researcher .... | 21 | 128.2 | 25.1 | 16 | 132.1 | 18.1 | 3.9 |
| 2. Teacher below university level ...... | 30 | 110.8 | 32.8 | 24 | 117.8 | 28.2 | 7.0 |
| 3. Authors and Journalists ....... | 14 | 113.6 | 30.7 | 8 | 127.8 | ... | 14.2 |
| 4. Lawyers ......... | 57 | 111.5 | 23.4 | 51 | 123.4 | 18.8 | 11.9† |
| 5. Physicians ....... | 23 | 112.5 | 26.0 | 21 | 120.2 | 19.9 | 7.7 |
| 6. Chemists ........ | 20 | 110.0 | 21.1 | 17 | 123.9 | 13.5 | 13.9‡ |
| 7. Engineers ........ | 32 | 102.2 | 23.6 | 30 | 122.8 | 23.0 | 20.6† |
| 7a. Twice-tested Engineers so-classed both times ...... | 22 | 103.7 | 24.1 | 22 | 121.4 | 24.5 | 17.7‡ |
| Differences between means: | | *CR* | *P* | | *CR* | *P* | |
| 1 vs. 2 ........ | | 2.13 | .03 | | 1.95 | .05 | |
| 1 vs. 5 ........ | | 2.03 | .04 | | 1.90 | .06 | |
| 1 vs. 7 ........ | | 3.77 | <.001 | | 1.51 | .13 | |

*A group of miscellaneous professions is omitted.
†Significant at the .01 level of confidence or better.
‡Significant at the .02 level of confidence.

TABLE XVII

CONCEPT MASTERY SCORES BY AMOUNT OF EDUCATION FOR GIFTED MEN.

| | | *Form A* | | *Form B(E)* | |
|---|---|---|---|---|---|
| *Education* | *N* | *Mean* | *S.D.* | *Mean* | *S.D.* |
| 1. Ph.D. degree ............. | 25 | 127.3 | 22.9 | 138.5 | 14.1 |
| 2. M.D. degree ............. | 21 | 111.2 | 24.0 | 120.2 | 19.9 |
| 3. LLB. degree ............. | 51 | 109.6 | 23.4 | 124.5 | 18.5 |
| 4. Other graduate degrees .... | 54 | 109.5 | 30.5 | 121.4 | 23.9 |
| 5. 1 or more years graduate work; no graduate degree .. | 35 | 107.9 | 30.4 | 122.5 | 25.5 |
| 6. Bachelor's degree ......... | 104 | 96.1 | 27.6 | 113.2 | 25.5 |
| 7. 1 to 4 years college; no degree | 75 | 82.4 | 28.4 | 104.5 | 26.4 |
| 8. High school and technical or business training ........ | 25 | 82.5 | 27.1 | 102.9 | 25.6 |
| 9. High school graduation or equivalent ............... | 32 | 81.1 | 30.6 | 98.2 | 27.7 |
| Difference between means: | | *CR* | | *CR* | |
| 1 vs. 9* ............. | | 5.37 | | 7.12 | |
| 1 vs. 6* ............. | | 5.87 | | 6.72 | |

*Significant above the .001 level of confidence.

findings indicated that there were significant increases on those tests titled "Practical Judgment," "Synonym-Antonym," "Disarranged Sentences," "Information," and probably "Analogies." In addition there was a significant increase on the total Army Alpha Score. In the cases of the other three tests there was no significant decrease in score but a picture of maintenance of an original level of performance over the thirty-year period.

This still left many gaps in our knowledge about the nature of the growth and change in intellectual behavior. Since the foregoing reports are concerned solely with originally superior adults, what would be the results with people who had discontinued intellectual pursuits and/or lived in relatively unstimulating and unrewarding environments? These are questions still to be answered but about which hypotheses may be derived. The way these questions are posed may suggest some of the hypotheses. For example, one might suspect that originally average adults would tend to maintain abilities but show greater variability than the gifted, or that the dull adult would show a decrease in abilities perhaps proportional to or greater than the superior adults. Again, people in occupations or following avocations which are less and less stimulating of intellectual activity might be expected to show less of an increase, if not an actual decrease in scores; and the same might be true of people according to their environments. (See Fig. 6-5.)

Studies at the Institute of Gerontology are attempting to relate life experiences and events at earlier ages to those of later periods of life. In these studies, the longitudinal approach has been employed in order to determine the direction and magnitude of changes in test scores over time and some of the factors related to such changes. In a doctoral dissertation in psychology completed at the Institute of Gerontology by Mir F. Zaman,[7] three subtests, Ability to Do Quantitative Thinking (QT), Ability to Interpret Materials in Natural Science (NC), and General Vocabulary (Voc.) of the Iowa Tests of Educational Development (ITED) were readministered in 1964 to a group of 196 subjects, who were high school seniors in 1947 to 1948 in Cedar Rapids and Davenport, Iowa. Along with these three subtests, a specially constructed attitude questionnaire was also administered for assessing the attitudes of the subjects toward intellectual activities. Also a

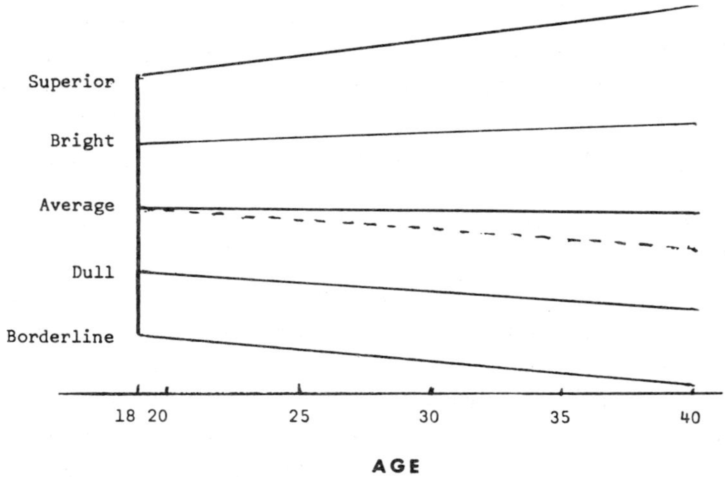


Figure 6-5. Hypothetical changes in adult intelligence with age.

Personal Data sheet was used to gather information about the intervening experiences of the subjects between the two test administrations. Altogether there were one hundred males and ninety-six females in the sample. One hundred and two were from Cedar Rapids and ninety-four from Davenport, divided almost equally between men and women.

In brief, analysis of the results indicated that the scores of all groups increased significantly. This, despite the fact that many of the subjects warned that they had not done anything like this since high school and thought they probably would do badly on the tests! The results are shown graphically. All groups increased, and it is especially significant that the vocabulary scores increased so steeply since vocabulary is commonly regarded as the best single measure of intelligence among all those usually included in batteries of intelligence tests.

Another result of even greater interest, however, refers to an analysis based on a subdivision of the subjects on the basis of their original test scores into "very high," "high," "low," and "very low" scoring groups. Our interest here concerns the retest scores of these groups and the results may be seen graphically in Figure 6-6. It is quite clear that all groups tended to increase on retest. This increase is particularly marked among the males and, again, the vocabulary test results are particularly striking.

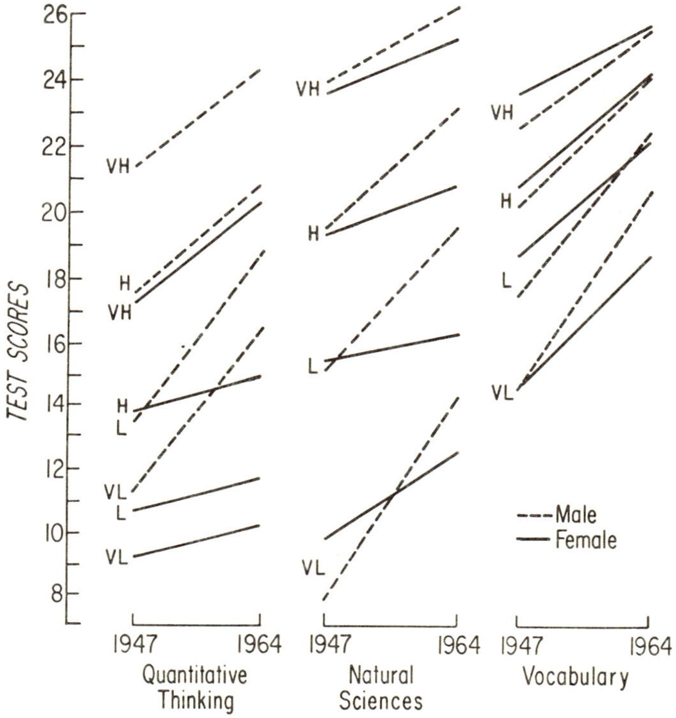


Figure 6-6.

Occupational pursuits, attitudes toward intellectual activities, and other intervening experience variables such as the amount of intellectual activities, reading books and writing, etc., and educational attainment were all related to increased test performance. Males tended to demonstrate a greater increase in test performance than females. However, working females (that is, those employed outside of the home for financial remuneration) performed better on retest than the nonemployed.

The results of this study are interpreted as supporting the view that the abilities measured by these tests do not decline with increasing age in early adulthood up to the age of 34. Furthermore, it was demonstrated that earlier and intervening life experiences do, indeed, bear a relationship to increased test performance. Probably of most significance is the new information concerning test score changes in relation to "original" level of functioning. Previous studies, especially those by Owens and by Bayley and Oden concerned only superior subjects ("gifted children" grown to adulthood and their spouses and 1918, 1919 college freshmen). In this study, we report not only on a more nearly "average" to "above average" group, but are able to demonstrate an increase in test results among even the very lowest scoring groups! It is planned to follow these same subjects so that additional longitudinal information will be available for analysis. Other studies should extend this method downward to include groups of below average abilities.

## THE CONCEPT OF SENILITY

Senility is another area of interest which has to do with mental hygiene and it has been said that "due to the nature of senility, older people cannot be helped by psychological or psychiatric treatment." The nature of senility referred to here is well illustrated in the following gloomy description offered in a standard textbook of clinical psychiatry:

> The prognosis of the senile psychoses is manifestly hopeless. No well-defined remissions are to be expected. . . . The course is progressive, the patient gradually becoming more demented, although life may continue for ten years or even longer before death supervenes.[8]

In large part, this opinion about senility is conditioned by the fact of organic brain changes and their importance in the mental health of the patient. But as Aring has said,

> The frequency with which our patients are said to be suffering from chronic brain syndrome these days leads me to wonder whether this rather elegant phrase isn't serving something besides diagnosis. House officers seem to be fond of it. It sounds so final. Chronic brain syndrome when combined with a diagnosis of cerebral arteriosclerosis represents senile dementia in modern dress. The indications usually are that an irrevocable mental state has set it.[9]

Again, concerning treatment of these patients, Aring says,

> As a young neuropsychiatric house officer, I had the usual introduction to the problem of taking care of many patients in a general hospital who were as rapidly as possible shunted to the state hospitals with what was then termed senile dementia.

> In the early 1930's, as today, these people were given the minimum of our time and were rapidly as possible shunted to the state hospitals and sanatoria for boarding the rest of their lives. As I try to recapture our thinking about these patients, we were as much embarrassed by them as any other feeling we may have had, a condition made tolerable for us by reason of the fact that they were soon to be gone. This state of affairs isn't much changed today; witness the frequency with which we move patients with chronic disorders out of the stream of medical consciousness, usually to somewhere in the suburbs or even more distant.
>
> It was only later that I became aware of *some of the social and economic factors that brought many of these patients to us.* The loosening of family ties with all that it implies, the relaxation of discipline with its depreciation of elders, the critical financial decade and the accompanying unemployment beginning in 1929, the urban shift of population, conscription, even the isolationism rampant after the first world war; these and many other factors played a part. However, a busy young physician earning clinical spurs had little time in those days for such concepts; it was only later that they entered my thinking about senile dementia.[10]

This conception of senility is quite at variance with the aforementioned textbook description of the senile psychoses. Furthermore, *it suggests environmental causative factors* which may be important in the production of or in the hastening of the production of senile changes. These suggestions are, in turn, in keeping with the thinking and research of Maurice Linden who has the following to say concerning the nature of senility:

> The author is of the conviction . . . that senility as an isolable state is not an inevitable biologic stage in the human life cycle, but is rather a cultural artifact, a product of prevalent social attitudes. It is the logical culmination of the combined social rejection of the late mature person and the senescent person's self-rejection.[11]

Linden describes the onset of the senile state as marked by a profound feeling of rejection and isolation, accompanied by a sense of insecurity and diminishing self-esteem, followed by a deep feeling of fatigue and melancholy. These beginnings seems to be successively followed by loss of environmental contact and periods of confusion during which memory and orientation are affected. If unchecked this proceeds into the terminal deteriorative state.

Now the emphasis in these viewpoints is upon social and intrapersonal stresses which impinge upon older people rather than inevitable, biological decline. If this were so, it should follow that the condition might be alleviated if attention were paid to the posited causative factors. This is the approach Linden took in proposing to do group psychotherapy with female patients of this type.

The patients with whom we are concerned here had a mean age of 70, three were younger than 60 and one was 89. The time spent in the hospital before treatment ranged from one month to forty years. The mean was about four years and ten months. Thirty-one of the total of fifty-one had been hospitalized for two years or less; twelve had been inpatients for eight years or more. In addition to their psychiatric diagnoses, a number and variety of other conditions were also present in these patients such as cardiac disease, arterial hypertension, nutritional anemia, diabetes, osteoarthritis, gynecological disorders, and arrested tuberculosis (see Fig. 6-7).

FIGURE 6-7
Total = 51

| *Diagnosis* | *No. of Patients* |
|---|---|
| Psychosis with Cerebral Arteriosclerosis | 12 |
| Senile Psychosis | 5 |
| Senile Dementia | 3 |
| Involutional Psychosis | 8 |
| Manic Depressive Psychosis | 7 |
| Schizophrenia | 6 |
| Paranoid Condition | 4 |
| Psychoneurosis | 1 |
| Character Neurosis | 2 |
| Huntington's Chorea | 1 |
| Psychosis with Intracranial Neoplasm (operated) | 2 |

Employing criteria of a clinical nature which were more a measure of *resocialization* than of complete remission of a psychosis, arrived at from physician and nurse observations, patients were classified as *much, moderately,* or *slightly improved,* or as showing no change whatever. None became worse.

Of the total group, the results were: twenty-two patients were much improved; eight were moderately improved; eleven showed slight improvement and only ten were unchanged. Twenty-three patients, or 45 per cent of the total, left the hospital for their own homes, county homes, or placements. (See Figs. 6-8 and 6-9.)

FIGURE 6-8

IMPROVEMENT STATUS OF ENTIRE GROUP

Total = 51

| *Type of Improvement* | *No. of Patients* | *% of Total* |
|---|---|---|
| Much | 22 | 43 |
| Moderate | 8 | 16 |
| Slight | 11 | 21.5 |
| No change | 10 | 19.5 |

FIGURE 6-9

IMPROVEMENT STATUS OF "HOME" GROUP

Total = 23

| *Type of Improvement* | *No. of Patients* | *% of Total* |
|---|---|---|
| Much | 17 | 73 |
| Moderate | 4 | 17 |
| Slight | 1 | 5 |
| No change | 1 | 5 |

A very rough comparison is made of these results with those of the other 279 patients in the same building who did not participate in therapy. Of these 13 per cent left the hospital as compared with the 45 per cent of the therapy group.

Again there is a theme evident here: There seems to be a relationship between earlier life experiences and environmental stresses and the development of so-called senile psychoses and, perhaps of even greater importance, there seems to be a relationship between the attitudes of responsible health personnel and the "fates" of the aged ill.

## THE FUNCTIONAL IMPORTANCE OF ATTITUDES

This section is concerned with the functional importance of *attitudes*—attitudes of people toward their own aging and those of others toward the aging.

All of us have some sort of an attitude or set of attitudes toward our own later years. Whether verbalized or not we have had such attitudes since our early years and these turn out to be pretty important. Speaking generally, it is probably safe to say that young people usually do not look forward with any particular relish to growing old. Without going into the whole history of the development of such attitudes, suffice it to say that there is this tendency to reject the idea of old age. Part of this may be determined by cultural mores and part, perhaps arises out of attitudes developed by children while growing up and passing through the socializing process required of them by their parents, teachers, ministers, truant officers and the other important elders in their lives. Too often during this process negative, antagonistic feelings toward these elders aid in the formation of elder-rejecting attitudes and feelings.

Theoretically, the next step would be that of not only a rejection of the idea of becoming old but in addition the rejection, passive or otherwise, of old people themselves, representing as they do symbols of the state of being which is both feared and rejected. Maurice Linden has described this state of affairs graphically as follows:

> In our society we are more subtle about such matters. We neither revere nor crudely discard the aged. But our passive neglect of them has caused annihilation just as surely as if our mode of action had been more direct. Witness youth who reject the protective caution of their elders as "conservativism and fuddy duddyism." Is not the reactive suffering of the older group, thus hastily by-passed in the stream of life, murderous? Witness industry that arbitrarily regards age 65 as the end of usefulness. Is not the mandatory retirement thus achieved a ticket to nowhere? Witness the physician, yes even the psychiatrist, the social worker, the counselor, who, annoyed with problems difficult of solution, says, "Well, what do you expect of older people? They're rigid, unyielding, unmodifiable, and cantankerous." Is not the resultant do-nothingness an invitation to indolence, stagnation and regression? [12]

It should not be surprising, then, that when these same people do reach that age at which they overtly or covertly say, "I am old," they must reject themselves. In other words, their feelings previously directed toward elders are now directed toward themselves. This is, almost by definition, depression and melancholy accompanied by all the feelings of uselessness, low self-esteem, loneliness, and reduced self-confidence usually associated with melancholia.

The roles of attitudes may be illustrated by two recent experiences. A group of some one hundred or more middle-aged and older women was asked quite spontaneously for a show of hands on the question, "How many of you are looking forward with positive attitudes (joy, pleasant expectations, enthusiasm) toward your later years?" One woman tentatively raised her hand and then took it down again. Afterwards she told me she would have raised her hand, but she didn't want to be the only one.

The second experience is related to this one. In lecturing to thirty-four senior nurses, the same question was asked with some elaborations. They were asked how many were looking forward with these same positive feelings toward their next five years (ages 20-25); then the next five years (25-30); then the next ten years (30-40); then the next fifteen years (40-55); and finally to the following ten years or more (55-65 or more). The results were about what would be expected; favorable attitudes were expressed by all thirty-four girls to the periods 20 to 25 and 25 to 30. These girls defected for the period 30 to 40. Only fifteen felt positively about the middle-age period from 40 to 55. None raised her hand for the 55 to 65 period!

In discussing their reasons for these latter feelings, their general picture of the later years was marked by such words and phrases as the following: gloomy, dependent, poor health, insecure, lower prestige and status, useless, nothing to do, end of the road, burden on others, etc.

Of equal, if not greater importance are the attitudes of others toward aging themselves. A short time ago, in the elevator of a large Iowa hospital, the following conversation between two young residents was overheard:

Resident No. 1: "Where are you going?"

Resident No. 2: "Oh, I have a real interesting 27-year old patient to see up on 7." (Followed by a brief description of the patient and his problem).

Resident No. 2: "Where are you going?"

Resident No. 1: "Oh, I have to see an 'old crock' on 5!"

This attitude, which is not uncommon, needs little comment. What is disturbing is that this attitude occurs so frequently among young doctors, psychologists, social workers, and even among teachers and ministers, though less outspokenly to be sure among the latter.

For a long period of years, a similar set of attitudes were quite common with reference to psychiatry and psychology. Patients tried to hide the fact of their needing psychological treatment. They would go to appointments as surreptitiously as possible and their behavior was marked by feelings of shame at having what they apparently regarded as defects in character requiring psychological or psychiatric help.

Over the past several years these attitudes have been slowly changing. One feature of the change seems to have been the increase with which people have been able to relax a little and poke fun at psychiatry and psychiatrists. The change is so pronounced that in some eastern cities a woman feels somehow left out of things at her afternoon bridge party if she cannot talk about "her psychoanalyst."

For the past several years we have seen many people working on, with, and for the aged and whenever the subject comes up it seems to be accompanied by a clenching of the fists and a setting of the jaw and an expression of the attitude that this business of aging is a grim business. Now there may be some change of attitudes about the grimness of it all and a little better acceptance of aging as a normal, developmental phase of the life process. Aiding in this development have been the relatively recent moves on the part of governments—local, state, and federal—to alleviate to some extent the economic problems in the areas of income maintenance and health care which have loomed large as specters affecting the attitudes of all of us as we look ahead to our own later years.

## CONCLUSION

The examples presented and many others serve to suggest that the problems ascribed to the aging are not novel problems, but have their roots in earlier life experiences. The study and understanding of these earlier life events should be the keys to understanding the aging process; indeed this approach carried with it the hope of *prevention* rather than merely the detection and handling of already existing problems. The suggestion is that we must emphasize the continuity of behavior, from normal to abnormal; and this applies also to personality development and to adjustment.

This dynamic concept of the aging process bears striking similarity to the following quotation from Leonardo da Vinci: "In youth acquire that which may requite you for the deprivations of old age; and if you are mindful that old age has wisdom for its food, you will so exert yourself in youth, that your old age will not lack sustenance."

Also on the theme of this conception of the process of aging, is the following verse from chapter twelve of the book of Ecclesiastes: "Remembers now thy Creator in the days of thy youth, While the evil days come not, nor the years draw nigh, When thou shalt say 'I have no pleasure in them.' "

A final expression of this same theme is found in one of the dialogues of Plato:

> There is nothing which for my part I like better, Cephalus, than conversing with aged men; for I regard them as travelers who have gone a journey which I, too, may have to go, and of whom I ought to inquire, whether the way is smooth and easy, or rugged and difficult. And this is a question which I should like to ask of you who have arrived at that time which the poets call the "threshold of old age"—is life harder toward the end, or what report do you give of it?
>
> I will tell you, Socrates, he said, what my own feeling is. Men of my age flock together; we are birds of a feather, as the old proverb says; and at our meetings the tale of my acquaintance commonly is—I cannot eat, I cannot drink; the pleasures of youth and love are fled away: there was a good time once, but now that is gone, and life is no longer life. Some complain of the slights which are put upon them by relations, and they will tell you sadly of how many evils their old age is the cause. But to me, Socrates, these complainers seem to blame that which is not really in fault. For if old age were the cause, I, too, being old, and every other old man, would have felt as they do. But this is not my own experience, nor that of others whom I have known. How well I remember the aged poet Sophocles, when in answer to the question, "How does love suit with age, Sophocles,—are you still the man you were?" "Peace," he replied, "most gladly have I escaped the thing of which you speak; I feel as if I had escaped from a mad and furious master." His words have often occurred to my mind since, and they seem as good to me now as at the time when he uttered them. For certainly old age has a great sense of calm and freedom; when the passions relax their hold, then, as Sophocles says, we are freed from the grasp not of one mad master only, but of many. The truth is, Socrates, that these regrets, and also the complaints about relations, are to be attributed to the same cause, which is not old age, but men's characters and tempers; for he who is of a calm and happy nature will hardly feel the pressure of age, but to him who is of opposite disposition youth and age are equally a burden.

## REFERENCES

1. FUNKENSTEIN, D.H.; KING, S.H., and DROLETTE, M.E.: *Mastery of Stress.* Cambridge, Harvard, 1957.
2. BUTLER, S.: *The Way of All Flesh.* New York, Dutton, 1916.

3. WECHSLER, D.: *Measurement of Adult Intelligence.* Baltimore, Williams & Wilkins, 1944, p. 55.
4. *Ibid.* p. 59.
5. BAYLEY, NANCY, and ODEN, M.H.: The maintenance of intellectual ability in gifted adults. *J Geront, 10*:91-107. 1955.
6. OWENS, W.A.: Age and mental abilities: a longitudinal study. *Genet Psychol Monogr, 48*:3-54, 1953.
7. ZAMAN, MIR F.: Factors Related to Test Performance: A Longitudinal Analysis. Ph. D. Dissertation, Iowa City, U. of Iowa, June 1964.
8. NOYES, A.P.: *Modern Clinical Psychiatry.* 2nd ed., Philadelphia, Saunders, 1939, p. 298.
9. ARING, C.D.: Senility. *Arch Intern Med, 100*:520, Oct. 1957.
10. *Ibid.*, p. 521.
11. LINDEN, M.E.: Group psychotherapy with institutionalized senile women: study in gerontologic human relations. *Int. Group Psychother, 3*:150-170, 1953.
12. LINDEN, M.E.: Emotional problems in aging. *Jewish Social Quarterly, XXXI*:81, Fall, 1954.

*Chapter 7*

# SOCIAL RELATIONS

FRANK ITZIN

SOCIAL RELATIONSHIPS cover the broad spectrum of activities that associate man with his fellow human beings and the society in which he lives. Four general statements can be made about social relationships, all of which have relevance to older persons.

First, the variety and nature of the social relations of individuals and groups form the essential fabric of social systems and society. Second, the nature of the social relationships determine to a large extent the contribution which can be made or the influence which can be brought to bear by individuals or groups to enhance or shape social institutions and society. Third, the nature of the social relationships in his attachment to social systems provide the individual with his self-image and self-conception, in fact provide him with his definition of his self. Fourth, virtually every human being has a point of view about what specific social relationships are or ought to be, a viewpoint based partly on the facts as he sees them, and partly on the values, hopes, fears, or other feelings he holds toward them.

## POINTS OF VIEW HELD ABOUT AGING AND THE AGED

One often hears, for example, some variation of the theme that older people are merely younger people or middle-aged people with a certain number of years added to their lives; carrying forward with them the myriad quantitative and qualitative differences in social relations which existed in earlier years. This viewpoint frequently is held by middle-aged persons and sometimes by older persons themselves. The essential validity of this assertion cannot be denied. But social forces and personal circumstances in the latter years may force modification of previous social patterns and life styles for many older persons.

A point of view popular in the not too distant past, and often held by younger persons today, is that older persons are the leading, most advantaged, most powerful, or even the most exploitive members of the community.[1] Cicero, in his essay on Old Age written in 44 B.C. praised certain of these characteristics in older life when he said the following:

> To begin with, I have always remained a member of a "club". . . .
> For myself, I take delight even in the old-fashioned appointment of master of the feast; and in the arrangement of the conversation . . . . These things I keep up even among my Sabine countrymen, and every day have a full dinner party of neighbors, which we prolong as far into the night as we can with varied conversation. . . .
> In fact, old age, especially when it has enjoyed honours, has an influence worth all the pleasures of youth put together.[2]

The results of community surveys of thirty to forty years ago gave graphic evidence that the control of the economic and civic club structure of communities was thought to be in the hands of older men.[3] This viewpoint also contains elements of truth. There are older persons in positions of political and economic power and influence, the elder statesmen. One can name scores of older persons who are leaders in the arts, entertainment, and the professions. But relatively few older people possess that combination of talent and personal resources, together with the opportunities within our social systems, necessary for these honored roles in their later years.

Still another picture is that of the aged as an infirm, socially isolated, shunned and forgotten, thoroughly deprived group in our society. This view is frequently held by persons whose work brings them in contact with deprived older persons. Anzia Yezierska dramatically portrays this isolation and social deprivation in his story, *A Window Full of Sky.*

> A few blocks away from the roominghouse where I live is an old people's home. "Isle of the Dead," I used to call it. But one day after a severe attack of neuritis, I took a taxi to that house of doom from which I had fled with uncontrollable aversion for years. Cripples in wheelchairs and old men and women on benches stared into vacancy—joyless and griefless, dead to rapture and despair. With averted eyes, I swept past these old people, sunning themselves like the timbers of some unmourned shipwreck.
> The hallman pointed out a door marked "Miss Adcock, Admissions." I rapped impatiently. Almost as though someone had been waiting, the door opened, and there was Miss Adcock trimly tailored with not a hair out of place. Just looking at her made me conscious of my shabbiness,

my unbrushed hair escaping from under my crumpled hat, the frayed elbows of my old coat. She pulled out a chair near her desk. Even her posture made me acutely aware of my bent old age.

The conflict, days and nights, whether to seek admission to the house or to die alone in my room, choked speech. A thin thread of saliva ran down from the corner of my mouth. I tried to wipe it away with my fingers. Miss Adcock handed me a Kleenex* with a smile that helped me start talking.

"I've been old for a long, long time," I began, "but I never felt old before. I think I've come to the end of myself.

"How old are you?

"Old enough to come here.

"When were you born?

"It's such a long time ago. I don't remember dates.

Miss Adcock looked at me without speaking. After a short pause she resumed her probing.

"Where do you live?

"I live in a roominghouse. Can anyone be more alone than a roomer in a roominghouse? I tried to look into her eyes, but she looked through me and somehow above me.

"How do you support yourself?

"I have a hundred dollars a month in Social Security.

"I looked at Miss Adcock and it seemed to me that her offer to visit me was the handclasp of a friend. . . .

"The prospect of Miss Adcock's visit gave me the strength to clean my room. Twenty years ago, when I began to feel the pinch of forced retirement, I had found this top-floor room. It was in need of paint and plumbing repairs. But the afternoon sun that flooded the room and the view across the wide expanse of tenement roofs to the Hudson and the Palisades beyond made me blind to the dirty walls and dilapidated furniture. Year after year the landlord had refused to make any repairs, and so the room grew dingier and more than ever in need of paint.

"During my illness I had been too depressed to look at the view. But now I returned to it as one turns back to cherished music or poetry. The sky above the river, my nourishment in solitude, filled the room with such a great sense of space and light that my spirits soared in anticipation of sharing it with Miss Adcock." [4]

Lack of functionally meaningful activity and social isolation, together with poverty, infirmity, and advanced old age are not the lot of all older persons in our society. But to varying degrees and in varying combinations these factors do effect the majority of older people.

---

* Kleenex is a registered tradename. This product is produced by the Kimberly-Clark Corporation.

On the basis of this brief exposure, one can readily infer that no generalization, stereotype, or point of view applies to all older persons. Vast differences do exist in the social lives of older persons. Membership in society at any chronological age involves a vast complex of reciprocal relationships, and it has been only recently that systematic attention has been devoted to the study of older persons. Specific consideration has been given to political, leisure time, and religious, activities, as well as to family relations in other chapters in this volume. In this chapter, some of the concepts or theories used in viewing the social participation of older persons, as well as some of the factors or variables which are related to social participation of older persons will be examined.

## SOCIAL ROLE CONCEPT

The concept of *social role* is frequently used in research and literature dealing with the social dimensions of aging and social participation of older persons. Social role is an interaction concept, defining or describing the attachment between the individual and a social system.

Social roles are the expected behaviors in the positions a person occupies which have meaning both to the community, and through community definition, to the person himself. The person's sense of adequacy, self-worth and self-expectation are inextricably tied up with how he occupies these roles. These roles determine to a large degree the extent and quality of the relations the person has with other human beings. The status accorded a role by the community or social system is important to the person filling the role.

Roles that are ill-defined, ambiguous or are in conflict with more accepted roles or values frequently cause conflict and uncertainty in the person performing the role and to those around him, and generally are not prestigious in the eyes of the community. To be roleless, that is to occupy no social roles that are defined as marginal, means to be unattached to a social system, to exist in a relative normless, formless social limbo. The person's subjective perception and evaluation of all his roles constitutes his definition of *self*. Conversely, the nature of the definition and the status which the community gives to the roles occupied by a person determines the person's influential potential in the social system.

Havighurst lists the roles of parent, spouse, homemaker and worker as first order roles, in that the behaviors of these roles have been most thoroughly internalized so they have become self-expectations.

> Second order roles are less deeply internalized, but they have enough reward value to be filled fairly well. These are the roles of friend and user of leisure time. Third order roles are not deeply internalized and have no great reward value for most people, consequently they are generally poorly performed. These are the roles of citizen and club and association member.
>
> Exceptions to these generalizations are found in the case of upper-middle class people who have more fully internalized the roles of citizen and club and association member, and consequently perform as well in these areas as in the second order roles. Exceptions are also found in some people in all classes with respect to the church member role. A minority of people of all classes have internalized this role deeply, but the majority have not.[5]

## OLDER PERSONS IN PRIMARY SOCIAL ROLES

How are older adults related to the first order social roles of parent, spouse, worker, and homemaker?

### Child Rearing Function Completed

Persons over age 65, except in rare instances, have finished the child rearing process and their children are out of the home. In fact, longer life expectancy together with earlier marriage and earlier child-bearing gives parents a longer period of time together after the departure of their children. Obviously social relationships with the departed children do not cease (see chapter on family relations). But it does mean that the primary reason for many relationships with other young people and their parents, informally and through school and youth club activities, no longer remain. The role of parent in terms of meaning and behavior has ceased to exist for older persons.

### Loss of Spouse in Later Years

Persons over age 65 show the effect of more marital disruption than those in any other age group. During the period of life between ages 35 and 44 nearly 90 per cent of both men and women are married. In contrast between ages 65 and 74, 79 per cent of the men but only 46 per cent of the women are married. Over age 75, 57 per cent of the men and only 20 per cent of the women are married. Between ages 65 and 74, about 12 per cent of the men and over 44 per cent of the women are widowed; over age 75 years, 34 per cent of the men and over 70 per cent of the women are widowed. For the age group of 65 through 74 years slightly over 10 per cent of both men and women are single or divorced, and this carries over into the 75 years and over age group with little change.

It is obvious that there is great loss of the role of spouse for older persons and that this loss occurs overwhelmingly in greater frequency for women. In fact, the role of spouse exists for only 46 per cent of the women between ages 65 and 74 and for only 20 per cent of the women over age 75 years. Men fare better in this respect because of the longer life expectancy of women; 79 per cent of the men between age 65 and 74, and 57 per cent of the men over age 75 retaining the role of spouse.[6]

For a woman, loss of a husband can be an extremely traumatic and overwhelming experience, particularly if close, intimate or dependent relations existed in the marriage. The process beginning with the numbing sense of loss and removal of self from ties with others, and the eventual reintegration and reinvestment with others is described by Marris. But the reintegration is more likely to include fewer social relationships stemming from the husband's work and community activities, and fewer of the more extended social relations shared previously by the married couple.[7]

The same personally traumatic experience and process faces the man who loses his wife. If the man is filling other roles in work and community activities, the reintegration process more likely will include a greater number of community integrative social relationships. Yet, Loeb, on the basis of a study of older people in Pepin County, Wisconsin, reports as follows:

> We found many men who upon the death of the wife, would move into a nursing home. They did this not because they were unable to take care of themselves, but because they did not want to live alone and have to look after themselves.[8]

For these men, the loss of their spouse meant relinquishing, or greatly altering their social relationships in the community.

Cummings and Henry, in their portion of the Kansas City Study of Adult Life, found that the problem of reintegration into a social system without husbands was not too difficult for many widows. Factors influencing widows' reintegration were the following: (a) widowhood is a socially honored state and certain supportive considerations are seen in society's general stance toward it, not found for example, toward retired men; (b) many widows tend to identify with prestige elements of their late husbands' careers; (c) having been the mediators with family and kin, this group is more open and accessible to the widows in the process of reintegration; and (d) "widows have a ready-made peer group in other widows, and there is reason to believe they join this very happily." But Cummings and Henry also stated the following:

> Some of our study group have low morale, and we know that the suicide rate is high among widows. Perhaps we are dealing, in our study group, with survivors of this transition, and have missed the depressed, despondent widows, because they did not meet our criteria of good health and economic stability.[9]

Kutner, in his study of older persons in the Kips Bay-Yorkville area of New York, found that widowhood tends to encourage social isolation but that three variables—social class, length of widowhood, and increasing age—affected the social relationship of widows.

> Within the higher status group, social relationships with friends continue through the years at a level only slightly below that found among the married group. Social isolation among upper status widows tends to become more noticeable with increasing age. In the low status group, social relations are at a low ebb in the years immediately following the death of the spouse, then increase. As age and length of widowhood increase, the difference in the relative degree of social isolation between the high and the low status widows tends to decrease. . . . [F]rom our data it would appear that the life circumstances of persons of higher social positions are not so drastically affected by widowhood as are the circumstances of people of lower social position. In time, however, these differences tend to decrease.
>
> In both status groups, outside social activities increase importantly with the length of widowhood. Church functions, organizational activities, and other more passive activities occupy the elderly widow. Finally, it is of great interest to note that feelings of deprivation remain about the same with lengthening years of widowhood.[10]

For widowers, Kutner found morale and social relationships remained fairly high, but were severely affected by loss of employment and poor health.

In summary, the role of spouse is an anchorage which does not exist for a large proportion of older persons, and is a role which is lost frequently during old age. This loss means a narrowing or shifting of social relationships or both. The losses and changes in social relationships, especially for women, are more likely to move the remaining spouse away from, rather than toward, community integrative activities. Social class or status, health, income, length of the period one is widowed, age, previous life patterns and presence of other social roles such as work appear to be variables which have a bearing on the amount of decrease and the nature of the changes in social relationships associated with the loss of the role of spouse.

## Loss of the Work Role

Of the primary social roles, the work role is the most important, both directly and indirectly, in providing social anchorage to men and through them to their families. The social definitions and values surrounding the work role, and the rewards accruing from it, comprise a large part of the hard core value system in our society. In fact, these values are so firmly rooted that occupation of the father constitutes the key factor in locating a family in the hierarchy of social class and status in the community. Conversely, performance in the work role is an integral part of the male's conception of himself and determines to a large extent his behavior and relational associations. In addition, one reward of work, *money,* provides the access to wide ranges of relationships and services, as well as positively affecting the self-concept of those who possess it sufficiently and predictably.

The work role is not held by many older persons, nor do older persons as a group share great monetary rewards from work. In March, 1966, only approximately 25 per cent of the men and 10 per cent of the women age 65 and over were actually engaged in the role of worker. These figures include both full-time and part-time participation in the worker role. A comparison with employment figures for March, 1960, which showed approximately 32 per cent of the men and 10 per cent of the women age 65 and over at work, indicates that the work role is a decreasing one for men.[11]

Most men do not retire voluntarily but rather for reasons of health or because they reach compulsory retirement age. The rate of voluntary retirement, however, is increasing. Men in low paid work are more likely to retire than men in the higher-paid occupations such as professional workers and proprietors.[12]

According to personal income figures for 1964, persons age 65 years and over had a median annual income of $2,037 as compared to a median annual income of $4,941 for persons in the 55 through 64 age group, and compared with a median annual income of $6,075 for the 45 through 54 age group.[13] The meaning of these figures would not be too important if older persons were already the possessors of considerable assets. However, the findings of the 1963 Survey of the Aged reveal quite the opposite.

> The median value of the asset holdings of couples aged 65 and over was $11,180; nonfarm homes accounted for almost one-third of total assets. When the equity in the home is excluded, the median value of their assets is reduced to $2,950. Nonmarried men and women had less than one-third these amounts.
>
> One-tenth of the couples and more than one-fourth of the nonmarried men and women had no assets.
>
> Widows had substantially lower median assets than nonwidows in all age groups. . . .
>
> In general, the proportion owning assets and median amount of these holdings declined with age.[14]

In summary, only a quarter of older men are in a work role on any basis and the trend is toward less participation of older men in the work role. Men occupying upper-class positions bringing higher monetary rewards are less likely to leave work roles and probably do so less abruptly than the poorer paid group. Most retirement from the work role is involuntary, due to health or reaching the mandatory retirement age. Income for the majority of older persons is low in absolute or comparative terms. Most older persons have modest assets or none at all. Assets held by most older persons consist chiefly of equity they hold in their homes. It is apparent that in terms of work, income, and assets that the majority of older persons are so marginally attached that they are in no position to significantly enhance or influence the social system.

Wide variations have been reported in the studies of retirement and the patterns of social relationships of older people. Wilensky points out that the mass of men view work as little more than a source of in come. The nature of their jobs offers little status or opportunity and thus there is little reason for close identification with the work role.

> To the extent that people are exposed to disciplined work routines yielding little gratification, or have careers which neither afford continuity of personal experience nor necessitate wide community participation, their retreat from work is accompanied by a gradual decline in the number and strength of secondary attachments.[15]

Simpson, Back, and McKinney found that status and orderliness of work history were factors associated with post retirement involvement.

> We found more loss of pre-retirement involvement by upper-white collar retirees than by any other status groups because less of their pre-retirement involvement could be meaningfully maintained outside the work setting.[16]

Kutner points out a sharp decline in the extent of social interaction between ages 65 and 69, the "retirement years."

> At varying lengths of retirement, there is no change in the relatively low morale and low level of social activity and social relationships that characterize the retired group.[17]

Cumming and Henry found retirement poses three problems in social relationships. First, men have difficulty moving to pure sociability, a woman's characteristic, but require some instrumental activity to mediate their relationships. The second problem is loss of status identity which accrued from the work role. The third problem is loss of peer group.

> The horizontal solidarity of a lifetime is seriously disrupted by retirement, and men must integrate themselves into a new membership group. . . . In our panel, only a tiny fraction of the retired men report keeping in touch with work colleagues. . . . When a man retires and loses membership in his group of work colleagues, he has to spend more of his time with his wife and her companions. But as men grow older, their wives tend to become more and more engaged with groups of widows because their friends and kindred have lost their husbands. This means that a retired male has difficulty finding a membership group unless he has a large kindred, because although it is possible for a man to be integrated into a kinship group of surviving women, it is impossible for him to be integrated into a group of widows to whom he is not related.[18]

If health care and economic independence are guaranteed, Cumming and Henry found retirement was not too much of a problem for most men. [I]t is the lack of horizontal ties and of a suitable way of relating, which retirement may carry with it, that seem to make trouble.[19]

In summary, loss of or absence of the work role brings a dimunition and change in social relations. Factors associated with these changes are many and include status and characteristics of previous work, level of income, health, and opportunities available for new relationships.

### Homemaker Role Least Affected by Age

The role of homemaker or household manager remains intact for more older persons than any other role. If changes do occur, the shift in role for many older women may not be severe. The homemaker role, although giving meaning and definition to the woman in the role and having some horizontal social relationship connotations, has no great extended community implications. Factors affecting how this role is held and the social relationship opportunities attached to it are presence of spouse, income, housing, and previous life patterns.

## OTHER FACTORS ASSOCIATED WITH SOCIAL RELATIONSHIPS AND SOCIAL PARTICIPATION

Many factors other than age which affect the social relationships and social participation of older persons have been noted so far in the discussion of older persons as participators in social roles. A more systematic review of these factors and their relationship to persons age 65 years and older will be considered in this section.

Kutner, in his New York Study, found that widowhood, unemployment and retirement, as previously noted, were associated with low participation and isolation. Other factors associated with social isolation of older persons were chronic illness of the older person or spouse, socioeconomic status, ethnic group membership, and education. Chronic illness and low socioeconomic status are related to low social participation and social isolation.

> In Czech, Hungarian, and especially Italian families, for example, protection of the elderly father or mother by inclusion in the household of the adult child is somewhat more common than among native-born, British, German, or Irish families. Hence, there is understandably a

> considerable difference in degree of isolation of members of these various ethnic groups.[20]

Isolating tendencies, however, were found to be less present in the higher strata of society among nearly all ethnic groups. "There is also a tendency at all age levels, but most marked in the group over 75 years of age, for those having had more education to be less isolated." [21]

Videbeck, on the basis of examination of data from the Baseline Study of Adult Participation in Nebraska, reported the following findings.

> The high participators live in urban places, have high educational levels, a higher occupational category, and a higher socioeconomic status than the low participators. In addition, the high participators tend to evaluate political activity as being efficacious and tend to hold higher ideals for themselves and have higher aspirations.[22]

O'Reilly studied Old Age Recipients in Chicago; therefore his findings apply to a particularly economically deprived group of older persons in a large metropolitan community. He found that less than half of his study group had belonged to social groups when younger and very few belonged to clubs for older people. Increasing old age seemed to have no appreciable effect on the amount of social contact of these older persons.

Race and sex were important factors which in many instances also affected other relationships. For example, Negroes had more friends than the white recipients; women more than men. "Living arrangements were found to have a definite effect upon social contact, with residential isolation relating to social isolation." [23] Other studies report no relationship between residential isolation and social isolation. However, housing is significantly related to the social relationships of older persons.

Carp has reported a comprehensive study of older persons of limited financial resources in San Antonio, Texas, many of whom were living in residential isolation. These older persons were studied intensively while they were on the waiting list of a housing project for elderly persons which was being built, and were studied intensively again after they had lived in the new housing project for a period of a year. The older persons on the waiting list who were not admitted were used as a control group.

> [R]esidents showed many changes in the patterns of their lives, generally toward increased activity and social interaction, not toward disengagement. Memberships in clubs and participation in less formal group activities multiplied, and seven-day diaries showed a significant rise in time spent at meetings. More residents had assumed leadership roles in groups. They were not surfeited. The number of groups they wanted to join increased. While there was a tendency for nonresidents to have fewer close friends than a year previously, residents tended to have more. Generally, the number of close friends, and the number of visitors, increased markedly for residents.[24]

Pihlblad, in his study of social adjustment of older persons in three small, rural Missouri communities, pointed out the influence of health.

> Health status will influence almost every aspect of the older person's life: his income and outgo, the degree to which he can remain independent or must rely on the help of others, his type of residence, his degree of mobility, the extent of his participation in the life of the community, and association with other people.[25]

The importance of health factors and personal mobility in social participation was stressed by Pihlblad but he could not distinguish poor health from poor morale in assessing low social participation.

Lack of money, like poor health, has a pervasive influence on the social activities of older persons. Gray and Moberg report that three out of seven reasons older persons report for not attending church were (a) they are unable to contribute financially, (b) they are not able to dress well enough, (c) they are unable to get transportation for one reason or another including inability to pay transportation charges without disruption of budget.[26] Smith, in his study of older persons in a Southern city, reports that of all persons mentioning one or more constrictions on level or style of life nearly 45 per cent attributed some or all constrictions on weakened financial positions. "Decisions to give up club memberships and to buy lower quality clothing were based on financial considerations in a clear majority of the cases." [27]

In summing up the research on formal participation of older persons Wilensky states as follows:

> [T]here is near-unanimity that the number of secondary attachments is closely related to education, social-economic status, and residence (urban and rural non-farm vs. rural farm). Those with high-school education

> or more, in higher economic brackets and higher occupational status living in urban areas participate most.
>
> [T]he unique effect of aging cannot be sifted out until we give closer attention to type of organization, type of community, and social-economic level—all of which condition the relationship of age to secondary attachments.[28]

It has been seen that a complex variety of factors affect the amount and nature of social relationships of older people. Some older persons, the personal isolates, have had few personal relationships throughout life and continue this pattern into old age. Some older persons belong to racial and ethnic groups where patterns of friendship and family relations remain active. Patterns of social relations differ for older persons living in urban areas or in smaller rural communities, or within urban areas depending upon whether they live in the dingy apartments and rooming houses in the "ghettos of the aged" in the poorer sections or whether they live elsewhere in the city. But it has been vividly evident that participation in primary social roles; being in a high socioeconomic grouping (that is, having high income, high job status, and a high educational level), and having good health are the overriding and interrelated prime determinants of the number and nature of the social relationships of older people. In terms of all three of these criteria, it has been evident that older persons constitute a disadvantaged group.

## Older Persons as a Group Lack Significant Social Roles and Resources

Older persons as a group are relatively roleless compared with other adults. They are removed from the primary social roles by social regulation, illness, or death of spouses; and through loss of primary roles, many of their secondary roll attachments disappear. Having lost these roles, older people have no place to go. Society has provided no role definitions for older persons which would attach them or keep them attached to the social system. Society has provided no role definitions around which their own personal activities can have social meaning. A certain freedom from role responsibility exists for older persons, but freedom achieved through rolelessness carries grave consequences for individual older persons and for older persons as a group. Several authorities in gerontology point out that a variety of substitute activities in themselves will not solve this problem. Rosow, on the basis of careful study of relationships between older persons and their children and friends concludes the following:

> [T]here is no general principle of compensatory association whereby parents see friends specifically to counteract any limited contact with children. Insofar as filial relationships spring from the most central social roles, this particular finding may be but a specific expression of a larger generalization: *there may be no effective substitutes for the loss of any major social role except the succession to an equally central status which is more highly valued and rewarded.* Consequently, strategies to relieve basic status loss in old age through such devices as Golden Age clubs or glamorizing retirement leisure are fundamentally bankrupt.[29]

Kutner came to a similar conclusion on the basis of his study in New York.

> It is not merely a matter of providing recreational or leisure-time pursuits that will help avoid boredom or prevent morbid reminiscing that is required. *Many older people require activities in retirement that will be substantial functional substitutes for the responsibilities of gainful employment, family rearing, and homemaking.* For many, mere leisure-time pursuits will be felt to be the expressions of indolence and of the useless role to which society has relegated them.[30]

The socioeconomic status of most older persons is, in a sense doubly negative. Many older persons have never had high socioeconomic status. Most older persons are not in a work role which makes this status a day-to-day reality. Older persons as a group have less education than younger adults. And transcending these factors is the low level of income received and the paucity of assets held by older persons. In other words, the level of income of most older persons would tend to lower their socioeconomic position; it is in itself an index of low socioeconomic status.

Finally, older persons as a group are more likely to suffer from chronic illnesses, and in the increased aged bracket more older persons are likely to be seriously impaired or handicapped. But the effect of chronic illness or handicap on the social relationships of older persons may be contingent on the social roles being held and the socioeconomic status of the older persons.

The orientation expressed in the discussion in this section is that the factors affecting social relations of older persons are largely social and as such are modifiable by society. Rosow sums up this position as a moral dilemma.

> By now it should be clear that the crucial people in the aging problem are not the old, but the younger age groups, for it is the rest of us who determine the status position of the old person in the social order. What is at stake for the future is not only the alienation of the young from each other and of man from man. There is no real way out of this dilemma, for young or old, without a basic reordering of our national aspirations and values, of which the aging problem is but a token.[31]

## THE NARROWING SOCIAL WORLD OF THE AGED: DISENGAGEMENT THEORY

The disengagement theory of aging has had rather wide popular acceptance since its appearance as the central theme of the book, *Growing Old: The Process of Disengagement,* by Elaine Cumming and William E. Henry in 1961. The theory evolved from and is supported by the authors' findings as part of the Kansas City Study of Adult Life. The theory is simply stated by Cumming and Henry.

> Starting from the common-sense observation that the old person is less involved in the life around him than he was when he was younger, we can describe the process by which he becomes so, and we can do this without making assumptions about its desirability. In our theory, aging is an inevitable mutual withdrawal or disengagement, resulting in decreased interaction between the aging person and others in the social systems he belongs to.
>
> The process may be initiated by the individual or by others in the situation. The aging person may withdraw more markedly from some classes of people while remaining relatively close to others. His withdrawal may be accompanied from the outset by an increased preoccupation with himself; certain institutions in society may make this withdrawal easy for him. When the aging process is complete, the equilibrium which existed in middle life between the individual and his society has given way to a new equilibrium characterized by a greater distance and an altered type of relationship.[32]

The hypotheses formulated which would support the theory were the following: (a) there should be a decrease in the number of persons with whom the individual habitually reacts, and decreases in the amount of interaction with them; (b) qualitative changes in styles and patterns of interaction should be seen which would reflect decreased involvement; and (c) changes in the personality of the individual that both cause and result in decreased involvement with others, and increased preoccupation with self should be observed. The sample for the study consisted of physically healthy adults who had no major economic worries.[33]

Results of their study support their hypotheses of disengagement. The number of social roles in which persons act become fewer with increasing age for men and women, the loss of the roles of worker and kinsman accounting for most of the decrease.

> The pattern for the whole population is quite stable between the ages of 50 and 64, about 60 per cent of this younger group act in six or more roles, but by age 65 only 39 per cent do, and the proportion decreases steadily until at age 75 and over, only 8 per cent act in more than five roles. The decline with age is significant. When we examine the men and women separately, we see that the women undergo some expansion before discarding roles, and although this slight difference in pattern is not significant, it adumbrates a pervasive difference between the sexes in the manner of growing old.[34]

The amount of interaction with other persons declines with age.

> There is a steady decrease in the percentage of people with a high daily interaction as we proceed up the age range. There is a slight difference between the women and the men paralleling the one we saw in the numbers of roles played; that is, in the middle of the age range there is an increase in the number of women with high daily interaction, but again it is not a significant difference. However, the ultimate decrease in interaction is highly significant, and this measure provides evidence of an age-related disengagement of the individual from his social system.[35]

The Lifespace measure employed in the study gave similar results. Their conclusions were as follows:

> As age advances, the involvement with society, by any of the measures we have employed, become less. The aging person sees fewer kinds of people, less often, and for decreasing periods of time as he grows older.[36]

One exception was noted. "Contacts with intimate kin do not diminish except when these kin are no longer available." [37]

And finally in relation to the third hypothesis, the authors' see their data supporting less social and more self-involvement and preoccupation as persons grow older.

> Generally speaking, these answers suggest a restructuring of life goals—calling for less responsibility and allowing more focus on the self. At the same time we see problems of health and approaching death becoming less bothersome as age increases. Although there is persistent frustration with decreased mobility and with role loss among men, the move is away from tight enmeshment with the social system where health and competence in the instrumental role are the important features.[38] It is suggested that the modal middle-aged, or engaged state is that of acting in a large life space and perceiving it as stable, while the aged, or disengaged state is that of acting in a small space and perceiving it as constricted.[39]

The authors' conclusion, which they state as a formal theory, is the following:

> Disengagement is an inevitable process in which many of the relationships between a person and other members of society are severed, and those remaining are altered in qualities.[40]

Smith, in his report of a study of older persons in Dunholme, a Southern city, supports the theory of disengagement.

> This review of contrasts between the two samples, in which the possible effects of aging on the social world of the aged can only be inferred indirectly, conforms to and enlarges upon the picture yielded by the data which provide more direct evidence that changes have resulted from aging. Despite the fact that the old sample (OS) members [older persons] tend to disidentify with and not to accept the status of older persons, the passage of time has done its damage. Our OS members [older persons] live in a narrower social world than others do.
> Their conceptions of their social selves have shrunk apace, and their interests have more and more turned inward. As these processes have operated, they have also suffered a related loss in their public and physical resources for claiming access to and acceptance in community affairs. Our methods of sampling may have yielded a more advantaged group than samples dealt with in other studies of the aged, but even it has not escaped the erosions and conversions of social aging.[41]

Williams and Wirths, as a result of continuing work in the Kansas City Study of Adult Life, reach a similar conclusion.

> After an intensive examination of the lives of one hundred sixty-eight

> people over the age of 50, during approximately a five-year span, and to some extent, over their entire life spans, we are convinced that disengagement is a characteristic process faced by the majority of people within the predominant pattern of American, and probably western European culture, and a problematic one for many.[42]

Most of the material previously cited in this chapter in connection with the social role concept certainly could be used to support the contention that most older persons are more disengaged from social roles and social relationships than middle-aged groups and than they, themselves, were in previous years.

## Evidence and Arguments Contraindicting the Theory of Disengagement of Older Persons

Although the disengagement theory has caught the fancy of many persons during the past few years, crucial questions have been raised about its validity. Kutner points out the following:

> Sociological research suggests that the decrements of aging are produced at least as much by circumstances (such as compulsory retirement, age-segregation, youth-oriented community facilities, death of family and friends) as by any intrinsic aging phenomenon.[43]

He says that the views expressed in disengagement theory suffer three basic defects.

> They assume (1) the universality of a trend which may describe only a fraction of the aging population . . . (2) the irreversibility of the decline of social competence, especially when health is a major intervening factor, and (3) that social aging is basically a decelerating, degenerating, linear process.
>
> We would suggest on the other hand, that aging be conceived of as a process of redifferentiation and reintegration. No assumptions of unidirectional change need be made; indeed, reversible or irreversible tendencies may be demonstrated to hinge on fortuitous circumstances, such as retirement or illness, rather than on aging; and a more nearly universal applicability will obtain.[44]

Rose also raises serious questions about the inevitability of disengagement, citing empirical evidence some of which will be considered in detail. He also challenges the value judgment implicit in the theory that disengagement is desirable for older persons, and points out that empirical evidence indicates "[T]hat the engaged elderly, rather than the disengaged, are the ones who generally, although not always, are happiest and have the greatest expressed life satisfaction." [45] His third line of criticism, an analysis of the disengagement theory in the context of social structure and social trends, finds the theory a poor interpretation of the facts. The fact that a large proportion of older people in the United States tend to lose many of their adult roles Rose sees as follows:

> [A] function of American culture in this phase of its organization, not a universal for all time. American culture accords a low status to the elderly; we have a youth-centered society. Many other societies accord special prestige and power to the elderly, do not disengage them from adult roles, or create new age-graded roles of importance for them. The situation of the elderly in the United States has been especially unfavorable in the past fifty years, with the decline of the self-employed occupations and the rise of compulsory retirement.
>
> These trends have meant that the major social role for men in the society is not open to most elderly persons. Forced disengagement in the occupational role has tended to cause disengagement in auxiliary roles, for example, in the occupational associations (trade union, businessmen's association, professional organization) and the "service clubs" which have a membership based on economic activity. Thus cultural values and economic structure have combined to create a condition in which a large proportion of the elderly people are nonparticipant. Those men who remain economically active past 65 years do not disengage, even in the unfavorable cultural value system of the United States. The politician, the employer, the self-employed professional, do not disengage until they become physically or mentally feeble. In fact, they often take on additional membership and leadership roles after they pass 65 years.[46]

Several pieces of research seem to contraindicate parts of the disengagement theory. Implicit in the theory is the notion that social competence, that is ability to perform roles, decreases in old age. Havighurst, on the basis of his investigations in the Kansas City Study of Adult Life, concluded as follows:

> There was no sharp decrease in role performance with age. . . . Thus, in the age range 40 to 70 we can conclude that people's social competence remains on a plateau which has been achieved in early middle age and slopes very slightly downward toward the latter years of life.[47] Apparently some people do not decrease at all in their social competence during these years, while others do fall off, thus causing a small decline

in the average role performance score with age. . . . The explanation for this selective falling off of role performance may be that some people are hit severely by the accidents of later middle-age—such as ill health, widowhood, loss of friends and family—and these people suffer a fall in social competence; while others escape these traumas and maintain their social competence with little or no decline.[48]

The results of Videbeck's investigations also raise questions about age being the crucial and determining factor accounting for declining social relations and social participation of older persons. In his conclusions, he states the following:

As we suggested earlier, the correlation between age and participation is a spurious product of their joint relationship to those major adult statuses which define one's life condition. Whether for research or policy issues, to treat the aging population as a homogeneous class of persons does violence to the facts of the matter. The aging population is not homogeneous in either history or participation, or the routes taken through the life cycle, or in the present conditions of life. These are factors which predict participation in any population.[49]

Some of the findings from Carp's study of economically disadvantaged older persons in San Antonio before and after living in a new housing project were cited earlier in this chapter.[50] Marked increases in social relationships and social participation by these older persons were seen to occur during a year's occupancy in the housing project. These findings would suggest that a process of engagement or reengagement, rather than disengagement, was taking place. An example described by Carp rather dramatically illustrates her findings:

A little old lady in a faded, misshapen bathrobe opened the door to her expected visitor. Apathetically she turned back into the room, allowing the caller to follow her. Shuffling in her dilapidated, run-over carpet slippers, she slowly made her way to the unmade bed and slumped down on its edge. The guest had to clear a chair of odd pieces of old clothing and torn magazines.

During most of the time they talked, tears ran unheeded down the old woman's cheeks. Occasionally she would brush a hand across her face, or run it through her uncombed gray hair. The air was stale and musty, dirty dishes were carelessly stacked in a corner, and the woman herself probably had not bathed or washed for several days.

She was worried about poor health and described her many ailments, including at least five heart attacks. For many weeks she had not been out of her home, and no one had been to see her except her son. The only good thing in her life was this son, who stopped to see her each morning on the way to work and every evening on the way home to his family. In addition, he paid for her phone and called her half a dozen times each day. Except for him, she had no reason to go on living, and his wife begrudged his attention. Fourteen months later, this woman greeted the same visitor with a bright smile and warm handclasp. She attentively seated her visitor at a small table, set with a spotless cloth, on which were a little bowl of flowers and a plate of homemade cookies. As they sipped and nibbled, the old woman spoke vivaciously of her busy and happy life, her many friends. (She was such a gad-about that many phone calls had been necessary to catch her at home to arrange this visit.) Later that day she was to attend a garden club meeting. She had invited an elderly bachelor in to share her supper, then both of them were going out to sing religious and old-fashioned songs with a group of people their age. Spry and cheerful, she had earned the nickname "Cricket" among her many new acquaintances.

Her skin was freshly washed and lightly powdered, her hair professionally groomed and nicely combed, her clothes carefully pressed. Asked about her health, she laughed and said she had not thought about it.

She spoke of her son with no less warmth than formerly, and of his wife without resentment. Last Sunday she had had dinner with them and the grandchildren; this Sunday they were coming to eat with her. "It does her (her daughter-in-law) good to get out, and you should see the children eat when they're over here! I love to see them come—and I love to see them go home!"

The many daily visits and calls from her son had dwindled to an occasional one. "I must have been a dreadful burden to him, always weeping and wailing. He's a good son, but I'm out so much now, or someone else is here, and he feels like he's in the way."

As she walked to the door with the visitor she said fervently, "Every day I get down on my knees and thank God for the wonderful life I have now. I only wish every person could be as fortunate."

This narrative presents a striking but by no means unique example of the kind of change which took place in the members of a group of older people.[51]

The point to be emphasized here is not that housing units for the elderly are the answers to all social problems of older people. Rather, social relations are associated with a wide range of factors, particularly the opportunities which are available to older persons for such relationships. If given the opportunity, older persons can establish or reestablish a wide range of social relationships and patterns of social participation.

In summary, virtually all research indicates a narrowing social world for most older persons, a disengagement from social institutions and social relationships. The disengagement theory states that *aging is an inevitable mutual withdrawal or disengagement resulting in decreased interaction between the aging persons and others in social systems they belong to*. The theory has been questioned on the following: (a) whether disengagement is inevitable; (b) whether disengagement is universal among older persons; (c) whether disengagement is a progressive lineal process; and (d) whether age in itself is a crucial, or a relatively incidental, factor in disengagement. Considerable empirical evidence supports the questions which have been raised about the disengagement theory as it is stated.

## SUBCULTURE OF THE AGING

Arnold Rose has suggested that a subculture of the aging might exist, or be in the process of developing, and urged that some study and research be directed to this possibility.[52] The suggestion seems timely. One characteristic of a subculture, and at the same time the principle reason for its existence, is that a group of people are excluded from interaction with other groups and lack effective participation in the major social systems and social institutions of a larger society. On the basis of the material presented in this chapter, it is evident that large numbers of older people meet this requirement at this time.

Subcultures have other characteristics. A group consciousness, that is, mutual recognition of a common element that the members have in common, is necessary. Third, there are usually interests held in common which bind or attach members to each other. These interests may be around gains to be obtained, interests to be protected, social bonds arising from physical proximity, or values held in common. Fourth, characteristics are usually found in the group which transcend regional, social class, educational, or other differences which the group might possess.

These common characteristics might be viewed as common adaptations to common problems of the members of the subculture. For example, Oscar Lewis has identified similarities in family structure, interpersonal relations, time orientation, value systems, and spending patterns among the poor. These characteristics of the poor transcend regional, rural-urban, and national differences and tend to indicate the existence of a subculture of poverty.[53] When the characteristics of a subculture are reasonably well developed there is usually some public awareness of the group which constitutes the subculture.

Little specific research has been directed at the concept of a subculture of the aging. Most studies of older persons living in communities tend to indicate that older persons lack group consciousness; that is, they lack awareness of the fact they are old and belong to a group of older persons. That large numbers of older persons identify themselves as younger is pointed out in many studies.

Little evidence can be gleaned from studies of older persons in communities that would indicate common interests or common characteristics of older persons other than those which tend to separate them from social participation. There is little evidence of a common adaptation to common problems. Aging group consciousness, common interests, and perhaps common characteristics are more likely to be found among older persons in age-segregated housing units and in retirement communities.

In spite of the lack of evidence of widespread age group consciousness, age related common interest or common characteristics at this point in time, it would be unwise to discount the potential value of the concept of a subculture of the aging.

Rose reports the results of a study of older persons in Minneapolis which raises some interesting questions. He found that older persons having an aging group consciousness cannot be distinguished on the basis of sex, education, or social class from those older persons who do not have such an orientation. The aging conscious group had much higher social participation and more social relationships than the group that was not aging conscious and in general were more satisfied with life.[54] If similar results were obtained from studies of older persons in other communities, some foundation would be established for the potential of the eventual emergence of a subculture of the aging.

## A LOOK TO THE FUTURE

Social relations of older people and their participation in social systems have been seen as related to many factors in addition to age.

Therefore, changes in the magnitude and patterns of social relationships of older persons in the future will be related to other changes as they affect older people.

Taking a long view, one might predict that social relationships of older persons will be less constricted and that older persons will more meaningfully participate in social systems and society. There will be more older persons. Increases in medical knowledge and improvement in the distribution of medical care, making it more available to all older persons, should at least mean that health should not be an increasing problem for older persons. An increasingly larger proportion of older persons will have higher educational levels. Older persons retiring in the future will have more retirement income, and even allowing for the depreciation of inflation, there is some likelihood that the income of the older group in the future will be relatively higher. In other words, the older persons in the future may possess or be able to command more assets in terms of social relations and social participation.

One might anticipate, also, some shifts in societal definitions and values attached to social roles. In the face of increasing industrialization and automation, some revaluation of the work versus leisure or other free-time roles may occur, and some new nonwork roles may emerge. Should these events occur, a quite different and undoubtedly a more favorable framework for participation of older persons in society would result. Another factor which might influence social relations and social participation of older persons in the future is the current rapid emergence of gerontology as a social movement. Social movements in the past have influenced, or at least were forerunners of, changes in social values and social systems.

If opportunities for more effective participation and integration in the larger society do not occur, or if age-segregation develops as a pattern for increasingly larger numbers of older persons, it would seem almost inevitable that a subculture of the aged will emerge. A group of older persons would under such conditions have to turn to a subsociety of their own for the development of meaningful social roles and satisfying patterns of social relationships.

No optimistic predictions can be made on the basis of a short-range view of the future. The social relationship and participation patterns of older persons will remain largely as they are today. There should be, at least on the basis of present knowledge, a shift away from the focus on the adaptive capacity of the individual older person to one which includes equal emphasis on the wide range of social supports which can be used by older persons when abrupt adaptations to changed life conditions become necessary. There should be a shift away from seeing institutional placement or congregate living as the only answers to social isolation or the social crises requiring reorganization of an older person's social world.

Loeb suggests that such reorganization has three essential characteristics: (a) that the various dimensions of a person's environment fit together in such a way as to maximize the individual's autonomy; (b) the pattern or reorganization has some continuity with the person's previous life style; and (c) any contraction of the person's social world occurs gradually.[55] A wide variety of social supports for older persons will need to be developed in communities.

Finally, older persons, like persons of any age, when afforded social opportunities, can utilize them in an infinite range of individualistic and creative ways.

## REFERENCES


1. Smith, Joel, and Turk, Herman: Considerations bearing on a study of the role of the aged in community integration. *Social Aspects of Aging.* Simpson, Ida, and McKinney, John (Eds.), Durham, Duke, 1966, p. 197.
2. *Cicero on Old Age and Friendship.* Shuckburgh, E. S. (transl.), Shuckburgh. London, Macmillan, 1900, pp. 68, 70-71, 86.
3. Lynd, Robert S., and Lynd, Helen M.: *Middletown in Transition.* New York, Harcourt, 1937, pp. 97-101.
4. Yezierska, Anzia: A window full of sky. *The Reporter, XXXI,* (1): 29-30, July 2, 1964.
5. Havighurst, Robert J.: The social competence of middle aged people. *Genet Psychol Monogr, LVI*: 319, Nov. 1957.
6. U.S. Bureau of the Census: *Statistical Abstract of the United States: 1966.* 87th ed., Washington, D.C., 1966, p. 31.
7. Marris, Peter: *Widows and Their Families.* London, Routledge and Kegan Paul, 1958, pp. 1-86.
8. Loeb, Martin B.; Pincus, Allen, and Mueller, B., Jeanne: A framework for viewing adjustment in aging. *Gerontologsit, VI* (4): 186, Dec. 1966.
9. Cumming, Elaine, and Henry, William E.: *Growing Old: The Process of Disengagement.* New York, Basic Books, 1961, pp. 156-158.

10. KUTNER, BERNARD, *et al.*: *Five Hundred Over Sixty.* New York, Russell Sage, 1956, pp. 65-66.
11. U.S. Bureau of the Census, *op. cit.*, p. 285.
12. PALMORE, ERDMAN. Retirement patterns among aged men: findings of the 1963 survey of the aged. *Social Security Bulletin, XXVII* (8): 3-4, August 1964.
13. U.S. Bureau of the Census, *op. cit.*, p. 343.
14. Assets of the aged in 1962: findings of the 1964 survey of the aged. *Social Security Bulletin, XXVII* (8): 3, Nov., 1964.
15. WILENSKY, HAROLD J.: Life cycle, work situation, and participation in formal associations. *Aging and Leisure.* Kleemeier, Robert W. (Ed.), New York, Oxford, 1961, p. 234.
16. SIMPSON, IDA H.; BLACK, KURT W., and MCKINNEY, JOHN C.: attributes of work, involvement in society, and self-evaluation in retirement. *Social Aspects of Aging.* Simpson, Ida, and McKinney, John (Ed.), *op. cit.*, pp. 147-148.
17. KUTNER, BERNARD, *et al.*, *op. cit.* pp. 89 and 111.
18. CUMMING, ELAINE, and HENRY, WILLIAM E., *op. cit.* pp. 147-148.
19. *Ibid.* p. 153.
20. KUTNER, BERNARD, *et al.*, *op. cit.* p. 112.
21. *Ibid.* p. 111.
22. VIDEBECK, RICHARD, and KNOX, ALAN B.: Alternative participatory responses to aging. *Older People and Their Social World.* Rose, Arnold B., and Peterson, Warren A. (Ed.), Philadelphia, Davis, 1965, p. 43.
23. O'REILLY, CHARLES T., and PEMBROKE, MARGARET M.: *OAA Profile: The Old Age Assistance Client in Chicago.* Chicago, Loyola, 1961, pp. 51-67.
24. CARP, FRANCES MERCHANT: *A Future for the Aged.* Austin, U. of Tex., 1966, pp. 131-133.
25. PIHLBLAD, C. TERENCE, and MCNAMARA, ROBERT L.: Social adjustment of elderly people in three small towns. *Older People and Their Social World.* Rose, Arnold B., and Peterson, Warren A. (Ed.), *op. cit.*, pp. 57, 64-72.
26. GRAY, ROBERT M., and MOBERG, DAVID O.: *The Church and the Older Person.* Grand Rapids, Eerdmans, 1962, pp. 96-117.
27. SMITH, JOEL: The narrowing social world of the aged. *Social Aspects of Aging.* Simpson, Ida, and McKinney, John (Eds.), *op. cit.*, pp. 229-230.
28. WILENSKY, HAROLD J., *op. cit.* pp. 221-222.
29. ROSOW, IRVING: The aged, family and friends. *Social Security Bulletin, XXVIII* (11): 19-20, Nov. 1965.
30. KUTNER, BERNARD, *et al.*, *op. cit.* p. 103.
31. ROSOW, IRVING: Old age: one moral dilemma of an affluent society. *The Gerontologist, II* (4): 191, Dec. 1962.
32. CUMMING, ELAINE, and HENRY, WILLIAM E., *op. cit.* pp. 14-15.
33. *Ibid.* pp. 15-16.
34. CUMMING, ELAINE; HENRY, WILLIAM E., and NEWELL, DAVID S.: Social-

structural evidence for disengagement. *Growing Old: The Process of Disengagement.* Cumming, Elaine, and Henry, William E., *op. cit.,* p. 39.

35. *Ibid.* pp. 46-47.
36. *Ibid.* p. 51.
37. *Ibid.* p. 63.
38. *Ibid.* p. 73.
39. CUMMING, ELAINE; HENRY, WILLIAM E.; DEAN, LOIS R., and NEWELL, DAVID S.: The evidence for disengagement in attitude and orientation changes. *Growing Old: The Process of Disengagement.* Cumming, Elaine, and Henry, William E., *op. cit.,* p. 101.
40. CUMMING, ELAINE; HENRY, WILLIAM E., and DAMIANOPOULOS, ERNEST: A formal statement of disengagement theory. *Growing Old: The Process of Disengagement.* Cumming, Elaine, and Henry, William E., *op. cit.,* p. 211.
41. SMITH, JOEL, *op. cit.* p. 241.
42. WILLIAMS, RICHARD W., and WIRTHS, CLAUDINE G.: *Lives Through the Years.* New York, Atherton, 1965, p. 195.
43. KUTNER, BERNARD: The social nature of aging. *Gerontologist, II* (1): 5, March, 1962.
44. *Ibid.* p. 6.
45. ROSE, ARNOLD M.: A current theoretical issue in social gerontology. *Gerontologist, IV* (1): 48, March, 1964.
46. *Ibid.* p. 48.
47. HAVIGHURST, ROBERT J., *op. cit.* pp. 340-341.
48. *Ibid.* p. 343.
49. VIDEBECK, RICHARD, and KNOX, ALAN B., *op. cit.* p. 48.
50. CARP, FRANCES MERCHANT, *Loc. cit.* pp. 131-133.
51. *Ibid.* pp. 3-5.
52. ROSE, ARNOLD M.: The subculture of the aging: a framework for research in social gerontology. *Older People and Their Social World.* Rose, Arnold M., and Peterson, Warren A. (Eds.), *op. cit.,* pp. 3-16.
53. LEWIS, OSCAR: *La Vida.* New York, Random, 1966, p. xiii.
54. ROSE, ARNOLD M.: Group consciousness among the aging. *Older People and Their Social World.* Rose, Arnold M., and Peterson, Warren A. (Eds.), *op. cit.,* pp. 19-36.
55. LOEB, MARTIN B.; PINCUS, ALLEN, and MUELLER, B. JEANNE, *op. cit.,* p. 186.

*Chapter 8*

# LEISURE AND AGING

Robert J. Havighurst

One hundred years ago the average working week in factories and mills and mines was about seventy-two hours, the average farmer worked from sunrise to sunset six days a week. The average worker continued in his old age to work until he died or became too feeble to work. Work was valued because it produced economic goods and also because it was thought to be morally valuable in itself. From the time of Luther, work came to be regarded as a way of serving God. And Karl Marx said, "Work is the essence of man."

Then, in the closing years of the nineteenth century, the sacred character of work came under question. People were beginning to get a vision of an economy of abundance. This would give men leisure. In 1883, Paul Lafargue wrote a pamphlet, *The Right to Idleness* (Le Droit a la Paresse). What was then a challenge to the established morality became a generally accepted goal of workers' organizations sixty years later, when Leo Lagrange could write in 1936, "We want the worker, the peasant, and the unemployed to find in leisure the joy of life and the sense of their own dignity." [1]

Thus leisure has become established as an element of value. A code of ethics for leisure is in the making. Some people are now deliberately choosing more leisure rather than more work to earn more money. Studies made in Europe and the USA indicate that an increasing proportion of people will choose the added free time if asked such a question as the following: If you could reduce your work week by two hours and draw the same money as you do now, would you do this rather than increase your income by working your present work week and being paid for two hours more work?

There is clear evidence that many workers now prefer to retire at age 65 or even earlier with a pension and social security benefits, rather than to work beyond age 65, thus earning more and increasing their pension when they do retire. Recent wages and working agreements between the automobile workers and the auto-makers in the USA have provided higher pensions and earlier retirement ages rather than increased wages.

Thus some people, at least, in modern society prefer the added leisure of retirement at 65 or 60, to the added money they could earn by working to a later age.

## DEFINITION OF LEISURE

Leisure activities may be defined as activities in which a person may indulge of his own free will either to rest, to amuse himself, to add to his knowledge or improve his skills without increasing his earning power, or to maintain his voluntary participation in the life of the community. This definition excludes the things a person is constrained to do in order to earn money, to maintain his health, or to keep house. It excludes sleeping, eating, dressing, cooking, cleaning, and travel to and from work.

Free time activities can be subdivided into several categories, as follows:

A. Activities complementary to work: study in preparation for promotion in one's career.

B. Activities of homemaking: cooking, keeping up the house, making it more attractive and more comfortable, studying to become a better cook.

C. Activities of family life: rearing children, entertaining relatives, visiting relatives, corresponding with family members.

D. Church activities: atending church, working on behalf of the church, reading the Bible or other religious literature.

E. Civic-political activities: active work for a political party, active work on behalf of charity, or a social welfare organization, membership in organizations that work for the improvement of the local or national or world community.

F. Professional activity: membership in a trade union or an association of professional men or of businessmen.

G. Social club activity: membership and participation in organizations that exist primarily for the social benefit of their members.

H. Informal personal-social relations: activity with friends, acquaintances, neighbors.

J. Purely free-choice activities which are not tied to any social role; hobbies such as gardening, stamp and coin collecting, arts and crafts, caring for pets, taking active or passive part in sports, reading, listening to music, watching television.

Studies of the free-time activities of older people show that they are active in all of these areas except that of activities complementary to work, together with some reduction in the category of professional organizations, which is related to the worker role. In other words, almost the entire range of leisure activities that is reported by middle-aged people is open to retired people.

## FREE-TIME PATTERNS

On the basis of interviews with several hundred people between the ages of 65 and 75, the writer has defined a set of free-time patterns that can be used to describe the leisure activities of older people. If the interview is reasonably adequate, it is possible to identify a person's pattern with such reliability that two different judges agree 80 per cent of the time.

The free-time patterns were initially identified and described with the aid of a factor analysis of the qualities and values characteristic of leisure activities of middle-aged and elderly people.[2] Most of the examples given below come from interviews with retired teachers and retired industrial workers in a cross-national study of retirement, together with interviews in the Kansas City Study of Adult Life.

### Challenging New Experience

This is the major factor in category J—purely free-choice activities that are not required by any of the social roles. The respondent does things for his own interest and pleasure and does them with such energy and quality that they bring him in touch with new people. For instance, a retired teacher works mathematical problems for fun, constructs mechanical toys for children, reads a good deal of history, and watches a variety of sports. He is known in his neighborhood as a man with a variety of active interests. Another example is a London teacher who has written two books on music since his retirement, (They are not moneymakers.) and plays the cello two hours a day ("Schubert is my main interest."). Still another is a Viennese teacher who does some sketching "but not seriously," has a garden which he tends in the morning on pleasant days, and is studying Italian with his wife in preparation for a long visit to Venice. Among the Kansas City group, the people who were outstanding in this pattern had as their favorite leisure activities: gardening, photography, breeding dogs, cabinet work, sewing, and playing the piano.

## Instrumental Service

When a person gives a large portion of his free time and energy to one or more of categories C, D, E, or F, he is performing according to pattern II. The main function of this activity is to accomplish something useful for the family, the church, the community, or one's occupational group. Among retired people, church work or service to the church is very frequent. Thus a retired Dutch teacher spends two afternoons a week calling on about forty families of the church and attends meetings on church business two nights a week. A Chicago teacher is Chairman of the Finance Committee of his church, and spends two mornings a week in the church office, filing materials for the pastor. Another Chicago teacher is a precinct captain for his political party, has run for public office, and works vigorously for a reform to the state constitution. A London teacher is vice-president of a local association for assistance to the blind, a committee member of the Anglican church council, and treasurer of the Old Students Association of his teacher-training college.

In the Kansas City sample, the favorite leisure activities of this group are home decorating and repairing, church work, club work, music, and League of Women Voters.

## Expressive Pleasure

In a way, this is the opposite of pattern II. The individual uses his free time for sheer pleasure, and not as a means to the improvement of society or himself. While all people do some things "just for fun," this pattern is present when a person is quite energetic and autonomous in his search for pleasure, through social clubs, theater, card-playing, music, handwork, and puttering around the house and garden. For instance, a retired Viennese teacher has season tickets for two theaters and the opera; still plays the piano for his own pleasure; reads many journals and books; and always goes with his wife to the Tyrol for a month in the summer. A Warsaw teacher (a widower), who still teaches eight hours per week, goes one night a week to the theater or cinema, spends at least one evening a week with male or female friends, plays his violin one and one-half hours a day, and reads widely. A Chicago retired steelworker has a room full of canaries in his basement, and a shop where he makes articles for his home. He likes to grow flowers in his garden, watches baseball and football regularly on television, and will go to California next summer. Categories G, H, and J contribute to this pattern.

Among the Kansas City group who had this pattern, the favorite leisure activities were flying, golf, bowling, fishing, hunting, oil painting, ceramics, photography, reading, sewing, and gardening. Men outnumber women in the Expressive group, while women outnumber men in the Instrumental group.

## Mildly Active Time Filling

This pattern consists of a routine leisure activity which takes two or three hours a day and requires a considerable amount of initiative on one's part, though it has become a routine with him. He may go to a park or tavern regularly every morning to play cards and talk with friends. This is a common pattern for Milanese steelworkers, who have a recreation center maintained by the company that formerly employed them. Another rather common example of this pattern is the daily walk of one to two hours. One German teacher visited all the new construction in his neighborhood every weekday afternoon, as a kind of "sidewalk superintendent." Another took a long walk in the wooded park known as the *Venusberg* which he said he knew "like the pockets in my jacket."

The difference between this pattern and II and III lie in the degree of activity, novelty, and autonomy shown by the person. Patterns II and III require more than routine attention. Among women who have this pattern, the favorite leisure activities are likely to be home centered, such as canning, cooking, visiting relatives, watching television.

## Ordinary Routines Expanded to Fill the Day and Week

In this pattern, the person exercises little or no initiative and does nothing unusual. The ordinary social roles expand to fill his day or his week, as his energy and tempo of action are reduced. For example, a 72-year-old steelworker goes to the market every morning with his wife. He says, "By the time you shop and come home and put your purchases away it seems to be a day's work." Another Chicago steelworker comments that he takes much more time than he did formerly for daily routines.

> You take three hours for breakfast and the newspaper. Then you fuss around in the basement or the garden. They're building a garage in back of us. The man next door is retired; the man over there is retired; we all three go over and supervise the job; I don't know whether it's leisure or wasted time; after all, I guess it's all leisure time if you have nothing to do.

## Apathetic

The person with this pattern has had no new interests for some time and does not initiate anything. Thus, a 74-year-old Chicago steelworker who is not well said, "All my time is free, but I can't do much with it." Another retired steelworker goes to six o'clock mass every morning with his wife. When the interviewer asked him what he does the remainder of the day he said, "Just what I was doing when you came here—sitting in that chair; and I sleep two hours every afternoon." This type of person stays home most of the time. He may enjoy visits from relatives, and may be quite comfortable in his family life. But generally he is unhappy and morose. For instance, a Kansas City man said he watches television but does not enjoy it, and he has no other leisure activity. In all the ordinary social roles this person is apt to be low in activity and low in satisfaction.

## Literally Has No Free Time

This is uncommon, but a few elderly men and women are still employed or they have so much responsibility for home and family roles that they have little time or energy for nonconstrained free-time activity. For example, a retired Chicago teacher works as an accountant and income tax consultant. He owned a half-block of land around his home and has sold thirteen lots in recent years, while he still cares for a large garden and lawn. He has some club activity, including a Country Club membership, but has no time to use it. A Milanese teacher works part time as inspector of schools for handicapped children. In the afternoon, he takes a nap, reads or helps grandchildren with their studies. Though he has a stamp collection, he does not have much time for it.

## FACTORS DETERMINING LEISURE ACTIVITY

The free-time patterns are obviously dependent on health, which permits some persons to be more active than others. They are also dependent on personality. Free-time activity is often taken as an expression of personality, since it is relatively unconstrained by the environment.

By the time a person reaches later maturity he has had enough experience with free-time activity to have some preferences, which he usually indulges when he retires from work and has more time at his disposal. The experience factor probably weighs heavily in differentiating middle-class from working-class people in their leisure activities. Just as middle-class people of middle age are more active in club activities, civic-political, church, and friendship activities, the same social class difference is found in older people. Consequently there is a socioeconomic difference in the frequency of the various free-time patterns. Middle-class people more often exhibit patterns I, II and III, while working-class people exhibit patterns IV (mildly active time filling) and VI (apathy).

Throughout the interviews with retired manual workers runs the refrain of a desire to "take it easy," to rest after a long life of hard and physically exhausting work. A retired Chicago worker says, "In the morning I do a little work around the house, and maybe I do some shopping for my wife. Then I eat my dinner and smoke a cigarette and go lay down. Then I get up, smoke a cigarette, and go outside again. . . . Saturday afternoon? Well, that's my real job. I take a bath, shave, dress up a little bit, and go outside and sit." A Viennese steelworker, age 71, had a heart attack at age 62, but kept working until 65. He says, "I have worked enough for my life." He gets a good deal of enjoyment from pattern IV. He shops at the local market just before noon every morning, where he enjoys gossiping with the women vendors. Generally, in mid-afternoon he and his wife go out and sit in a neighboring park.

A London teacher has a rather similar pattern of smooth adjustment, though a little more urbane. Retired at 62 because he was tired, and could not get around comfortably due to an old World War I wound in the leg, he has adopted at age 72 a comfortable routine. For breakfast, he says, "I have an egg and one rasher of bacon 350 mornings a year I should think—the other fifteen I like a change." After breakfast he reads the London Times and then brushes his cocker spaniel. He reads a good deal on the history of art, as well as ephemeral literature such as that of Ian Fleming. "There's a lot of zest in James Bond." he says.

Retired middle-class people, who were much more *engaged* than manual workers in social interaction outside of the family sphere in middle age, probably tend to retain the patterns of social engagement after they retire. If they have the physical energy as well as a liking for these activities, they can easily continue them, whereas manual workers would have to learn new kinds of behavior. Workers tend to fill up their added leisure time upon retirement with family and informal social relations, while middle-class people may draw from their experience with a wider variety of free-time activity.

## The Opportunity Factor

It is probably a combination of past experience with opportunity which mainly determines the free-time pattern in later maturity.

A person's physical location becomes more important as a factor in the meaningful use of time as he grows older. If he lives in a metropolitan apartment, he has the facilities of the city but no space or opportunity for gardening, work around the house, and little opportunity to enjoy the outdoor life. If he lives in a suburb of a city, he has opportunity for gardening and being outdoors; but he may find it increasingly difficult to see his friends from other parts of the city and to enjoy the amenities of metropolitan life. A retired farmer may deliberately move into the county-seat when he retires, so as to be close to things and people that his farming life did not allow for. If a person is in a warm climate, he may be active outdoors all year long; but if he lives in a cold climate, his winter activity is likely to be limited.

The opportunity factor can be increased by a community which cares to provide facilities for free-time activity for older people. This can be done by a church which provides weekday activities in the form of a Golden Age Club or some other group for seniors. It can be done by a YMCA, or through a community center sponsored by the County Farm Bureau or some other group with a program for older people. Under the Older Americans Act, the Federal Government assists the states to support local community recreation centers for senior citizens.

### Leisure and Loneliness

The loneliest people generally have the most leisure. Living alone is the lot of some 30 per cent of women over 65, and of 15 per cent of men over 65. These people are at all economic levels. Some live in semiluxury in small apartments or apartment hotels in middle-class areas. Others have a bare but clean room in a second-rate hotel with two meals a day, for which they pay roughly the amount of their social security benefit plus a little more. And many have a small room in a rooming house, with a gas burner to cook meals on and a window box to store food. More than half of these lone people get along on a hundred dollars or less a month, and often are fully dependent on welfare payments from the state.

While they are accustomed to being alone and to doing very little with their time, many of them are pathetically anxious for simple forms of social intercourse, but do not know how to make social contacts.

## CONCLUSION

Retirement is a crisis in the meaningful use of time. It forces a person to shift his major activity out of the customary work role into other roles and to seek more satisfaction in these other roles which are still open to him—the roles of homemaker, parent, spouse, citizen, friend, association member, church member, and user of leisure time.

We know enough about the variety of personality types among older people to know that they do not and cannot all enjoy a high degree of social-civic free time activity, nor can they all enjoy a life of disengagement from their activities. What the community can do is to provide facilities for leisure activity and to encourage older people to try them out for their possible satisfaction value.

## REFERENCES

1. DAMAZEDIER, JOFFRE: Current problems of the sociology of leisure. *Int Soc Sci J, 12* (4): 522-531, 1960.
2. HAVIGHURST, ROBERT J.: The nature and values of meaningful free-time activity. *Aging and Leisure.* Kleemeier, Robert W. (Ed.), New York, Oxford, 1961, pp. 309-344.

## ADDITIONAL READINGS

DUMAZEDIER, JOFFRE: *Toward a Society of Leisure.* New York, Free Press, 1967.

HAVIGHURST, ROBERT J.: The leisure activities of the middle aged. *Amer J Soc, 63*:152-62, 1957.

KAPLAN, M.: *Leisure in America: A Social Inquiry.* New York, Wiley, 1960.

KLEEMEIER, ROBERT (Ed.): *Aging and Leisure.* New York, Oxford, 1961.

LARRABEE, E., and MEYERSOHN, R. (Eds.): *Mass Leisure.* New York, Free Press, 1958.

MEAD, MARGARET: The patterns of leisure in contemporary american culture. *Ann Amer Acad Political Soc Sci, 313*:11-15, Sept. 1957.

*Chapter 9*

# RELIGION IN THE LATER YEARS

David O. Moberg

Religion either covers all of life or almost none of it, depending upon the scope of one's definitions and interpretations. Philosophers, theologians, and others have produced hundreds of definitions of "religion," many of which seem inconsistent with others.[1] Instead of surveying them, we shall simply assume that religion, for our purposes in this chapter, has two chief orientations, one personal and the other institutional. The personal beliefs, values, and activities pertinent to that which is supernatural, mysterious, and awesome, which transcends immediate situations, and which pertains to questions of final causes and ultimate ends of man and the universe, are closely related to group behavior in the church and many other social institutions.

The specialization of institutional roles in modern society has delegated the religious questions largely, but not exclusively, to churches, synagogues, and related religious institutions and agencies. Nevertheless, religion continues to play an active and important role in many families, schools, welfare agencies, civic organizations, custodial institutions, hospitals, and community associations. It is not confined to the segment of society that is customarily labeled as "religious," for in essence, religious values and commitments cut across all human affairs. Just as even the most personal aspects of religion are profoundly social,[2] the most "secular" of contemporary institutions, organizations, and activities have their religious implications, can be subjected to religious evaluation, and may be interpreted as parts of the "religious" life of their participants. Whether they are dealt with thus or not is less a product of their "true nature" than of the attitudinal stance and intellectual-emotional frame of reference of the interpreter.

In the past, many social scientists have neglected religion in comparison to other major facets of man's social life. This was done for many reasons,[3] some of which are relevant to home economists. If religion as customarily defined and observed seems to be irrelevant to one's own life, he tends to assume that it is irrelevant to others also. This is probably one of the underlying reasons why religion is sometimes considered a "taboo topic" in American society.[4]

The clients, patrons, or subjects of one's demonstration, research, and action programs should always be foremost in one's planning. Although there are great variations by age, locale, religious preference, and other characteristics, more older persons in the United States belong to churches than to any other kind of voluntary agency. Other indicators of religious interest also demonstrate its great significance to large proportions of the aged population, as we shall see. To ignore the religious component of their philosophical life-orientation and practical life-style is to overlook a very significant source of understanding, helping, and motivating them.

Of course, it must be recognized that the language used to express religious orientations and activities varies considerably by religious group, by region, by ethnic background, by educational level, and by social class characteristics of people. Everyone working with people should be aware of that fact and should understand the specialized local argot of his clients together with the numerous attitudes, prejudices, values, and normative standards which they implicitly and explicitly convey.

## FUNCTIONAL ANALYSIS

The effects of most human behavior and social events are very complex. Sometimes they coincide with the desires and expectations of those who acted to bring them about, but sometimes they fail to produce such results or even contribute to diametrically opposite effects. Religious behavior is no exception.

The study of the effects of social action is known among social scientists as *functional analysis.* This involves determining the direct and indirect consequences of an act, group, role, organizational pattern, or event for the larger social system of which it is a part. Functional analysis may be made on many different levels of interpretation. A social role of John Doe, for instance, has consequences for his personal self-conception and self-integrity, but it also is pertinent to his family and the other social groups of which he is a part. These consequences, in turn, have implications for the entire society. We hence may speak of the consequences of an organization or event for the individual, for a given institution, or for society. The effects of the religious beliefs, institutions, and behavior of older persons may be analyzed on all three levels.

Some of these consequences contribute constructively to the integration, adjustment, or adaptation of the person, institution, or society which is the focus of attention. These are called *functions*. Others have disintegrative and destructive results, decreasing adaptation or stimulating maladjustment; they are *disfunctions*. Some of the functions and disfunctions are *manifest,* that is, deliberately intended, desired, and recognized by participants. Others are *latent* (unanticipated, unintended, not desired, concealed, or not recognized).[5]

Very few, if any, of man's activities, including his religious behavior, are completely functional, and few are totally disfunctional. Mixed effects are typical. To complicate the situation even more, what is functional for a person may be disfunctional for his religious group, and what is functional for a church congregation or denomination may be disfunctional for the society of which it is a part.

Although they may not use social science terminology, the critics and debunkers of religion tend to stress its manifest and latent disfunctions, while religious leaders and other apologists praise its manifest functions! Any objective appraisal must recognize both, but it must also seek out the latent functions that apologists as well as critics usually overlook.

Even though we all have a tendency to do so, it is dangerous to make sweeping generalizations about the functions and the disfunctions of religion. There usually is a wide range of personalized religious beliefs and behavior within any specific religious group, to say nothing of the great variations among them. None can be certain that his beliefs are identical to those of another person. It is likely that few people engaging in the same ritual have exactly the same subjective interpretations of and reactions to that experience. The consequences of the behavior are therefore likely to be somewhat different for each. What is functional for the personality integration of one may be disfunctional for the other. What draws one person into closer identification with his group could drive the other away from it. What brings happiness and joy to one may produce sadness and despair in the other.

Despite these problems, which must always be taken into account in the functional analysis of any specific phenomenon, some generalizations about typical personal and social consequences of religion among the older generation of our society may be made.

## FUNCTIONS AND DISFUNCTIONS OF RELIGION

In times of stress, religion provides meaning for life to those who in faith accept its teachings. Comfort is offered in the midst of sickness and suffering, death and bereavement, financial distress and unemployment, accidents and disability, famine and pestilence, mental illness and deficiency, poverty and discrimination, and other common or rare experiences related to the human condition. Problems of the meaning of life and of society itself are proffered. The true believer finds his self-identity in the context of his religious group; he may either live at peace with himself and the world as a result or be driven by powerful inner springs of conviction to try to "turn the world upside down" on behalf of his religion through efforts to convert others to his faith, to compel them to conform to his moral convictions, or to force society into the mold of standards or structures established by his sect.

### Values and Value Conflicts

Values essential to the survival of society have been developed and sustained in religious groups. These values, in turn, provide the basis for the social rewards and punishments designated by society. The ultimate values may be distinguished from those that are derivative, with religious institutions obviously concentrating on the former. Yet in establishing a value-hierarchy with certain values ranked higher than others, religious groups often draw into an integrated system diverse objectives that by themselves might otherwise have appeared unrelated and meaningless. In this manner, they give meaning to life, promote the ability of men to understand their values, and thus increase the chances that consensus will prevail with regard to social goals. By making clear to the individual what is "right" and "wrong," "good" and "bad," morally "pure" and "impure," religious groups thus contribute indirectly to the integration of society.

Reinforcing political, economic, moral, and other social goals in the minds of individuals, churches help to increase the social solidarity or cohesiveness of society itself.[6] When, however, they sharply disagree with one another's conclusions on such matters, they are a divisive force within the social order.

Religious institutions tend to be conservative influences in society because of their orientation to traditional values. At times, however, this conservative orientation has a revolutionary impact when prophetic leaders point to inconsistencies between the basic values of the religion and society's established institutions and customs.

When the religious world is divided on such matters, as in the case of the current civil rights movement, some churches are militantly revolutionary while others dogmatically resist change. Each group condemns the other as "inconsistent"; each feels the other has betrayed "true religion"; each believes the other is promoting values and actions which will lead to the downfall of society. In fact, both may be to some degree correct, for the functions and disfunctions of social action are tightly interwoven with each other and seldom appear in unadulterated form. Older people, whose basic religious orientations were first developed two generations ago, tend to take the conservative stance whenever such internal disagreements arise.

## Social and Psychological Consequences

It is in the church more than in any other type of social institution outside the family that the aged are most likely to find personal friendship and other resources to curb their loneliness and despair. It is to the church that many of them look for alleviation of the fear of death. Some of them find physical or psychological healing in prayer and in the tenets and rituals of their religion. They may feel the envigorating or stultifying influence of the controls their religious group exerts over their personal behavior.

Many older people are the recipients of church-sponsored volunteer services, institutional care, and welfare programs. Their personal religious experiences may be facilitated by the programs and services offered through the church. As a result, they may believe that they have discovered the will of God for their life, are experiencing daily fellowship with him, have found meaning for life, and are secure in the midst of a troubled world because God is the Sovereign of the

Universe. Many esthetic, educational, therapeutic, economic, recreational, and other functions are similarly provided them by their churches.[7]

The very religious activities which have functional consequences for most participants may produce disfunctions for others. Those who believe themselves to be incapable of extending their faith to receive the blessings promised by their religious leaders and sacred literature may be fiilled with despair that would not have been theirs had they never heard the promises. The person whose faith seems too little to be rewarded may languish in the fear that he is predestined to eternal damnation. In an effort to earn salvation he may submit himself to legalistic rules and regulations which make his own life and the lives of associates exceedingly miserable, or he may feel that he has committed an unpardonable sin.

## Implications for Action

Reactions to the religious message and program are thus highly dependent upon the recipient; automatic results cannot be guaranteed in contemporary American society. Whether religious teachings, projects, and programs are functional or disfunction for the older person depends largely upon the recipient, although the understanding or lack thereof with which these services are provided undoubtedly makes a significant difference. Even such apparently minor matters as the types of food served at a club's luncheon for "senior citizens," the manner in which it is distributed, and seating arrangements while eating may greatly influence the adjustive or maladjustive reactions of the guests because, among other things, their religious conditioning predisposes them to react in sterotyped ways.

Religious symptoms occasionally appear in cases of senility. In such instances, past religious experiences of the patient may have played a part in bringing on the illness, or they may merely have contributed to its external expression. Therapists and others who work with such patients must be cautious about their references to religious topics and their use of treatment which is related to religion and the church. Sometimes a religious reorientation is called for, but there also are instances in which religious reinforcement is needed.[8]

The staunch individualism which has been fostered by many American religious groups is often entrenched most strongly in the older generation. Focusing solely on the virtues, activities, attitudes, and relationships of individuals rather than those of groups, institutions, and society, this orientation neglects the social implications of religious doctrines and contributes to a pietistic otherworldliness that hinders social progress. It is often linked with the viewpoint that conditions in the world will get worse and worse in spite of all of man's efforts, so any attempt to improve world conditions or social life is doomed to failure.

Persons who hold such perspectives may be extremely optimistic about their future in eternity, but their pessimism and despair about the present may make them maladjusted personally as well as socially in this life. Those who work with older people must be prepared to recognize this problem, to cope with the hypocritical self-righteousness of both the members of such groups and their critics, and to be a wholesome mediating influence reconciling people of divergent religious views to one another.

Most of the leaders in movements to protect interpretations of the Bible which appear inconsistent with modern science are older persons. Insistence on a six-day creation, on a flood that covered the entire earth, on evil spirits as the cause of mental illness, and on rigid moral codes of recreation, hair styles, clothing, and ornamentation also is typically the most pronounced in the older generation. Those who work with such people must be judiciously gracious in dealing with such viewpoints and not make an issue of moot points of intrepretation. To work effectively with their clients, they must begin with them where they are, not where they would like to see them.

The social functions and disfunctions of religion are thus closely interrelated on both the personal and social level. There are great variations between persons as well as between communities and denominations in the religiously-tinged issues of recreational programs, food, clothing, service projects, and other activities which are the concern of home economists. Recognizing differences is a first step toward coping successfully with them.

## MAJOR DIMENSIONS OF RELIGION

The religion of any person can be seen from the perspective of many different aspects, components, or indicators. Professor Glock of the Survey Research Center at the University of California in Berkeley has developed a classification of five "dimensions of religiosity," [9] to which must be added a sixth if one wishes to cover the totality of personal religion. We will briefly survey these, with special reference to older people.[10]

## Religious Practices

The *ritualistic* dimension of religion pertains to people's religious practices or acts. Perhaps because these are relatively easy to observe, there has been much research on this.

Studies in a large number of American communities consistently indicate that more older people are members of churches than of all other voluntary community organizations together. Public opinion polls have found consistently higher figures for Bible reading, praying, and church attendance among adults past the age of 50 than among younger adults. The precise statistics vary considerably by region, type of community, ethnic background, religious faith and denomination, and other factors, but invariably a higher proportion of women than of men are members, attend church, and participate in other religious activities.

In most communities, there tends to be some decrease in church attendance with advancing years past the age of 65, but this usually can be attributed to increasing problems of health, disability, and economic limitations rather than to lack of interest. Participation in other social organizations declines at a much more rapid rate than church participation. As church attendance decreases, regular Bible reading, listening to religious programs on radio, and viewing them on television tend to increase.

Both by personal choice and as a result of social pressures, there is a pronounced tendency for older people to drop positions of leadership in churches and other religious organizations. Sometimes these are relinquished with great relief, but in other instances their loss is interpreted by the person as a mark of failure and a sign of diminished worth. Major posts like the papacy and bishoprics are typically held by older people, but most other positions of religious leadership are held by middle-aged persons.

In summary, religious practices outside the home generally decrease with the advance of age past the sixty-fifth birthday, but those which occur within the home tend to increase. Physical condition seems to be the chief intervening variable responsible for these ostensibly contradictory trends.

## Religious Feelings

The *experiential* dimension of religion pertains to religious feelings. The emotions deemed proper vary widely from one religious group to another, with certain groups claiming to have a totally rational, nonemotional religion and others emphasizing an open display of emotions as something far superior to all intellectual achievements. Religious feelings in the later years have not been studied systematically, so there is but little empirical evidence on this dimension.

In most samples which have been studied, there appears to be a greater interest in religion among older than among middle-aged and younger adults. The Terman Gifted Group, for example, revealed a greater interest in religion at the median age of 56 than they had ten and twenty years earlier.

When asked, people are more likely to say that religion has become more helpful to them with increasing age than to state it has become less helpful, but this conclusion may be attributed to a "halo effect" in American culture which makes it desirable or respectable to make such statements. Regardless of the cause, as the end of life approaches, expressions of interest in religion become more common in most segments of the population.

## Religious Beliefs

The *ideological* dimension deals with religious beliefs. The beliefs members of a religious group are officially expected to hold do not always coincide with those they actually hold. For some persons, beliefs are more important and salient than for others.

Generally, older people have more conservative religious perspectives than younger adults. A higher proportion of them believe in a life after death, in God as a loving father, and in the importance of preparing for life after death. They also are more certain of their religious beliefs. Whether such differences are due primarily to divergent experiences of the generations during childhood and youth, which are the most formative ages of the life cycle, or to actual changes linked with the aging process is not known because currently available research data are insufficient to answer that question.

## Religious Knowledge

The *intellectual* dimension of religion concerns information and knowledge about the basic tenets and sacred writings of one's faith. Relatively little research has been done on age differences in religious knowledge, but the writer's personal impressions are that older church members tend to hold their information and misinformation more tenaciously and are more likely to have memorized scripture passages than younger adults; the latter are more likely to have read widely in theological and religious literature outside of the Bible and are more apt to recognize divergent viewpoints as valid. People past the age of 55 participate less in adult education than other age groups, but when they do participate, they are more interested in studying religion.[11]

## Results of Religion

The *consequential* dimension is on a different conceptual level from the other four, for it includes all of the secular effects of religious practices, feelings, beliefs, and knowledge. The Christian concept of "works" in contrast to faith is one of its major components. Rewards, punishments, expectations, obligations, commandments, and promises linked with religion may also be included under the consequential dimension.

Fearful attitudes toward death tend to be more common among those who have little religious activity and give little evidence of religious commitments. Religious beliefs and faith in God also have helped disorganized members of group therapy sessions overcome their grief.

Certain studies have shown that happiness is related to the frequency of church attendance among both Catholics and non-Catholics. The "very happy" attend church the most frequently, the "moderately happy" next most often, and the "less happy" attend the least of all. Religion brings feelings of satisfaction and security to many people.

On the other hand, hospital patients who flaunt a Bible are often troublesome to their physicians, possibly because they tend to be insecure, unstable persons who are members of fringe-type religious sects.

Numerous studies have been made of personal adjustment in old age. These have shown a direct relationship between good personal adjustment and religious indicators like church membership, church attendance, Bible reading, regular listening to radio church services, belief in an afterlife, and religious faith. The best evidence supports the conclusion that it is not church membership as such but the religious activities and beliefs associated with it that are responsible for this relationship.

On a different level, another consequence of religion is the large number of clubs, clinical centers, retirement and nursing homes, volunteer service projects, educational programs, and other activities for the aged which are sponsored by churches. Religious perspectives have also contributed indirectly to much of the private and public welfare system. Humanitarian perspectives and activities are inspired and supported by religious teachings. Of course, we must also recognize that certain religious groups oppose such programs on the grounds of their interpretations that only the church should be involved in welfare, that believers should not cooperate with nonbelievers, that he who will not work should not eat the food that is produced by the labors of others, or that children and not the government should take care of retired parents.

When relationships like these are considered, it is necessary to keep in mind the possibility that they may not represent direct cause-effect relationships. We know, for instance, that church members are more likely than nonmembers to belong to and participate in other voluntary community associations, and officers in churches are more likely than other members to be leaders in other organizations at all ages. Gregarious personality orientations and leadership ability may be the basic factors underlying such correlations; to what extent they are an effect of the religious factor *per se* is open to question.

Similarly, well-adjusted older persons may engage in many religious activities and poorly adjusted people may not. The relationship between adjustment and religious activities, in other words, could be a spurious consequence of common third causes. Future research should include specific tests of that possibility. On the other hand, most of the relationships observed on the consequential level are consistent with the goals of religious groups and can be considered manifest functions until solid contrary evidence has been provided.

## The Spiritual Component of Religion

The five "core dimensions of religiosity" distinguished by Glock do not, however, cover the totality of religious commitment. There is also a *spiritual* component that cuts across and is woven into all the others. It is the realm of faith, revelation, illumination, and insight which some have labeled the sacred, the holy, the supernatural or the transcendental. It is what theologians label the vertical, I-Thou, or man-God relationship. Within Christianity, it is reflected in such biblical concepts as regeneration, being "hid with Christ in God," and "written in the book of life."

Sturzo, an Italian sociologist, has labeled this "the true life." He indicated that the supernatural and the natural meet in man. The supernatural is not something juxtaposed to the natural as a separate section of social life that people may accept or reject at will. It is rather a total "atmosphere" within which the natural exists.[12]

The spiritual dimension is currently beyond the scope of direct empirical research, but its correlates and effects are as proper a subject of scientific study as numerous other phenomena that can be investigated only indirectly. Such evidence can come from self-reports of subjective spiritual experiences, case studies of believers, the apparently universal grasping of men for some kind of ultimate commitment or concern, and the tests of the validity of personal religious experience used by many religious groups in screening membership applications.

Even though these data are no more solid scientifically than much of the content of other sociopsychological research, home economists and others who sense no personal experiences related to the spiritual or supernatural component of man's nature should take seriously the claims of religious people instead of assuming that there is nothing but illusion involved in them. They will then be in a much better position to serve their clients effectively; adjusting to their their religion will help to establish relationships of rapport that can never come through attempts to compel them to fit the contrary personal predilections of their leaders.

A person may, obviously, be "very religious" on the basis of certain indicators and very "irreligious" or even "antireligious" on the basis of others. Religion is not a unitary phenomenon; it has many dimensions despite the daily tendency to simplify it by processes of labeling, classifying, and stereotyping.

## RELIGIOUS INSTITUTIONS SERVE OLDER PEOPLE

Even religious leaders sometimes overlook the multidimensional nature of religion. There are sectarian groups, as well as individual clergymen of major denominations, which emphasize one or two of the six dimensions of religion and neglect or minimize all the others. Balanced church life should give attention to all of them; fortunately this increasingly seems to be the case in most churches of the United States.

In addition to lending support to personal faith through preaching, teaching, social activities, and pastoral services, churches also sanction many community programs to help meet the needs of older people. They have often been in the vanguard of significant community projects like the one in Earlham, Iowa, to innovate new services on behalf of the aging.[13] Numerous community centers for "senior citizens" are located in church facilities. Religious bodies have given their moral support through official resolutions and other action to civic, state, and national programs to resolve the economic plight, housing problems, and health needs of older people. Although they have not moved as a solid political bloc on such matters, their influence generally has been on the side of enhancing the welfare of the aging, despite the contrary voices among them in our religiously pluralistic society.

A wide variety of programs, projects, and services are provided older persons by churches, in many of which home economists have or can have a part. Some of them are possible only by the cooperation of all churches in a community or of churches with other social agencies and institutions, while others can be fulfilled by a single congregation or even by a suborganization within a local church. Details pertinent to some of these possibilities are discussed elsewhere in this book; others are more fully presented in the references at the end of this chapter.

The following list of church-related activities summarizes some of the most obvious ways in which churches can and do help to satisfy the needs of older people and thus contribute functionally to their welfare. Imaginative leadership will suggest numerous other possibilities related to the specific needs of any given community.

1. Churches provide institutional and personal opportunities for cultivating and fulfilling the ritualistic, experiential, ideological, intellectual, consequential, and spiritual dimensions of religion to which we have referred earlier.

2. Churches educate children, youth, and adults to prepare for old age and, in the later years of life, to cope with the needs and problems typical of that stage of the life cycle.

3. Churches help to develop wholesome personalities by providing meaning for life, fellowship with other people, mental hygiene resources, and an opportunity to be useful.

4. Churches exert their influence in civic affairs on behalf of the needs of older people in the community.

5. Churches meet social and recreational needs of older people through friendly visiting, camping programs, sightseeing excursions, and specialized clubs, centers, projects, and other activities, as well as through the conventional programs and social organizations in the church.

6. Churches provide transportation to their worship services, plan their facilities to meet the physical problems of the handicapped, and in other ways facilitate participation of those older people who need assistance or special consideration in order to enjoy the benefits of the regular church program.

7. Churches provide pastoral ministries, counseling resources, and referral services to help older people solve their personal problems of adjusting to retirement, physical and mental illness, social and economic deprivation, housing, bereavement, loss of friends, and the approach of death.

8. Churches sponsor and support retirement homes and villages, nursing homes, and other institutions for the care of older people.

9. Churches sponsor numerous projects to meet other needs of the aged, including homemaker services, reassurance telephone calling, meals-on-wheels, transportation to health services, rides to the polls on election day, handiman household and odd-jobs assistance, playing the recorded worship service in the homes of shut-ins, and gospel team visits to institutionalized people.

10. Churches provide older people an opportunity to serve, thus enhancing their usefulness, reinforcing worthy self-concepts, and extending the effectiveness of the congregations' ministries of service.

## OLDER PEOPLE SERVE THEIR CHURCH

Many older people are given responsible positions of service in churches, even though they tend gradually to withdraw from official leadership positions. Perhaps the most obvious of these involve services to their peers in the church and community, but there are many other levels on which such service can be donated for the benefit of the church, the people it serves, and, reciprocally, those who serve. Examples of such service possibilities include the following:

1. Older people can help others by active participation in worship services and in other activities of their church. This gives encouragement and blessing to others.
2. They can teach Sunday school classes, sponsor youth groups, aid the church nursery supervisors, work on scouting projects, assist in children's club work, and help furnish portions of the programs of other church organizations.
3. They can help in the visitation program of the church, finding prospects for membership, following up requests for visits, or fulfilling the need for friendly visitors to disabled, hospitalized, and infirm people in the community.
4. They can help maintain the building, grounds, and properties of their church.
5. They can assist the pastor or church secretary with mailings, records, and other clerical needs.
6. They can collect information about alternative resources and costs pertinent to the purchasing of supplies and other business affairs of the church.
7. They can serve as a "telephone brigade" for special announcements as well as for a regular telephone reassurance service to check daily on the welfare of handicapped and aged people who live alone.
8. They can provide transportation to church activities, medical facilities, shopping centers, and other places which handicapped people and infirm aged persons otherwise cannot reach.
9. They can take care of the church library.

10. They can help cook and serve church suppers.

11. They can represent the church in community programs, inter-church projects, and civic committees.

12. They can donate volunteer services in hospitals, nursing homes, social welfare agencies, and other organizations.

13. They can help recruit and train others for volunteer services to the church and community.

14. They can serve as consultants and resource people in areas related to their special vocational and other competencies.

15. Even when they are personally disabled, they can continue to serve through praying for others, maintaining a wholesome perspective on themselves and their problems, and thus giving satisfactions and cheer to people who serve and visit them.

No person can perform all of the above services, for individual abilities, to say nothing of interests, greatly vary. Everyone who wishes to serve can, however, find a place of service if only he is sufficiently resourceful to see the needs in relationship to his abilities. Home economists, religious leaders, and others can greatly stimulate the insights and expand the opportunities for helping other people and the church.

Service for others and service from others are thus complementary. When offered within a wholesome framework of attitudes and objectives, each helps to improve the effectiveness and efficiency of the other. He who gives the most to his fellowmen is also he who receives the most from them.

Religion is important in the later years partly because it provides an opportunity both to give and to receive. Its orientations may have been implanted early in life and reinforced throughout the years even in the minds of nonmembers. The religious components of self-concepts and other important influences on personal adjustment and social interaction which have been affected by churches and by personal religious experiences and commitments are of great importance to anyone who is involved in professional or voluntary work with older people.

## REFERENCES

1. FERM, VERGILIUS (Ed.): Religion, the problem of definition. In *Encyclopedia of Religion.* Paterson, Littlefield, 1959, pp. 646-647.
2. MOBERG, DAVID O.: *The Church as a Social Institution.* Englewood Cliffs, Printice-Hall, 1962, pp. 3-7, 513-514.

3. *Ibid.* p. 13.
4. FARBEROW, NORMAN L. (Ed.): *Taboo Topics.* New York, Atherton, 1963.
5. GOODE, WILLIAM J.: *Religion Among the Primitives.* New York, Free Press 1951, pp. 29-34; Merton, Robert K.: *Social Theory and Social Structure.* New York, Free Press 1957, pp. 21-84.
6. NOTTINGHAM, ELIZABETH K.: *Religion and Society.* New York, Random, 1954, pp. 12-18, 28-55.
7. MOBERG, *op. cit.* pp. 127-178.
8. See OATES, WAYNE: *Religious Factors in Mental Illness.* New York, Assn. Pr., 1955.
9. GLOCK, CHARLES Y.: On the study of religious commitment. *Religious Education.* July-August 1962, vol. 57, No. 4, pp. 598-5110.
10. MOBERG, DAVID O.: Religiosity in old age. *Gerontologist,* 5(2):78-87, 111-112, June 1965. (For the original sources of most data in this section see the 51 references cited in that article.)
11. JOHNSTONE, JOHN W. C., and RIVERA, RAMON J.: *Volunters for Learning.* Chicago, Aldine, 1965, pp. 79-81.
12. STURZO, LUIGI: *The True Life: Sociology of the Supernatural.* Carter, Barbara Barclay (transl.), London, Geoffrey Bles, 1947.
13. Earlham onference on Aging, Earlham, Iowa, Sept. 25-26, 1964.

## ADDITIONAL READINGS

CHAKERIAN, CHARLES G.: *The Aging and the United Presbyterian Church in the U.S.A.* New York, Division of Health and Welfare, United Presbyterian Board of National Missions, 1964.

Committee on the Aging: *Judaism, the Synagogue and the Aging.* New York, Union of American Hebrew Congregations, 1962.

CULVER, ELSIE T.: *New Church Programs with the Aging.* New York, Assn. Pr., 1961.

Department of Public Welfare: *Ministries in Aging: Survey Report, Planned Church Programs for Older Persons.* Santa Fe, New Mexico, 1966.

GRAY, ROBERT M., and MOBERG, DAVID O.: *The Church and the Older Person.* Grand Rapids, Eerdmans, 1962.

JACOBS, H. LEE: *Senior Citizens in the Church and Community.* 3rd ed., Iowa City, Institute of Gerontology, U. of Iowa, 1960.

PETERSON, MIRIAM A.: *The Church's Ministry with Senior Adults.* Valley Forge, Pennsylvania: Division of Christian Education, American Baptist Convention, n.d.

SCUDDER, DELTON L. (Ed.): *Organized Religion and the Older Person.* Gainesville, U. of Fla., 1958.

STOUGH, ADA BARNETT: *Brighter Vistas: The Story of Four Church Programs for Older Adults.* Washington, D.C.: Administration on Aging, U.S. Department of Health, Education, and Welfare, 1965.

# PART IV

# BIOLOGICAL ASPECTS OF AGING

*Chapter 10*

# THE BIOLOGY OF AGING

NEILL SOLOMON, NATHAN W. SHOCK,
AND PATRICIA S. AUGHENBAUGH

## THE SCIENCE OF GERONTOLOGY

UNLIKE OTHER SCIENCES, gerontology has no one specific method or technique. Rather its uniqueness arises from the fact that the science of aging has time as the independent variable. Instead of varying experimental conditions, one has as the sole variable the age of the experimental subject. The biological aspects of gerontology deal with the changes in physiological function that occur with age, and which, like reproduction, are universal. With few possible exceptions such as the anemonae, no organism escapes the aging process.

Although we seldom think of aging on a macrocosmic level, the evolution of the world and universe is, in the most basic sense, an example of the aging process. Here aging consists of the evolutary adaptation and change of an organism so that it is best equipped for survival. On this general level, aging brings refinement and a constant struggle for the biological "perfection" of a species over thousands of years.

Even on the microcosmic level, where one usually considers aging within a finite span of time, the process which is a normal part of the life cycle can be considered as an adaptive one of the organism as well as a destructive one. When we hear the term "old" or "aging," we immediately think of someone in the later phase of his life, but actually aging begins from the time of conception. The first period of life, from conception to about age 30, is one of growth, development and adaptation. At about 30 years of age, the time that is ironically called the "prime" of life, the degenerative process starts, and man starts to deplete the reserve capacity that has been established in his youth. However, the rest of man's life is still adaptive in the sense that his body compensates physiologically for the decrease in reserve.

## RESEARCH IN GERONTOLOGY

Only recently has any major investigation into the area of the physiology of aging been undertaken. Whereas most scientific disciplines have been studied for centuries, it was 1941 before investigations in the field of gerontology were undertaken systematically with the establishment of the Gerontology Branch of the National Institutes of Health at Baltimore City Hospitals in Baltimore, Maryland. Until this time, aging was considered a necessary evil and research into the area neglected. However, with the continuous increase of the average length of life, it has become increasingly important to enable older people to be active participants in family and community life, and it is the aim of gerontological research to make this a reality.

Because time must be the only variable in a gerontological study, research in the field poses many problems. Individual differences at any given age must be taken into consideration, and the most desirable way to obtain accurate data is through the establishment of a longitudinal study such as the one recently created at the Gerontology Branch. Here subjects come in annually for evaluation of physiological and psychological function and for biochemical determinations. The study is of recent conception, but eventually each individual's performance will be compared with that of his younger years. Through analysis of many subjects over a period of years, definite patterns and trends in the aging process can be more clearly delineated.

## REDUCTION IN PHYSIOLOGICAL RESERVES

Investigators feel that the decrease in reserve capacity exhibited by a decrease in actual cell number is a key characteristic of the aging process. Studies under resting conditions show that although older subjects do not function as well physiologically as do the younger ones, they can at least maintain a physiological balance which cannot be maintained under stress or disease. Figures 10-1 and 10-2 quantitate the physiological decline which accompanies aging. Age changes, such as decreased visual and auditory acuity, should be expected as evidenced by the increased number of glasses and hearing aids in the older population. Although many older people can perform many tasks as well as younger ones when not under stress, the time required for completion increases with age. However, in a stress situation, the

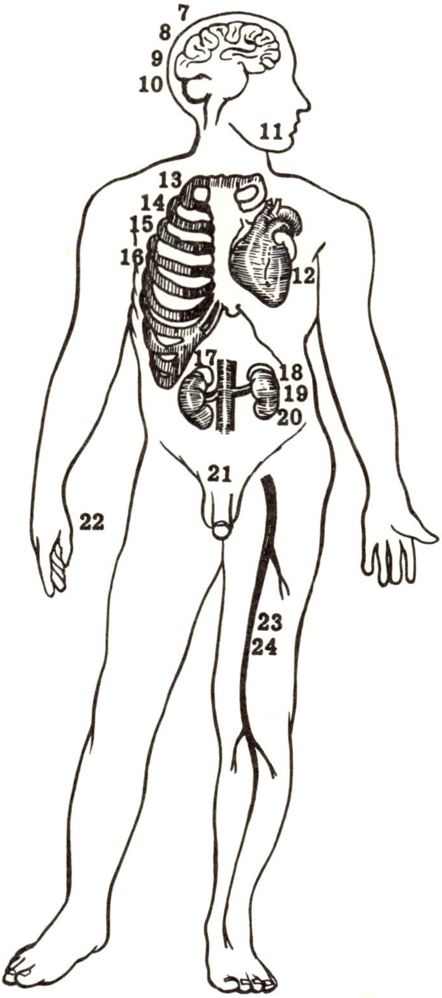


1. Speed of return to equilibrium of blood acidity (17)
2. Maximum work rate (70)
3. Maximum work rate for short burst (15)
4. Basal metabolic rate (84)
5. Body water content (82)
6. Body weight (male) (88)
7. Brain weight (56)
8. Recent memory loss (50)
9. Slower speed of response (50)
10. Blood flow to brain (80)
11. Number of taste buds (36)
12. Cardiac output (at rest) (10)
13. Maximum oxygen uptake (exercise) (40)
14. Maximum ventilation volume (exercise) (53)
15. Maximum breathing capacity (voluntary) (43)
16. Vital capacity (56)
17. Less adrenal activity (75)
18. No. glomeruli in kidney (56)
19. Glomeruli filtration rate (69)
20. Kidney plasma flow (50)
21. Less gonadal acitivity (83)
22. Hand grip (55)
23. No. nerve trunk fibers (63)
24. Nerve conduction velocity (90)

Figure 10-1. Physiological decline accompanying age appears in many measurements throughout the body. Changes are great in some cases, small in others. The figures in brackets following most of the labels in the key at left at the approximate percentages of functions or tissues remaining to the average 70-year old man, taking the value found for the average 30-year old as 100%.

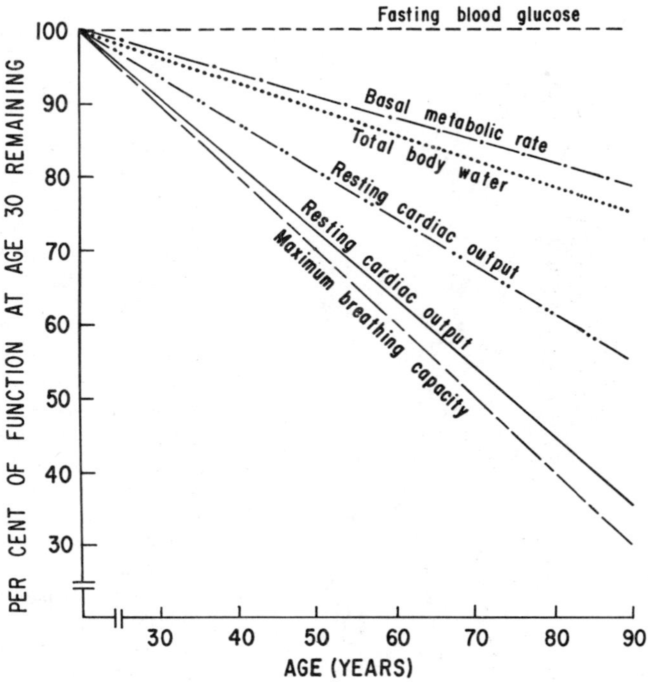


Figure 10-2. Average age differences in physiologic functions. For each function values are expressed as the per cent of the mean value for subjects aged 25-35 years. All subjects were males.

older person functions poorly and exhibits difficulty in task completion.

Under conditions of severe exercise, the loss of reserve capacity, which is often detectable under rest conditions, becomes appreciably accentuated. The 70 year-old man functions only approximately 15 per cent as well as the 30 year-old when doing severe work, which is attributable to several factors. One important factor is that the actual muscle strength of the older individual is decreased to 55 per cent of that of the 30 year-old, which is a reflection of the decreased muscle mass due to the attrition of individual muscle cells.

## The Aging Heart

A decrease in effective heart function also accompanies the aging process. At rest, the old heart has a slower rate, and the cardiac output, the amount of blood pumped from the heart per minute, is decreased to 70 per cent of that of the individual in the prime of life. However, even with the decrease in heart function, there is still an adequate supply of blood to vital organs as evidenced by the number of individuals who live for years after reaching an age where heart function is considerably reduced. Under stress conditions the old heart becomes greater. When a young individual exercises, his cardiac output increases significantly due to the increase in heart rate, and more blood is pumped from the heart per minute, which allows more oxygen to reach vital organs and peripheral areas and of course clears away the increased waste products which build up during heavy exercise. It is interesting that an athlete's heart-rate does not increase as much in severe exercise, and ejects more blood by pumping more forcefully. In the older individual, there is also an increase in cardiac output under extreme working conditions. However, it is much less than in the young person because in the older person heart-rate does not increase to as high a level. This, in a sense, is compensatory because the slower heart-rate allows a longer period for blood to enter the heart, therefore allowing more blood to be pumped out per unit time and also allowing the heart a greater amount of time to rest before the next beat. Studies show that more time is required for the old heart to return to its resting state. Experiments on animals have shown that the old heart cannot sustain an increased work load for as long as the younger heart can.

The aged heart also exhibits more frequent arrhythmias or irregularities in electrical conduction and hence in rhythm. This means that both filling and pumping are distorted, and oxygenation of the heart itself is poor. Under stress conditions, arrhythmias occur more frequently, and when the heart muscle needs oxygen the most, it is unable to receive it. Obviously, if the arrhythmia is severe enough, it can lead to the death of the individual.

Another interesting fact about the old heart is the increase in cell size called hypertrophy. This is a direct result of the increase in blood pressure with age which forces the heart to do more work in order to maintain sufficient blood flow to vital organs. Since each cell is significantly larger and since the capillary bed nourishing the heart probably remains constant, the facility of oxygen diffusion is impeded. This could account for the increased number of arrhythmias in the older heart described previously. Our laboratory is engaged in active investigation to determine the degree of oxygenation of old hearts.

## The Aging Lungs

The lungs, too, show a decrease in function with age. At rest, the old subject has a rate of exchange of air in and out of the lungs only 56 per cent of that of a young one although the breathing rate of both old and young individuals is equal. The decrement in exchange is because of the decreased elasticity of the lungs and particularly the chest wall due to infiltration and deposition of collagen as one grows older. Under stress situations, the 70 year-old cannot increase his breathing rate as much as the young person, and his maximum breathing capacity is reduced by 57 per cent. However the oxygen diffusion across his lung is less than that in the young individual due to both the increase in collagen and scar tisue of the lung and the decreased blood flow to the lung. The decreased amount of oxygen in the blood could also contribute to the arrhythmias mentioned earlier. However, even this reduced amount of oxygen is sufficient to keep the individual alive. Since the blood flow in the old individual is slower, there is more time for each cell to extract the needed oxygen from the blood, and therefore there is a significant decrease in the oxygen content of venous blood, the blood returning to the heart.

## The Aging Kidneys

There is also a decrease in kidney function and adaptability with age. It is less able to remove waste products from the blood due to a decrease in the number of kidney cells to 56 per cent of that present in younger years. However, the remaining cells function normally. The blood flow to the kidney is reduced by 50 per cent due to the decreased cardiac output and more importantly due to the increased resistance which is caused in part by cholesterol deposits along the arteries. However, if the old body did not compensate by increasing blood pressure, the flow to the kidneys would be even more impaired. It is important to realize that even though the number of cells in the kidneys is decreased, the remaining kidney cells are not normally overloaded because the total number of cells in the rest of the body is also decreased, thereby decreasing the total production of waste products. This assumes that old cells do not increase production of waste products. Therefore, kidney failure does not result from the attrition of cells due to the aging process, but rather due to some external manipulation or process such as disease which either overloads the kidneys or destroys a critical number of the remaining kidney cells. The younger person can compensate for these stochastic accidents because of the greater reserve capacity of functional kidney cells. The ratio of kidney cells to total body cells is less in the senescent than in the young individual.

## The Endocrines

In addition to the decrease in function of specific organs, there is a decrease in coordination of metabolic processes, or a decrease in the effectiveness and interaction of hormones. This decrease is again exaggerated under stress. For example, there is a decrease in the overall utilization of glucose with age if the individual is subjected to large doses. This is not surprising since the older subject has fewer cells available for glucose utilization even though the production of insulin is not impaired. As a result, there is no increase in fasting blood sugar levels, and blood sugar is elevated in older people only after administration of large amounts of glucose; this, rather than being an aberration is something to be expected. There is also a decrease in adrenal activity which hampers the older person in adapting to a stress situation. This is probably secondary to either a decrease in ACTH, adrenocorticotropic hormone, which is secreted from the pituitary gland and stimulates the adrenals to secrete steroid hormones or to a decreased adrenal response to ACTH.

The basal metabolic rate (BMR) which is an index of total oxygen consumption of the cells (which in turn is an index of the amount of work done by the cells) is decreased in age to 84 per cent of that of a young man. However, there is also a decrease in body water to 82 per cent which is exhibited by the decrease in body weight of individuals as they grow older. This exemplifies the fact that the remaining cells must function 100 per cent normally, for the decrease in BMR approximates the decrease in cells. As mentioned above, this was also true of the kidneys.

Another interesting point governed by the endocrine system is exhibited by the reproductive organs. Women in later years cease to menstruate because the egg cells cease to mature. This is accompanied by a significant decrease in female hormones and pituitary hormone imbalance. However spermatozoa are depleted at a much later age in life, and the cessation of sperm production is not accompanied by a decrease in male hormones.

## The Nervous System

The nervous system is one of the most vulnerable to the aging process for several reasons. The cells of the central nervous system begin to die early in life and are not replaced while other organs are still growing and producing new cells. It also takes a greater length of time in an older person for an impulse to travel across the connections linking nerve fibers (synapses), and therefore specific response to input is delayed. In addition, the nervous system, as the coordinator of body processes, receives input from other parts of the body, and as areas or organs deteriorate, so does their input to the central nervous system, thus exaggerating the existing deterioration.

The main detriment to the nervous system does not occur to the peripheral nerves, but to the brain itself. The decrease in brain weight as represented by cell loss is 44 per cent. This decrease is manifested most noticeably in the area of recent memory, which is in turn correlated with a decrease in electrical activity of the brain or brain waves. We are all familiar with older individuals who relate detailed stories of their childhood but who cannot seem to recall that they have just told one.

Older people who are confronted with tasks requiring both reaction and decision-making responses show an increase in reaction time and an even greater increase in decision making time. This increase in decision time is also correlated with the decrease in the electrical activity of the brain waves. Another interesting point is that blood flow to the brain is decreased by 20 per cent per unit of remaining brain cells. This is not as great a dimunition as occurs in other parts of the body because of compensatory responses which shunt blood to the brain, an all important organ, at the expense of other less vital parts.

## Homeostasis

Another detriment to function in the elderly occurs with homeostatic mechanisms or the ability of the body to restore equilibrium or the normal state once it has been disturbed. This increase in time required for the body to return to normal is the result of a decrease in functional capacity as well as a decrease in the optimal function of the coordinating systems of the body. One example of lowered ability to cope with disturbing elements is manifested by the acid-base balance. Blood is normally slightly on the alkaline side of neutrality. However, strenuous exercise results in excessive acid production, and the acidity increases. The speed of the blood's return to normal is decreased to 17 per cent in the old individual. The reasons for this deficiency are manifold. Already mentioned is the decrement in the ability of the lungs to blow off acid in the form of carbon dioxide with age as well as the decreased kidney function which retards the elimination of acid or hydrogen ions from the blood stream. The integrative systems here play a role of vital importance. When one organ is decreased in function, more stress is put on another organ which is unable to meet the compensatory demands placed upon it. When environmental processes disturb the body so far from equilibrium that homeostasis becomes impossible and the organism can no longer compensate, death occurs.

## Mortality Rates

Because of the decrease in homeostatic and functional capacity, the older subject is prone to an increase in disease and death becomes more likely. Figure 10-3 graphically depicts the increased incidence of mortality with advancing age. However, many older people can adapt well to disease and disturbance of equilibrium. Some individuals at 70 function as well as or in some cases better than others at 30. One should always consider an old person's ability on an individual basis. Too many older people fail to work to maximum capacity solely because they are old. Many perfectly capable individuals retire to their rockers long before they need to, and unfortunately prolonged failure to use a tissue results in wasting or atrophy. Thus, muscles become weak and bones fragile which even further limits the physical activity of sedentary older people.

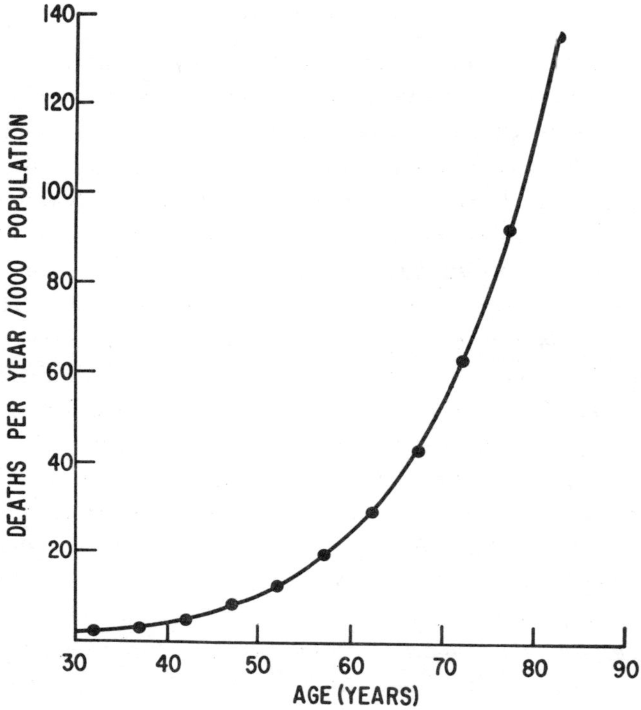


Figure 10-3. Age specific death rate from all causes as a function of age for U. S. males, 1949 (13). (*From* U. S. Atomic Energy Comm., Brookhaven Nat. Lab., *34*: (BNL 854) (T 340), 1-11, Mar. 18, 1964).

## BIOLOGICAL THEORIES OF AGING

Many descriptive aspects of aging have been documented experimentally, but the basic cause or theory of aging is unfortunately more elusive. Although many suggestions have been made, no theory has to date been verified. The exhaustion-accumulation postulate, as the name implies, is dual in nature and maintains either that an essential intracellular substance is exhausted or that a deleterious substance accumulates within the cell. According to the exhaustion part of this hypothesis, the supply of cellular energy might decrease and according to the accumulation portion, the process for detoxification, ridding the cell of its waste products, might become inadequate. There would then, as one aged, be a quantitative accumulation of cellular waste products which would finally become so great that cell function would be inhibited and death would ensue. There is an increase in cellular pigments with age; however, there is no proof that this is the cause of aging or of death.

Another popular subdivision of the exhaustion-accumulation postulate is the eversion hypothesis which states that after molecules are formed some critical intramolecular chemical reaction no longer continues normally. This results in an energy level below that required to maintain cell life, so cellular death ensues. In support of this theory, evidence has been accumulated showing a decrease in the number of enzymes (organic catalysts that increase biochemical reactions within the cell) in old rat cells which do not readily reproduce themselves such as those of heart, muscle, and kidney. Enzymes needed for energy production in the flight muscles of the common housefly also decrease with age.

Compatible with this theory is the increase in stiffness of the older man's lungs, muscles, skin, blood vessels, and heart due to changes in the collagen tissue after the molecules have been formed.

Although one would like to accept the eversion theory, in all fairness, it should be noted that the experiments done to date have been conducted on extracellular proteins, and there are no data available to document such changes within the cell.

Another popular concept is the error hypothesis. According to this view, the cell produces a useless kind of protein by mistake along with normal proteins. In order to supply the body with the necessary kind of protein to sustain life, the cell must increase protein synthesis. When the amount of ineffective protein produced becomes greater than the essential protein, or when ineffective protein reaches a critical level, death ensues. A currently popular variation of the error hypothesis is that desoxyribonucleic acid (DNA) or the genetic material necessary for both reduplication and coding of cellular protein synthesis is programmed with an inherent defect which becomes manifest at some late period in life (senescence) and produces error protein until death ensues. The authors feel that this is doubtful because if DNA were not so rigidly constructed, more genetic abnormalities would occur than do presently.

Life span can be reduced genetically by breeding litter mates. However, this decrease is entirely reversible in the succeeding generation by breeding into outside blood lines.

## PROLONGATION OF LIFE SPAN

Several experimental attempts have been made to increase life span, but to date life has been prolonged by varying only three environmental conditions: temperature, food supply, and the amount of radiation present.

Starvation increases the life span of rotifers, microscopic organisms, as well as rats. Starving prolongs the duration of the egg-laying period of life, but has no effect on the length of senescence.

Decreasing the environmental temperature increases the life span of cold-blooded (poikilothermic) animals but not of warm-blooded animals such as man. For example, the life span of rotifers is increased by decreasing the temperature of the solution in which they live. The decrease in temperature seems to have no effect on the growth period or egg-laying period of the organism. However, the time from the cessation of egg-laying to death, or the period of senescence is increased significantly. Nonlethal doses of radiation can significantly increase the life span of the female fruit fly. This is because reproduction is stopped, and the female has the protein that would ordinarily be used for reproduction on which to live. On the other hand even in the fruit fly, extensive doses of radiation are lethal and in man, radiation is life shortening. However, under any of the extreme methods employed, it would be difficult to vouch for the biological integrity of the organisms used. Prolongation of life does not necessarily imply increased ability to withstand the stresses of a normal environment, nor can these findings be transferred to man to increase health, prosperity or happiness.

## SUMMARY

The one significant generalization of the aging process is the reduction of reserve capacity which results from the loss of individual cells in various organs and tissues of the body. However, although individual organs exhibit decreased capacity, the greatest reduction in function occurs in the most complex organs and in integrative functions. Because of this, homeostasis or the body's ability to readjust to the equilibrium state is reduced with age. Although the aging process is inevitable and part of the normal life cycle, some individuals seem less impaired over the period of years and should be treated in accordance with their capacity. However, it becomes increasingly important to avoid extreme environmental conditions with age.

## REFERENCES


1. Bjorksten, J.: A common molecular basis for the aging syndrome. *J. Amer Geriat Soc, 6*:740-748, 1958.
2. Book, J. A.: Congenital malformations in children of mothers aged 42 and over. *Nature, 181*:1545-1546, 1958.
3. Boothby, W. M.; Berkson, J., and Dunn, H. L.: Studies of the energy metabolism of normal individuals; a standard for basal metabolism with a nomogram for clinical application. *Amer J Physiol, 116*:468-484, 1936.
4. Chvapil, M.: Connective tissue. In *Perspectives in Experimental Gerontology*. Shock, N. W. (Ed.), Springfield, Thomas, 1966, pp. 134-155.
5. Cohn, J. E., and Donoso, H. O.: Mechanical properties of lung in normal men Over 60 years old. *J Clin Invest, 42*:1406-1410, 1963.
6. Curtis, H. J.: The late effects of radiation. *Proc Amer Philosophical Soc, 107*:5-10, 1963.
7. Curtis, H. J.; Tilley, J.; Crowley, C., and Fuller, M.: The role of genetic factors in the aging process. *J Geront, 21*:365-368, 1966.
8. Davies, D. F., and Shock, N. W.: Age changes in glomerular filtration rate, effective renal plasmo flow, and tubular excretory capacity in adult males. *J Clin Invest, 29*:496-507, 1950.
9. Duncan, L. E.; Solomon, D. H.; Rosenberg, E. K.; Nichols, M. P., and Shock, N. W.: The metabolic and hematologic effects of the chronic administration of ACTH to young and old men. *J Geront, 7*: 351-374, 1952.
10. Elden, H. R.: Aging In collagen. In *Perspectives in Experimental Gerontology*. Shock, N. W. (Ed.), Springfield, Thomas, 1966, pp. 212-223.
11. Gregerman, R. I., and Solomon, N.: Acceleration of thyroxine and triiodothyronine turnover during bacterial pulmonary infections and fever; implications for the functional state of the thyroid during stress and in senescence. *J Clin Endocr, 27*:93-105, 1967.
12. Hall, D. A.: Connective tissue—its role in the aging process. In *Perspectives in Experimental Gerontology*. Shock, N. W. (Ed.), Springfield, Thomas, 1966, pp. 125-133.
13. Jones, H. B.: A special consideration of the aging process, disease and life expectancy. In *Advances in Biological and Medical Physics*. Lawrence, J. H., and Tobias, C. A. (Eds.), New York, Academic, 1956, vol. 4, pp. 218-336.

14. Kirk, J. E.: The urinary excretion of neutral 17-ketosteroids in middle aged and old men. *J Geront, 4*:34-38, 1949.
15. Landowne, H.; Brandfonbrener, M., and Shock, N. W.: The relation of age to certain measures of performance of the heart and the circulation. *Circulation, 12*:567-576, 1955.
16. Medvedev, Zh. A.: Erros theories of aging. In *Perspectives in Experimental Gerontology.* Shock, N. W. (Ed.), Illinois, Thomas, 1966, pp. 336-350.
17. Mittman, C.; Edelman, N. H.; Norris, A. H., and Shock, N. W.: The relationship between chest wall and pulmonary compliance and age. *J Appl Physiol, 20*:1211-1216, 1965.
18. Norris, A. H., and Shock, N. W.: Exercise in the adult years—with special reference to the advanced years. In *Science and Medicine of Exercise and Sports.* Johnson, W. R. (Ed.), New York, Harper, 1960, pp. 466-490.
19. Rockstein, M., and Brandt, K.F.: Enzyme changes in flight muscle correlated with aging and flight ability in the male housefly. *Science, 139*: 1049-1051, 1963.
20. Shock, N.W., and Yiengst, M.J.: Experimental displacement of the acid-base equilibrium of the blood in aged males. Abstract. *Fed Proc, 7*:114-115, 1948.
21. Shock, N. W.: The physiology of aging. *Sci Amer, 206*:100-110, 1962.
22. Soloman, D.H., and Shock, N.W.: Studies of adrenal cortical and anterior pituitary function in elderly men. *J Geront, 5*:302-313, 1950.
23. Strehler, B.L.: Origins and comparisons of the effects of time and high energy radiations on living systems. *Quart Rev Biol, 34*:117-142, 1959.
24. Gordon, Tavia: Blood pressure of adults by age and sex; United States, 1960-1962. *Vital & Health Statistics.* U.S. Department of Health, Education, and Welfare, Public Health Service, 1964, Ser. 11, No. 4, pp. 1-40.
25. U. S. Department of Health, Education and Welfare: Weight, height, and selected body dimensions of adults; United States, 1960-1962. *Vital & Health Statistics,* U.S. Department of Health, Education and Welfare, Public Health Service, 1965, Ser. 11, No. 8, pp. 1-44.
26. Verzar, F.: Aging of the Collagen Fiber, In *International Review of Connective Tissue Research.* Hall, D. A. (Ed.), New York Academic, 1964, vol. 2, pp. 243-300.

*Chapter 11*

# HEALTH ASPECTS OF AGING

Austin B. Chinn and Edith G. Robins

In recent years, the subject of health of aged persons has captured the atention of the public as well as health professionals. With attention focused on the pros and cons of Medicare prior to its passage in 1965, and on program development since enactment of this landmark legislation, major concern has been for the needs of the aged who are chronically ill and disabled. Invariably, discussions on health of the aged have centered totally or primarily on problems of the sick-aged; health needs of apparently well-aged persons have received minimal, if any, attention. However, a new trend is emerging. The focus is being broadened to embrace the area of "wellness," as well as "sickness," of the aging and aged, and increasing emphasis is being placed on development of preventive measures to implement this concept.

## CHANGING CONCEPTS OF ILLNESS IN THE LATER YEARS

Facts belie the popularly accepted stereotype of the aged individual. The vast majority of the elderly are not in poor health; they are not significantly dependent; they are not institutionalized. Only 4 per cent are in nursing homes, chronic disease hospitals, homes for the aged, or mental institutions. Some 96 per cent of persons over 65 live in the community and, of this group, 82 per cent are able to carry on the normal activities of daily living. (If you consider only those between 65 and 74, the figure rises to 88 per cent.) Admittedly, many in this age group have physical problems of one sort or another—but they function. *Function* is the key word. The terms *wellness* and *health* as applied to the elderly connote the ability to function with reasonable independence, despite ailments and impairments.

Thus, the great challenge to those in the health professions is not only to care for the sick-aged, but to maintain the health status of the well-aged to the degree our present scientific knowledge will permit.

Chronic disease, long-term illness, and disability comprise the bulk of the health problems of adults in their later maturity. Most prevalent are cardiac, cerebral and arterial disease, mental disorders, cancer, and diseases of the joints. Where these are accompanied by disability or invalidism, they can take a heavy toll of the resources of the patient, the family, and the community.

## New Approach to Chronicity

Stated in terms of "chronic conditions" and "most prevalent diseases," the process of aging would seem to lead inevitably toward debility, dependence, and despair. However, if we look at the aging person in terms of his or her capacity to function physically, mentally, and socially, we see great resources for adaptation, and great potential for independent and happy living.

At the present time very little is known about how to prevent or cure chronic diseases. We do not know how to prevent or cure chronic diseases. We do not know how to prevent atherosclerotic heart diseases or diabetes. We do not know how to prevent arthritis, or cancer, or glaucoma, or a host of other chronic diseases which affect the elderly. However, we have an abundance of knowledge on how to prevent or modify illness and disability resulting from these chronic conditions.

Most medical people believe that early detection of these diseases, followed by prompt provision of proper care, may prevent, postpone, or minimize many of their disabling effects. The population of particular concern in this regard is the 82 per cent of the elderly who are not sick, although many of them may be affected by a chronic condition. The measures to be taken to keep these people from getting sick call for a totally new approach to the traditional pattern of preventive health services.

In any discussion of maintenance of health and prevention of illness, it is important to recognize the basic difference between the terms *disease* and *illness*. Although these terms describe two very different conditions, they frequently and mistakenly are used interchangeably. Disease is a pathologic process which may not necessarily produce obvious symptoms. Indeed, there are few persons beyond middle life who do not have some disease process, although it may not be clearly evident. Sickness or illness is a manifestation of disease, and often it is only when symptoms become evident that the underlying disease process is recognized. For example, an individual may have atherosclerosis with no obvious symptoms of the disease. He thus has a chronic disease without chronic illness. Or he may be subject to hay fever—a chronic sensitivity or disease process—but have no manifestations except during the high pollen count season. It is only then that sickness enters the picture.

## Impairment versus Disability

Two other terms, *disability* and *impairment,* also are frequently used interchangeably despite the fact that they are not synonymous. Disability is the inability of the individual to cope with or adapt to the physical, intellectual, social, and economic demands of his environment. Impairment or handicap is anatomical or functional loss, although such a condition may not necessarily be accompanied by disability. For example, the individual who is blind has a sight impairment. However, if he remains functional, even though he cannot see, his disability is less extensive than the disability of another person with the same impairment who has not been able to make such an adjustment.

The older person with disability vitally needs restorative services to help him hold his own in the world, even if the ultimate goal can be only self care. Without support in his adjustments, he tends to move increasingly into isolation, accelerating the loss of adaptability and capacity to function. A chain reaction occurs: dependency in one category—physical, social, psychological, or economic—leads to dependency in other categories. Fortunately, the chain reaction can work in the other direction. When an elderly patient who was bedfast becomes physically independent, new avenues of social, psychological, and possibly even a certain degree of economic independence are open to him. In other words, success is attaining independence in one sphere can pave the way to independence in other spheres.

A brief review of some of the pertinent facts about the steadily increasing numbers of aged in the population and in the changing health profile of our Nation reveals the broad scope of the total problem.

## Increasing Number of Elderly Persons

Almost one in ten Americans is 65 or older, about nineteen million persons. Census experts predict increases. By 1975 there will be twenty-two million aged—more, if breakthroughs occur in treatment or prevention of cancer and cardiovascular-renal diseases. By 2000, at least thirty million will be 65 or older.

These figures clearly foretell part of the need for comprehensive services to the aged. There is more. People are living more often into the oldest ages. This is not to say that the outermost limits of human lifespan are expanding; more likely it means that more people are approaching the limits as we have known them.

About six million of today's nineteen million aged are over age 75. This one-in-three proportion will grow. By 1980, nine million of the aged will be over 75, and by 2000 more than thirteen million will be at least 75. By then the Nation will have as many people over 75 as it had over 65 in 1950.

## HEALTH STATUS OF THE AGED

The dramatic rise in the number of the old and of the "older" old persons in our population provides only one dimension of the total problem. A great alteration also has occurred in the health profile of persons at all age levels, but particularly among the elderly.

Examination of their health status gives important added perspectives. Many of the acute infectious diseases have been eliminated or drastically reduced. This has come about largely through improved medical treatment coupled with public health measures such as sanitation, quarantine, and immunization. Our successes in this area have insidiously created the newer problem of an increase in chronic degenerative diseases—and it is these disabling diseases that hit hardest at the older population.

An important consideration of the effect of any disease is the limitation of activity imposed by the resulting illness. The National Health Survey reveals that the extent and intensity of physical disabilities associated with chronic disease increase sharply with age, starting with the middle years. While more than half (54%) of the eighty-six million persons in the total population who are affected by one or more chronic conditions are under 45, the prevalence of disability from illness is greatest in the 45-and-older age group. Of those under 45 who have one or more chronic conditions, 14 per cent have some limitation of activity as compared with almost 30 per cent in the 45-to-64-year age group, and over 59 per cent of those 65-and-older.

Only 1 per cent of those under 45 who have one or more chronic conditions are so disabled that they are unable to carry on any major activity, as compared to 4 per cent in the 45-to-64-year age group, and almost 18 per cent in the 65-and-older age group.

### Individual Differences in Illness

While statistics on health status of the aged help us to appreciate the scope of the problem, these do not give the true picture because older people are not alike. Their abilities, attitudes, and problems differ. Bodily changes occur differently and at different times in various individuals; however, these changes do not necessarily impair the efficiency of the body or lead to disease or death. To be sure, there are modifications with aging in the body's resiliency and power of adaptation and in its ability to function well under strain.

Not only does aging proceed at different rates in different individuals, it proceeds at different rates in different systems of the same individual. Manifestations of disease are modified to some extent by old age. People can reach extreme old age, however, in perfect health, with no evidence of earlier disease—provided they began with a favorable genetic endowment and lived in a favorable environment. Many others, however, bear the scars of earlier disease and deprivation.

Aging appears to involve a gradual increase in vulnerability to disease and a diminution of functional reserves. Thus, illness and disability are not caused by aging alone. While we cannot reverse the human aging process, we can deal with specific diseases and their consequences. We can deal with them in terms of prevention, cure, and rehabilitation. We can aim at achieving the maximum function and the maximum physical and social effectiveness of which the individual is capable.

Capabilities, personal needs, health status, attitudes and social conditions vary among the elderly as they do among the young. So, too, is there variety in ability to adjust, adapt, repair, and restore. Although these abilities are modified with age, they are not lost.

## UNIQUE ASPECTS OF HEALTH PROBLEMS OF THE AGED

When the health profile of older persons is compared with that of younger persons, certain factors and differences become apparent.

Qualitatively, there is usually no significant difference in basic illness among the aged as compared to that found among younger age groups. The quantitative differences, however, are great. It is quite common for old people to have more than one disease at a time, and the possible combinations are great. The interactions of these conditions must be understood for the implications to management and treatment.

Other basic differences exist. From a physical standpoint, the elderly have lowered resources, they respond more slowly and to a lesser degree to therapy, and they lack resistance to stress. From a socioeconomic point of view, the lowered income of the elderly affects the amount and kind of health services they receive. Low income is also a reason that a greater proportion of this age group lives in housing that is undesirable from a health standpoint. Psychologically, the elderly do not respond in the same manner as younger persons to community health promotion programs, and they may not understand the need for or may lack the motivation to seek or follow through with rehabilitation or restorative services.

In view of these basic differences, the categorical and general health services programs of communities frequently need modifications in order to meet efficiently the unique health needs of the aging and aged. Moreover, doctors, dentists, nurses, social workers, and representatives of other health and health-related disciplines who are interested in the health of this age group have emphasized the fact that the problems of the elderly will be adequately met only when the health disciplines have been oriented and trained to meet these problems.

## Psychological and Sociological Factors Affecting Health

Total health is so closely interrelated with psychological and sociological aspects of aging that it is impossibe to view physical health as a compartmented entity. An understanding of these interrelationships is essential to all who are concerned with health of the aged.

Economic Insecurity. This is an important consideration. For many Americans, old age is a period of a declining standard of living, often reaching the point of real economic deprivation. Even when extreme poverty is not involved, economic insecurity may affect the self-esteem and position in society of the older person, and this, in turn, can and does have adverse effects on the mental and physical health of the individual.

INACTIVITY OF RETIREMENT. This has serious implications for the aged and for increasing numbers of aging. Growing numbers of persons in their fifties and even in their forties are being displaced in the labor market as a result of automation, and are in the unenviable position of being "too old to work, too young to retire." Our culture provides few sanctioned patterns of work expectations for the transition from middle to old age. Older people who can no longer keep in step with the standards set by the American youth-dominated culture tend to be forced to give up all meaningful participation in the Nation's economic life. Studies indicate that prolonged inactivity has deleterious effects on both mental and physical health; and, conversely, that such a trend can be reversed when programs of meaningful activity are superimposed on such a situation.

The prestige loss that often comes with aging can have a pronounced impact on the health of the individual. This is, of course, psychological, but gives rise to withdrawing and disengagement from the main stream of life. Certainly there have been conspicuous exceptions to the rule in such political, business and scientific leaders as Winston Churchill, Bernard Baruch, or Albert Schweitzer. But, for the most part, these are exceptions and as such must not be permitted to befog the generalization that prestige loss is directly related to other losses such as income and influence, and that self-esteem of the vast majority of the elderly therefore suffers.

Older persons, particularly those residing in urban areas, often become *socially isolated* and lonely. Here again, studies point to the fact that social isolation and loneliness can lead to mental and physical deterioration, and that the process can be reversed when opportunities are provided for meaningful social participation to the limit of individual physical and social capabilities.

PHYSICAL AND MENTAL CAPABILITIES. These generally decrease in old age. For many persons, this process is accompanied by severe psychological shock reactions which are culturally nurtured. It is significant that studies of the aged underscore the fact that some of the physical complaints of older persons reflect more psychological than physical difficulties. It would be a mistake to oversimplify or shut our eyes to the many changes that are a part of the normal aging process. At the same time, it would be a serious mistake to disregard or treat lightly all those factors which affect physical health and well-being in the later years.

Thus, when considering the health status and the health needs of aged persons, the term *health* should be used in the broadest sense—to embrace well-being and the many related factors which bear directly upon health—inasmuch as psychological, sociological, and economic problems that exist or arise independently of or along with physical illness must be considered an intrinsic part of the total health problem.

## HEALTH CARE

Health care of the older population classically may be divided into two general types of service: therapeutic and preventive. Both types are obviously closely related, but for the sake of clarity will be described separately.

### Therapeutic Care

Therapeutic care is required for illness which has already developed in the individual, and is applicable to three very broad and interrelated categories: physical, mental, and social illness.

Physical Illness. Almost all diseases can be seen in the elderly. However, in this age group, certain diseases occur more frequently. The most common diseases are those associated with the circulatory system and arteriosclerosis. Arterial disease is the most frequent cause of cardiac, renal, and neurological problems. The elderly are especially susceptible to acute infections of the respiratory tract, and increasing numbers are affected by emphysema and other chronic lung diseases. Many diseases of the gastrointestinal tract occur, most commonly functional gastrointestinal distress. Cancer is a frequent cause of death in the aged population; often the cancers are of many years' duration.

In concert with the processes that occur as a natural accompaniment of aging, there are important patho-physiological changes which are present more frequently and to a greater degree in the aged person than in the younger person. These changes of disease are classically represented in many forms: changes in the walls of arteries which produce arteriosclerosis; changes in the joint spaces which result in arthritis; or changes in the functioning of certain endocrine glands which cause various disorders such as diabetes. Although such disease processes occur in persons of all ages, it is important to remember that they are more likely to occur in the older person and usually are more severe.

From time to time, these disease processes give rise to clinical signs and symptoms. For example, heart failure or stroke may stem from arteriosclerosis; painful or swollen joints may result from arthritis; and weakness, weight loss, and infection may occur because of diabetes. The older individual beset with a deficit in his functional cell mass reacts to these abnormal states in a manner which is typical of the aged—that is, he demonstrates an inability to compensate or adjust to the stressful situation imposed by illness. In contrast, the younger person has a far greater ability to cope with this kind of stressful situation.

MENTAL ILLNESS. Mental illness may assume the same manifestations in the older person as in the younger, although the underlying or contributing cause more often is organic. Particularly prevalent among the aged are the major psychoses resulting from organic brain injury following strokes and other vascular conditions. Delusions, hallucinations, and other signs of marked brain decompensation are among the outstanding symptoms that occur. At times, a psychosis may manifest itself in an extremely mild form, presenting such symptoms as foregetfulness and confusion. Even mild mental disorder, however, may be disabling to older persons. From a numerical standpoint, the most common mental problem which affects the elderly is caused by a functional minor neurosis, with anxiety either as the sole symptom or associated with depression.

SOCIAL ILLNESS. Many may question the propriety of classifying social illness as a specific illness category. However, in dealing with the health of older persons, one becomes keenly aware of their social problems, and one comes to view these problems as a form of illness—just as surely as heart problems are regarded as physical illness and brain impairment problems as mental illness.

Social disabilities which affect the aged may take many forms, including strained family relationships, lack of status in the community, monetary problems, housing problems, or an occupation incompatible with health status. Decompensation of any of these social aspects of a person's life can be an important cause of his lack of good health.

## MULTIPLICITY OF ILLNESSES AMONG THE ELDERLY

Comprehensiveness in the care of older people is essential not only because older people have different kinds of illnesses or even more severe illnesses than younger people, but rather because almost invariably they have more of these illnesses at the same time. Multiplicity of physical illness probably is related to the lack of resistance to stress referred to earlier. In other words, one major illness lowers resistance sufficiently to allow others to appear. For instance, severe brain injury from a stroke is almost always accompanied by other problems such as urinary tract infection, pulmonary complications, and disturbances in nutrition. Not only are there often multiple physical illnesses in the same person, but along with these there frequently appears some manifestation of mental illness and social illness. For example, and once again using the stroke patient to illustrate a point, this type of patient often suffers from mental confusion, agitation, and delusions, as well as possible social abnormalities such as unsuitable housing and inadequate financial resources.

### Interrelationship of Health Problems

The interrelationship of many of these problems adds to the complexity of the situation. Who can dispute the interdependence of heart disease in an older person and the necessity for him to climb three flights of stairs to get to his room? Or the interdependence of serious structural diseases of the brain and social decompensation?

Obviously, no one person trained in a single profession can possibly bring about solutions to the multiplicity of problems so often presented. In order to meet these many and varied health problems of the individual sick older person, representatives of many professional competencies are necessary.

### Need for Coordination and Collective Action

The only practical approach is through collective action from a group representing a broad range of disciplines. The sick older person may require services from one or more of the following: physicians, dentists, nurses, nutritionists, medical social workers, physical therapists, occupational therapists, vocational counselors, clinical psychologists, and spiritual advisers. The real challenge is to get all these persons working together in a coordinated fashion with a common goal. Coordination should properly be the responsibility of one member of the health team. In most instances, this responsibility falls on the physician, the nurse, or the social worker. Which of the three serves as coordinator is really unimportant; what really matters is that there be coordination.

## The Role of Community Resources

The multidisciplinary focus on the health needs of the older person is only part of the answer. There also must be adequate community resources which enable professional people to carry out the services. There must be suitable and adequately equipped facilities such as hospitals, rehabilitation facilities, nursing homes, and homes for the aged. There must be community programs to provide out-of-institutional care such as visiting nurse services, homemaker services, home care services, nutrition counseling, social services, and friendly visitor services.

The role of community resources underscores the fact that implementation of comprehensiveness in health care for the elderly goes beyond the direct services given by professional personnel. Development and continued support of essential community facilities and resources depend upon interest and support from public-spirited citizens, community leaders, business, labor, religious groups, government, and voluntary and professional organizations.

The essence of comprehensive care for the olderly is development of a mechanism to assure that the older sick person will be in the right place at the right time in order to receive the right services from the right people. This applies to all types of health care, regardless of whether such care assumes the form of (a) treatment of heart failure by proper medication, (b) treatment of a musculoskeletal defect by physical therapy techniques, (c) treatment of a problem with mastication of food by dental services, (d) treatment of a stroke victim at home by visiting nurse service, or (e) treatment of a serious family problem by social counseling. No one single service can suffice to meet the total needs of the individual; *all* phases of poor health in the older person must be attacked.

## Preventive Care—Health Maintenance

Preventive care, or health maintenance, for the older person calls for no less a comprehensive approach than does therapeutic care. One might conservatively say that the necessity for therapeutic care, to some extent at least, is the result of deficits in preventive care. This is in no way meant to imply that all diseases and their accompanying illnesses can be prevented; but it is generally accepted that early detection of chronic diseases, followed by prompt and proper care, can prevent, postpone, or minimize many of the disabling effects of these diseases.

## Essential Preventive Services

To achieve a comprehensive program of preventive care for the elderly, older persons and their families must be made aware of the importance of giving attention to health *before* the onset of serious illness, and adequate numbers of health personnel must be available to provide the essential preventive services. Here, too, a broad range of health professionals is needed.

As in therapeutic care, coordination is all-important. Efforts to prevent a physical disability may be completely nullified by failure to meet a housing problem. Efforts to prevent or alleviate a mental problem may be totally unsuccessful because of failure to meet a problem in disturbed family relationship. Halfway measures or a haphazard approach will not suffice; the total problem can be resolved only by attacking it on a broad front with a broad range of professional personnel and community resources.

This calls for the expenditure of much time, effort, and money. It requires a basic change in attitudes and concepts—an acceptance of the fact that chronic illness and disability are *not* inevitable by-products of aging. A positive feeling about health maintenance and the potential of restorative services for the elderly must be instilled in all concerned—the aging, their families, and all health practitioners who serve the aged. Education is the key.

Health practitioners can play an important role in educating the elderly person on measures he can take to protect his health. Responsibility for implementation, however, rests with the individual.

Accidents represent one of the greatest threats to the aged who are well. Accidents are the third most frequent cause of death among aged males, the fifth among aged females. For every fatal accident there are probably two hundred nonfatal but disabling accidents.

The automobile is the No. 1 villain—not to drivers but to the aged pedestrian. The second most common type of accident is falls, 60 per cent of which occur in the home, most frequently falling down stairs. Burns rank third, especially frequent among women.

## Effects of Physical Age Changes

The risk of accidents among the elderly is increased by such general physical changes as impaired vision and hearing, loss of the sense of smell, and slower reflexes. Older persons should be made aware of the possible effects of these physical changes and of their own specific limitations.

Climate is not significant in the maintenance of good health or on the process of aging. To be sure, certain conditions — respiratory diseases, for example—are less prevalent in warm climates; arthritics often feel more comfortable in warm places. Nevertheless, older persons do quite well in colder climates. In fact, contrary to popular belief, the states with the highest percentages of 65-and-over residents are such northeastern states as Vermont and Maine, such midwestern states as Iowa and Missouri. The older person should understand that with appropriate clothing and proper heating and ventilation of the home, he can live anywhere.

Although climate may not be a decisive factor in health of all the aged, it is true that as the body ages, it loses some of its ability to adjust to extreme temperature variations in the environment. Elderly persons should be advised to protect themselves against extreme heat (which upsets normal fluid and mineral balance), extreme cold (which causes narrowing of blood vessels and may therefore put a greater strain on the heart), extreme dampness (with its higher incidence of upper respiratory infections), and overexposure to sun, heavy winds, or any other extreme of weather (among other reasons, in the case of sun, to keep a healthier, less wrinkled, more attractive skin).

## The Vital Role of Mobility in the Later Years

Mobility—the ability to get about—is basically important to the older adult's independence and feelings of self-esteem. It has a very direct bearing on his physical health. Mobility is essential to the business of daily living—such as shopping, visiting a clinic or one's physician, taking care of one's business and other activities. Mobility is essential to maintaining one's relationship with family and friends. Mobility makes possible new interests and activities, and therefore adds zest to living.

### NUTRITION AND HEALTH

It will hearten the aging person to know that if his food habits are basically sound, little change in diet is necessary in later years. It may be necessary to change shopping habits to adjust to a smaller family, or learn how to prepare appetizing menus for two persons, or only one. But the kinds of foods one eats need not change with age. Nor is it necessary to have vitamin pills, if a balanced diet is maintained. Thus, vitamin purchases generally are an unnecessary burden on the incomes of the elderly.

Digestive processes slow down, and older persons should be encouraged to adjust meal size and frequency. They may find that small frequent meals are better than the customary two or three large meals a day. Where necessary, older persons should be advised to reduce caloric intake to a level consistent with the degree of activity. A suggested optimal weight is the same as one's weight at age 25; there should not be any marked increase. The criterion for caloric adequacy should be an intake which maintains optimal weight. Fasting or drastic dietary restriction is not desirable.

Undernutrition may be responsible for the older person's complaints of general weakness, irritability and other psychological symptoms. Specific food deficiencies lie principally in an inadequate intake of protein and calcium, and in an inadequate supply of essential vitamins. Sometimes these deficiencies are a consequence of reduced income and the resultant increased proportion of carbohydrates (usually cheaper than meats) in the diet. They may result also from poor cooking and eating habits.

Eating is very important to older persons. It should be enjoyed.

The older individual who lives alone should be encouraged to invite a friend or relative to dinner as often as is feasible, so that eating becomes a social occasion. Anything else that adds to the pleasure of eating should be encouraged—for example, the use in moderation of spices, coffee or tea, wine or other alcoholic beverages.

Eating and food intake are closely entwined with emotions and moods. Thus when a person is tense, he may overeat. Or the angry or hurt elderly person may eat very little, expressing his protest through a sort of self-imposed starvation. Emotional good health is important to good eating and adequate sustenance; good eating and adequate sustenance are important to emotional good health.

Personal health habits are developed early in life and generally do not change as one ages. Health education and group experiences can be used to encourage personal habits which contribute to well-being. Individuals can modify their mode of living and, in turn, affect positively their total adjustment to aging.

## Periodic Health Appraisal and Counseling

Essential to good health are a continuing relationship with a personal physician and a regular program of physical examinations and disease detection. All health practitioners should remind the elderly of this fundamental need. When periodic health appraisal and counseling and guidance are utilized as protective measures, it is possible to view the physical, mental, and social health of older people in a far more positive sense. These measures can be looked upon as the maintenance of wellness rather than the treatment of sickness.

How much can be done to control or manage a chronic disease is dependent in a large measure upon how soon after onset it is detected. Chronic diseases often begin in the young middle years, during the thirties and forties. They develop insidiously, at first showing no obvious symptoms. When symptoms start to appear, they are often confused with the minor aches and pains of advancing years.

The real threat lies in the fact that when these diseases are permitted to develop unchecked, they can be cripplers. The real hope lies in the fact that much knowledge is available to assist in their control if they are detected and treated at an early stage. Fortunately, laboratory tests and diagnostic procedures are available which will assist the physician in the detection of many chronic diseases in their pre-clinical stages.

## Pre-Clinical Approach to Disease Detection

It is estimated that as many as 25 per cent of the nation's adults currently are afflicted with heart disease. The electrocardiogram is an important clinical diagnostic tool to demonstrate subtle abnormalities that may indicate a developing serious heart condition.

The chest x-ray is commonly associated with examining for tuberculosis. But such an x-ray is valuable also in detection of lung cancer, and of changes in the size and shape of the heart and large blood vessels in the chest cavity, changes in the mediastinum, and changes in the bony structure of the chest.

Another test measures changes in pulmonary function, often indicative of early chronic bronchitis and pulmonary emphysema—diseases especially prevalent among cigarette smokers over 45.

The tonometer is a simple instrument that quickly indicates abnormal intraocular pressure, the earliest sign of glaucoma—a disease which is the second leading cause of blindness and hits hardest at persons over 40. Blindness caused by glaucoma usually can be prevented if the disease is detected early and treated promptly. Yet it is estimated that there are well over a million undiscovered cases of glaucoma in the population today.

Diabetes is another disease which can be identified early in its course and usually controlled to prevent some of the serious complications. Screening for possible diabetes simply involves testing of a small sample of blood. It is estimated that there are approximately two million cases of undetected diabetes in the population, primarily adults.

Still another simple, rapid, and effective test is the Papanicolaou smear to detect cancer of the uterine cervix. These cancers, when discovered before they become invasive, are almost always curable. Yet approximately ten thousand women each year die of cervical cancer detected too late.

The development of automated, computerized screening techniques for the early detection of chronic diseases, utilizing recent advances in medical technology, represents an important step forward in the practice of preventive medicine for the aging and aged population. Automated medical screening provides a mechanism by which a self-administered medical history is combined with selected physiological measurements and laboratory tests to obtain a health profile of the individual. Generally this is completed prior to a visit to the physician, and thus saves the physician's time in establishing a diagnosis or in determining a state of wellness.

There is a significant difference between the new technology and the traditional screening programs carried out in the past. Historically, each laboratory test in a disease-detection program was designed to assist the physician in determining whether or not an individual was likely to have a specific disease process. In contrast, the health assessment techniques which recently have been developed go several important steps further. In addition to providing specific tests for specific diseases, it now is possible through the use of automated equipment and computers to collect from each individual a broad range of physiologic measurements and pertinent psychological and sociological information.

These data should aid the practicing physician by indicating first the probability of the presence of one or more chronic disease conditions which the physician would want to clarify by more definitive diagnostic procedures. Secondly, when health appraisal is carried out periodically, the physician can observe changes taking place over a period of time. For example, he is able to observe gradually-changing blood chemistry levels or progressive increases of pressure in the eye. These may provide patterns essential to the early detection of diseases which otherwise could not be diagnosed with certainty until they became fully developed.

Multiphasic screening of the asymptomatic or "well" population offers the opportunity for early detection of disease, for establishing a baseline health information pattern of the individual, for a study of the natural history of disease, for health education, and for a way of getting people into the mainstream of medical resources systems to minimize the disabling effects of disease and restrain the cost of health care.

In the basic development of these techniques, a significant step forward was taken a few years ago when the United States Public Health

Service provided research and development support to the periodic health appraisal program being conducted by the Kaiser Permanente Health Foundation in California. In essence, this program is an updated version of the traditional disease detection tests, streamlined and coordinated, and with many special features. Using a battery of automated procedures with built-in computer analysis and readout results, the multitest laboratory completes in less than three hours clinical tests and health history that would require much greater time by conventional methods. Thoroughness, speed, accuracy, and economy of money and personnel time, particularly physician time, are special features of this approach.

### Model Adult Health Maintenance Centers

The Public Health Service has provided support for the creation of four model Adult Health Maintenance Centers which will utilize the automated equipment and computer techniques for health testing developed at Kaiser Permanente.

These four centers are not intended to determine the feasibility of the "technology" or "machinery" for such services — this has been amply shown in the Kaiser Permanente and other programs. The main purpose of the demonstrations is to determine how automated health screening programs can be integrated most effectively into a community's complex medical care structure. In each community, work is being carried on in close collaboration with the state and local health departments and with local medical societies. In each program, emphasis is being given to the development of techniques and methods to be employed in motivating and recruiting participants for the health appraisal service, as well as other behavioural and educational factors.

## APPROACH TO NEEDS OF WELL OLDER ADULTS

The well-aging need protection against infectious diseases as do any other members of the community. In general, infectious diseases involve a greater threat of serious morbidity or mortality among the aged than they do in younger age groups.

In considering immunizations for the aging population, it is important to differentiate among those diseases for which the aging are likely to have had earlier protection; those for which immunity may have waned but which are no longer crucial, such as measles or mumps; and those which deserve continuing attention, such as smallpox, diphtheria, tetanus, poliomyelitis, and influenza.

Age per se is no contraindication to any immunization. Age may actually be a strong indication. However, the physician must take into account the individual needs and tolerances as determined by his knowledge of the vaccine end of his patient. For this reason, the private physician or a special geriatric clinic is preferred to the routine immunization clinics where programs are handled on a mass or standardized basis.

Retirees are engaging increasingly in foreign travel; immunizations should be brought up to date. It is important to begin these programs well in advance, so that small, repeated doses of one agent at a time may be given. This will minimize reactions to the multiple inoculations necessitated by last-minute rush. This is undesirable at any age, and particularly so for the aged.

The following immunizations should be given attention:

SMALLPOX. Vaccinations should be repeated throughout life at intervals of five to ten years. Those traveling abroad should be vaccinated every one to three years. Those with a known exposure to smallpox should be vaccinated immediately. Vaccination scars never should be considered as evidence of current immunity, nor should the physician take the patient's word about having had the disease.

DIPHTHERIA. If exposed, the elderly can get the disease; therefore, immunization should be done. Because of possible severe reactions, toxoids should be administered in small doses over a period of weeks.

TETANUS. This still has a high mortality rate, especially in the over-40 age group. Immunization is particularly important for retired persons who engage in "do-it-yourself" activities and gardening. Booster doses should be given at five-year intervals, and immediately after occurrence of a tetanus-prone wound. The physician should consider use of tetanus antitoxin of human origin (immune globulin) which is devoid of the hazards of horse serum.

POLIOMYELITIS. This is still a hazard to the adult. Complete vaccination is recommended using all three types of polio vaccine, even for patients who have had a diagnosed case of one type earlier in life.

Oral vaccine is preferable. It should be administered directly on the tongue, as the elderly patient may break teeth or dentures, may gag or choke on a sugar cube.

INFLUENZA. Flu hits harder at the elderly than at other age groups. Annual immunization is recommended, early each fall, in advance of any epidemic. Should an epidemic occur late in the season, or be prolonged, a booster dose given six months after the first one may be advisable to assure a high level of protection.

GAMMA GLOBULIN. This should be considered for the prevention of infectious hepatitis.

## Health Protection and the Community

The goal of practitioners is to help the individual maintain and improve his health. The community's responsibility is to provide the range of coordinated services that support this goal.

Types of activities that could be included in a community's health maintenance program for the aged are as follows:

1. Diagnostic centers.
2. Geriatric hospital facilities, including daytime nonresident care.
3. Hospitals with ambulatory and home-care programs.
4. Nursing and convalescent homes.
5. Visiting nurse programs.
6. Programs lending hospital equipment for home use.
7. Vocational rehabilitation and counseling services.
8. Physical rehabilitation units.
9. Homemaker, friendly visitor, home-delivered meals, and other home services.
10. Housing projects and placement facilities, including listing of good quality foster homes, nursing homes, and a variety of public and private dwellings.
11. Programs for financial assistance, income maintenance, and employment opportunities.
12. Information and referral services that tell the individual where to obtain legal, family, recreation, and welfare help.
13. Counseling services in mental health and family needs.
14. Leisure time facilities and programs.
15. Public health clinics and other facilities offering health infor-

mation, screening and immunization programs, and safety and accident prevention programs.

## Community Leadership Planning

The community can be particularly effective in activities relating to health education, safety and accident prevention, and multiple screening efforts.

In developing health education programs, practitioners and other community leaders should define the important information to be communicated, such as nutrition, first aid, safety, and where to go for health assistance. The content of the health education program should be evaluated in terms of the audience. Do the elderly need a lot or a little information on certain points? Is the material prepared so as to be easily understood?

It is essential to evaluate in advance what the follow-through needs may be. For example, if an education effort is successful in informing and motivating the audience to obtain health examinations, will these be available in a convenient place and at a price they can afford?

The most effective ways of reaching the elderly must be determined. For example, union groups, nationality groups, churches, and community and neighborhood centers can be effective channels.

In safety and accident prevention, a community should review—from the standpoint of the characteristics of the aging—whether its housing and building codes provide for maximum safety and are thoroughly enforced. Traffic hazards should be eliminated. Public transportation can be improved by making routes and stops easily accessible to the elderly. Driver-education programs in high schools can emphasize consideration for the elderly driver and pedestrian.

For the early detection of chronic illnesses—such as glaucoma, diabetes, and cervical and uterine cancer—multiple screening examinations can be effective, rapid, and economical. The examinations can provide an opportunity for influencing the individual's attitude toward health.

Effective planning is needed to avoid limitations and deficiencies of multiple screening efforts. Programs have been fragmented and isolated, have met resistance from physicians (who often are omitted in planning), have been ineffectual in encouraging periodic health examinations by a private physician or clinic, and often have been oblivious to the personality, attitudes, and socioeconomic status of the older person.

Announcing a multiple screening effort is not enough. The older person must be motivated to come. Health education efforts by personal contact and group work may be necessary. In addition, the effectiveness of multiple screening examinations to health maintenance can be enhanced by the well-aging conference. Here, a physician will look over the screening tests and a medical history, listen to the individual, and then give advice. Further, physicians of the community should be encouraged to use screening tests prior to physical examination. This may involve them more in health maintenance of the well-aging.

Thus, periodic multiple screening examinations, combined with meaningful medical conferences and physical examinations, can help maintain the well older individual.

## CONCLUSION

Increased longevity and the enlarging aging population confront society with many difficult problems. Certain generalizations can be made in attempting to find effective solutions. In considering the health of the aged, increased emphasis should be given to the terms *health* and *wellness,* and greater attention directed at activities which protect and maintain the health of the elderly. Complicating the total problem is the prevailing attitude toward the abilities and potentials of the elderly from the standpoint of health and social worth. Health practitioners should gain understanding about the changes inherent in the aging process and the unique health needs of the aging and aged.

A vital first step in approaching the total problem is a comprehensive program of education for all concerned with the health and well-being of our older citizens. Understanding can lead the way to action. All of us—young and old, rich and poor—can reap the benefits, providing we live long enough. And, according to statistics, the majority of us will!

## REFERENCES

Birren, James E.: *The Psychology of Aging.* Englewood Cliffs, Prentice-Hall, 1964.

Blumenthal, Herman T. (Ed.): *Medical and Clinical Aspects of Aging.* New York, Columbia, 1962.

Bortz, Edward L. (Forum Chairman): *Positive Health of Older People.* 1960 Health Forum of the National Health Council Proceedings, National Health Council, 1790 Broadway, New York, New York, 1960.

Burgess, Ernest W. (Ed.): *Aging in Western Societies.* Chicago, U. of Chicago, 1960.

Dasco, Michael M.: *Restorative Medicine in Geriatrics.* Springfield, Thomas, 1963.

*The Dilemma of a Social Role for the Aging.* Brandeis University Papers in Social Welfare, No. 8, Waltham, Massachusetts, 1965.

*Five Hundred Over Sixty.* New York, Russel Sage, 1956.

Howell, Trevor H.: *A Student's Guide to Geriatrics.* London, Staples, 1963.

Kastenbaum, Robert: *New Thoughts on Old Age.* New York, Springer, 1964.

Tibbitts, Clark (Ed.): *Social and Psychological Aspects of Aging.* New York, Columbia, 1962.

Tibbitts, Clark, and Donahue, Wilma: *Aging in Today's Society.* Englewood Cliffs, Prentice-Hall, 1960.

# PART V

# BASIC NEEDS OF PEOPLE

*Chapter 12*

# NUTRITION OF THE AGED

MARGARET O. OSBORN

A growing sense of responsibility for the 9.3 per cent of the population of the United States who are 65 years and older has been shown by the immeasurable investments of time and energy that have gone into research seeking answers to the problems of man's health and well-being as influenced by his food.[1] Much of the early research concerned itself with causes of nutritional deficiency diseases, food sources of the various nutrients and man's requirements for these nutrients. The science of nutrition is relatively new compared to many other sciences, but its role as an important factor contributing to health is well recognized. The results of good nutrition are not dramatic and are not achieved overnight, but a life time of good eating habits has contributed to the vigor and well-being of many of the healthly elderly today.

## DIETARY SURVEYS

The nutritional status of the aged has been studied by dietary intake, biochemical and clinical examinations either singly or in combination. Dietary intake information often obtained through an interview has been evaluated in terms of nutrient intake or by use of food groups.

One of the findings of dietary surveys has been the general trend toward a decrease of energy intake with age and often a decrease in nutrient intake.

One of the most comprehensive studies of the nutrition of older people in the United States was the cooperative regional project "Nutritional Status and Dietary Needs of Population Groups." In this study, 2800 women and 250 men were surveyed. Batchelder in summarizing the study reported that many people with low energy intakes also were consuming diets with low amounts of nutrients.[2] In the

North Central Region, Ohlson *et al.* found that not only calories but also protein and phosphorus were reduced in each successive decade and the intake of each nutrient was highly correlated with intake of calories.[3, 4] In Iowa, the average energy value of women 70 years of age and over as reported by Swanson *et al.* was 1440 calories per day as compared to 1740 calories for women of all ages 30 years and over. The average protein intakes for the group of 70 and over age group was 44 gms with calcium 0.4 gm.[5]

An aging population in San Mateo County, California, has been studied over a period of fourteen years. The original study was part of the "Nutritional Status" survey. The last report showed that food intake decreased with increasing age and while there was a reduction in nutrient intake, few subjects consumed nutrients in amounts significantly lower than recommended. About one-fourth consumed two-thirds the recommended level for calcium and niacin. The ascorbic acid and vitamin A were low in at least one of the years studied. Another finding of interest was the fact that although 35 per cent used vitamin or mineral supplements, they were usually taken by persons with adequate food nutrient intakes. Also approximately 30 per cent were 10 per cent or more overweight.[6]

A nationwide survey of food consumption in 1955 conducted by the U.S. Department of Agriculture revealed that the use of meat items, poultry, fish and commercially frozen vegetables declined in persons aged 60 and over compared to younger age groups, and the use of fats, oils, and salad dressings was lower in homes with older homemakers.[7]

Other studies reveal similar findings. Jordon *et al.* evaluated the diets of seventy-six women and twenty-four men, 65 years or older using a check list. They found the outstanding lack was yellow and leafy green vegetables. Also dairy products and citrus fruits were excluded more frequently than desirable.[8] In Nebraska, Fry and coworkers reported decreased nutrient intakes with increasing age, particularly calcium, iron and riboflavin.[9] In Boston, one-fourth of those interviewed were found to be consuming less than 75 per cent of the recommended allowances for calories, riboflavin, iron and ascorbic acid. Milk or its equivalent were the foods most often slighted by both men and women.[10]

In a study of predominantly low-income households in Rochester, New York, with one or more individuals 65 years of age or over it was found that about one-fourth of the households had food supplies that furnished less than two-thirds of the recommended allowances of one or more of eight nutrients studied. Calcium and ascorbic acid were the two nutrients in shortest supply.[11] Similar findings regarding these nutrients were reported in a study in Washington State.[12]

Changes in living circumstances frequently change food habits of the aging. Davidson *et al.* reported that many people had reduced their usual intake of milk, eggs, meat and fish because of changed circumstances of living related to aging. Many had low intakes of protein, the B-complex vitamins and ascorbic acid as measured by "Recommended Dietary Allowances" of the Food and Nutrition Board.[13]

The dietary intake of institutionalized older subjects has been studied by Rafsky and Newman along with laboratory analyses of the vitamins and minerals in the food. They found lowered serum levels for some nutrients but concluded, "We must look elsewhere than an inadequate diet for the explanation of 'biochemical avitaminosis' which exists in normal aged individuals." [14]

Several studies have been reported outside the United States. In London, Pyke reported that elderly women in his survey in 1947 consumed 1034 to 2313 and elderly men 1903 to 2273 calories. The amounts of vitamin A and ascorbic acid consumed by many of the subjects were small but calcium and iron appeared to be reasonably adequate.[15] Also in England, Bransby found vitamin A intakes of women to be lower than standards set by the British Medical Association for the adult.[16] In a more recent British study, findings showed a reduction in caloric intake with age associated with a general reduction in food intake.[17]

In Jerusalem, vitamins A and C were found to be low in diets of older people living in their own homes. The total food consumption was low with men living alone consuming less fruits and vegetables than men living with their spouses.[18]

## SUMMARY

Energy and nutrients of the diets of elderly living in the United

TABLE XVIII

NUTRIENTS PER DAY IN THE DIET OF ELDERLY PEOPLE LIVING IN THE UNITED STATES

(expressed as averages unless indicated as range)

| *Subjects* | *Region* | *Age* yrs. | *Sex* | *Calories* gms | *Protein* gms | *Calcium* gms | *Iron* mg | *Vitamin A* I.U. | *Thiamine* mg | *Riboflavin* mg | *Niacin* mg | *Ascorbic Acid* mg | *Year Reported* | *Reference Number* |
|---|---|---|---|---|---|---|---|---|---|---|---|---|---|---|
| 44 | New York | 67-88 | M | 1710-2008 | 77.4-85.2 | | 6.9 | 6,933* | .81 | 1.26 | 10.2 | 44 | 1948[a] | 14 |
| 21 | | 68-88 | F | 1604-2260 | 66.6-97.4 | | 6.9 | 2.433† | .81 | 1.26 | 10.2 | 44 | 1948[b] | 3 |
| 10 | Iowa and | 40-70 | F | 1824 | 61.0 | .93 | | 6,933* | | | | | | |
| 54 | Michigan | | F | 1658 | 56.0 | .65 | | 2,433† | | | | | | |
| 22 | | | F | 1464 | 48.0 | .56 | | | | | | | | |
| 6 | | | F | 1786 | 56.0 | .59 | | | | | | | | |
| 8 | | | F | 1122 | 41.0 | .41 | | | | | | | | |
| 40 | North | 50-59 | F | | 62.0[c] | .83 | | | | | | | 1952[d] | 19 |
| 25 | Central | 60-69 | F | | 57.0 | .82 | | | | | | | | |
| 11 | | 70-79 | F | | 50.9 | .65 | | | | | | | | |
| 1 | | 80-89 | F | | 56.7 | .98 | | | | | | | | |
| 170 | Iowa | 60-69 | F | 1700 | 55.0 | .50 | | | | | | | 1955 | 5 |
| | | 70 & over | F | 1440 | 44.0 | .40 | | | | | | | | |
| 232 | California | 50-75 + | M | | | | | | | | | 99 | 1955[e] | 20 |
| 293 | | 50-75 + | F | | | | | | | | | 86 | 1955[f] | 21 |
| 40 | | 50-54 | M | 2613 | 92 | | 15 | | | | | | | |
| 45 | California | 50-54 | F | 1817 | 60 | | 10 | | | | | | | |
| 39 | | 55-59 | M | 2624 | 95 | | 16 | | | | | | | |
| 50 | | 55-59 | F | 1742 | 62 | | 11 | | | | | | | |
| 34 | | 60-64 | M | 2504 | 89 | | 15 | | | | | | | |
| 55 | | 60-64 | F | 1786 | 62 | | 11 | | | | | | | |
| 38 | | 65-69 | M | 2370 | 80 | | 14 | | | | | | | |
| 51 | | 65-69 | F | 1815 | 64 | | 11 | | | | | | | |
| 33 | | 70-74 | M | 2138 | 76 | | 13 | | | | | | | |

| | | | | | | | | | | | | | | |
|---|---|---|---|---|---|---|---|---|---|---|---|---|---|---|
| 37 | | 70-74 | F | 1685 | 65 | | 11 | | | | | | | |
| 16 | | 75-79 | M | 2160 | 77 | | 15 | | | | | | | |
| 24 | | 75-79 | F | 1514 | 53 | | 9 | | | | | | 1955[e] | |
| 15 | | 80 & over | M | 2223 | 75 | | 13 | | | | | | | |
| 12 | | 80+ | F | 1426 | 47 | | 9 | | | | | | | |
| 100 | Boston | 65+ | M | 2458 | 87.6 | 1.06 | 13.5 | 10,973 | 1.29 | 2.0 | 15.69 | 105 | 1956[g] | 10 |
| | | | F | 1831 | 65.8 | 0.87 | 10.0 | 8,571 | 0.94 | 1.58 | 11.60 | 95 | | |
| 39 | Michigan | 40-85 | F | 1802 | 58 | 0.53 | 1.01 | 4,433 | 0.93 | 1.26 | | 53 | 1957[f] | 22 |
| 28 | | 40-85 | F | 1179 | 44 | 0.37 | 0.82 | 4,493 | 0.67 | 0.89 | | 42 | | |
| 40 | Boston | 70.9 | F* | | | | | 7,538 | 1.12 | 1.75 | 13.13 | 80 | 1962[h] | 13 |
| 60 | | 68.4 | F† | | | | | 10,912 | 1.18 | 2.11 | 13.61 | 132 | | |
| 32 | Nebraska | 65-80 | F | 1669 | 66.1 | 0.81 | 10.1 | 4,885 | 1.1 | 1.68 | 21.4[i] | 102 | 1963[j] | 9 |
| 11 | Iowa | 39-59 | M | 2375 | 106.3 | .78 | 15.1 | 6,798 | 1.5 | 1.78 | 18.8 | 90 | 1963[k] | 23 |
| 22 | | 40-69 | F | 1917 | 79.8 | .76 | 11.8 | 8,123 | 1.1 | 1.55 | 14.5 | 75 | | |
| 98 | California | 50+ | M | 2075 | 76 | 0.8 | 12 | 7,961 | 1.1 | 1.7 | 14. | 82 | 1965[l] | 6 |
| 131 | | 50+ | F | 1605 | 62 | 0.6 | 10 | 8,065 | 0.9 | 1.4 | 12. | 90 | | |

*Carotene.

93†Vitamin A.

[a]Vitamin and mineral values are averages of analyzed data; institutionalized subjects were interviewed.

[b]86 white and 14 negro; all active living in own homes; all economically independent.

[c]Calculated from nitrogen data (n x 6.25).

[d]Active, living in own homes; middle and low socioeconomic but not indigent; self-selected diets; menus of food samples for analysis.

[e]Lived in own homes.

*Averages of subjects who scored lowest in food faddism.

†Averages of subjects who scored highest in food faddism.

[f]Data obtained from 3 to 7 day food intake records; some subjects lived in own homes, others in county homes.

[g]Low to moderate economic level; data obtained by interview.

[h]Interviewed healthy middle class subjects.

[i]Niacin equivalents.

[j]Seven day dietary records and weighed food intake records; subjects lived in own homes.

[k]Dietary pattern obtained at two different seasons by interview.

[l]Subjects lived in same area as 1955 California studies.

States are shown in Table XVIII. A review of the studies reveals that nutrient intakes do not always meet suggested levels when evaluated in terms of the "Recommended Daily Allowances." The general trend toward a decrease of energy intake appears to be a common finding. However, many of the studies, in which clinical evaluations were also made, revealed that overweight was often a problem, suggesting caloric intakes were higher than required.

Calcium and ascorbic acid were nutrients frequently below recommended levels. This reflects the fact that milk, fruits and vegetables were frequently used in lesser amounts than desirable.

## NUTRIENT REQUIREMENTS OF THE ELDERLY

Since 1940, the Food and Nutrition Board of the National Research Council, National Academy of Sciences, has developed and published recommendations of daily nutrient intakes judged to be adequate for maintenance of the nutrition of people of the United States including elderly persons.[24] (Table XIX.) The allowances afford a margin of safety to cover variations among individuals. The Food and Drug Administration has established "Minimum Daily Requirements," for certain vitamins and minerals, which were developed for the purpose

TABLE XIX

NATIONAL RESEARCH COUNCIL RECOMMENDED DAILY DIETARY ALLOWANCES FOR MEN AND WOMEN 55 TO 75+ YEARS, 1968

| *Energy and Nutrients* | *Men* | *Women* |
|---|---|---|
| Weight | 70 kg (154 lbs.) | 58 kg (128 lbs.) |
| Height | 171 cm (67 in.) | 157 cm (62 in.) |
| K calories | 2400 | 1700 |
| Protein, gm | 65 | 55 |
| Vitamin A, I.U. | 5000 | 5000 |
| Vitamin E, I.U. | 30 | 25 |
| Ascorbic acid, mg | 60 | 55 |
| Folacin, mg | 0.4 | 0.4 |
| Niacin, mg equiv. | 14 | 10 |
| Riboflavin, mg | 1.7 | 1.5 |
| Thiamine, mg | 1.2 | 0.9 |
| Vitamin $B_6$, mg | 2.0 | 2.0 |
| Vitamin $B_{12}$, mcg | 6 | 6 |
| Calcium, gm | 0.8 | 0.8 |
| Phosphorus, gm | 0.8 | 0.8 |
| Iodine, mcg | 110 | 80 |
| Iron, mg | 10 | 10 |
| Magnesium, mg | 350 | 300 |

of labeling food and should not be confused with recommendations of the Food and Nutrition Board.[25]

## Energy Requirements

Energy requirements decline progressively after the years of early childhood. It has been well established that metabolic rate declines with age after maturity as expressed in calories per square meter of body surface per hour.[26] Reduction in physical activity is also associated with advancing age.

Durnin studied the difference in energy expenditure of young and older men. He found highly significant differences between the two groups in treadmill exercises and suggested that the higher rates of energy output by the older men were due in part to their greater weight. However, he believes walking involves coordination of joints and control of balance and these may be less perfectly regulated in the elderly than in the young.[27]

## Fat

There is insufficient evidence for the Food and Nutrition Board to make decisions as to desirable amounts of fats or fatty acids for persons of any age. Gillum found that dietary fat and cholesterol were positively associated with serum cholesterol with different patterns in older men and women.[28] Dietary substitution of fats rich in polyunsaturated fatty acids for saturated fats can induce a lowering of plasma cholesterol in a large percentage of individuals.[29]

Interest in the relationship between diet and blood lipids has stimulated experiments such as those conducted in New York and Chicago in which attempts were made to limit animal protein and fat and increase the ratio of polyunsaturated to saturated fatty acids.[30] However, conclusions with regard to the relationship of fat intake to human atherosclerosis have not been determined. Considering that obesity is a problem in many late middle-aged individuals, moderate reduction in total fat may be beneficial.

## Protein Requirements

Studies of protein requirements are conducted usually by one of three approaches: (1) determination of amount of protein required to maintain nitrogen balance, (2) determination of the amount of an essential amino acid required to maintain nitrogen balance in subjects receiving an otherwise adequate diet, and (3) estimation of losses of nitrogen that must be replaced by dietary protein. It is also necessary to correct any values because of variation of individual requirements and the quality of protein and hence its utilization.

The literature of the subject of protein requirements for the elderly is in conflict with advocates for both high and moderate intakes. An extensive study was carried out in 1952 by five north central agricultural experiment stations using as subjects 136 women ages 30 to 85 years in which balance periods lasted seven to ten days. The average nitrogen intakes for the various decades ranged from 9 to 11 gm daily. The protein intake was correlated with the intake of calories with approximately eighteen hundred calories per day being required to maintain nitrogen equilibrium.[32] In this study, considerable individual variation was found. The authors concluded that, "The present recommended allowances for nitrogen are not excessive for aging adult women under the conditions of the self-chosen diets described in this paper."

The work of Tuttle suggests that the efficiency of protein utilization may decrease with age and requirements may increase.[33, 34] He fed five healthy males ranging in age from 52 to 68 years a mixture of the natural form of the essential amino acids. All subjects were in positive nitrogen balance on the natural diets but in negative balance when a basic amino acid mixture was substituted. When the basic amino acid mixture was doubled, all subjects attained nitrogen equilibrium. This study also confirmed the need for calories to support nitrogen equilibrium. In further studies, Kountz reported nitrogen balances on a number of older people and found 1 gm protein per kg body weight was required for equilibrium and that infection and other illnesses tended to produce negative retentions.[35]

Watkin, who has done considerable research in this field, concludes the following:

> The assessment of protein nutrition in the aged is difficult because of the small magnitude of change per unit of age, the large variability both among individuals and within an individual, and the differences of the experimental design.[36]

At the present time, protein allowances suggested by the National Research Council are the same as for younger adults.

## Calcium

Attempts to appraise the calcium needs of older adults like similar investigations in early maturity have been numerous, but the results have not been in agreement. The wide individual variations found among adults is pointed out by Steggerda and Mitchell, and these differences increase in the aged as suggested by studies of Ohlson *et al.*[37, 38, 39] The problem is complicated by the ability of man to adapt. Studies such as that of Hegsted in Lima, Peru, show that a racial group that has existed for generations can adapt and maintain balance on levels as low as 200 to 400 mg of calcium per day.[40] On the other hand, Daum and others found that calcium balances of elderly men 53 to 83 years old, on generous intakes of calcium ranged from 1.46 to 2.62 gm per day.[41] The following illustration by Mitchell describes man's ability to adapt:

> It is often said that man is a creature of habit. If he consumes a quart of milk daily he may boost his requirements of calcium and ribroflavin to high levels, in part by a wasteful use of abundant supplies available to him. If he eliminates milk from his diet, his body will in time become more thrifty in assimilating the diminished supply of these nutrients and in using them for its needs. He adapts himself to his new diet with no permanent damage to himself.[42]

The metabolism studies of Roberts, Kerr and Ohlson on middle-aged and elderly women receiving freely chosen diets suggest daily intakes of 0.90 to 1.0 gm daily as adequate to prevent loss of calcium.[43] The authors describing studies with diets containing less than two thousand calories warn that, "Reduced caloric intakes without attention to selection of nutrients may be the key to understanding many cases of nutritional instability."

The number of cases of broken bones among the aged and the high prevalence of osteoporosis in older persons in the United States is of much concern. Osteoporosis is four times more common in women than men and usually is not seen before the age of fifty.[44] This is a condition in which the absolute amount of bone is decreased but the chemical composition of that remaining is in the same proportion as normal bone. The possibility that a minimal intake of calcium over a long period of years may contribute to osteoporosis is suggested by studies of Lutwark and Whedon.[45, 46] Stearns reported that severe osteoporosis at the time of menopause may be reversed by attention to improved diets increased in intakes of calcium.[47] Dairy products are the best source of dietary calcium. While milk drinking is often distasteful to the older person, a diet with milk included in cooked foods, in addition to cheese, and generous supplies of vegetables, the 0.8 gm calcium recommended by the National Research Council can be supplied.

## Iron

The Food and Nutrition Board suggests that 10 mg of iron daily will meet the needs of the adult male and postmenopausal female (Table XIX). It is not known to what extent iron-deficiency anemia exists in the elderly in the United States but diet can influence hemoglobin levels in the aging as shown by Gillum and Morgan.[48] Physical examinations, medical and dietary histories, seven-day diet records, blood and urine analyses for 577 men and women all over 50 years of age were done. The majority of the higher intakes of both protein and iron were found in the group with the higher levels of hemoglobin and the lowest values of hemoglobin for those with the lowest intakes.

Ordinarily, the needs for iron can be met by the iron of the diet. However, the "availability" of iron for intestinal absorption varies from one food to another. Regulation of iron absorption in the intestine is a complicated matter which is not thoroughly understood and varies among individuals.

Recommendations for the man 55 to 75-plus years are the same as the younger adult male but are reduced for the older woman from that of the nonpregnant menstruating female (Table XIX).

## Other Minerals

Studies of the elderly as regards other specific minerals are few. Data from a study of 1,015 persons over 45 years of age, living in North Dakota, suggest that fluorine may lessen the prevalence of osteoporosis and collapsed vertebrae and may play a role in preventing calcification of the aorta.[49] However, a study in New York State did not support the hypothesis for women of postmenopausal age at the time fluoridation was initiated.[50] The needs for other minerals are thought to be essentially similar to those of younger adults.

## Water

Water is often taken for granted and thus it is the neglected nutrient. The standard of 1 ml/calorie of food is suggested by the Food and Nutrition Board, but thirst usually will serve as an adequate guide.[51] However, the elderly frequently drink limited amounts and complain they do not like to drink water. Encouraging older people to drink fruit juices, soft drinks, tea, coffee and other beverages will help to supply the needs. Stieglitz, Thewlis and others have emphasized the importance of water.[52, 53]

## Vitamins

There is little clinical evidence to lead us to believe that fat-soluble vitamin deficiencies are present in the aged. The tendency toward a decrease in serum vitamin A level with aging has been reported by Rafsky and also by Gillum, Morgan and Sailer.[54, 55] Other researchers have found no differences between aging and younger individuals.[56, 57, 58] Gillum *et al.* found both dietary and serum values slightly higher for the major group of subjects who lived in their own homes than a smaller group who were institutionalized.[59] They believe the subjects who lived in institutions "were possibly survivors of more or less stressful lives." All other men and women in the four above studies lived in nursing homes or county homes. Rafsky believes results of his study were a manifestation of liver dysfunction in normal aged individuals.[60]

Thiamine requirements allow 0.5 mg per one thousand calories for all adults. This provides a satisfactory buffer for the older woman who frequently has reduced caloric intake. Some indication is suggested that thiamine requirements may be slightly increased in the elderly. Oldham determined minimum thiamine requirements for ten women, 52 to 72 years of age and compared these with eight women 18 to 21 years of age.[61] In both groups, thiamine intakes were gradually increased first from less than four hundred to five hundred, then to 810 $\mu$gms daily. As judged by thiamine excretion, the older women reacted more rapidly to thiamine depletion. On the basis of this study, the authors conclude that the minimum requirement for thiamine is greater for older women and a higher thiamine-calorie ratio may be needed. This observation is of interest since Kirk found a slight tendency for the thiamine value of blood to decrease with age, whereas the pyruvic acid level, which is elevated in instances of thiamine deficiency, showed no change with advancing years.[62]

The therapeutic use of vitamins, especially the B-complex, has often been prescribed to improve physical and mental health. In the studies of Wexburg and also Stephenson, positive improvement was reported.[63, 64] Horwitt and co-workers studied a group of mental patients at the Elgin State Hospital from 1943 to 1946 in which they found that old men can absorb nutrients as efficiently as young men and that requirements for the B-complex vitamins were no greater for older men than younger men.[65] However, the aged were less resistant than the young to ill effects of restriction. They concluded that a very liberal provision of B-complex vitamins was of no therapeutic value in the treatment of mental disease.

Regarding the retention of vitamin $B_{12}$, Watkin has found it to be greater in old men than young men when the general dietary intakes of the two groups were essentially similar.[66] Continued studies of absorption and metabolism of this vitamin will give us the answer to whether or not the diet of the elderly needs special consideration.

The observations of Morgan *et al.* indicate a direct relation between serum levels of ascorbic acid and dietary intake, with the requirement of men beyond 50 years of age greater than women.[67] The work of Kirk and Chieffi would seem to confirm this sex difference when they found ascorbic blood concentration in young men was twice, and young women two and one-half times as high as the average value of institutionalized middle-aged and old persons.[68] A direct relation of intake to serum levels was shown in the North Central Regional Cooperative project in which age did not influence either mean intake or its mean serum concentration.[69] The recommended allowance of 60 mg daily of ascorbic acid for older men and 55 mg for older women provides a safe margin above intakes known to protect against signs of scurvy (Table XIX).

## SUMMARY

Energy needs diminish with age as the metabolic rate declines and activity decreases. Obesity is frequently a late middle-age problem. However, reduced caloric intakes should not be made without attention to selection of nutrients. Also adjustment of caloric intakes needs to be made on an individual basis to maintain normal weight.

The efficiency of protein utilization may decrease with age and the requirements for some of the amino acids may be increased. Considerable individual variation in utilization and requirement is found at all ages. The present recommendation of a similar amount for adults of all ages allows for individual needs and adaptation. If calories are lowered, the proportion of protein to calories in the diet needs to be increased.

The prevalence of osteoporosis in older persons, especially women, has led many researchers to suggest that minimal intakes of calcium over long periods of time may be a contributing factor. The finding that fluorine may lessen the prevalence of osteoporosis and may play a great role in preventing calcification of the aorta is of extreme interest.

There appears to be no evidence that requirements for the fat-soluble vitamins change with advancing years. Some indication is suggested that thiamine and ascorbic acid requirements based on saturation tests may be slightly increased in the elderly. Some physicians have found both physical and mental improvement using vitamin supplements. However, others found no therapeutic value in the treatment of mental disease. Present recommendations of the Food and Nutrition Board allow a margin of safety for the vitamins.

## FACTORS WHICH CONTRIBUTE TO THE NUTRITION OF THE ELDERLY

### A Lifetime Accumulation of Food Habits

Food likes and dislikes influence the nutrition of people of any age, but the elderly have had a longer time to form food habits. Most of us relish familiar foods and those we learned to eat in our childhood. In addition to individual preferences, every section of the United States has its own food preferences.[70] We are all familiar with foods considered typical of a particular region. Attempts to change food habits are difficult and require a very active and vigorous approach over a period of time.[71] As an example, food sent to starving people in foreign countries is often not acceptable because it is unfamiliar to them.

The problem of unfamiliarity is not limited to people living in countries in need of food. Sebrell points out the fact that the elderly person in the United States may dislike many modern processed foods because "to him they just don't taste the same as the foods that were obtained from the family garden and prepared in the farm kitchen." He notes that no one in our society who has passed military draft age had frozen orange juice as a baby and no one beyond high school age established his food preferences at a time when frozen foods were on the market.[72] Ford found in a recent survey that low-income families in a Mississippi town used only limited amounts of dried skim milk although it was available as a commodity product.[73] Many families used it only in the preparation of corn bread and biscuits because they were not familiar with it and no one had shown them how to use it.

## Food Fads and Fallacies

Over five hundred million dollars is wasted on unnecessary or falsely represented vitamin products and so-called health food yearly.[74] The elderly are especially susceptible to such misrepresentations, which can be costly to the elderly person on a limited income. Unfortunately, individual food faddists may be sincere in their beliefs but often want fervently to convert their friends to their way of eating. Worse than the financial loss is the false sense of security which may cause delay in proper health treatment. Even the term "health foods" is misleading because it implies that the products have special health-giving properties when they merely have the same nutrients as found in common foods. Yoghurt has the same nutritional value as milk; vegetable juices have no more vitamins than the raw vegetables from which the juices were made. Garlic has no magical powers in curing high blood pressure and safflower capsules will not prevent strokes. The calories in food do count in weight control.

The food faddist has abused the phrase "natural foods" and goes to the extreme in disapproving of such food items as milled and enriched cereals, canned foods and pasteurized milk.

Vitamin pills certainly have a place for those whose needs have been diagnosed by a physician. However, the thousands of dollars spent annually by the elderly for self-prescribed vitamins in hopes they will cure all their aches and pains would better be spent for good wholesome food.

## Poor Dental Health

A serious factor affecting the eating habits of the elderly is poor dental health. Dental caries is the chief cause with peridontal disease as the second. It is estimated that 50 per cent of Americans have periodontal disease by age 50 and that nearly 100 per cent have it by age 65.[75]

A high percentage of older people have lost their own teeth, and the quality of their dentures varies greatly. The U.S. Public Health Service estimates that 20.1 million Americans—eighteen in every one hundred persons in the United States—wear dentures.[76] Many of these persons have never learned to use their dentures for adequate mastication or they are so poorly fitted that they can never be used. The result is that many keep their dentures in their pockets or they stay in a dresser drawer rather than in their mouths. Missing teeth and ill fitting artificial teeth can influence what people eat and the level of their nutrition. Yurkstas and Emerson compared the number of times a food was eaten by denture patients to the number of times it occurred in the diet of patients with natural teeth.[77] The results indicated that denture patients tended to avoid foods that were difficult to chew, such as meats, raw vegetables, some sandwiches and salads.

Green, Drigen, and Spies gave 446 patients who came to a nutrition clinic complete oral and physical examinations.[78] They found that patients with insufficient masticating capabilities had significantly higher incidence of constipation and other gastrointestinal complaints than persons with sufficient masticatory ability. Dahlberg believes "an increase in the number of strokes used to masticate a bolus of food does not compensate for masticatory impairment." [79]

It is hoped that preventive measures such as oral hygiene, adequate nutrition, fluoridation of water and regular dental treatment will reduce the incidence of periodontal disease, lessen loss of teeth and provide better quality teeth for the elderly.

## Loneliness, Shopping Problems, and Reduced Incomes

As has already been pointed out, nutrient intake of the elderly living in their own homes does not always meet "Recommended Dietary

Allowances." Whether the diets of these persons would be improved if their physical setting were changed is not known. Such factors as loneliness and other emotional feelings probably play a role in their nutrition. The older woman who is suddenly left to eat alone after the death of a husband for whom she enjoyed preparing food may change her pattern of eating because of a lack of incentive to prepare an adequate diet. Psychological factors may also influence utilization of nutrients. In studies with older women, Swanson reported negative nitrogen and calcium balances during episodes of anxiety over the terminal illness of a relative and during periods of living alone.[80]

Shopping for food may become a real problem. Many elderly living in their own homes must depend upon friends or relatives to do their food shopping. The older person who never gets to the food market does not have the stimulus of seeing the array of well displayed foods offered today in the modern supermarket or grocery store.

With reduced incomes after retirement, many become overly concerned about finances and reduce their food purchases or select foods poorly because of a lack of knowledge of the nutrient content of food. An adequate diet can be purchased by those with limited incomes.[81, 82]

## NUTRITIONAL ASSISTANCE FOR THE OLDER PERSON

### Home-Delivered Meals and Retirement Homes

A number of communities have established a program of providing home-delivered meals for the ill, handicapped and the elderly. The first of such programs was started in the early 1950's. However, the phrase "meals-on-wheels" taken from the British program is the name of almost every nonprofit project for home-delivered meals in the United States. The National Council on Aging in 1965 summarized recommendations and guidelines. The eighty-six-page project report included guidelines for home-delivered meal programs, recommendations to national, state and local organizations as well as a factual summary of programs surveyed in five communities. Programs in the communities differed widely from one another. For example, in one community there was a close meshing of the program with other community services, while in others the social and health agencies were virtually ignored. The report recommends that the program should be tied in with other health and welfare programs and the portable meals program, if not able to provide meals seven days a week, should help clients to make suitable alternate plans for meals that are not delivered.[83]

Home Economists with their training and experience can give valuable service to any community in helping to initiate this type of service for the elderly and to provide support for those programs already in existence.

Many retirement and nursing homes serve excellent food to their residents. In others, the picture is just the opposite, too often due to a lack of trained personnel. The use of the "shared dietition" has helped to improve food service in a number of retirement homes.

## Nutrition Education

Good food habits can best be achieved by people who have correct knowledge of nutrition and are motivated to use it.

A number of pamphlets written in simple language are available for the elderly. Examples are "Food Guides for Older Folks" and "Food Hints for Mature People." [84, 85]

Educational techniques such as programmed instruction, and dietary counseling services, have successfully been used with adults.[86, 87] The "Dial-a-Dietitian" service is viewed by clients as a readily accessible and valuable resource for nutrition information in those communities where it is available.[88]

Mass media of radio, television, newspaper and magazines are far-reaching as a means of informal education of the public. Most of such information is correct. However, those who read, look and listen should seek authoritative help if they have questions.

## SUMMARY

Nutrient intakes of older persons do not always meet suggested levels when evaluated in terms of the "Recommended Dietary Allowances." Calcium and ascorbic acid frequently are below recommended amounts reflecting the inadequate use of milk, fruits and vegetables.

The nutrient needs of the elderly are similar to those of all adults except for a reduction in caloric intake. Present recommendations of the Food and Nutrition Board provide a margin of safety which allows for individual needs and adaptation.

Such factors as food habits, poor dental health, emotional stress, and reduced income influence the nutrition of the elderly.

Community programs such as home-delivered meals, and the increased number of retirement and nursing homes which serve well-planned and nutritious food contribute to the health and well-being of this group in our population. Nutrition education during the whole life span as well as during the later years of life is needed.

Great progress has been made toward an understanding of the many facets of nutrition of older people, but more research is needed.

All professional workers who have responsibility for older people should promote programs and activities for the improvement of their nutritional status.

## REFERENCES


1. Metropolitan Life Insurance Co.: The population of elders. *Statist Bull, 46*:1-3, 1965.
2. Batchelder, E.L.: Nutritional status and dietary habits of older people. *J Amer Diet Assoc, 33*:471-476, 1957.
3. Ohlson, M.A.; Roberts, P.A.; Joseph, S.A., and Nelson, P.M.: Dietary Practices of 100 Women from 40 to 75 Years of Age. *J Amer Diet Assoc, 24*:286-291, 1948.
4. Ohlson, M.A.; Jackson, L.; Boek, J.; Cederquist, D.C.; Brewer, W.D., and Brown, E.G.: Nutrition and dietary habits of aging women. *Amer J Public Health, 40*:1101-1108, 1950.
5. Swanson, P.; Willis, E.; Mairs, P.; Roberts, H.; Angus, R., and Pohm, A.: Iowa State College nutritionists report on the diets of Iowa women. Reprints of articles published in *Iowa Farm Sci,* Oct. 1954 and Sept. 1955. (Home Economics Research, Iowa Agriculture Experiment Station.)
6. Steinkamp, R.C.; Cohen, N.L., and Walsh, H.E.: Resurvey of an aging population—fourteen-year follow-up. *J Amer Diet Assoc, 46*:103-109, 1965.
7. U.S. Department of Agriculture: Household Food Consumption Survey, 1955. *Food consumption and Dietary Levels of Households as Related to the Age of Homemaker, United States—by Region.* Report No. 14, 1959.
8. Jordon, M.; Kepes, M.; Hayes, R., and Hammond, W.: Dietary habits of persons living alone. *Geriatrics, 9*:230-232, 1954.
9. Fry, P.C.; Fox, H.M., and Linkswiler, H.: Nutrient intakes of healthy older women. *J Amer Diet Assoc, 42*:218-222, 1963.
10. Lyons, J.S., and Trulson, M.F.: Food practices of older people living at home. *J Geront, 11*:66-72, 1956.

11. Lebovit, C.: The food of older persons living at home. *J Amer Diet Assoc, 46*:285-289, 1965.
12. Vanslyckle, C.: Food consumption of older families. *J Amer Geriat Soc, 5*:603-611, 1957.
13. Davidson, C.S.; Livermore, J.; Anderson, P., and Kaufman, S.: The nutrition of a group of apparently healthy aging persons. *Amer J Clin Nutr, 10*:181-199, 1962.
14. Rafsky, H.A., and Newman, B.: A quantitative study of diet in the aged. *Geriatrics, 3*:267-271, 1948.
15. Pyke, M.S.; Holmes, R.; Harrison, R., and Chamberlin, K.: Nutritional value of diets eaten by older people in London. *Lancet, 2*:461-464, 1947.
16. Bransy, E.R., and Osborne, B.: A social and food survey of the elderly living alone or as married couples. *Brit J Nutr, 7*:160-180, 1953.
17. Exton-Smith, Stration, Newman, B.R., and Ramsey, M.: Report of an investigation into the dietary of elderly women living alone. King Edwards Hospital Fund for London, 1965. *Nutr Rev, 24*:236-238, 1966.
18. Guggenheim, K., and Margulec, I.: Factors in nutrition of elderly people living alone or as couples and receiving community assistance. *J Amer Geriat Soc, 13*:561-567, 1965.
19. Ohlson, M.A.; Brewer, W.D.; Jackson, L.; Swanson, P.; Roberts, P.H., Mongel, M.; Leverton, R.M.; Chaloupka, M.; Gram, M.R.; Reynolds, M.A., and Lutz, R.: Intakes and retention of nitrogen, calcium, and phosphorus by 136 women between 30 and 85 years of age. *Fed Proc, 11*:775-783, 1952.
20. Morgan, A.F.; Gillum, H.L., and Williams, R.I.: Nutritional status of the aging. III. Serum ascorbic acid and intake. *J Nutr, 55*:431-448, 1955.
21. Gillum, H.L., and Morgan, A.F.: Nutritional status of the aging. I. Hemoglobin levels, packed cell volumes and sedimentation rates of 577 normal men and women over 50 years of age. *J Nutr, 55*:265-288, 1955.
22. Kelley, L.; Ohlson, M.A., and Harper, L.J.: Food selection and well being of aging women. *J Amer Diet Assoc, 33*:466-470, 1957.
23. Stevens, H.A.; Bleiler, R.E., and Ohlson, M.A.: Dietary intake of five groups of subjects, 24-hour recall diets vs. dietary patterns. *J Amer Diet Assoc, 42*:387-393, 1963.
24. Food and Nutrition Board: *Recommended Dietary Allowances,* 7th ed., Washington, D.C., National Academy of Sciences-National Research Council, 1968.
25. *Code of Federal Regulations, Title 21.* Parts 125.1, 125.2, 125.3, 125.4. Label statements concerning dietary properties of food purporting to be or represented for special dietary uses. Washington, D.C., U.S. Government Printing Office, 1967.
26. Berkson, J., and Boothby, W.M.: Studies of the energy of metabolism of normal individuals. A comparison of the estimation of basal metab-

olism from (1) a linear formula and (2) "surface area." *Amer J physiol, 116*:485-494, 1936.

27. Durnin, J.V.: Energy expenditure in the elderly. *Proc Nutr Soc, 15*:89-99, 1956.
28. Gillum, H.L.; Morgan, A.F., and Jerome, D.W.: Nutritional status of the aging. IV. Serum cholesterol and diet. *J Nutr, 55*:449-467, 1955.
29. Jolliffe, M.; Rinzler, S.H., and Archer, M.: The Anticoronary club, including a discussion of the effects of a prudent diet on the serum cholesterol level of middle-aged men. *Amer J Clin Nutr, 7*:451-462, 1959.
30. Stamler, J.; Berkson, D.M.; Young, Q.D.; Lindberg, H.A.; Hall, Y.; Miller, W., and Stamler, R.: Approaches to the prevention of coronary heart disease. *J Amer Diet Assoc, 40*:407-416, 1962.
31. *Ibid.*
32. Ohlson, *et al., op. cit.*, p. 775.
33. Tuttle, S.G.; Swendseid, M.E.; Mulcare, D.; Griffith, W.H., and Bassett, S.H.: Essential amino acid requirements of older men in relation to total nitrogen intake. *Metabolism, 8*:61-72, 1959.
34. Tuttle, S.G.; Swendseid, M.E.; Mulcare, D.; Griffith, W.H., and Bassett, S.H.: Study of the essential amino acid requirements of men over fifty. *Metabolism, 6*:564-573, 1957.
35. Kountz, W.; Hofstatter, L., and Ackermann, P.G.: Nitrogen balance studies in four elderly men. *J Geront, 6*:20-33, 1951.
36. Watkin, D.M.: The assessment of protein nutrition in aged man. *Ann NY Acad Sci, 69*:902-915, 1958.
37. Steggerda, F.R., and Mitchell, H.H.: Further experiments on the calcium requirement of adult man and the utilization of the calcium in milk. *J Nutr, 21*:577-588, 1941.
38. Mitchell, H.H.: Adaption to undernutrition. *J Amer Diet Assoc, 20*:511-515, 1944.
39. Ohlson *et al., op. cit.*, p. 775.
40. Hegsted, D.M.; Moscoso, I., and Collazos, C.: A study of the minimum calcium requirements of adult men. *J Nutr, 46*:181-201, 1952.
41. Daum, K.; Tuttle, W.W.; Warren, B.; Sabin, M.; Imig, C.J., and Schumacher, M.T.: Nitrogen utilization in older men. *J Amer Diet Assoc, 28*:305-307, 1952.
42. Mitchell, *op. cit.*, p. 511.
43. Roberts, P.H.; Kerr, C.H., and Ohlson, M.A.: Nutritional status of older women: nitrogen, calcium, phosphorus retentions of nine women. *J Amer Diet Assoc, 24*:292-299, 1948.
44. Lutwak, L.: Osteoporosis—a mineral deficiency disease? *J Amer Diet Assoc, 44*:173-175, 1964.
45. *Ibid.*
46. Whedon, D.C.: Effects of high calcium intakes on bones, blood and soft

tissue: relationship of calcium intake to balance in osteoporosis. *Fed Proc, 18*:1112-1118, 1959.
47. Stearns, G.: Recent investigations in mineral nutrition. *J Amer Diet Assoc, 18*:366-369, 1942.
48. Gillum, H.L.; Morgan, A.F., and Jerome, D.W., *op. cit.*, p. 265.
49. Bernstein, D.S.; Sadowsky, N.; Hegsted, D.M.; Guri, C.D., and Stare, F.J.: Prevalence of osteoporosis in high- and low-fluoride areas in North Dakota. *JAMA, 198*:499-504, 1966.
50. Goggin, J.E.; Haddon, W.; Hambly, G.S., and Hoveland, J.R.: Incidence of femoral fractures in postmenopausal women. *Public Health Rep, 80*: 1005-1012, 1965.
51. Food and Nutrition Board, *op. cit.*
52. Stieglitz, E.J.: Nutrition problems in geriatric medicine. *JAMA, 142*: 1070-1077, 1950.
53. Thewlis, M.W.: *The Care of the Aged.* St. Louis, Mosby, 1946.
54. Rafsky, H.A., and Newman, B.: A study of vitamin A and carotene tolerance tests in the aged. *Gastroenterology, 10*:1001-1006, 1948.
55. Gillum, H.L.; Morgan, A.F., and Sailer, F.: Nutritional status of the aging. V. Vitamin a and carotene. *J Nutr, 55*:655-669, 1955.
56. Campbell, D.A., and Tonke, E.L.: Vitamin A, total carotenoids and thymol turbidity in plasma. *Brit Med J, 2*:1499-1501, 1949.
57. Haig, G., and Patek, A.J.: Vitamin A deficiency in Loennec's cirrhosis: the relative significance of the plasma vitamin A and carotenoid levels and the dark adaption time. *J Clin Invest, 21*:309-317, 1942.
58. Kirk, J.E., and Chieffi, M.: Vitamin studies in middle-aged and old individuals. I. The vitamin A, total carotene and A + B carotene concentrations in plasma. *J Nutr, 36*:315-322, 1948.
59. Gillum, H.L.; Morgan, A.F., and Sailer, F.: *op. cit.*, p. 655.
60. Rafsky, H.A., and Newman, B., *op. cit.*, p. 1001.
61. Oldham, H.G.: Thiamine requirements of women. *Ann NY Acad Sci, 98*: 542-549, 1962.
62. Kirk, J.E., and Chieffi, M.: Vitamin studies in middle-aged and old individuals. III. Thiamine and pyruvic acid blood concentrations. *J Nutr, 38*:353-360, 1949.
63. Wexberg, E.: Neurometabolic deficiency in old age. *Amer J Psychiat, 97*: 1406-1418, 1941.
64. Stephenson, W.; Penton, C., and Korenchevsky, V.: Some effects of vitamins B and C on senile patients. *Brit Med J, 2*:839-844, 1941.
65. Horwitt, M.K.: Dietary requirements of the aged. *J Amer Diet Assoc, 29*:443-448, 1953.
66. Watkin, D.M.; Lang, C.A.; Chow, B.F., and Shock, N.W.: Agewise differences in the urinary excretion of vitamin $B_{12}$ following intramuscular administration. *J Nutr, 50*:341-349, 1953.
67. Morgan, A.F.; Gillum, H.L., and Williams, R.I., *op. cit.*, p. 431.

68. Kirk, J.E., and Chieffi, M.: Vitamin studies in middle-aged and old individuals. XI. Concentration of total ascorbic acid in whole blood. *J Geront, 8*:301-304, 1953.

69. Roderuck, C.; Burrill, L.; Campbell, L.J.; Brakke, B.E.; Childs, M.T.; Leverton, R.; Chauloupka, M.; Jebe, E.H., and Swanson, P.P.: Estimated dietary intake, urinary excretion and blood vitamin C in women of different ages. *J Nutr, 66*:15-27, 1958.

70. Steibling, H., and Dreis, T.A.: Habit—and more in food. *The Yearbook of Agriculture*. 1959, p. 631.

71. Pilgrim, F.J.: What foods do people accept and reject? *J Amer Diet Assoc, 38*:439-443, 1961.

72. Sebrell, W.H.: It's not age that interferes with nutrition of the elderly. *Nutr Today, 1*:15-18, 1966.

73. Ford, W.B.: Dietary Practices of Low-Income Families as Indices for Nutrition Education. Unpublished thesis. Iowa City, University of Iowa Libraries, 1967.

74. Food and Drug Administration: Your money and your life. *F.D.A. Publication* No. 19, Washington, D.C., U.S. Department of Health, Education and Welfare, 1963.

75. Robinson, H.B.G.: Oral diseases and the aging patient. *Amer Geriat Soc, 11*:120-129, 1963.

76. Kelly, J.E.; Van Kirk, L.E., and Garst, E.: Total loss of teeth. *Vital and Health Statistics,* No. 27, U.S. Department of Health, Education, and Welfare, Oct. 1967.

77. Yurkstas, A.A., and Emerson, W.H.: Dietary selections of persons with natural and artificial teeth. *J Prosth Dent, 14*:695-697, 1964.

78. Greene, H.I.; Dreizen, S., and Spies, T.D.: A clinical survey of the incidence of impaired masticatory function in patients of a nutrition clinic. *JADA, 39*:561, 1949.

79. Dahlberg, B.: Masticatory habits. *J Dent Res, 25*:67, 1946.

80. Swanson, P.: Adequacy in old age. I. Role of nutrition. *J Home Economice Assoc, 56*:651-734, 1964.

81. U.S. Department of Agriculture: Food guide for older folks. *Home and Garden Bull,* 1959, vol. 17.

82. Cofer, E., and Clark, F.: Food plans at different costs in food. *The Yearbook of Agriculture,* 1959, p. 576.

83. National Council on the Aging: Home-delivered meals for the ill, handicapped and elderly. *Amer J Public Health, 55*:1086, 1965.

84. U.S. Department of Agriculture: Food guide for older folks.

85. King, C.G., and Britt, G.: Food hints for mature people. *Public Affairs Pamphlet No. 336.* New York, Public Affairs Pamphlets, 22 East 38th Street, 1962.

86. Downing, C.B.: What is programmed instruction? *J Amer Diet Assoc, 46*:39-42, 1965.

87. PIPER, G.M.: Planning new community nutrition services. *J Amer Diet Assoc, 44*:461-464, 1964.

88. WAGNER, M.C.; HUYCK, M.C., and HINKLE, M.M.: Evaluation of the dial-a-dietitian program. II. Impact of the program on the community. *J Amer Diet Assoc, 47*:385-390, 1965.

*Chapter 13*

# HOUSING NEEDS

WALTER K. VIVRETT

HOW DO MIDDLE-AGED, and how do older people want to live? What are their particular needs, and what should be the public policy with regard to meeting those needs? What is the relationship between the needs of older individuals and families, the needs of younger families?

Within a single generation, dramatic changes have occurred in our social, economic, and political life—and in the physical environment in which these changes have taken place. Pressures of war, boom and recession, pressures of acceleration of family formation and increased birth rates, and pressures of technological development appear to have worked to the advantage of *younger* age groups more than of *older* age groups. Concern for the housing of new and expanding families—coupled with an easy acceptance of the *status quo* of older, contracting households—has meant that the situation of the older people has not improved with the generally rising standards of living. Instead, it has brought about an increasing concentration of older people in some of our communities and has created others devoid of them; it has aggravated the accessibility of community services and facilities at the same time that it has also provided increased comforts and conveniences. Thus it has come about that many aspects of the present environment are not ideally suited to the patterns of life in later maturity and in old age.

## HOUSING NEEDS OF THE ELDERLY

Typically, an individual spends his early life in the household of his parents. As a young adult, he may live alone or with friends in an apartment or a rooming house. With marriage, he establishes his own household and becomes a parent. When children have grown and left home, the family contracts to its original size. With the death of spouse, the surviving individual may elect to live alone again, continuing in the family residence or moving to an apartment; or he may choose the household of a married son or daughter. There are, of course, variations in this sequence of events; but it is this process of family formation and dissolution that provides the basis for changes in living arrangements.

Each situation suggests some rather specific household needs for the several age periods in life. If we add to them the multitude of external and environmental influences that shape our lives, we begin to create a backdrop against which to determine the housing needs of any age group.

## Housing Over The Life Cycle

In its typical cycle, the household expands and then contracts. Adjustments in living accommodations are commonly made in order to meet the needs of the family and its members as conditions make such changes feasible and advantageous.

Present Generations of the Old. Present generations of the old were born prior to the turn of the century at a time when life expectancy at birth was *less* than 50 years, at a time when it was also to be expected that one of the parents in the family would have died before the last child married and left home, that less than a fifth of one's lifetime would occur after the dissolution of the family. At that time it seemed natural that a major emphasis in adult life should be upon family living, frequently embracing a three-generational pattern.

As it happened, a greater number of people than was expected have lived into old age. They have lived longer with more years of married life after their children left home, as well as more years of widowhood. Thus, among *men* 65 to 74 years, about 78 per cent and over 75, 61.4 per cent are still married and living with their wives. Those widowed are 11.2 per cent for the 65 to 74 age group and 29.8 per cent for the over 75 age group. The separated or divorced comprise about 4 per cent of the male 65 and over population and 7 per cent are single, that is, never have married. On the other hand, among *women* 65 years and over, about 34 per cent are married and living with husband, about 55 per cent widowed, about 3 per cent are separated or divorced, and about 7 per cent are single.

Patterns of living arrangements of these present generations of old people are closely related to their marital status. Most of these (approximately 61% of those over 65 live in their own households with spouses, with relatives or friends, or alone. Another large percentage (approximately 35% of those over 65) live in households other than their own. Many live entirely alone, that is, as one-person households.

A relatively small remaining group live in quasi-households such as institutions, hotels, clubs, large rooming houses, and the like. Acknowledging that the institution is society's primary means of meeting some characteristic needs of the aged, a relatively low percentage of people for a relatively short period of time live in institutions. A small but increasingly significant number of old people are being attracted by the noninstitutional environment of such quasi-households as the hotel and the residence club.

ONCOMING GENERATIONS OF OLD. For those adults approaching their later years, in addition to an extended life expectancy, there looms the probability of thirty years of life for women, and twenty-one years of life for men after the last child has married and left home. Thus one-third of married life will be lived after the years of child-rearing. The aging couple and the widowed individual with today's expectancy of so many years ahead, are more likely to plan for this period. Such an extension of the adult years of life makes it possible for the oncoming generations of the old and their married children to provide mutual assistance and intermittent sociability; but it points up the fact that in the later years of life, when one might think of living with members of a younger generation, one must also consider whether that arrangement is for only a few years or whether it is to extend over a long time. It means that on occasion, two generations of a family both, of whose child-rearing roles have been completed, may arrange to live together. For example, a widowed mother may have a son or daughter whose children have left home, and whose home is sufficiently large to provide her with a place to live.

From the time childbearing is completed until the children leave home, the number of persons in the family remains unchanged, but the roles and requirements of the members change rather steadily. Similarly, when the children leave home, the husband and wife change their roles and requirements as they approach retirement years, and then again as one of them experiences lowered energy reserves or increased physical infirmity. Finally, with the death of one's spouse the shift to a one-person household occurs.

Thus the changes produced by family formation and dissolution influence the choice of living arrangements.

## Changing Patterns of Living—Rising Standards of Housing

These changing social patterns, abetted by technological and medical advances, are bringing about a new independence of action for the later years of life. This is being expressed in the choice of an independence and a separateness of living arrangements which seem to become increasingly desirable up through old age.

FACTORS INFLUENCING PATTERNS OF LIVING. With earlier marriage, earlier completion of childbearing and child rearing, and the relatively free movement of adult children in search of economic opportunities, many parents are left alone while still in their prime, still working, and frequently with their own homes. Single people, on the other hand, grow into middle age and into later maturity living alone or at least with considerable independence in their living arrangements. Then too, the difference of interests among recent generations contributes to a separateness of living arrangement, and these different patterns of living are being extended into later life.

Along with extensive urbanization in the United States, some of the sense of family belongingness has been replaced in many cases by one of community belongingness, and this has made the individual more independent of the family. Moreover, society's increasing assumption of health and welfare responsibilities is providing a security outside the family circle, a security quite differenct from that once offered at the almshouse or the poor farm.

Earlier generations of the old were satisfied merely to wait out their remaining days. But today's shorter work week, leisure, and longer period of retirement emphasize the need for additional ways to occupy one's time and for the optimal environment in which to spend this time.

The fact that virtually no older person need be without some cash income has perhaps influenced the patterns of living arrangements more than has anything else. Social security payments, pensions, and annuities backed up by old age assistance grants provide at least part of the cost of living. Although the housing market is by no means a buyer's market, this feeling of economic security has caused recent generations of the aging to declare their wants and needs; for until disaster comes (extended illness, disability or death of spouse) such finds are frequently sufficient to secure a measure of independence for the individual.

Medical techniques of treatment have pointed toward rehabilitation and restoration of the patient in the home, particularly in the younger age group; similar techniques are not being developed for older people. The rapidly evolving philosophy of rehabilitation for the old with its understanding of the values of milieu therapy not only fosters but actually demands the extended use of the independent living environment of the home. Thus, such advances indirectly encourage living outside the walls of the institution and extending the home environment into still later years.

The medical profession and the supporting human services of the community are concerning themselves with the ratio existing between the needs of the community and the resources for meeting those needs. They recognize that techniques of service must make every hour and every piece of equipment count for a maximum. This means concentrating technical skill and specialized equipment with increasing emphasis upon outpatient therapy. Thus, frequently the individual becomes accustomed to seek medical service in the physician's office or in the clinic, or on occasion in the hospital for brief but intensive treatment. It is natural that he will follow such patterns into later life, seeking out the service he requires but continuing to reside as long as possible in his home in the community.

At the same time, the communities in which we live have also undergone major physical changes. Superhighways and airways have shortened the time-distances and thereby have provided better access to specialized resources once considered out of reach. Improved transportation and communication open up new potentials for the individual in terms of the location of his residence and of the resources of the urban center.

Within the home, countless advances make life easier—automatic heat controls, washers and dryers, precooked and frozen foods, improved refrigerators. These encourage independent living yet minimize effort and worry, and these advances have been incorporated into the homes of some of the old with valuable results.

Evolving Standards in Housing. During the first half of the century, tremendous changes took place in our social consciousness of the housing needs of the population, and in the standards of quantity and quality of housing.

During these years, progressively higher standards of living were set, and with them have come demands for higher standards of housing—of space and of equipment. Thus today a family expects to find in its home a living room and perhaps a recreation or family room, a dining area and a kitchen, separate bedrooms for the parents and children, and bathrooms suitable for bathing and dressing. How tragic it is, then, if the space standards of the homes for older people are permitted to fall—to fall just when social opportunities have lessened. And these older people must spend more and more hours at home! At such an age, it is distressing to have to forego the private toilet and private bath in the home and to share antiquated fixtures at the rear of a rooming house hall or institutional corridor. Similarly, the dormitory cubicle is a poor substitute for the home in which even the smallest child's bedroom was more commodious.

The common conditions of ill health and infirmity which beset all of us as we grow older—beginning in middle age and often intensifying in the later years—demand that the standards of the home take into particular account such factors as failing eyesight and hearing, slowness or unsureness of gait, and general dwindling of energy reserves.

We must also concern ourselves with some of the less frequent and more serious conditions of failing health—wheelchair existence, or total blindness, or forgetfulness. Thus, for example, we should take another look at the entry halls in our small homes and apartments and acknowledge that they should be large enough to permit one to open and close the door without being trapped and to put on coats and overshoes as well as to get them out of the closet—large enough for the person in the wheelchair as well as the ambulant person; we may even question the actual necessity of having an entrance hall at all. In some cases, particularly where economy is a factor, it might be desirable to enter the living quarters directly. The importance of such considerations doubles when we consider the philosophies and the potentials of rehabilitation and restoration, for we must find in the home the sort of environment that will contribute to continuing rehabilitation.

## Particular Housing Needs Of The Older Individual

The failure of our society to meet some of the particular needs of older people is due to at least three things: (1) the lag between stated goals of income maintenance and security and the actual economic situation of large numbers of older individuals; (2) the failure to anticipate the evolving needs of the aging individual in relation to the home and the community; and (3) the emphasis in recent decades upon the environmntal needs of *younger* age groups.

Economic Status of Older People. Adequate housing is, for financial reasons alone, beyond the reach of large numbers of older people. One obvious indication of the seriousness of this situation is the generally low level of their incomes. Since a large percentage of elderly persons have incomes which fall at about current estimates of "minimum" or "subsistence allowance" budgets, they must allocate an unreasonable portion of their incomes for housing, or they must depend on some form of subsidy or assistance from the community, or they must accept substandard housing.

For some older people, savings and ownership of homes constitute partial relief from this economic burden. But an examination of their assets and net worth, particularly in the light of the rate of their *dis*-saving, suggests that this represents for many only a temporary security in the later years of life. For the cost of living—including the cost of home ownership as well as of renting—eats away at net worth at an alarming rate; and when illness or disability strikes, the economic resources of most aged persons are insufficient.

Physiological and Sociopsychological Needs. Man's sensations of heat or cold, of moisture or dryness, of purity or contamination, of drafts or stillness depend greatly upon his physical condition, his food intake and activity level, and upon the relative changes involved. In the literature, one repeatedly finds statements of optimal conditions of environment; but most of these so-called "guidelines" are based upon assumptions and not upon objective research. Present levels of gerontological knowledge of body environment and the external milieu, show that most of the work to date has dealt with visual and auditory senses, that little describes the tolerances of the aged for changes in thermal conditions and the nature of the basic mechanisms upon which these changes demand.

Most people recognize the value of proper artificial illumination for they know that, as eyesight begins to fail, inadequate illumination may adversely affect not only seeing efficiency but also mental and physical health. The light intensity required by the old person for reading is higher than that required by the student in school; the source and distribution of this light must properly relate brightness contrasts within his line of vision. Similarly, in the home there must be appropriate control of the brightness contrast in the several spaces through which the individual moves.

While excessive noise is disturbing, excessive quiet may be even more troublesome, particularly if one's sight is poor and he must depend on sound for his cues. And, from a slightly different point of view, with loss of hearing, one may desire increased volume from the radio or TV; and unless he is living in isolation, such intensity of sound must not be allowed to annoy those about him.

Some of the general reactions of the aging person as they pertain to the air about him have been observed: (1) a desire for increased warmth and freedom from drafts, (2) an inability to tolerate extremes of heat or cold, and (3) a concern about air pollution and excessive humidity or dryness as they relate to comfort and range of toleration.

With the increased leisure of retirement, the saving of time is less important to the older person than it is to the younger. On the other hand, reduced energy reserves mean that the facilities of the home and techniques of accomplishing daily routines should be organized for conservation of energy. With advancing age, one has greater difficulty reaching, lifting, pulling, bending over, and getting up and down. Exercise which induces unnecessary fatigue and hardship all too frequently results in the curtailment, or abandonment of activities and routines.

Accident prevention has an increased significance in the housing of the old. Failure in sight or hearing, unsureness of gait or sense of balance, unsteadiness of hand, and lapses of memory bring about a higher incidence of accidents in the home, particularly falls, among old people. Among those 65 to 74, for instance, the accidental-death rate due to falls in the home is about 15.6 per 100,000 population, and among those over 75, the death rate is 113.2 per 100,000, as compared to six per 100,000 persons for the general population. Some hazards can certainly be reduced: resilient nonslippery floors can be substituted for highly polished wood or terrazzo; scatter rugs and "scattered" furniture can be kept out of circulation paths; unnecessary stairs and changes of level can be avoided in the design of housing; drafts and driving rain at entrances can be controlled without a four- to six-inch high step at the door or even a "tripping" threshold; mechanical appliances and contrivances can be selected on the basis of their proved safety; and adequate convenience outlets appropriately located will obviate the use of extension cords and lamp wires that stretch across one's path in the house.

Even though the range of some interests may contract, space needs continue to be closely related to the earlier patterns of living. The dormitory cubicle can hardly be expected to fill these needs and, although some of them may be met through the use of indoor and outdoor communal facilities in group living arrangements, the old person clearly requires a place to which he can retreat and over which he is lord and master—one place, no matter how limited, where remaining vestiges of independence may find expression and where irritations and resentments can be minimized.

Privacy in the individual dwelling unit is requisite to reduce the irritations and resentments which tend to build up. The "open plans" of some current day housing—plans in which sleeping space and living space are only separated by a partial partition or a screen are questionable. Certainly, where two persons must occupy the same dwelling unit, even though they be husband and wife, the need is clearly for a minimum of two separate rooms—a bedroom as well as a living room. In the case of the individual living alone, however, perhaps the visual control will suffice.

For most people, the living patterns of early adulthood are extended with few changes into late middle age. Although some change in housing needs is suggested by reduction in the size of the family, seldom do the evolving situations of middle age *demand* modification in living arrangements, or in housing. Not until age 60 or 70 does a concern about living arrangements appear, along with changes in mental and physical health, in marital status or income. It is then that other living arrangements are likely to be sought.

THE INDIVIDUAL DWELLING UNIT. What do such evolving needs imply in terms of the house or the apartment which is to provide for independent living in the late years?

It is generally agreed that the dwelling unit must be as good as, if not better than the individual's customary living quarters of earlier years. It must obviously be suitable not only to his living patterns in optimum health, but also to the conditions of failing health and illness frequently observed in the aging, failing eyesight or hearing, slowness or unsureness of gait, or dwindling of energy reserves and changing physical capacity. In addition, the dwelling unit must have maximum adaptability to the less frequently observed conditions of failing health such as blindness, wheelchair existence, or forgetfulness; finally, it must contribute to continuing rehabilitation of the individual who is returned to the home.

SOCIAL AND LIVING AREA. A minimum of up to four people may be expected to use the living area at one time, even in the dwelling of the single or widowed person. For the most part, visitors will take part in conversation, play games, and have light refreshments. If the quarters are small, a sofa or couch might be a welcome accommodation for an overnight guest, or for an attendant who might be needed during illness or other emergency.

COOKING AND EATING. The number of people to be accommodated at a table will probably range from one to four. For conservation of energy and assurance of use, the table should be close to, if not in the kitchen. Ideally, it would be close enough to permit taking a pan from the stove without getting up. Occasional light snacks and lunches are the order-of-the-day. Since individual food requirements are usually small, ample refrigerated and frozen food storage are particularly necessary to insure that a loaf of bread can be kept fresh until it is used up, or a half package of frozen vegetable can be saved for the next meal. Because eating assumes a major part in the daily life of older people, table and chairs should be arranged in surroundings that are pleasant and relaxing.

Sleeping and Dressing Area. Since the sleeping area is also a major facility to be used in case of illness or convalescence, it should be large enough to permit minor nursing operations and the use of a wheelchair or walking aid. There should be enough space (at least 3 feet) at sides and foot of the bed to allow bed-making with the minimum of reaching and stretching. A table or a chest and a lamp are necessary at the head of the bed, and when possible, a telephone or other communicating device—particularly as the infirmities increase and there is need to summon help. A sturdy chair with arms should be placed near the closet-wardrobe dressing area; shades, draperies or other darkening devices are required from time to time, if not daily. A simple direct route, without right angle turns from the bed to the toilet becomes important with increasing infirmity or incontinence.

Bathing-Toilet Space. The requirements for the bath are among the most important if the living unit is to continue to serve as an independent one. The doors must be wide enough to accommodate a wheelchair, and bathroom fixtures should be arranged so that a typical wheelchair could be maneuvered into suitable position for a person to transfer to the toilet (one side as well as front) or to the tub, or to use the lavatory while still seated in the wheelchair. For a bathroom with the three basic fixtures, this means a room area of approximately fifty-six square feet (in contrast to the more customary bathroom area of 35 square feet). Most people, regardless of age, find some sort of grab, or rail handy when getting in and out of the bathtub, and this like all the accessories (towel bars, soap holders, and curtain rods) should be capable of withstanding the sudden pull which bodyweight might occasion. Where a particular infirmity occurs, local tradesmen can usually advise on the installation of other special rails or aids which might be needed.

Personal Interests, Activities, and Hobbies. Not all older people like to read, but those who do will want shelf space for books and magazines. People who like to write will want a writing desk or table. Older women who sew will need space for a sewing machine and a chair. And if these activities are to be truly available to the older person, the required "props" must be at hand in the living quarters, not put away somewhere so that they need to be gotten out, or so that they will be pushed away in the course of the daily routine.

To provide for every eventuality is obviously not possible; but personal interests or activities rarely demand any more space than that required by the usual writing desk or chair. Even in minimum standards, it would seem necessary that one such space allowance be made for each individual.

General Criteria. There are, of course, many established criteria for housing in general, such as the relationship or orientation to sunlight, prevailing breeze and natural ventilation; there are the standards related to sanitation and hygiene, and to safety. All these apply with special force to housing of old people. Similarly, in the equipping of the home, our basic guideposts should prevail, and new developments should bring new advantages to the older householder. Unfortunately though, while in many houses today, gadgets and mechanical conveniences are plentiful, few of them are found in houses of older people in a way to support independent living or to add to the amenities of living. Seldom do we find remote control TV's in the homes of the old, or telephone jacks at convenient points, or garbage disposals in the kitchens, or revolving shelves in the cupboards. Housing for old people should bear less resemblance to the minimum filtered-down dwellings of 1900; they should present intriguing settings such as those depicted in the colored pages of the magazines of young homemakers.

Neighborhood and Community Settings. Outside his home, what does the old person expect to find? What resources does he expect to find in the community? Even at the turn of the century, individual contacts were seldom limited to the immediate household or neighborhood; and, with the significant shift from an agricultural to an industrial economy, these contacts have expanded to a veritable constellation: physical contacts with other people, visual contacts with the world at large through TV, auditory contacts through telephone and radio, and written and spoken contacts through correspondence, books, magazines, and recordings—all of these have become an integral part of our daily lives.

Clearly, man, as a social being, needs the recognition of his fellow man. As his sphere of social, professional, and vocational activity becomes limited, he naturally will attach increasing importance to his belongings—his home, his furnishings, his knickknacks. Deprived of these too, he may seek satisfaction in dreaming and talking of the accomplishments of the past. Obviously then, it would be advantageous for him to remain in his original home if possible, not only because of what the home itself represents, but also because of the need to salvage those few contacts left in the community. If he should be forced to move to another neighborhood, another city, or another section of the country, he must find new ways to satisfy his social needs; he must also develop new patterns of activity and endeavor; he must seek new opportunities for participation and social experience.

What are the new patterns of activity, of participation to be? The disappearance of the household economy has deprived older people of some of the occupational roles within the family; urbanization and industrialization have further reduced the number of hours and days spent at work, so that young as well as older age groups have been forced to alter significantly their patterns of living.

Extended holidays and longer vacations have resulted in a reorganization of the lives of present middle-aged people, bringing increased personal freedom and search for activities. Sports, social activities, useful work, and hobbies have generally broadened the interest in community life. When these leisure hours are supplemented by retirement, the amount of free time is increased by about one-half. It may well be that future generations of the old, accustomed to these new patterns of leisure, will find less difficulty in working out full and satisfying lives for themselves in retirement. Certainly among the foremost supports to this pattern of life will be the physical environment of the home and the community, and the opportunities they present for maximum participation.

Variations in Need, Propensity to Change, and Ranges of Toleration. Older people form a heterogeneous group whose needs vary with the inherent differences in their natural, ethnic, and cultural backgrounds, and with the differences in the physical environments in which they have lived. Frequently, in our zeal to meet some particularly acute need, we overlook the attendant readjustment in the living patterns of the older person, which, while seemingly slight, may exceed the bounds of his toleration when added to other difficulties. In the past, individuals generally found it necessary to adjust themselves to their environment; but in the future, with the patterns of mobility of the younger population, with the conscious search for housing and living situations to suit individual needs (sometimes minor), they may find it feasible to adjust the environment to their needs, or directly to seek a more appropriate environment. Because with age, there seems to be such an acceleration of change, and of concomitant needs, it may be that some environmental adjustment will have to come with traumatic changes, but certainly through education and planning, we can ease the burden of these experiences.

Continuing to live in the same place under as nearly as possible the same conditions seems almost always the easiest thing to do. In fact, frequent change of residence or living arrangements is regarded as undesirable, if not abnormal, pattern. Unfortunately, a change in living arrangements is often less the result of careful planning or deliberate choice than the result of some change in the individual's circumstances. An obvious case is that of the middle-aged couple whose grown children have left to establish homes of their own. The older couple, with their home paid for and with many friends in the community, settle back and prepare to do the things they have always wanted to do. In this way, life continues evenly until the husband or the wife dies and the other (usually the wife) is left alone. Dramatic change is then thrust upon the widow.

Personal factors are also likely to motivate changes in living arrangements. The breadwinner retires, his income is cut in half, and as he looks at his expenditures for daily living, housing suggests itself as one of the areas in which costs could be cut. Or the widow, surveying her insurance funds, savings, and other assets, finds that even though the three-bedroom family home is comfortable and easy to run and well located, it is too much of a financial burden, so she looks for a small apartment or a hotel room. Even as the oldest generation is going through such change, the next generation is following with a twenty- or twenty-five-year lag. Thus with three, four, and sometimes even five generations of a family all living at the same time, it is not uncommon to make suitable living arrangements other than the storybook three-generation family.

A change in physical health is a common and most dreaded cause of change in living arrangements, for, with increasing infirmity or with partial or full disability, the decision to move is often thrust upon the individual against his will. Thus people who in middle age or later maturity prefer living alone may later choose to live with relatives with whom they have strong ties of affection, or they may select the institutional environment because of their impaired mental or physical health.

On the other hand, unfavorable change in the neighborhood environment may motivate a change in living arrangements. This is particularly true in or near the centers of cities where forty- or fifty-year old houses are located in neighborhoods characterized by incipient blight if not by actual slum conditions. Part of this problem may be that since houses this old will not have been properly maintained, they are likely to have deteriorated and thus to have contributed to creeping blight in the neighborhood. Or it may be that the residential neighborhood has been subjected to the effects of "progress"; the front door of the house is within fifteen or twenty feet of the whizzing traffic of a major thoroughfare, and industrial establishments have changed the pace of the neighborhood. Old families move out of the neighborhood to the suburbs as lower social and economic classes move in. All these help to make a neighborhood unfavorable; and even though such conditions may not be primary, they frequently encourage changes in living arrangements.

Other older people may change their living arrangements not to escape urban blight but to seek out a warmer and more favorable climate because of their health requirements or because of the obvious attractions that such climates offer.

## Some Common Emerging Objectives

Today most older people want and can live independently in their own homes. Some of them, as age advances, prefer the group setting of a hotel or a residence club; a still smaller number, particularly in the very late years of life as infimities increase, accept residence elsewhere in the same community. Others prefer to migrate to favored climates or to move to another place to live with a friend.

There is general agreement among professional workers in the major fields of endeavor that human services should be geared to treat and to restore all individuals to optimum health and to help them maintain themselves insofar as possible in their own homes. Whether in independent houses or apartments, or in some form of group setting, the basic objective of independence for the individual is the same, the only difference being in the extent to which it is capable of realization. In assuming the responsibility for human services, society supports the corollary that older people should remain an integral part of the community in which they spent their earlier years and should be encouraged to live the most independent lives possible for the longest practicable period in their own communities.

We have already observed that the patterns of living in early adulthood are extended with few changes into late middle age. Although some change in housing needs is suggested by reduction in the size of the family, seldom do the changes of middle age demand modifications in living arrangements or in housing. Moreover, it is unlikely that very many families would abandon their three- or four-bedroom homes for smaller ones as the children grow up and leave home, for it is part of the American dream that children will return to the homestead with children of their own; moreover, a personal status value is implied in owning a home that is more than big enough to meet one's basic needs. It is not actually until later maturity (age 60-70) that initial concern about living arrangements is likely to appear. Along with changes in mental and physical health, in marital status or income, other living arrangements are more likely to be sought.

What objectives must the house or the apartment fulfill for independent living in these later years? It must be as good as if not better than the individual's customary living quarters of earlier years: it must be suitable to the conditions of failing health and illness frequently observed; it must also have maximum adaptability to the less frequently observed conditions of illness, disability, and convalescence; and, finally, it must contribute to continuing rehabilitation of the individual.

Much of the available housing does not fulfill such objectives. Some of its shortcomings can be overcome by minor adjustments or remodeling, but more generally, barring some outside help, these shortcomings will continue on into the years because of the habits and reduced energy which are characteristic of old age.

## THE HOUSING SUPPLY

In the previous section, the particular characteristics of older people and of their housing needs have been described. In the present section, the available supply of housing will be discussed.

With the demonstrated impact of maximum independence of action and the continuing emphasis on maintenance of individuality in later maturity and old age, housing and other aspects of the environment logically seem classified in terms of relative degree of independence which they afford the individual. Further, because the relative degree of independence of living is a major criterion in choosing living quarters, a twofold classification of housing for middle-aged and older people seems particularly suitable for the present discussion.

## Housing for Independent Living

Living quarters in which the dwelling unit is separate and self-contained, according to the Bureau of Census definition, includes units that have separate kitchen or cooking facilities or units with a separate entrance from the outside or through a common hall. Thus, it includes such types as houses, apartments, flats, occupied trailers, and boats.

## Housing for Group Living

All other living quarters including living accommodations in institutions, and other quasi-household accommodations such as large rooming houses, hotels, tourist courts, dormitories, residence clubs, Y's and shelters such as the Salvation Army or mission shelters.

Under this classification, it should be noted that some institutions catering to the retired provide housing for independent living, many others offer group housing, and still others provide a variety of accommodations ranging from single-family houses to the group setting of the home for the aged and the nursing home. Thus, under group housing, the organization as an administrative and operational unit is to be distinguished from the institution as a place of residence. The latter has been defined by the Bureau of Census as places such as homes for delinquent or dependent children, homes or schools for the mentally or physically handicapped, places providing long term medical care, homes for the aged, prisons and jails. Persons in such places are ordinarily not in the labor force, have no income and are not in the housing market.

HOME OWNERSHIP. The special 1960 Census tabulations indicated that 68 per cent of householders over 60 owned their own homes in 1960.

Size of Dwellings. A comparison of size of households with size of dwellings is helpful in indicating the adequacy of space in the dwellings of older households, for 75 per cent of the households with heads 65 and over are one- and two-person households. Thus, since their households are generally smaller, older people who live in their own homes are less likely to live in crowded conditions than are younger families. The larger size of the dwellings of those 65 and over relates, of course, to the number of older people, particularly couples, who have continued to occupy a homestead purchased earlier when their children were growing up. Also, it relates to the number (albeit small) of older people of higher incomes who are able to afford a relatively high standard of living. In general, the proportional distribution of heads of households under age 65 follows fairly closely that of those for persons age 65 and over.

Valuation of Housing. Studies have shown that the value of homes owned by heads of households aged 65 and over is slightly lower than that of homes owned by younger heads of households. The median value of all owner-occupied homes in the 1960 census was $12,600 while the median value of homes owned by persons 60 to 64 was $11,000, persons 65 to 74 was $9,900 and persons over 75 was $8,600. A similar pattern is evidenced in rental housing where the median rental paid by persons under 60 years was $76 per month, persons 60 to 64 was $67, persons 65 to 74 was $61 and those over 75 was $56. These low-rental figures obviously reflect the number of heads of households in the old age group who have incomes of less than $1,000 per year. A sharp drop in income upon retirement obviously can only mean that many older people who did not already own their homes could not afford to purchase or rent adequate housing.

Condition of Dwelling Units. A slightly larger proportion of the nonfarm dwelling units of older household heads are listed as "dilapidated," than those of younger household heads. Such facilities as private toilets, baths, and running water, are increasingly apt to be missing from households as the age of the head runs beyond 60 years.

In understanding the characteristics of the housing of present generations of older people, some of the more detailed surveys of specific segments of the population are more helpful than are the Census data. Studies by academic, civic, and governmental groups have generally concerned themselves with individual communities or with specific categories of older people in the community.

Availability of Housing to the Aging Population. An examination of individual cases (as well as of generalized data) discloses that a large percentage of the older population currently reside in homes in which they have lived for the past thirty years or more, and that these were obviously bought originally as homes for younger families. Similarly, in recent years many individuals and families have bought new homes for their later years. In theory, housing on the market is just as available to the older population as to the younger population. An examination of the market and of past housing production, however, point up the following facts about major housing efforts: (1) During the 1930's it was in behalf of younger families; (2) In the early 1940's it was in behalf of defense and war workers (usually younger families); and (3) In the post war years, it was in behalf of returning veterans and newly-formed families. Thus, it stands to reason that the older population, consisting of one- and two-person households, finds itself poorly accommodated in the housing market.

If we define the housing needs of one- and two-person older households as dwelling units of one- or two-bedrooms, and examination of the total housing supply (both old and new) suggests that many of the dwelling units originally built for younger families during the 1930's and the postwar years, are nonetheless fairly suitable in size to the older population. Similarly, the one-room efficiencies and one-bedroom apartments swell the inventory of housing which may be particularly suited in size for older families.

If, however, we examine the housing situation of older one- and two-person households in terms of their finding *housing they can afford,* the situation appears far more critical; for the great majority of older people cannot afford to pay either purchase or rental prices of housing available in most of our cities today. This situation appears even more urgent when one considers that the economic position of the aging is a declining, or at best a constantly low one, compared to the economic position of younger families and individuals, which is more likely to rise with the general economy of the country.

In some communities, rental agencies and management cooperatives have been observed to discriminate against older tenants in several ways: (1) An increasingly large proportion of older residents in multi-unit housing projects was presumed to give those apartments an "aged" reputation. Many younger families, dreading the environment which a situation might create, tended to segregate themselves from older families, indeed, the presence of a high percentage of widows seemed to discourage occupancy by single and widowed males, and by couples. (2) Some rental agencies and cooperative managements, fearful that possible illnesses among older people would bring about excessive demands in terms of service and attention or that incomes might be insufficient (a) set exorbitant rentals for older people, or (b) denied them rentals outright. In the case of (a), an increase in the housing supply, plus the introduction of quota systems, has served to allay fears that projects will achieve an "aged" reputation. In the case of (b), the improvement of community medical care facilities has alleviated some of the concern about the abilities of the aged resident; moreover, experience has convinced many rental agents that the older tenant seldom defaults in the payment of his rent, is generally a longer term term resident than other tenants, and frequently takes better care of his quarters.

## Housing for Group Living: Hotels, Residence Clubs, and Rooming Houses

Those people who do not want, or are unable to live independently in their own homes (either alone or in a household with others), obviously need group housing. This is especially true for many of the increasing number of widowed and single unattached older individuals. To some extent our group housing, such as the hotel, the residence club, and the boarding house which serve the general population, can continue to serve a segment of the older population. But because individuals do tend to seek the company of their peers, because it is a convenience in management and operation to serve individuals of the same approximate age (and frequently of the same sex), group housing in our communities tends to become segregated by age.

Expressed Preferences. It is frequently presumed that the older person selects the group setting—and particularly the institution—as a last resort because of declining physical and mental health or a lack of personal security. But a number of other reasons cause some to prefer group housing.

Some people, and particularly older people, choose to live in the residence club or the hotel in order to avoid the burden of housekeeping chores. The older person living alone may find such routines at best boring, and at worst an excessive drain on his energy. The executive who is accustomed to pressing the buzzer for whatever he wants, or the well-to-do woman who devotes hours to her favorite charity while others do her household chores, may well find independent living undesirable. The traveling salesman may prefer continued residence in a hotel to living in an independent house in Florida.

The loss of spouse, death of contemporaries, moving of grown children to another part of the country, and the individual's own incapacity for maintaining his former social status are frequently pertinent reasons for the older person's choosing a group living situation. There he may find opportunities for new social contacts and may have companionship at will. The costs of maintaining the family home may be all too often beyond the older person's means. Social security and pension and retirement programs seldom permit one to live out his life in the manner to which he has been formerly accustomed.

Furthermore, some group settings offer a higher quality of housing and a more congenial environment than do independent dwellings of comparable cost. Some hotels and residence clubs offer more stimulating living environment than do some of the available small apartments—an environment in which there is less tension and more commonality of interest than in the household of a relative.

Objectives for Group Housing. Those specialized forms of housing which cater to the aging population (the residence club, the hotel, the retirement home, and the home for the aged) are inextricably bound by the overall housing goals of *separateness* and *independence,* and by their counterparts of communality and dependence. Such needs become even more pronounced in group housing than in independent housing because of the physical arrangements involved and the consequent necessity to rely upon communal facilities and service.

Individual Living Quarters. The requirements for individual living quarters within the group setting are closely akin to those of the independent dwelling unit. Those within the group setting have a similar overall objective of providing the most independent pattern of living practicable for the individual; the only difference is the grouping, physically and/or administratively, for the purpose of accomplishing certain supportive services, particularly the serving of food and the assumption of some housekeeping responsibilities. Within individual quarters, the same basic clues are applicable in planning, in establishing its size, and in selecting furnishings and facilities. But here the characteristics of individuality and independence assume an even greater importance because group effort too easily may produce stereotyped results. Then too, where an increasing number of functions are conducted as a community venture, or by management, those elements of individuality and independence which remain as the individual's own prerogative, assume an increasing importance.

For some, individual quarters within the group setting will differ from independent housing only that they do not contain full facilities for housekeeping, or for the preparation of food and serving. For others, quarters within the group setting may have to be tailored to special needs, such as the inability of the arthritic to move about freely, or the necessity for the cardiac patient to avoid certain types of exercise. In some cases, the more independent type of living quarters may be manipulated or reordered to serve this purpose; in others the specifically designed environment may be indicated.

Characteristics of the Group Setting. The arrangement of the living quarters, in relation to one another and to the facilities of the group setting, provides the physical framework that should complement the capacities of the individual to maintain himself in residence, to relate himself to other individuals within the group setting and to the community of which the group setting is a part.

The overall environment of the group setting should reflect the intended social use at the same time that it provides a framework within which the functions of service to residents may be carried on. The hotel and the residence club most simply express the group setting with services perhaps limited to housekeeping and the preparation and serving of food. The institution such as the home for the aged may also offer a wide range of facilities such as the beauty shop, the chapel, the hospital, or others provided by the community at large. Where the services are fewer, there may be a greater freedom in ordering of the individual living quarters, but, on the other hand, the desirable characteristics of the former need not be sacrificed because of number of the services which might be embodied in the latter.

Two basic aspects of the physical environment appear particularly pertinent in establishing a desirable social framework of the group setting: (1) *the pattern of communication and circulation within the setting,* and (2) *the focus, or focii of individual and group endeavors.*

1. *The pattern of communication and circulation.* The thread of communication (the telephone or the intercommunication line) make it possible for the older person to maintain contacts of earlier years and also to reach the management either for routine or emergency requests. The circulation routes, the walkways and the halls or corridors are the physical routes which relate the older person to other residents in the group, to management, and its services within the setting, and finally to the community outside. Now we need research to show how interior functions and space can be organized so as to foster increased socialization within the group setting.

Excessively long and monotonous corridors make for an "institutionalized" feeling; but even when the length of the corridor is cut to a reasonable dimension or to the minimum prescribed by a building or fire code, the greatest concession made to the older inhabitants is a handrail down either side of the corridor. What would be more important would be to make the corridor a place conducive to positive relationships between individuals, as cheerful and well illuminated as their living quarters or the communal spaces to which it leads. Ways must be found whereby the older residents can meet together informally and naturally, simulating perhaps family and neighborhood living. This will probably require not only the small, cozy sitting room, but also some public yet casual place that does for the group setting what sidewalk, streets and back doors do for the residential neighborhood.

2. *The focus, or focii of individual and group endeavors.* Just as the general store with its potbellied stove was a focus of yesterday's informal community contacts, so today, there needs to be a focus for contact—cultural, recreational and social—in the group setting. In the community at large, day centers, and recreational and hobby centers are attempting to meet such need. Some group settings may

be able to use community facilities outside the institution; others may find it necessary to establish their own.

What is important is that the need be recognized, in a way that is suitable to the particular requirements of those older people. Social and recreational facilities do not have to be very elaborate or even extremely spacious. As a matter of fact, some of our less admirable and less successful efforts have gone into building spacious public lounges where 50 to 100 people can be seated, but where many people talking at once, or worse, unoccupied emptiness, makes it impossible for two or three persons to visit with the dignity and grace which should be accorded adults. While there is value in having space for a large group on occasion, there may be other, more pressing needs of individuals for the total number of their waking hours!

In the small grouping of apartments, which relies upon the established facilities across the street or down the block, there need be no more than a lounge near the mailbox where residents may wait for the postman, or a little larger space near the entrance or the manager's office. On the other hand, larger populations may require a variety of communal use spaces—sitting rooms, dining rooms, group activity rooms, and rooms in which organized therapies can be conducted.

Some early, and too eager enthusiasm over the potentials of group therapy has caused, on occasion, the sacrifice of the quality of individual living quarters for the satisfaction of having provided a space for each activity listed in current literature. Institutions particularly have subscribed to such a notion, and agencies (including public ones), in establishing criteria, have been guilty of following the same trend. The realistic relationship between the quantity of space allocated for residential purposes, and that allocated for communal use needs to be determined. Even where there are ample funds for building activity spaces and for hiring the personnel to staff them, their efficiency in terms of the total population which is to use them must be found. Finally, it is important that the services of the group setting are being used to supplement, not to supplant, the services provided by the community or the resources of the individual.

Group Size. Concepts of optimum size in group endeavor are in a state of flux. Today's sense of scale and number has expanded beyond yesterday's. Although professional workers in psychology, social work, and planning have variously indicated that an ideal social grouping contains nine to fifteen people, there is little data to confirm these figures for older people in the group setting in terms either of the inherent virtues of such group sizes or of the physical characteristics of the architectural spaces such a group requires.

In architecture, it is possible to order the environment in such a way that it is composed of a number of distinct individual parts, each constructed on a human scale and each producing a feeling of neighborliness. If there is validity in the group size of nine to fifteen people, carefully documented research would certainly guide the architect who believes that a large number of rooms on a floor give strength and boldness to the overall exterior expression, or the religious or fraternal groups who feel that concentrating their resources in one large institution will give them prestige and stability.

Access to the Community. The more nearly the front walk and the entrance give access to individual quarters, the more free and comfortable the older person and his visitors will probably feel in leaving and entering. The present popularity of the motel type of structure among retired people is in part an indication of such a preference. One of the basic objectives for the group setting is the ordering of the environment in such a way that individual residents will function as an integral part of community life. Thus there is a relationship of the entrances and walkways between various sections of the group setting, and between the group setting and the community in which it is located. Unfortunately, it is frequently felt that the structure which provides for a number of individuals should be set back from the street a little further than the usual residence; or, because so much was said in earlier years about spatial tensions, it is thought desirable that standards of distance between building units be further and further increased. Or, another example: entrances to individual dwelling units are sometimes located on opposite sides of buildings—privacy for the individual being sought just when the need is for an increase in opportunity for casual and informal contact.

## CONCLUSION

Our knowledge of the environment in which middle-aged and older people live is fragmentary. Most of it is based upon personal observation of a limited number of cases in both the independent and group setting. The basic data which are available are far too scant to make many of the broad assumptions which are necessary for effective action.

How do middle-aged and older people want to live? To perhaps no other question are so many contradictory answers given. Even acknowledging that people seldom have the opportunity of choosing their living environments freely, present indications are that they desire and need a variety of living environments.

There is a general paucity of knowledge about housing and in particular about how people use their housing. Organomic research with emphasis on method of research design is needed. Little is known about the relationships between individuals as mediated by the neighborhood environment and by housing design considerations. Needs-demands studies are desirable, not only of present generations, but of future generations of older individuals—individuals who have experienced higher standards of living, and increasing amounts of leisure time, and have been planning ahead for their retirement.

In the efforts to better understand the problems and issues that relate to the neighborhoods and the housing in which older people live, one question should remain foremost: How can situations be best achieved in each of our communities, in which as many individuals as possible might find for *themselves* dignified and meaningful ways of life up through their old age?

## REFERENCES


Bernadette de Lourdes, Moth M.: *Where Somebody Cares.* New York, Putnam, 1959.

Burgess, Ernest S. (Ed.): *Retirement Villages.* Ann Arbor, U. of Mich., 1961.

Carp, Francis: *A Future for the Aged.* Austin, U. of Tex., 1966.

Carp, F.M., and Burnett, W.M. (Eds.): Patterns of living and housing of middle-aged and older people. Proceedings of Research Conference on Patterns of Living and Housing of the Middle-Aged and Older People, March 21-24, 1965. *Public Health Service Publication No. 1496.* Washington, D.C., U.S. Dept. Health, Education and Welfare, 1966.

Chapin, F.S.: Some housing factors related to mental hygiene. In *Social Policy and Social Research in Housing.* Myrton, R.K.; West, Patricia S.; Jahoda, Marie, and Selvin, R.C. (Eds.), New York, Assn Pr., pp. 164-71.

DONAHUE, WILMA (Ed.): *Housing the Aging.* Ann Arbor, U. of Mich., 1954.

DONAHUE, WILMA; HUNTER, W.W., and COONS, DOROTHY H.: A study of the socialization of old people. *Geriatrics, 8*:656-666, 1953.

FESTINGER, L.; SCHACTER, S., and BACK, K.: *Social Pressures in Informal Groups: A Study of Human Factors in Housing.* New York, Harper, 1950.

FESTINGER, L: Architecture and group membership. In *Social Policy and Social Research in Housing.* Merton, R.K.; West, Patricia S.; Jahoda, Marie, and Selvin, H.C. (Eds.), New York, Assn Pr., 1951, pp. 152-163.

GILBRETH, LILLIAN M.; THOMAS, O.M., and CLYMER, E.: *Management in the Home.* New York, Dodd, 1955.

GINZBERG, R.; BRINEGAR, W.C.; DUNN, F.K., and OLSVARY, VILMA: Improvisations in rural Iowa. In *Housing the Aging.* Donahue, Wilma (Ed.), Ann Arbor, U. of Mich., 1954, pp. 91-103.

KLABER, E.H.: *Housing Design.* New York, Reinhold, 1954.

Massachusetts State Housing Board: *Standards of Design: Housing for the Elderly.* Boston, The Board, 1954.

MAXWELL, JEAN M.: *Centers for Older People, Guide for Programs and Facilities, a Project Report.* New York, The National Council on the Aging, 1962.

MUSSON, NOVERRE, and HEUSINKVELD, HELEN: *Buildings for the Elderly.* New York, Reinhold, 1963.

National Safety Council: *Accident Facts.* Chicago, The Council, 1965.

NEUGARTEN, BERNICE L.: The Kansas City studies of adult life. *Newsletter (Geront Soc), 4*(4):9, 1957.

ORBACH, H.L., and SHAW, D.M.: Social participation and the role of the aging. *Geriatrics, 12*:241-246, 1957.

PEACOCK, J.F.: Detached dwellings. In *Housing the Aging.* Donahue, Wilma (Ed.), Ann Arbor, U. of Mich., 1954, pp. 64-71.

ROSOW, IRVING: *Social Integration of the Aged.* New York, Free Press, 1967.

RUSK, H. A. and TAYLOR, E. J.: *Living with a Disability.* Philadelphia, Blakiston, 1953.

SCHRAMM, WILBUR, and STOREY, RUTH T.: *Little House, A Study of Senior Citizens.* Stanford, Stanford University Institute for Communication Research, 1962.

WARREN, ELLEN: After discharge from the hospital, how do older people get along at home? *Geriatrics, 12*:233-240, 1957.

WILLIAMS, RICHARD H., *et al.* (Eds.): *Processes of Aging.* New York, Atherton, 1963, vols. 1 and 2.

WILNER, DANIEL M., *et al*: *The Housing Environment and Family Life, A Longitudinal Study of the Effects of Housing on Morbidity and Mental Health.* Baltimore, Johns Hopkins, 1962.

VIVRETT, WALTER K.: Designing a retirement community. In *Housing the Elderly in Retirement Communities.* Burgess, E. W. (Ed.), Ann Arbor, U. of Mich., Division of Gerontology, 1960.

VIVRETT, W. K.; ORBACH, H. L., and SHAW, D. M.: Planning study, housing

*Handbook of Social Gerontology.* Tibbets, Clark (Ed.), Chicago, U. of Chicago, 1960, pp. 549-617.

Vivrett, W. K.: Orbach, H. L., and *Shaw,* D. M.: Planning study, housing for the aging. Unpublished studies of retired persons of Minneapolis and St. Paul. Minneapolis, U. of Minn., School of Architecture, 1955.

Vivrett, W. K.: Specially designed housing for elderly persons. A report to the Federal Housing Administration. Minneapolis, The Author (Mimeographed).

*Chapter 14*

# CLOTHING

ADELINE M. HOFFMAN

CLOTHING IS A subject of universal interest in which numerous people claim a degree of expertise or authority. Among them are the designers, manufacturers, retailers and fashion forecasters, and the social scientists and home economists. According to George Hartman, clothing is a "persistent center of interest in everyone's life" and though it varies greatly in intensity and manner of expression, it is a fundamental life interest.[1] Clothing has always been regarded as one of the essential needs of people but it has only recently become an area of serious scientific research among the social scientists and home economists. Both popular writers and psychologists have recognized the psychological value of being well dressed at any age and in any environment, and the desire for approval in people of all ages. Thus, it has often been pointed out that we dress for other people, for their approval, and that in their approval we find our sense of well-being, self-confidence and social acceptance.

Lawrence Langner, in his book, The Importance of Wearing Clothes, wrote that "one of the greatest spiritual needs of people is the admiration of their fellow men and women and here clothing plays a major role." [2] Such expressions of the significance of clothes are found in the writings of others from various walks of life. Thorstein Veblen, in his classic of economic thought, *The Theory of the Leisure Class,* wrote that "the need for dress is eminently a higher or spiritual need" and referred to the relationship of dress to canons of good taste and reputability.[3] Likewise, Ralph Waldo Emerson, in his essay on Social Aims, said "the sense of being well dressed gives a feeling of inward tranquility which religion is powerless to bestow." In the Shakespearean plays, there are many references to the significance of clothing, the most familiar of which is probably one from *Hamlet* in which Polonius said "costly thy habit as thy purse can buy, but not expressed in fancy, rich, not gaudy; for the apparel oft proclaims the man."

Among the various roles of clothing is the expression of personality of the wearer. In commenting on clothing as an expression of personality, George Dearborn, an early twentieth century psychologist said "we might consider clothing as a vicarious artificial skin, almost an extension of the individual boundary, involving important relationships between the person and his environment, spiritual as well as material." [4] Evidence of aesthetic sensitivity is expressed in clothing in the choice of color, design, texture, decoration and distinctiveness, all of which contribute to setting each individual apart from others. Thus, clothing may become a source of aesthetic enjoyment. Clothing that is attractive and wins the approval of others provides an important measure of ego support, and compliments on clothes take on a decidedly positive value. Those who are not sensitive to the aesthetic values, fail to gain maximum enjoyment from their clothing.

In certain periods of history, masculine attire was rich, colorful and ostentatious and had a greater claim to beauty than did feminine attire. However, this is not true today, and when we speak of fashion in clothing, it is generally in terms of feminine wear. Even though there has been much recent effort to emphasize fashion in men's clothing and greater differentiation in its use, most fashion interest is still centered on womens' clothing. Fashion in womens' clothing changes more rapidly, womens' wardrobes are generally larger than those of men, and womens' expenditures for clothing are usually larger than mens' expenditures. Also, women have more problems in satisfying their clothing needs than do men and are more concerned with the social significance of their clothing. Thus, most of the writing and research in the field of clothing for older people has been concerned with older women rather than older men. This chapter will deal with the clothing problems of older women and their clothing behavior.

## SPECIAL SIGNIFICANCE OF CLOTHING FOR OLDER WOMEN

In developing new social relationships, in maintaining a positive self-image, and in providing ego support, clothing has special significance for older women. There was a woman who came to live in a retirement home in Iowa who wired her son-in-law shortly after she moved into the home to tell him that she would need at least six new dresses if she was to associate with the other women in the home. Here was a woman who recognized the importance of clothing in social acceptability. The need for new social contacts, for affection and personal dignity become particularly important for older women because of the loss of family members and friends and the resultant feelings of loneliness and uselessness. Loss of status as a result of termination of employment at retirement age may become a drain on the ego, especially when it is accompanied by sharply reduced income. Under such circumstances, effective use of clothing to create attractive appearance can do much to provide ego support and greater assurance of social acceptance and to retain a positive self-image.

Jane Baird points out in her book, *The Harvest Years,* that one of the chief drawbacks of growing old is the physical changes that take place in appearance. Even at best, appearance (a) is a very elusive thing, (b) is important at every age, and (c) is ever changing from childhood to old age. If the gradual process of aging is understood and accepted by older women, the changes brought about by aging need not be accompanied by feelings of hopelessness and despair. Almost every woman, even every older woman, has a secret desire to be beautiful, and the effect of aging should be thought of not as beauty departing but rather as beauty changing.[5]

In appraising the special significance of clothing for older women and the importance of beauty in their appearance, some consideration might be given to the wearing of hats. The hat is one of the most misunderstood and underestimated accessories of feminine dress, and in the casualness of today's standards of dress, the hat is rapidly decreasing in importance. Yet, the wearing of a hat still carries with it a certain sense of dignity, formality and authority no matter what the season. A hat is more than protection for the head. It is adornment—it is a frame for the face and the single most important accent to a smart appearance. For the older woman, the hat works wonders in appearance and provides a culminating touch to the ensemble. More than any other item of adornment, the hat proclaims the status of the wearer. A psychologist, in discussing hats, said, "a hat is not a thing, a hat is an idea—it is a crown." It is woman's concession to the Goddess of beauty. A hat has little practical utility, but it has much psychological utility.

### Clothing in Retirement Homes and Nursing Homes

What is said of clothing in relation to older women applies equally to those living in their own homes and in retirement homes with the exception that clothing may become more important in some retirement homes where there is daily contact with many of the residents in the home. Also in some retirement homes, there is more active social life than older women may experience while living in homes of their own. In nursing homes, however, there is drastic change in activities and in social life which adds another dimension to the importance of clothing. In addition to the social values, there are therapeutic values in clothing and its effective use. Good appearance of women in nursing homes is an important source of compliments which add to the individual's sense of well-being. There is likely to be little eventfulness in the lives of women in nursing homes, but the little there is can be highlighted through dressing up and thus adding to the importance of an otherwise common-place occasion. The tone of the occasion even in a nursing home can be set by the clothes that are worn, thereby adding a measure of stimulation and enjoyment.

Under favorable conditions, daytime clothes should be worn during the day in preference to night clothes or lounging wear to create a feeling of recovery to normal health rather than that of being ill. Women in nursing homes should have the opportunity to choose their own clothing since choice in itself has the therapeutic value of achievement, personal control and expression of individuality. Even though most women in nursing homes have less need for new clothes than do those in normal health, there is some therapeutic value in newness itself. New clothes create a feeling of anticipation, of looking ahead rather than backward into the past when one's old clothes were new and perhaps in fashion. In this way, new clothes become a link with the outside world and convey a sense of the future rather than of the past.[6]

## PROBLEMS INVOLVED IN SATISFYING CLOTHING NEEDS

The clothing needs of older women, by and large, are similar to those of middle-aged women and the problems they encounter in providing themselves with suitable clothing are similar to the problems encountered by middle-aged women. However, they also have some needs and some problems which may be age-related and which fall mainly into three categories. They consist of (a) the economic problem (or ability to pay), (b) the suitability in terms of design, color, and fabric, and (c) the fitting standards.

## Economic Problems

It is difficult to make a general statement concerning the economic problems of older women or their ability to pay, since figures on income levels of older women taken from various sources are not in agreement. Even though percentage figures are available for older people at specific low income levels, they do not provide a basis for generalizing for all old people.[7] What we do know is that the incomes of wage earners are greatly reduced after retirement and that this is also true among many professional people, and that in the use of limited incomes, expenditures for food, housing, and health maintenance take priority over expenditures for all other needs. However, in a recent study in Iowa, in which the wives of retired professional men were interviewed, 12 per cent reported an increase in income following retirement, 28 per cent no change and 60 per cent a considerable decrease.[8]

On levels of expenditure for clothing among older women as compared with younger women, authorities agree that expenditures for clothing decrease regardless of income and social and cultural level of the older women.[9] Reasons given for this pattern of expenditure are that the need for clothing decreases with curtailed social activity resulting in less wear and tear on clothing and less need, therefore, to replace clothing. Reluctance to accept fashion change and the purchase of more casual clothing are other reasons given for reduced expenditure for clothing among older women. However, some research findings are not in agreement with this pattern of clothing expenditure and with the reluctance of older women to accept fashion change. How much less older women spend on clothing compared with other age groups depends somewhat on the specific groups represented in the statistics from which generalizations are drawn. It is reported that among the very low-income groups, there is practically no expenditure for clothing at all and that these groups depend on used clothing given to them by individuals and community groups. Among older people with fixed incomes from various sources including retirement systems, insurance and the like, it has been pointed out in some market research that expenditures for clothing are higher because many of the older people do not need to save money from current income, since their living expenses are easily covered by their incomes.[10] This depends very much on income levels of groups to which reference is made.

While age 65 is generally accepted as retirement age and it is typically the group age 65 and over that is referred to as the older people, those in this age category do not necessarily regard age 65 as a dividing line separating them from those regarded as middle aged. We do know that the change from the middle years to old age is gradual and that the rate of change varies among individuals. Some people are obviously young in their 70's, some are obviously old in their 50's and the self-image of the individual has its effect on clothing needs and clothing expenditures. In a study by Bader, in a community in Iowa, it was found that in a sample of sixty women age 65 and over, 70 per cent reported that they considered themselves middle-aged and only 20 per cent that they considered themselves old. The remaining 10 per cent could not quite place themselves in an age category, but they did not consider themselves old.[11] In the study of wives of retired professional men in Iowa, in which the wives were age 60 to 90, 12 per cent considered themselves as being young, 65 per cent as middle aged, 25 per cent as old and 7 per cent as elderly.[12]

## Design Problems

Research reported by home economists and marketing specialists shows that one of the problems encountered by older women in shopping for clothing is that of finding clothing suitable in design, color and weight.[13] In our youth-oriented society, designers and manufacturers, for the most part, apparently accept the general idea that all American women are young regardless of age and that they want to appear as young as possible, despite the fact that every day hundreds of women pass their sixty-fifth and seventy-fifth birthdays. And while it may be easy to accept the youthful American ideal, it must be recognized that there are also the grandmothers who resist the attempts of Madison Avenue to keep them forever young.[14] Those who are proud of their years and the dignity and authority which are the rewards of age, resent the encumbrance of youth which is being thrust upon them.

Specific design features preferred by older women have been reported in preference studies made by home economists in which there is general agreement.[15] Older women prefer gored skirts rather than very slim straight skirts or those gathered or pleated. While some preferences may reflect fashions from the past to which women have become accustomed, most preferences stem from need for becomingness and functional convenience. They prefer sleeves that are three-quarter length or just below the elbow and they do not like sleeveless dresses or those with very short sleeves. Neckline preference is the V shape without collars and round necklines starting a few inches below the neck. In dresses, front openings to below the waist or all the way are preferred rather than side openings or back openings and back openings are the most disliked of all design features. Back zippers from the neck to below the waistline are difficult even for younger women, and they are especially difficult for older women who may have a touch of arthritis and therefore have a problem in reaching and manipulating zippers. Dressing and undressing is strenuous exercise for some older women and the design of garments is an important factor in contributing to the ease of this daily routine.

Color is another factor important to older women in the selection of clothing, especially dresses. Many older women who are overweight and wear large sizes, resent the nondescript little floral prints that often appear in large size dresses and they also resent the lack of interesting stimulating color in large size clothing. Perhaps manufacturers still believe that large women should wear dull middle-value colors to make them less conspicuous and that only small size women should wear colorful clothing, thus penalizing women who wear large sizes. Color provides stimulation which is needed by women of all sizes and aesthetic sensitivity is not determined by body size. But small size women also have problems in terms of color selection. Because of their small size, they are often directed to childrens' departments were colors may be particularly lavish, loud and gay and not appropriate for older women. While it is generally accepted in theory that there is some relationship between color preference and personality, it is interesting to note that in some of the recent studies which have touched on color preferences, older women have indicated a preference for blue. In the Bader study, which was done in a rural area in Iowa, a majority of women claimed blue as their favorite color for clothing and this was also true in the Houston study.[16, 17]

## Fitting Problems

Recent research by home economists reveals that good fit is the factor of greatest importance to older women in selecting their clothing, that becomingness is the next most important factor, and that durability and ease of care are of least importance.[18] Perhaps the main reason why good fit is so important is because it is so difficult to achieve. Most of the fitting problems of older women stem from changes in body proportions which usually begin in the middle years and tend to become accentuated with time. This means that the older woman no longer fits into standard sizes and therefore complains that she cannot find clothes that fit. Someone, making light of the problem of changing body proportions said, "birthdays do not change us, but they surely rearrange us." Typically, the face thins out, the abdomen and hips expand, the legs get thinner and the waistline almost disappears. This makes it difficult to keep belts in place on dresses with waistline seams, and women often complain that belts are too short. Finally, the figure with sloping shoulders takes on a pear-shaped appearance and the figure with broad shoulders takes on the appearance of a barrel on stilts.

Some older women do maintain their normal body weight and proportions throughout life and thus have no special fitting problem in the selection of clothing, but the typical problem is that of added weight. There are also those older women who lose weight and get noticeably thinner, but obesity is a much greater problem. In addition to changes in weight, there are some other changes that effect clothing. The skin becomes dry, thin and inelastic as a result of a decrease in glandular secretion. Thus the skin becomes sensitive to rough textures and heavy fabrics and to changes in temperature both in winter and in summer. As a result, older women often feel the need of a sweater, stole or jacket and they avoid going out of doors in the very hot and very cold weather. While these body changes are taking place, a slight decrease occurs in height which is probably one reason why so many older women wear half sizes (which are shorter both in the waist and the skirt).

In the Houston study, three-fourths of the women in the sample of sixty over age 65 changed dress sizes from the time they were age 40.[19] In this study, half of the women in the group changed to larger sizes and half to smaller sizes, but well over three-fourths of the women wore half sizes. In the Bader study, three-fourths of the sample of sixty women age 65 and over wore half sizes though they ranged in actual size from ten to forty-eight.[20] In both studies, it was found that the most common alteration needed in dresses was the enlargement of the waistline. Whether or not designers and pattern makers for manufacturers of large size clothing take into consideration these special needs of older women is not known. However, there are women's clothing stores in some of the larger cities which specialize in large size clothing which can be adapted to the needs of older women, but the price lines of these stores limit the patronage to those with substantial incomes.

## Reaching the Older Market

It has been suggested by people concerned with the needs of older women, that clothing be specially designed and proportioned for older women, but at the same time, they are not in favor of identifying this particular age group. The problem is, therefore, how to reach this group without labeling it in terms of age. Marketing specialists see great potential in what they call the older market, but they regard it as a touchy one to approach, and they carefully avoid any mention of age, since many older women resist age-related identity which reflects a certain unavoidable stigma in a youth-oriented society.[21] How many women, they ask, would want to publicly admit to their years and seek out a department in a store set aside for older women?

In the Bader study, women were asked how they felt about a special department in a store for older women, and they were evenly divided as to those in favor and those not in favor of such departments. Those in favor thought this might help to cut down on shopping effort and those not in favor thought the clothing would not be smartly designed if it were intended for older women and also that the colors would not be interesting.[22] One solution to the problem might be a special size range proportioned to reflect changes in body proportions, using a name that would not suggest age identity. The immediate solution, at least for the present, appears to be selection within the current fashion picture in the most suitable size range. Specially proportioned clothing is available in other size categories such as petites, half sizes and talls, and it is not inconceivable that specially designed and specially proportioned clothing will be made for older women in the future and be marketed successfully without age identification.

## CLOTHING BEHAVIOR

Most of the early gerontological research was done in the health related fields and little had been done until recently in the area of clothing behavior. Those in marketing research have been interested in finding ways of reaching the older market and home economists have been interested in clothing preferences, problems in satisfying clothing needs of older women, their use of clothing and their attitudes concerning clothing. In much of this research, samples have been relatively small and have been limited in terms of socioeconomic levels. No longitudinal research has been reported in the area of clothing behavior.

It has been said that "we are what we are because of all our yesterdays and that as we grow older, we become more like ourselves." In a study of clothing behavior done in Pennsylvania in 1954 and 1955, relationships were found to exist between clothing behavior and certain social, cultural and economic background factors.[23] In this study, women with urban backgrounds were found to be more interested in clothes, to have larger wardrobes, and to spend more money on clothes than women with rural backgrounds. Also it was found in the same study that high educational level correlated with high aesthetic sensitivity as expressed in the selection and use of clothing, and that dressing up for home entertaining during childhood could be linked with dressing up for social occasions in adulthood. Thus it appeared that the roots of clothing behavior in older women may be found in their childhood. However, circumstances of the later years and also changes in one's hierarchy of values may serve to modify earlier influences in clothing behavior.

The manifestations, usually cataloged as clothing behavior, include interest in clothing, attitudes toward clothing, use of clothing, purchasing of clothing and possession and accumulation of clothing. In research, we attempt to measure these manifestations of clothing behavior, some of which can be measured with a high degree of accuracy and others which are much more difficult to measure. Clothing expenditure and volume of wardrobe can be measured objectively, but no one has yet devised a satisfactory instrument for the measurement of interest in clothing.[24]

Many variables can effect interest in clothing, which make such measurement an intricate process at best, and even then, one is not sure that what is being measured is actually interest in clothing. However, in terms of interest in clothing as it has been measured in some recent studies, Bader found that there was little loss of interest among older women until age 75, that older women were interested in clothing, that they wanted smartly styled attractive clothing and that they have a tendency to retain clothing attitudes and behavior patterns from the middle years.[25] Over half the women interviewed in this study felt that clothing was just as important to them as it was when they were younger, and over one-fourth of them felt it was more important, and a smaller proportion of the women felt it was less important. Concerning reaction to fashion change in the Bader study, there was evidence that older women were highly selective and deliberate in accepting fashion change and that they made serious judgment of what was suitable for them as older women and as individuals.

The effects of the husbands' retirement on interest in clothing were found in the study of wives of retired professional men. Three-fourths of the women felt that their husbands' retirement had no effect on their interest in clothing while the remaining fourth felt that it had decreased their interest. Reasons given by those who did not lose interest were the following: (a) their appearance was just as important as ever, (b) they still loved clothes, (c) they liked to appear well before their children, and (d) they were still clothes conscious and their husbands' retirement had nothing to do with their clothes. Among the reasons given by those who did not maintain their interest were that they had fewer occasions for public appearance and less need for dress up clothes. Concerning their attitudes toward dress up affairs, three-fourths of the women liked them for the following reasons: (a) dressing up made them feel good, (b) they enjoyed beautiful clothes, (c) being all dressed up made one feel like a different person, and (d) they responded to the dignity, formality and graciousness of the occasion. Those who didn't like dress-up affairs felt they were too much trouble, took too much energy to get ready; they disliked crowds and were bored with teas and luncheons.[26]

### Wardrobes

Clothing behavior is manifested in many ways in the individual wardrobe, the most important of which are: expenditure level, variety of garments, and frequency of purchasing clothing. Although clothing expenditures decrease with age increments regardless of social, cultural and economic level, exceptions appear in some studies. In the Bader study, two-thirds of the women purchased the same amount of clothing and better quality than they did before and in the Houston study two-thirds of the women had more money available for clothing and purchased more clothing.[27, 28] It may be worth noting that many of the women in a research group at this time must have been 30 to 40 years of age during the depression, and this would affect the relationship between amount spent on clothing at that time and after age 65. In the study of wives of retired professional men, a small proportion of the women spent more for clothing after their husbands retired, and almost half the group purchased clothing more frequently, but purchasing garments for special occasions dropped off following retirement of the husbands. Very little change occurred in the variety of garments in wardrobes, with a very small percentage reporting greater variety and less variety.[29]

## HAIR CARE AND GROOMING

Closely related to clothing behavior are grooming and other efforts to enhance personal attractiveness, the most important of which are care of the hair and judicious use of cosmetics. In the study of wives of retired professional men, about one-third of the wives increased their beauty shop patronage after their husbands' retirement and a very small fraction decreased their patronage. For those who increased their beauty shop patronage, the main reason was their greater need at this time of their lives to maintain a high level of appearance. For the smaller number who decreased their patronage, the reasons were that it took too much effort to get ready to go, the problem of transportation and cost which they avoided by taking care of their needs at home.[30]

## CONCLUSION

Clothing is a persistent center of interest in the lives of all people, and for older women, it can be an important source of ego support and enhancement of the self-image as well as a basis for social acceptability and expression of personality. Many of the problems older women face in finding suitable clothing for themselves will be relieved when designers, manufacturers and retailers recognize the needs and potential of the older market and the increasingly large segment of the population which is represented in the older market.

In conducting research in the clothing behavior of older women, it is difficult to isolate variables and to make measurements that are entirely objective. To determine sources of clothing behavior in the later years, it would be important to have some background information on the women concerned to determine whether specific factors of clothing behavior were age related or related more directly to influences from social, cultural and economic background. There is need for longitudinal studies of many different kinds of groups of women, representing a range of socioeconomic and cultural levels before generalizations can be made about clothing behavior of older women. Only as we are able to see common clothing behavioral patterns among diverse groups of older women will we be able to make general statements that relate to all older women.

## REFERENCES

1. Hartman, George W.: Clothing: personal problem and social issue. *J Home Economics, ILI* (6):295, June 1949.
2. Langner, Lawrence: *The Importance of Wearing Clothes.* New York, Hastings, 1959.
3. Veblen, Thorstein: *The Theory of the Leisure Class.* New York, Macmillan, 1899.

4. Dearborn, George Van Ness: The psychology of clothes. *Psychol Monogr, XXVI* (112):172, 1918.
5. Baird, Janet K. (Ed.): *These Harvest Years.* Garden City, Doubleday, 1951.
6. Hoffman, Adeline M.: Clothing: social and therapeutic values. In *Nursing and Retirement Home Administration.* Jacobs, H. Lee, and Morris, W. W. (Eds.), Ames, Iowa State, 1966, chap. 8.
7. Dodge, Robert E.: Purchasing habits and market potentialities of the older consumer. *Law and Contemporary Problems, XXVII* (1):142-156, Winter 1962.
8. Hoffman, Adeline M.: Clothing problems and clothing behavior of wives of retired professional men. Unpublished research, Department of Home Economics and Institute of Gerontology, University of Iowa, 1965.
9. Gidlow, Elsa: The senior market. *Sales Management, LXXVII* (9):35-39, 108, 110-111, Oct. 20, 1961.
10. Brill, Emil E.: Your billion dollar market—our over 16,000,000 senior citizen customers. *The Credit World, XLIX* (10):6-10, July 1961.
11. Bader, Iva M.: An Exploratory Study of the Clothing Problems and Attitudes of a Group of Older Women in Iowa City, Iowa. Master's Thesis, University of Iowa, 1963.
12. Hoffman, Wives of retired professional men, *op. cit.*
13. Dodge, *op. cit.*
14. Chay, Marie: Sempre Giovani. *Vogue, CXXX* (6):89, 91, 100, Oct. 1, 1957.
15. Tate, Mildred Thurow, and Glisson, Oris: *Family Clothing.* New York, Wiley, 1961.
16. Bader, *op. cit.*
17. Houston, Peggy Stiles: Changes in Clothing Behavior of Older Rural Women. Master's Thesis, University of Iowa, 1965.
18. Tate and Glisson, *op. cit.*
19. Houston, *op. cit.*
20. Bader, *op. cit.*
21. Gidlow, *op. cit.*
22. Bader, *op. cit.*
23. Hoffman, Adeline M.: Clothing Behavioral Factors for a Specific Group of Women Related to Aesthetic Sensitivity and Certain Socio-Economic and Psychological Background Factors. Ph.D. Dissertation, Pennsylvania State University, 1956.
24. *ibid.*
25. Bader, *op. cit.*
26. Hoffman, Wives of retired professional men, *op cit.*
27. Bader, *op. cit.*
28. Houston, *op. cit.*
29. Hoffman, Wives of retired professional men, *op. cit.*
30. *ibid.*

*Chapter 15*

# FAMILY RELATIONS AND THE AGED

MARVIN B. SUSSMAN

MODERN TECHNOLOGY, preventive medicine, and improved techniques of health care, hospital treatment and rehabilitation have had a profound effect upon the age structure of our society. More individuals today than their grandfathers survive beyond four score and ten. In 1900, the life expectancy for white males was 48 years; for females, 51 years; nonwhite males, 33 years; and females, 35 years. In the early sixties, white males could expect to survive to age 68; females, 74; nonwhite males, 62; and females, 67.[1] With this trend continuing, the necessity to consider the role of the aged in society becomes more pronounced. What rapidly becomes obvious is that neither are most of the aged "prepared" for aging, nor is society ready for them. Although industrialized society has made the retirement period possible, it has not provided positive roles for its older citizens. As a consequence of inadequate social definitions of what it means to be past the active parental and work-centered years and the ambiguity over the place of leisure in a work-oriented culture, older individuals are often assigned "roleless roles in American society," [2] and some find their fate is to "step into social nothingness." [3]

While feeling useful can result from activities other than engagement in the labor market, the dominant cultural value is the utility of work; a value intertwined with social status and social class postures; a value which by implication castigates nonworkers as useless and shiftless. The forced retirement of the aged and the joblessness of the underclassed, the poor, epitomizes the absolute rejection and removal of individuals from the mainstreams of society. The aged person's range of choice to participate in society is externally limited by these factors as well as by increasing physical limitations.

---

Special appreciation is given to Donna Siegel for her assistance in the preparation of this chapter.

After struggling for livelihood in a work-oriented and money-oriented society, persons reaching the crossroads of 65 are sometimes forced to stop many of the activities that have become habit or the paramount focus of concern to them. First their yearly income is reduced markedly. The Social Security Administration reports that in 1960 the median income for two-person families was barely half as large when the family head was aged 65 or over as when he was under 65. The median personal income for a male household head over 65 was $1,900; and the median total income of the families they headed $2,900, compared to $5,900 for families headed by a person under 65. Persons aged 65, not institutionalized, living alone or with nonrelatives, had a median income of slightly over $1,000.[4]

Secondly, without much preparation and with few opportunities to be socialized into retirement roles they are turned loose to work out schedules for using work day time and to develop their own interests and activities or to take on new ones. Complicating the adjustment into retirement is the dominantly held view that the space left in an individual's life after 65 cannot be considered "leisure" in the ordinary sense, but rather is "time which has to be filled." [5] The stereotype is that productivity in any form is impossible and to some, even undesirable.

A higher proportion of retired professionals, farmers, and self-employed persons continue their middle-adult years' activities on a reduced scale, than salaried people, wage earners, public service employees, clerical and industrial workers, and business people. The latter groups are less able to mould former work patterns to suit their own inclinations.[6] Health, of course, is a crucial factor, and debilitating conditions have more effect on manual, compared to sedentary or "intellectual" type activities. Another major reason for the difference between the two groups is economic capabilities. Members of higher social classes have more alternatives to choose activities which enhance preservation of functions. Thus far, research has yielded some evidence that activity is preservative.[7] In the realms of both work and leisure, more information is needed on what kinds of activities are physically and mentally suitable for older individuals, and what is the range of alternatives available to individuals of different class backgrounds.

## THE AGED AS A CATEGORY

### Heterogeneity: A Necessary Emphasis

It is important to keep in mind that the aged are *not* a homogeneous population. While there is a disproportionate number of sick, chronically disabled, isolated, and poor people among the aged, a sizeable number are well-to-do, have few health problems and carry on active lives with friends or kin. In considering the application and potential uses of sociology in the field of gerontology, Streib and Orbach stress that "it is absolutely essential that the fundamental heterogeneity of these people be recognized and made a basic assumption in planning for them." [8]

As the aged are not a homogeneous group, both their material and sociopsychological needs vary and are conditioned in large part by each individual's own socioeconomic position. However, they do share a common tie in relation to other groups in society: they are bound not only by advanced chronologies but also by the meanings, statuses, and stigmatizations attributed to their age group by community and society. Despite whatever "achieved" status a specific individual has by nature of past activities and position, he also has "ascribed" to him a certain place in the broader societal structure, which exists despite past history. It is a place involving limited participation in the mainstream of society. He is expected to be "out of things" and with as much grace as can be mustered allow the younger generation to take over societal affairs. How this is accomplished, what are the precise mechanisms deployed or the processes whereby intergenerational shifts in power, status, and responsibility occur are researchable questions.

STEREOTYPING. Furthermore, this "ascribed" position of marginality has quite far-reaching ramifications despite its resistance to precise definition. In fact, it is the very ambiguity of the role of the aged which presents the greatest problems, for in lieu of facts, policies tend to revolve around assumptions. Planners, too, become susceptible to the stereotypes covering the "old people"; and the common man in the street, who may have an aged family member residing in his home or close by, comes to think and act in terms of the stigmatizations associated with aging. There are some similarities in the ambiguity of the role of the aged with that of the divorcee, especially in reference to interaction situations. In the case of divorce or retirement there are no institutionalized norms as one finds in bereavement to handle the situation. Does one congratulate the retiree or recently divorced person or does one convey sympathy? In contrast, when death occurs there is one major sentiment which encompasses the event regardless of the saintly or sinful characteristics of the deceased; condolences are extended and thus uncertainty and ambiguity in the situation and role performance are reduced perceptibly.

As Cavan and Tibbits have noted, the vagueness clouding the roles of older individuals makes their continued social participation, seen as a basic need, quite difficult to achieve. Consideration of family relations and the aged, the focus of this chapter, must include recognition of the problem of ambiguity. Kin interaction as with other types of participation in any social network, hinges crucially on the *actual* and *perceived* positions of persons within the social system. For example, an aged individual by nature of his education, previous occupation and income may be posited in a certain bracket. While his age typically alters factors such as income, he retains an identifiable position as a retired custodian or a retired executive, each title representing a definite place in a hierarchy. However, the *perceived* position and role are related to how the person is viewed by himself and others—here an issue of status, as well as class.

The key aspect is that his advanced age separates him from the mainstream of activities and allows reference to the older person, not just as a "retired custodian" or a "retired executive," but as *a member of a social category called the aged.* The same labeling process is applied to the physically and mentally disabled, racial and ethnic minorities. Simple as these aspects may appear, they are central to the dynamics of social interaction. Moreover, the process of referring to a person as a member of a certain category, thereby attaching to him the connotations and stigmatizations of that category, without attention to individual variation, is essentially bound up with the dynamics of stereotyping.

Stereotyping is an identifying process based usually on less than accurate information which enables the individual to handle varied interactional situations with minimum effort in analyzing the context or issues involved in the interaction. The use of diagnostic categories in the health field is a good illustration of this process. One salient ingredient in stereotyping is power. Users are in a constant struggle to enhance or gain an advantage in the interaction situation and to find ideological and more bases to maintain or gain the upper position. Within this context, one can surmise that the social category of aged has the effect of speeding the transfer of the mantle of power from the old to the young in our society. This may not be the most sophisticated and highly intellectualized method, but few individuals or groups are willing to leave a preferential status willingly or with any degree of grace.

## SOCIALIZATION: A MISSING LINK

It is well to emphasize the perhaps obvious but easily overlooked fact that man is a *social* being. His culture is constructed and maintained through interaction among men. His own entrance onto the societal stage is rendered possible through his socialization into the values, attitudes, norms, goals—and quite importantly, language—of the specific society. During childhood and youth he learns the appropriate roles for functioning in society. This type of learning and socialization continues throughout adulthood as various roles such as husband, father, employee or employer are assumed. The individual learns how to perform, what others expect of him, and what to expect of others. When one reaches the later stage of life, however, the framework for actions, attitudes, and expectations is less clear.

Moreover, not only does the older person need a definite role, but he also needs individuals who will become responsible socializing agents. While it is obvious that the child receives the bulk of his socialization within the family, that other roles are learned in school, on the job, in the community and so forth, there are few generally accepted socializing vehicles specifically for the aged. The fact that many older people live with their children or other kin does not guarantee that their kin are prepared or equipped to guide the aged from one life stage to another. Indeed, the aged may be "in the way," considered a burden, and merely "maintained," rather than presented with new participatory channels and active roles within the family system. Considering the issue of the transfer of power and the value orientation of work there is lack of clarity as to what should be the goals of resocialization during retirement. The task for the socializing agent is to harmonize the functional needs of the family and society with the particularistic requirements for ego-maintenance of the aged person.

Social Disability. In a certain sense, the aged may be considered as "socially disabled" — a notion that centrally relates to Merton's observations on the incongruity between cultural goals and structural opportunities. This concept, as used by Gary Spencer, refers to those individuals who may be physically and emotionally "normal," but are ill-equipped with the necessary values and opportunities for independent functioning. Social disability results from a combination of "(1) failure to internalize normative values and goals; (2) blocked opportunity structures for achieving normative goals; and (3) the existence of alternative structures for learning alternative values or goals." [9] One additional factor which is similar to Spencer's "blocked opportunity structure" but one which does not assume that there exists an opportunity structure is the organized effort by those in power to suppress or control the individuals or groups in the lower levels of the social structure. This is a normal condition and activity in all societies; labeling and stigmatizing are processes employed to reinforce the pattern of differentiation and to handle dissenters by classifying them as social deviants.

While Spencer was concerned with specific problems of rehabilitation in poverty settings, these notions are somewhat applicable to the problems of the aged. Undoubtedly many aged have failed to internalize the values and goals associated with later life, because these values and goals are vague, and perhaps deliberately so; some who desire to actively engage in work or community spheres often encounter "blocked opportunity structures" for achieving these goals; and alternative values, e.g., "the aged are useless," are perpetuated by means of the machinery of stereotyping, prejudice and stigmatization. Behind these exclamations is the growing power struggle between the generations and the insufficiency of knowledge of "best practice," the appropriate mechanisms for making this transfer of power and authority judiciously, efficiently, and humanely.

Thus, while considering the family as a resource, it must be remembered that its effectiveness is contingent upon the broader societal arena, including the imagery, ambiguities, and stigmatizations therein contained and transmitted. Due to the aged persons' forced separation from the work spheres, the family stands out as an appropriate channel for integration and participation. Particularly in the essential realm of socialization, the family can perform crucial functions—functions which are inherently central to its composition, orientation, and resources. It is further emphasized that not only may the family *per se* offer instrumental and emotional resources to the aged, but also as a system interacting both independently and dependently with other societal institutions—and thus presenting links with various other resources. If necessary, it can furnish "simulated" work experiences which provide gratifications similar to those experienced in prior work roles. The potentials of the family, however, are at times obscured by the stereotypes of aging, as well as by certain misconceptions concerning the kin network.

## THE FAMILY AS A SOCIAL SYSTEM

Various writers have advocated that an increasing number of functions, previously assigned to the family, are being taken over by other institutions which have grown up in the modern period nurtured by the forces of industrialization, urbanization, and specialization. Some contend that in relation to other social institutions, the family increasingly assumes a less significant, more submissive, and dependent role. In family studies, primary attention is focused on the nuclear unit, composed of husband, wife and progeny, with less concern for relations between other kin or the extensiveness and functions of the network as a whole. However, new empirical evidence is emerging which proves the existence of a viable extended kinship system, highly integrated within a network of social relationships and mutual assistance, that operates along bilateral kin lines and vertically over several generations.

The establishment of this kin network as an on-going social system requires alterations in current family theory. That this network was not recognized before is due to several errors of earlier theorists. One mistake was in assuming that the rural-to-urban transition signaled a permanent breakdown of social structures. Actually, deviant behavior, marginality, and disruption of structures and functions are not equivalent to permanent social change. The new prominence of the nuclear unit did not mean that the kin structure was doomed to eventually disappear. Furthermore, anthropologists such as Murdock have demonstrated in cross-cultural studies that kinship structures confronted with equal or advanced technologies do not dissolve, but evolve and adjust, assuming new activities and functions, usually consonant with the emerging social system.

On the contemporary landscape we can see these processes of adaptation at play in the growth in importance and extensiveness of the educational system, accompanied by the family network's increased financial support of young members through an extended, though altered, period of dependency. Similarly, such trends as an increased number of "early" marriages reveal, not simply a breaking away from the family of procreation, but the formation of a new unit, which is bound to the parent unit through a reciprocal exchange of goods and services.

## Functions of Kin Network Structure

Since 1950, numerous studies undertaken in a variety of disciplines have supported the notion that a viable kin network structure exists and that it has numerous functions supportive of the goals of other social systems. An outline of the major findings has been prepared by Sussman and Burchinal: [10]

### *Help Patterns*

1. Help patterns take many forms, including the exchange of services, gifts, advice and financial assistance. Financial aid patterns may be direct as in the case of the young married couples Burchinal interviewed; or indirect and subtle, such as the wide range of help patterns observed by Sussman[11] Sharp and Axelrod.[12]

2. Such help patterns are probably more widespread in the middle and working class families and are more integral a feature of family relationships than has been appreciated by students of family behavior. Very few families included in available studies reported neither giving nor receiving aid from relatives. . . .

3. The exchange of aid among families flows in several directions, from parents to children and vice versa, among siblings, and less fre-

quently, from more distant relatives. However, financial assistance generally appears to flow from parents to children.

4. While there may be a difference in the absolute amount of financial aid received by families of middle and working class status, there are insignificant differences in the proportion of families in these two strata who report receiving, giving or exchanging economic assistance in some form.

5. Financial aid is received most commonly during the early years of married life. Parents are probably more likely to support financially "approved" than "disapproved" ones, such as elopements, interfaith and interracial marriages. Support can be disguised in the form of substantial sums of money or valuable gifts at Christmas, anniversaries or birthdays. High rates of parental supported are probably associated with marriages of children while they are still in a dependency status; those among high school or college students are examples.

## *Social Activities*

Social activities are principal functions of the kin family network. The major forms are interfamily visitation, participation together in recreational activities, and ceremonial behavior significant to family unity. Major research findings are as follows:

1. Disintegration of the extended family in urban areas because of lack of contact is unsupported and often the contrary situation is found. The difficulty in developing satisfactory primary relationships outside of the family in urban areas makes the extended family *more important* to the individual.[13]

2. Extended family get-togethers and joint recreational activities with kin dominate the leisure time pursuits of urban working-class members.[14]

3. Kinship visiting is a primary activity of urban dwelling and outranks visitation patterns found for friends, neighbors, or co-workers.[15]

4. Among urban middle classes there is an almost universal desire to have interaction with extended kin, but distance among independent nuclear related units is a limiting factor.[16]

5. The family network extends between generational ties of conjugal units. Some structures are identified as sibling bonds,[17] "occasional kin groups,"[18] family circles and cousin clubs.[19] These structures perform important recreational, ceremonial, mutual aid, and often economic functions.

## *Services*

Services performed regularly throughout the year or on occasions are additional functions of the family network. The findings from empirical studies are as follows:

1. Shopping, escorting, care of children, advice-giving and counseling, cooperating with social agencies on counseling and welfare problems of family members, are types of day-to-day activities performed by members of the kin network.[20]

2. Services to old persons such as physical care, providing shelter, escorting, shopping, performing household tasks, sharing of leisure time, etc. are expected and practiced roles of children and other kin members. These acts of filial and kin responsibility are performed voluntarily without law or compulsion.[21]

3. Families or individual members on the move are serviced by units of the family network. Services range from supplying motel-type accommodations for vacationing kin passing through town, to scouting for homes and jobs for kin, and in providing supportive functions during the period of in-migration and transition from rural to the urban pattern of living.[22]

4. Services on occasions would include those performed at weddings or during periods of crisis, death, accident, disaster, and personal trouble of family members. A sense of moral obligation to give service or acknowledgment of one's kin appropriate to the occasion is found among kin members. The turning to kin when in trouble before using other agencies established for such purposes is the mode rather than the exception.[23]

5. General supportive behavior from members of the kin family network facilitates achievement and maintenance of family and community status.[24] Supportive behavior of kin appears to be instrumental in affecting fertility rates among component family members.[25]

FAMILY AND MOBILITY. That extended family relations are essentially antithetical to democratic, industrialized societies, a hypothesis advocated by Talcott Parsons, has been challenged by Litwak and Sussman. Litwak contends that the extended family has an important function in providing aid across class lines, thereby allowing the nuclear unit to retain extended kinship contacts despite differences in class position, attributable in part to varying occupational activities. The aid given through family channels is isolated from the occupational system and thus does not hinder mobility based on merit. In this sense, the "modified" extended family is consonant with occupational mobility in an industrial economy.[26]

Sussman has posited the formulation that the nuclear family and its kinship network influences as well as adapts to the normative requirements of nonfamily societal systems. In economic activities involving family operated businesses and corporations there is integration of bureaucratic norms with familial concerns.[27] Influence of the kin network upon the structure, policy and activities of other societal systems is being studied cross-culturally, in which the family and its kin network is conceived as both an independent and dependent variable. The kin network is conceived as a voluntary system based upon exchange and reciprocity and one which competes with nonfamily systems for the interest and attention of its members.[28]

Some have argued that urbanization and widespread geographic mobility have negative effects on family structure. However, quite to the contrary, Key finds that in urban areas, large numbers of people and the fleeting and specialized nature of most interpersonal contacts tend to diminish the formation and maintenance of primary relationships. In rural areas, spatial isolation, rather than social isolation, hinders primary interaction. Thus the immediate and extended family is important in both regions because of the difficulty of making satisfactory primary contacts outside the kin network.[29]

Adams was also concerned with kinship in urban settings and the effects of geographic mobility on family relationships. He found that with young adults and their parents, "distance is but a qualifier, not a deterrent." [30]

> "Small numbers or residential distance from the bulk of one's kin do not necessarily result in kin being considered unimportant, since significant relatives may be considered intimate and a vital part of the individual's life regardless of their location." [31]

Intergenerational Exchanges. Involvement with parents is the dominant focus of relations between young adults and their kin; this relationship is termed by Adams "intentional" as distinguished from the qualities of "interest" and "comparison" which characterize adult sibling relations and from the "circumstantial" or "incidental" ties which typify relations with more distant kin. The interchange serves the function of primary relations, including intimate communication and the relationship for its own sake, accompanied by ties of mutual affection and obligation. A basic concern for each other's welfare find tangible and intangible outlets in financial and service forms of mutual aid.[32]

In considering the aid exchanged between parents and adult children, a somewhat asymmetrical pattern emerges, in that financial assistance tends to flow from parent to child, while parents place more emphasis on ties of affection.[33] Streib's data on intergenerational relations reveals that parents are unwilling to jeopardize close family ties with their children by expecting financial assistance from them. On the question of which is more important—affection or financial responsibility—65 per cent of the parents and 35 per cent of the adult children cited affection, while one-third of the parents and two-thirds of the children stated that affection and financial aid were equally important. Supporting these findings was the stronger desire on the part of the older generation, compared to the younger, for more contact between the two groups.[34]

Some caution is always required in assessing the results of attitude studies, since people are affected by the manner in which questions are framed, and also tend at times to give contradictory answers.[35] One study of aged family members served by a New York City social service agency found that nearly three-fourths of the clients agreed that "a family should be willing to sacrifice some of the things they want for their children in order to help support their aged parents." However, more of the same sample agreed than disagreed that "it is humiliating for parents to be supported by their children in later life." Thus the clients expressed that *ideally* financial assistance should go from parents to children and that *ideally* the older generation should remain independent.[36]

This example illustrates the power of dominant societal values emanating from the active work system and the ideologies of democracy and individualism. Simultaneously, the "humiliating" aspects of dependency surface in a denial of the principle of reciprocity. According to some authors, ideally, in the healthy family, the balance of responsibility shifts as older members, once responsible for the maturational growth of dependence-independence in their children, become "dependents" of these children who assume quasi-parental roles.[37]

The increasing prevalence of three generations is mitigating the apparent discrepancy between belief and practice in matters of support. It is a case of serial reciprocity. The middle generation is supporting both the younger and older ones. The expectation is that as changes in one's status occur along the life cycle, such as movement from the middle to the old age category, that one's children now in their middle years will provide services. Inheritance patterns support this notion.

Property dispositions occur over generational lines with the largest share going to those family members of the middle generation who provided all or most of services required by aged parents.[38]

Relevant now is an examination of some of the intricacies involved in this responsibility transference, including the problems posed for intrafamily relations by the introduction of the aged person into the home of adult children or other kin.

## Competing Generations: Their Needs and Orientations

Each age group—children, parents, and grandparents, has particular needs and orientations, and the interplay of individuals at differing life cycle stages may not always be harmonious. There are natural and expected discrepancies in the attitudes and behavior of the family members. Cavan mentions the difficulties which sometimes arise between grandparents and grandchildren, especially adolescents. A conflict of values may be more severe between these two groups than others—particularly in cases where the grandparent moves from a rural to urban setting or comes originally from another culture. Accompanying the values conflict are differing mobility rates, aspirations and routines.[39]

A different situation exists when children have left the home, and the middle-aged couple are confronted with the introduction of an aged parent into the home. One promising theoretical approach to this arrangement is using Simmel's distinctions between the dyad and the triad;[40] this perspective points up how the introduction of the third element, here the grandparent, can profoundly affect the relationship between the set of two. The situation provides an excellent opportunity to study shifts in interaction and socialization processes from those involving children to those relative to parents.

Middle age carries its own set of adjustments, prompted in part by biological and nutritional changes associated with advancing age and changes in social relationships, opportunities, and adult responsibilities. Furthermore, the major role changes for women and men do not occur at the same time;[41] women are usually affected first by changing patterns; when children leave the home, their schedules become less demanding. At the same time males are typically reaching a peak of their activities in the work sphere, resulting in a pronounced discrepancy between husband and wife. This is the time when many women return to the labor force, some to pursue "second careers,"[42] or to resume earlier endeavors. The emergence of a new value which stresses "personal happiness," something every individual is entitled to regardless of age or sex, makes middle aged individuals less enraptured with or inclined to take on the full responsibility for aged parents.

What these aspects indicate for the aged person is that he or she may not find a stable situation in the home. Adjustment to aging is thus only one facet of the total picture. While the family may be viewed as a totality, as when it is referred to as a general resource, each member has his own specific needs, and has his own way of adapting to and participating in changing realities. The example of the grandparent-grandchild conflict in values is a case in point. A person born circa 1900 may still retain an earlier epoch as his base of orientation due mainly to the particular impact of the socializing process during the stages of youth when the "self" is crystalized; and this orientation sharply conflicts with that of the modern teenager who has not only a different milieu but also a new set of tools and techniques for dealing with the world. For example, alterations that have occurred in the communications system alone have radically affected man's relationship to his environment. While an older person who has grown up in and lived through the announcement of the first television, the breaking through the sound barrier, and the introduction of all types of electrical gadgets, the world may appear more of a progression from one development to the next. A younger person, emerging head-on into a ready made "electric" world must build an identity amidst an unprecedented array of stimuli. The telephone, airplane and computer are his taken-for-granted tools, not wonders or blessings. His ideology is complicated by alternatives and contradictions presented by such trends as secularization, urbanization, industrialization and bureaucratinization, which, again, are set on the societal stage full blown, massive and almost uncontrollable and impenetrable.

The theoretical relevance of this position is obvious. However, the degree to which such differences in generational perceptions, attitudes and experiences creates cleavages between grandparents and grandchildren is still an empirical question. Returning to our notions regarding power and its transfer over generational time, one can hypothesize that in some instances there evolve coalitions between grandparents and grandchildren in the power struggle, with attendant rewards. The older generation, if cast in the minority-deviant role, can take an "I have nothing to lose" posture and reach consensus on objectives and means with the youngest generation in handling the middle one.

However, the different nature of the social worlds of each generation must not be underestimated, despite the increasing closeness of age groups deriving from such trends as early marriage and early child-bearing. Each child is taught during socialization how to handle and interact within the social world. The lessons are altered and amended during various resocialization periods occurring throughout the life cycle, but the initial base remains distinct for each person—set within a particular historical period. In analyzing the interaction of family members, one must consider the family structure as a whole and its place in a particular setting (e.g., rural or urban) and in the overall social structure (e.g., social, economic, and political themes); also to be considered are the various ideologies, life styles, ranges of experiences, and techniques of handling reality of the family members individually. One consideration to be kept always in mind in any analysis of aged roles and family behavior is the situation and circumstances under which interaction occurs. Such situational and conditional factors as financial means, stage of family cycle, illness condition, previous network activities, personality traits, ideological and value postures, determine the extent and quality of intergenerational relationships and the effectiveness of resocialization into aged roles.

## ADJUSTMENT TO AGING: SOME VARIABLES

In confrontation with social changes, some individuals are more socially and psychologically equipped than others to carry out effective adjustments. This point is well illustrated by Brissette's monograph on the significance of life goals in aging. In this study of elderly persons requiring psychiatric care after the age of 60, it was suggested that "a study of this older generation is a lesson in the fate of value systems and their adherents under the impact of a series of unprecedented social changes." [43] An individual's attitudes, behavior, and "happiness" or "success" — whatever the flavor of his aspirations — are dependent on the totally unique combination of endowments, environment, and structural opportunities.

One hypothesis tested by Brissette implied that "internalized stress, perceived as self-blame or defeatism, probably generates mental illness in old age, whereas stress that is externalized and perceived as a conflict with one's environment does not wreck destruction as great as mental illness upon the aging individuals." [44] This finding supports the thesis that challenge, conflict, and confrontation may have some therapeutic functions. Contests for preferred status and rewards conducted by the aged with friends or kin such as grandchildren against institutional constraints and other family members may be the means for physical and psychological maintenance in old age.

## Subgroup Variations

In another study, concerned with the racial attitudes of older adults, Thune found that compared to older white groups, older Negro groups were less prejudiced; considered themselves different from other Negroes and whites in valuing personal qualities rather than material objects or pleasure-oriented behavior; and felt less personal control over the environment and more controlled by outside forces.[45] While this might appear to forecast less "self-blame" or internalized stress on the part of the Negro aged, it is noted that "outside forces" often revolve around severe economic depression—prompting day-to-day struggles for survival. Moreover, the Negro is experienced in handling racial stigmatizations and is accustomed to deprivation and frustration. Consequently he is more apt to stress the need for personal kindnesses and intimate social relationships than material comforts and pleasurable activities, if only because the latter seem more distant possibilities. Active participation and acceptance within a kin group appear to be more important to the Negro than the white aged.

The precise interplay of these factors requires greater elaboration. Much remains to be learned, such as how the family functions in this context as a sector of the aged's environment, what it can do to alleviate internalized stress, and moreover, what it can do to help prevent mental illness among its aged members.

Needed Research on the Negro Aged. In the literature on

aging there is a noticeable gap on studies of the aged Negro. Jackson has emphasized the need to develop more appropriate methodological instruments and techniques in studying this group. The major emphasis has been on the relevance of race to aging, but there is lack of data on the actual behavior patterns of the Negro aged subgroups and the patterns to which they and others feel they ought to conform.[46] There is some evidence that the economic deprivation central to some Negro groups tends to heighten the active participation of old people within the family.[47]

Jackson suggests more refinement of data is needed on the proximity of kin to the aged person, as well as the quality and content of familial interaction processes. It is important to consider how the color of the data-collecting agent affects the sample; what are the conditions under which data on the Negro aged should be analyzed separately, included within larger samples, or compared with other age groups. Jackson notes the tendency to exclude comparison of Negro aged groups with one another and cautions that homogeneous Negro groups can only be identified when race is held constant.[48] One might hypothesize that the Negro aged have fewer problems than whites in accommodating the normative demands of the kin group because of previous experience and identification within it. The service orientation is more pronounced among the Negro subculture, especially the lower class and undoubtedly there are heightened reciprocal activities among its members and a useful service role for the aged Negro.

## Uniting Rival Theories

In the literature there appear to be certain conflicts over exactly what constitutes successful aging; moreover, measures of successful aging are diversely based upon the views of the aged themselves and the views of others. The two major rival approaches are the "activity" and "disengagement" theories. The most viable approach appears to be that of Havinghurst who stresses that both of the main theories are relevant; he strikes an appropriate balance between the two by holding that "life satisfaction" will be positively related to activity for some kinds of people and to disengagement for others.[49]

This view avoids the pitfall of considering the aged a homogeneous group, whose satisfactions are measured unidimensionally with no regard for the varied panorama of past activities, inclinations, and capabilities. For example, a "passive" type person who has progressed to the latter stages of life with infrequent and non-intense involvements outside his work and family spheres, may readily accept the decelerated pace of retirement, being quite satisfied with "disengagement" from the work sphere and from the burdens of family responsibility. For such an individual, the kin network could offer ongoing ties of emotional, and where necessary, financial support. Especially if he lives alone, the family would thus be somewhat of a bulwark against extreme isolation, while by nature of its primary interaction it presents itself as one of the most solid sources of integration.

Another individual, after carrying an "active" schedule of involvements in various spheres during his younger and middle years, and who is above everything else a "work addict," may find the coming of age 65 a jolting experience, fraught with displeasure at retiring not only from work but other pursuits as well. Some aged persons especially those of the middle class discover that previous club and committee involvements were more than tangential to the work spheres, often hinging greatly on occupational involvement. In these cases, "roleloss" may be severe, as the individual finds his usefulness to organizations as well as his status diminished by the severing of the work connection. For such persons, satisfaction during retirement depends heavily upon continued activity. Here the family emerges not only as a resource for engagement in itself, but also as a link with other social systems. An activity-oriented person may find satisfaction in participating in ongoing family functions, visiting with kin and offering services to other members. The family, through the participation of young and middle adult members in the work and community spheres, may learn of opportunities and demands for older citizens to which they may refer the aged member for further involvement. The kin network thus can perform linking of activities, arranging the proper mix of the aged person with the institutional system in reference to the emotional and physical needs of its aged members.

Thus, for both the active and passive types, the family stands as an available resource. Its effectiveness is enhanced by the fact that intimacy and familiarity characterize this system, rendering more possible the tailoring of services and interaction patterns to fit individual needs.

## Institutionalization

As Brody and Spark explain, "homes" for the aged originated as last refuges for the homeless and economically deprived *who lacked family ties.* Today, strictly custodial care is being replaced by dynamic treatment and service oriented approaches.[50] For a great number of clients in modern institutions, the family as a resource is in some way deficient.

Characteristics of applicants to one home for the aged cited by Brody show that 45 per cent sought entrance because of their own mental or physical impairment; 25 per cent, death or impairment of spouse; seven per cent, poor neighborhoods, loneliness, or relationship problems; and 23.5 per cent, death or severe illness of their adult child or the child's spouse.[51]

Scott's study of factors in the adjustment of institutionalized and noninstitutionalized aged demonstrated significant differences in the personal adjustment level between the two aged groups. Compared to nonnursing home residents, the nursing home sample contained twice as many never married people and twice as many separated, widowed, and divorced persons. The nonresident sample had three times as many living children.[52]

Furthermore, maintenance of rehabilitation gains in the post-hospital period among elderly disabled is a function of family members' involvement as emotional and physical caretakers. Individuals who are isolated from family and kin and are low on social particiapation after hospital discharge are low in maintaining hospital rehabilitation gains and survive for shorter periods of time than social participating individuals and those linked with family and kin networks.[53]

ALTERNATIVES. Mensh's approach to the psychiatric problems of later life suggests that home care has many advantages; older persons like to be with families and often feel that they can contribute to the welfare of the group. He cites several alternatives to total institutionalization: "day hospital plans" where persons participate in therapeutic hospital activities and sleep at home at night; and "night hospital plans" where patients sleep at the hospital but participate during the day in community programs. In Colorado, some older persons are being placed in "foster homes." Medical and psychiatric supervision are available and the resident "hosts" are paid; the "guest" is allowed the opportunity to actively participate in the family and thereby maintain healthy social contacts, as well as gaining a feeling of usefulness to the family unit.[54]

In their discussion of how sociological concepts and research are used in establishing programs for the family and older persons, Streib and Orbach refer to a project initiated by the Government's Office on Aging, which attended to the needs of two disparate age groups simultaneously. Research on human growth and development, indicating that children need sustained affectionate contacts with an adult and observations on the diffuseness of the aged person's role in society led to a program, formulated by sociologists Marvin Tabes, Donald Kent, and Clark Tibbits, in which low income elderly were paid an hourly rate to spend time in close association with orphaned and institutionalized children. This plan allowed the aged to assume a definite, useful social role and the young to receive vital warmth and attention.[55] In a sense, this format simulates a family situation in which the aged becomes "foster grandparents" and the young are, at least for several hours a week, "adopted" by a kin surrogate. This program has demonstrated its utility sufficiently to become incorporated into many big city OEO programs.

We would suggest one further development of this use of the "roleless" aged, namely as a worker to care for the emotionally and physically disabled child. In our search for untapped groups of individuals to meet the severe shortages of service workers among the blind, we postulated the idea that the aged, especiallv the aged blind might be a "colleague" worker with the retarded child. Under a reciprocal arrangement the retarded child could receive the long experience and folk wisdom of the aged person who in turn could receive the loving care of the child.[56] The family could be the means through which such relationships could be initiated and supported.

## CONCLUSIONS

The foregoing discussion has attempted to emphasize untapped resources of the family and kin network for the support and integration of its aged members. The family is a viable structure within which aged members may meaningfully interact and participate in satisfying and useful ways. Furthermore, as a social system the family-kin network wields power which may be channeled into mediation with other societal institutions on behalf of the aged member.

The internal and external potentials of this system are, as yet, obviously not fully realized, and are to a certain extent contingent upon a recognition of the dynamics of social interaction. Conflict and contention within the family system are not necessarily deleterious to the well-being of the aged, since in general such conditions customarily accompany any transfer of power within a social structure.

Moreover, understanding the mechanisms of stereotyping is an essential advance toward achieving a more comprehensive perspective on the aged as a heterogeneous group with varying needs and orientations. The aged are most similar in that they all confront the stigmatizations of a work-centered society. The preferred and actual activity patterns of and roles played by the aged are related to individual personality characteristics, previous occupational and leisure experiences, kin-network involvement, and situational variables.

The aged person is simultaneously a socialization novice and agent in that, due to the ambiguity surrounding the goals of and the means to socialization, he must "work his way through" reitrement. To a large degree he is bound by the "law of fortuitous circumstances." Chances for satisfactory retirement often hinge on the possibility that an individual is in the right place at the right time—that he has ongoing contact with his family network, which includes him in its activities and provides ties to other societal resources; that his community has advanced beyond the "uselessness of the aged" ideology and actively attempts to coordinate community needs with untapped manpower strength. While efforts are required on many levels, the family network heads the list of available resources. With research increasingly supporting its extensiveness and adaptability, the kin system is equipped to help meet and supplement the varied needs of the aged.

## REFERENCES

1. U. S. Bureau of the Census: *Statistical Abstract of the United States*: 1964. 85th ed., Washington, D. C., 1964, p. 56.

2. Tibbits, C.: The older family member in American society. In *The Older Person in the Family: Challenges and Conflicts.* Jacobs, H. L. (Ed.), Iowa City, U. of Iowa, Institute of Gerontology, June, 1955, p. 9.
3. Cavan, R. A.: A sociologist looks at the role of the older person in the family. In Jacobs, *op. cit.,* p. 36.
4. U. S. Department of Health, Education, and Welfare, Social Security Administration: The financial position of the aged. *Research and Statistics Note No. 1.* Feb. 16, 1962, Tables 1 & 2.
5. Anderson, J. E.: Placing the adult years in proper perspective in development through the life span. In *The Middle Years: Proceedings of the Sixth Annual Iowa Conference On Gerontology.* Morris, W. W. (Ed.), Iowa City, Iowa, 1957, p. 5.
6. *Ibid.*
7. *Ibid.,* pp. 11-12.
8. Streib, G. F., and Orbach, H. L.: Aging. In *The Uses of Sociology.* Lazarsfeld, P. F.; Sewell, W. H., and Wilensky, H. L. (Eds.), New York, Basic Books, 1967, p. 621.
9. Spencer, G.: *A Comparative Study of the Reduction of Dependency in Four Low-Income Housing Projects.* Monograph No. 4, Northeastern Studies in Vocational Rehabilitation. Boston, Northeastern University, August 1967, p. 29.
10. Sussman, M. B., and Burchinal, L. G.: Kin family network: unheralded structure in current conceptualizations of family functioning. *Marriage and Family Living, 24*:236-238, August 1962.
11. Sussman, M. B.: The help pattern in the middle class family. *Amer Sociol Rev, 18*:22-28, Feb. 1953.
12. Sharp, H., and Axelrod, M.: Mutual aid among relatives in an urban population. In *Principles of Sociology.* Freedman, R. *et al.* (Eds.), New York, Rinehart, 1956, pp. 433-439.
13. Key, W. H.: Rural-urban differences and the family. *Sociol Quart, 2*:49-56, Jan. 1961.
14. Dotson, F.: Patterns of voluntary association among urban working-class families. *Amer Sociol Rev, 16*:687-693, Oct. 1951.
15. Axelrod, M.: Urban structure and social participation. *Amer Sociol Rev, 21*:13-18, Feb. 1956.
16. Frazier, E.F.: The impact of urban civilization upon negro family life. In *Cities and Society.* Hatt, P.K., and Reiss, A.S., Jr. (Eds.) New York, Free Press, 1957, pp. 495-496.
17. Cumming, E., and Schneider, D.M.: Sibling solidarity: a property of American kinship. *Amer Anthropologist, 63*:498-507, June 1961.
18. Ayoub, M.: American child and his relatives: kindred in southwest Ohio. Project supported by the United States Public Health Service, 1961.
19. Mitchell, W.E.: Descent groups among New York City Jews. *Jewish J Sociol, 3*:121-128, 1961.
20. Sussman, The help pattern in the middle class family, *op. cit.*

21. Koza, J.; Rachiele, L.D., and Schommer, C.O.: Sharing the home with relatives. *Marriage and Family Living, 22*:129-131, May, 1960.
22. Sussman, M.B., and White, R.C.: *Hough: A Study of Social Life and Change.* Cleveland, Western Reserve U.P., 1959.
23. Sussman, M.B.: Family continuity: selective factors which affect relationships between families at generational levels. *Marriage and Family Living, 16*:112-120, May 1954.
24. Barber, B.: Family status, local-community status, and social stratification: three types of social ranking. *Pacif Sociol Rev, 4*:3-10, Spring, 1961.
25. Goldberg, D.: Some recent developments in fertility research. *Demographic and Economic Change in Developed Countries.* Reprint No. 7. Princeton, Princeton, 1960.
26. Litwak, E.: Occupational mobility and extended family cohesion. *Amer Sociol Rev, 25*:9-21, February, 1960.
27. Sussman, M.B.: The compatibility functions of the kin family network in modern urban industrial society. Paper presented at a meeting of the American Sociological Association, Montreal, Canada, September 4, 1964.
28. Sussman, M.B.: The urban kin network in the formulation of family theory. Paper presented at The Ninth International Seminar on Family Research, Tokyo, Japan. Forthcoming in Konig, R. (Ed.): Yearbook of the International Sociological Association.
29. Key, *op. cit.,* p. 55.
30. Adams, B.N.: *Kinship in an Urban Setting.* Chicago, Markham, 1968, p. 169.
31. *Ibid.,* p. 30.
32. *Ibid.,* pp. 164-165.
33. Sussman, The help pattern in the middle class family. *op. cit.*
34. Streib, G.F., and Thompson, W.E.: The older person in a family context. In *Handbook of Social Gerontology.* Tibbitts, C. (Ed.), Chicago, U. of Chicago, 1960, pp. 447-488.
35. Schorr, A.L.: *Filial Responsibility in the Modern American Family.* Social Security Administration, U.S. Department of Health, Education, and Welfare, Washington, D.C., U.S. Government Printing Office, 1960.
36. Leichter, H.J. and Mitchell, W.E.: *Kinship and Casework.* New York, Russell Sage, 1967, pp. 83-84.
37. Brody, E.M. and Spark, G.M.: Institutionalization of the Aged: A Family Crisis. *Family Process, 5*:78, March 1966.
38. Sussman, M.B., Cates, J., and Smith, D.: The Family and Inheritance. New York, Russell Sage, Forthcoming.
39. Cavan, *op. cit.,* pp. 43-44.
40. Simmel, G.: *The Sociology of Georg Simmel.* Wolff, Kurt H. (Ed. and transl.), New York, Free Press, 1950.

41. MARTEL, M.: Changing marriage relationships and adult sex roles. In Morris, *op. cit.*, pp. 21, 26.
42. HAUG, M.R., and SUSSMAN, M.B.: The second career—variant of a sociological concept. *J Geront, 22*:439-444, Oct. 1967.
43. BRISSETTE, G.G.: *The Significance of Life-Goals in Aging Adjustment—A Pilot Study.* California Mental Health Research Monograph No. 9. Bureau of Research, California Department of Mental Hygiene, 1967, p. 23.
44. *Ibid.*, p. 2.
45. THUNE, J.M.: Racial attitudes of older adults. *Gerontologist, 7*(1):182, Sept. 1967.
46. JACKSON, J.J.: Social gerontology and the negro: a review. *Gerontologist, 7*(1):168-178, Sept. 1967.
47. FLORES, A.: The new status of old people in the family and their relationships. In *Age With a Future.* Hansen, P.F. (Ed.), Philadelphia, Davis, 1964, pp. 455-458.
48. JACKSON, *op. cit.*, pp. 172-173.
49. HAVINGHURST, R.J.: Successful Aging — Definition and Measurement. Paper for the International Research Seminar on the Social and Psychological Aspects of Aging, August 1960.
50. BRODY and SPARK, *op. cit.*, pp. 76-77.
51. BRODY, E.M.: The Aging Family. *Gerontologist, 6*:203, Dec. 1966.
52. SCOTT, F.G.: Factors in the Personal Adjustment of Institutionalized and Non-Institutionalized Aged. *Amer Sociol Rev, 20*:538-546. Oct. 1955.
53. SLATER, S.S.: The Functions of the Urban Kinship Network Under Normal and Crisis Conditions. Ph.D. thesis, Western Reserve University, Sept. 1966.
54. MENSH, I.N.; WEISS, J.M.A.; DAVIS, D., and GILDEA, E.F.: Psychiatric problems of later life: III. Treatment and rehabilitation. *Amer Practitioner Dig Treatment, 10*:225-228, Feb. 1959.
55. STREIB and ORBACH, *op. cit.*, pp. 627-628.
56. SUSSMAN, M.B. and HAUG, M.R.: New Sources for Workers in the Blindness System. Paper delivered at the Workshop Conference on Rehabilitation and Visual Impairment, New York City, Dec. 1967.

## ADDITIONAL READINGS

BELL, W. and BOAT, M.D.: Urban neighborhoods and informal social relations. *Amer J Sociol, 62*:391-398, Jan. 1957.

BELLIN, S.S.: *Family Kinship in Later Years.* New York, State Department of Mental Hygiene, Mental Health Research Unit Publication, 1960.

BOTT, E.J.: *Family and Social Network.* London, Tavistock, 1957.

BROWN, J.S.; SCHWARZWELLER, H.K., and MANGALAM, J.J.: Kentucky Mountain Migration and Stem Family: An American Variation on a Theme by LePlay. Paper given at the American Sociological Association, Sept. 1961.

GREER, S.: Urbanism reconsidered: a comparative study of local areas in a metropolis. *Amer Sociol Rev, 21*:19-25, Feb. 1956.

KLEEMEIER, R.W. (Ed.): *Aging and Leisure.* New York, Oxford U.P., 1961.

KOOS, E.L.: *Families in Trouble.* New York, King's Crown, 1946.

MILLS, C.W.; SENIOR, C., and GOLDSEN, R.K.: *The Puerto Rican Journey.* New York, Harper, 1950, pp. 51-55.

QUARANTELLI, E.L.: A note on the protective function of the family in disasters. *Marriage and Family Living, 22*:263-264, August, 1960.

ROSSI, P.H.: *Why Families Move.* New York, Free Press, 1955.

SHANAS, E.: Older People and Their Families. Paper given at the American Sociological Association, Sept. 1961.

STREIB, G.F., and THOMPSON, W.E. (Eds.): Adjustment in retirement. *J Soc Issues,* 1958, vol. 24.

SUSSMAN, M.B.: Activity patterns of post-parental couples and their relationship to family continuity. *Marriage and Family Living, 27*:338-341, Nov. 1955; The isolated nuclear family: fact or fiction. *Soc Problems, 6*:333-340, Spring, 1959; and Intergenerational family relationships and social role changes in middle age. *J Geront, 15*:71-75, 1960.

# PART VI

# CITIZEN RESPONSIBILITY IN SOCIAL GERONTOLOGY

*Chapter 16*

# VOLUNTARY ORGANIZATIONS

JEROME KAPLAN

ALL OLDER PEOPLE are not alike. Their interests differ, their abilities vary, their attitudes are multiple and their needs are not simultaneous.

So it also is with the citizen voluntary organization. It, too, varies and its specific goals relate to both the historical background of the sponsor and/or those who guide the organization in its evolvement. A voluntary organization serves special needs which have become accentuated in our contemporary industrial American society. Thus, it makes special services available within a relatively short period of time.

## VOLUNTARY ORGANIZATIONS DEFINED

A voluntary organization is created when a small group of people find they have a purpose or interest in common and subsequently agree to meet and then act in concert so as to achieve that purpose or satisfy that interest.

The usual definition of a voluntary organization excludes profit making for its membership. This does not, however, preclude the fact that numerous voluntary organizations are developed to obtain economic benefits for members although the organization per se is nonprofit.

Voluntary organization presumes free choice for both entrance and withdrawal on the part of its membership. And yet, we are cognizant of the social forces in effect which, in reality, dictate that certain individuals will join certain voluntary organizations. The individual will weigh the advantages and disadvantages of joining a collective enterprise. This deliberation is affected by the formal and informal ways of social control of our society and the peculiar culture of any one community.

## Classification of Organizations

The voluntary organization is essentially a *secondary* association rather than a *primary* grouping. In this context we look upon the latter as receiving most of its membership through natural reproduction such as the family followed by the religious body or country to which the family belongs, even apart from the intimate face to face contact which provides the basic principles that shape an individual's behavior; the former is dependent for its survival upon the continual recruitment and involvement of new members into the organization.

MAJORAL, MINORAL AND MEDIAL ORGANIZATIONS. It may be helpful at this point to consider classification of voluntary associations as noted in a major study involving five thousand voluntary associations. A distinction was made between *majoral, minoral* and *medial* organizations. Majoral associations are those associations which serve the interests of the major institutions of society. Business, professional, scientific, educational, labor and agricultural associations belong to this category. Minoral associations, on the other hand, are those which serve the interests of significant minorities in the population. Women's clubs, fraternal groups, hobby clubs, and various associations formed to protect the rights of women, children and the aged or to protect rights of different ethnic or racial minorities in the population are all examples. Finally, medial associations mediate between the community and underprivileged population. Veterans' groups which mediate between war veterans and the Government or voluntary health associations, which mediate between individuals suffering from a disease and the medical practitioner or scientist, are examples of medial associations.[1]

The American Association of Homes for the Aging is an example of the majoral classification; the golden age club and senior citizen center are illustrative of a minoral association; and, the Gerontology Society, Inc. exemplifies the medial organization. Membership in majoral associations is usually adjunctive to occupational performance. Most eligible people apparently join majoral organizations because it is a matter of self-interest as one relates to occupational colleagues. Membership in minoral associations is more likely to be a matter of individual initiative. Members join and drop as the intensity of their personal interest varies. Membership in medial bodies comes about primarily as a result of active recruitment by the organization. Therefore, for members, it often makes use of relationships which were established for other purposes such as a medical gerontological research unit established within a major university.

ORGANIZATIONS MORE THAN TOTAL OF INDIVIDUAL MEMBERS. In a major study of the principles underlying formal organizations, it was noted that when "the efforts of five men become coordinated in a system, that is, an organization, there is created something new in the world that is more or less different in quantity and quality from anything present in the sum of the efforts of the five men." [2] It follows that organizations evolve into social structures with certain needs of their own apart from being merely instrumentalities for individuals to fulfill their own needs.

An organization may be then defined as a rationally conceived system for coordinating the activities of a number of individuals toward a selected objective or purpose. Typically, the participation of individuals in organizations is segmental for they do not devote a major share of their time and energy to organizational activities. In these two respects, namely, the coordinated character of the activity and the segmental involvement of individuals, organizations differ markedly from such aggregates as communities and families, in which the activities of individuals are not only coordinated informally but also require a more nearly total commitment on the part of the individual.[3]

The "ideal" nature of such a description is apparent upon further analysis. As it has already been pointed out, the ideal clashes with the "real" for individuals within the system tend to resist being treated as means. They interact as wholes, bringing to bear their own special problems and purposes; . . ." [4] In resisting manipulation and in reacting as if their segmental commitment were a total one, the individual members of an organization usually determine its ultimate character. The ultimate character of the organization may well differ from that envisioned by its founders, since the specific interests and aims of individuals do not necessarily match perfectly to the aim of the organization.

CORPORATE AND FEDERATION TYPE NATIONAL ORGANIZATIONS. From a structural viewpoint, national associations may be of three general types, namely, those with local units, those with membership residing anywhere in the United States and those with a combination of local units as well as general membership.

The terms *corporate* and *federation* seem to summarize the difference between the first two types. The latter type obviously as a combination, could use a term such as *corporate-federated.*

Some national states are loose federations of semi-autonomous component units while others are highly centralized. Churches may also be classified in a similar way. At one extreme are the churches which conform to the congregational model, in which each parish is responsible for its own affairs; at the other extreme are the episcopal type churches, in which ultimate sovereignty resides in the parent organization.

Most studies of national organizations have related to the corporate structure. The categories of structural types used in industrial management or public administration texts are also based upon the assumption that ultimate power in an organization rests entirely in the hands of the top administrators. This was implied by Max Weber who, as the instigator of the scientific study of bureaucracy selected highly centralized governments and churches as his primary models for the discussion of large-scale organizations.[5] Weber looked upon bureaucracy as an administrative form to be found within all highly developed societies. With several important exceptions, contemporary scientific sociological studies of large organizations have been limited to analyses of industrial organizations and government bureaucracies.[6] Few studies of voluntary associations have apparently directed specific attention to the authority structure of organizations.

Perusal of publications of social welfare point out that both corporate and federated structural types exist. Wayne McMillen, for example, describes these two types of organizational structure and delineates problems which arise in the relationship of national offices to local units and vice versa.[7]

EMPIRICAL STUDIES OF VOLUNTARY ASSOCIATIONS. Three contributions from empirical studies of voluntary relationships of the formal structure of associations are worthy of mention here among the many undertaken.[8]

Martin Lipset notes that there are two ideal-type patterns through which trade unions and other voluntary associations are created, to wit, organization "[F]rom the top down, where the group which originally starts the association organizes other individuals or branches into a larger structure. . ." and organization "[T]hrough the successive but autonomous formation of one group after another. . ." [9] Lipset believes that the possibilities for democracy are much greater in the second type of organization since there is a built-in opposition within the organization. He concludes his comments on structure with a general hypothesis that "[T]he greater the number of independent sources of power and status in an organization, the greater the possibility that alternative factions or parties will be established to oppose the incumbent part." [10]

Ray Johns' study of national social agencies, which is chiefly concerned with the conditions under which national organizations embark upon cooperative ventures with other organizations, suggests that cooperative ability and formal structure are directly related. Organizations organized along corporate lines more often than not have more limited relationships with other organizations than do those which have a federation-type structure.[11]

David Truman has undertaken an analysis of the role of pressure groups in the governmental process. In his comparison of federated and unitary forms of structure, he concludes that organizations which seek to mould public opinion are less effective if they have a federated structure for a united front becomes quite difficult to attain. He states that federated organizations sanctify subcenters of power by "acknowledging in formal terms certain spheres of local or constituent autonomy. . ." [12] He cites, to back up this point, several cases of internal dissension in such federations as the AFL and CIO, the American Medical Association and the American Farm Bureau Federation.[13]

IMPORTANCE OF HISTORICAL ORIGINS. It is significant to note that the writers cited above stress the point that historical factors determine a national organization's structure. McMillen notes "[F]ederation structure develops when a national organization is formed by a combination of local units. . ." [14] An educational journal states that local units of corporate-type organizations are organized at the initiative of an existing national group, "while federations are said to have created a national office to give them services they needed. . ." [15] Johns reports on organizations which are "federations of already established local agencies. . ." in contrast to those which "developed a national organization before local affiliates were organized." [16] Truman writes that the problem of cohesion—which he regards as academic to federations "almost invariably arises where the constituent units antedate the federal body. . ." [17] Further, Lipset comments that "[T]he variation in historical origins of different trade unions and other voluntary organizations may determine subsequent temporary or long-term variations in their organizational structures." [18]

Local Organizations. The history of modern gerontological associations can be traced primarily since 1948 albeit the decade of greater happenings has evolved essentially since 1958. While there has been a sizeable growth in national organizations in recent years, local organizations which range in size and importance as well as the extent of formality/informality are the most numerous. The majority of participants in specially designed voluntary association opportunities for the elderly and retired are involved locally rather than nationally. The characteristics of voluntary organizations which follow are applicable to both local and national organizations.

## AMERICAN DEMOCRACY AND VOLUNTARY ORGANIZATIONS

Participation in voluntary activity has been regarded as having its origins in the democratic nature of American society. It has been stated time after time that this is essential for the survival of democracy in America. It has also been stressed that the voluntary organization is peculiarly American. Many other societies, however, exhibit similar characteristics as demonstrated by Austria, Germany, Great Britain and the Scandinavian nations. Eastern countries, too, have a large number of voluntary associations, especially the rural Japanese society.[19] It is also to be noted that voluntary associations are not of equal importance in all Western countries.[20]

A second consideration is the recognition that participation in voluntary activities is by no means a universal phenomenon in America. Studies have shown that from one-third to one-half of the adult population does not belong to any voluntary associations, and that at best perhaps only one-fourth of the population belongs to more than one organization. Apparently, a large majority of people of higher status belong to voluntary organizations while a majority of people of lower status do not.[21]

## Membership Participation

The usual finding with respect to voluntary organization participation is characterized by an active minority which controls and an inactive majority which participates occasionally in activities and/or is apathetic. Even Lord Bryce, who stated voluntary associations were an important component of American democracy, recognized the "near-universality of minority rule in all assemblies and groups and organized bodies of men. . ." [22]

Philip Selznick has described the typical voluntary association in the following terms:

> Most voluntary associations . . . are skeletal in the sense that they are manned by a small core of individuals—the administration, the local subleaders, a few faithful meeting-goers— around whom there fluctuates a loosely bound mass of dues-payers. This type of membership has, on the whole, only a very limited relation to the organization; its agreement with it may be of the vaguest sort; it may give little or no time to the organization nor be guided by its pronouncements save, as in unions and professional groups, on very narrow issues; in short, the power implications of membership are minimal.[23]

Bernard Barber, a student of membership apathy among voluntary associations, has cited evidence of the existence of an active minority and an inactive majority.[24] Further, Broom and Selznick conclude that in most trade unions, the majority of members have little interest in the functioning of the union, and fewer than 10 per cent attend union meetings.[25] Riesman and Glazer have said the following:

> The discussion of apathy—and its converse, the responsibility of the citizen—has overflowed the boundaries of traditional political science and become the concern of the sociologist, the psychiatrist, the social psychologist, and, recently, the atomic scientists.[26]

An active minority and a passive majority may exist in organizations without interfering in any way with progress toward goals, just as widespread membership participation does not necessarily indicate an adherence to democratic practices. Membership apathy may be deplored because democratic values are violated, but an organization itself may not be adversely affected.[27] As long as services for the membership are provided, the inactive majority will generally be satisfied.

On the other hand, membership participation is crucial for the achievement of goals in other voluntary associations, particularly those which are dependent upon fund-raising campaigns for their financial support, as distinct from support via membership dues. The generic problem of maintaining membership involvement in voluntary associations is related to the concern one has in that when members lose interest, an active minority can easily gain control and move in directions other than the main goal of the organization.

Affect of Age on Participation. Contemporary characteristics of the aged give indications of their changed position in the emerging society as compared to that in the society of the past and the present. Greater free time in our society is coming at a point of longer life, better health, reduced economic pressure, and an earlier age of retirement for more and more old people. For most, it is no longer possible to work at their jobs with progressively decreasing work hours. Unless they move into a second job at retirement, retirement is then complete. With more free time, older people are theoretically more able to participate in voluntary associations than younger people although free time—i.e. time away from one's job—is increasing for all age groups.

The long-run trend in modern society has been toward the breakdown of the extended family and the community. Of the traditional institutions which provide the social contacts for the individual, the nuclear family alone has remained at least as strong as it was in the pre-industrial period. Yet, even the nuclear family has broken down for the aged. While children still feel responsible for their parents, it is a different kind of responsibility than in past decades. The loss of the family social contacts thus suggests participation in the voluntary associations of modern society.

Considerable descriptive literature is available suggesting some of the psychological needs of older people for participation in voluntary associations, especially reported by Kaplan.[28]

The voluntary association appears to be well structured to satisfy those who desire social contact in modern society. Insofar as this emergent society has become increasingly anomic, the voluntary association has become an acceptable antidote against loneliness by an individual or loneliness by being part of a not completely accepted group.

The age at which one becomes *older* may be defined in economic terms, chronologic age, health status or in terms of free time. Glick shows that child-rearing functions of parents have been taking place at an increasingly earlier age, until now the average woman bears her last child at the age of 26 years.[29] This means that when the present generation of young parents reach their mid-forties, their children would, in the average situation, have already moved away from the parental home. The opportunity and the responsibility to spend free time with one's children is being grossly diminished. Consequently, by the mid-forties, the emergent average American parent is entering into the ranks of older people insofar as free time is concerned. Most women in their mid-forties increase their participation in all sorts of voluntary organizations while some women utilize voluntary association activities for a major part of their lives. The degree of involvement may well relate to the extent of employment by the woman. In general, then *older people* or those age 65 and over have special needs for the activities and social contacts which voluntary organizations provide, but, in this social sense, being an "older person" is becoming significant for the average man and woman in their middle forties.

Affect of Organizations on Participation. As an institution of our society, the voluntary association has increased need of the individual as a participant in the modern democratic social setting. Just as the extended family and the community are no longer quite so able as they once were to provide social contacts, so these same institutions similarly are not now able to provide some of their earlier protection and welfare benefits. As their own functions shifted, the voluntary organizations have not only taken over the long time functions of the community and the extended family to a certain extent, but there are also newer and emergent functions due to increased sensitivity of the needs of people in our society. In some instances, the voluntary association is able to perform such functions more efficiently than government, and in other instances the voluntary organization must perform the function a free society is to continue.

Society, therefore, has greatly increased need for volunteers so as to fulfill those functions of the voluntary associations. The vast growth in free time of all Americans and especially older Americans is an increasingly esteemed societal value. A steady increase in the proportion of older persons becoming members of voluntary organizations is probably an emergent trend, although there is no systematic collection of statistics yet available to verify this hypothesis.

## SPECIAL VOLUNTEER ORGANIZATIONS OF OLDER PEOPLE

It is significant that there were few voluntary associations of or for the aging before 1930. The major exception was the old people's home, generally under religious auspices and sometimes under a service association as a philanthropic endeavor if it were not a governmental institution.

Older people appear to take both increasing satisfaction in associating with each other, and in undertaking group action with regard to their common interest areas. Older people are moving from being almost wholly family oriented as the extended family has faded, to being older-person oriented, while the nuclear family has taken hold. Older persons are likely to come together for sociability and to get personal satisfaction from associating with one another regardless of the purpose of their coming together.

As increased awareness of older people problems has come to the general public attention, voluntary organizations have responded to the need in an ever increasing manner.

The emphasis will be placed here, then, in two directions, namely, local volunteer organization involvement by older people themselves through golden age clubs and senior citizen centers followed by national organizations, both for older people themselves as well as to serve older people exclusively or importantly.

### Local Associations

Local or community based organizational efforts are, for purposes of this section, confined to involvement by older people themselves in golden age clubs and senior citizen centers.

Golden Age Clubs. The purpose of a golden age club is multiple. It is designed to offer opportunity to make new friends, recreate old hobbies, develop new interests, to mix with people interested in one's self, to serve other people among a whole host of reasons. In short, it is geared to provide a purpose for living in the retirement years. The term golden age club has come to refer to a group of older people who have banded together in a formal organization, self-sponsored or sponsored by a public or private agency or organization, for the purpose of a social outlet. The majority of the members usually are aged 65 to 75. This is in contrast to the age grouping of homes for the aged residents who usually are at least in the middle 70 years and that of nursing homes where the late 70's and 80's can be found to predominate.

The majority of the clubs in Canada are of the type that meet periodically, once a week or once a month, but there are centers which are open almost every day, such as the Second Mile Club in Toronto, the Senior Club in Hamilton, and the Good Companion Fellowship Center in Ottawa. Activities range from the games and sing-songs of small groups to extensive programs of handicrafts, lectures, concerts, discussion groups and home visiting of the more developed associations.

The National Council of Jewish Women and the Soroptomist Clubs have taken a leading role in the development of these activities in a number of Canadian cities. The Ontario Division of the Canadian Red Cross has offered a number of recreational services including drives, movie tickets, and entertainment in homes for the aged. Other sponsoring groups include churches, trade unions, local women's clubs and service clubs. Some firms such as the T. Eaton Company and Bell Telephone Company have sponsored clubs for retired employees and also make company recreational facilities available to them, an arrangement designed to provide some continuity in the lives of employees following their retirement. The Old Age Pensioners Association, at least in the western provinces, include recreational and social activities at their branch meetings.

In Metropolitan Toronto, a Senior Citizens League was formed, made up of representatives of the more than thirty clubs for older people in that area.

The golden age club movement in the United States began in the late 1940's and swelled considerably in the 1950's. The Retmen's Club of Mansfield, Ohio is one such illustration, having been founded by a retired citizen himself in 1953. The group meets twice a month with a male membership of almost five hundred and an average active participation of 175. Other clubs in the United States meet in churches, settlement houses, YMCA, YWCA, Salvation Army headquarters and a variety of auspices.[30] Attention is hereby called to other selected resource materials which describe golden age club involvement in detail.[31, 32, 33]

SENIOR CITIZEN CENTERS. The development of golden age neighborhood and interest clubs has usually preceded the center movement. In other instances the latter has either assumed precedence or has taken the leadership in organizing interest groups and neighborhood clubs.

The history of the senior citizen center, exclusively for older or retired people, is even more of a new phenomenon than the golden age club. While it is true that the modern golden age movement began in the late 1940 period, clubs for older people have been known to exist as far back as 1870 in Boston.[34] The first senior citizen center, however, was created in 1944 by the Welfare Department of New York City. Regardless of its origin, centers have been established primarily through volunteer auspices and cater to older people from all social, educational, economic and religious backgrounds. While centers began for socialization, they have evolved into providing a meaningful purpose for retirement living.

The Conard House of Mansfield Memorial Homes (Mansfield, Ohio) provides opportunity for both socialization and service, as one wishes. Council House in Minneapolis serves as a parent agency to other organizations throughout the city.

The center, as distinct from a club, is "a program of services offered in a designated physical facility in which older people meet at least two days or more each week, under the guidance of paid leaders performing professional tasks.

"The basic purpose of such centers is to provide older people with socially enriching experiences which would help preserve their dignity as human beings and enhance their feelings of self worth." [35] In 1962, there were at least 218 centers in the United States. It is safe to state this number has at least been doubled by January, 1968. Attention is drawn here to the Maxwell Study of the National Council on the

Aging as the best single source to date on centers.[36] Other material of value is also available.[37, 38, 39]

The Ohio Senior Centers Association, organized in 1958, was the first statewide voluntary organization of centers in the United States. It serves as a stimulator, educator and catalyst in developing new Ohio centers and in assisting existing centers to refine and expand their program.

## National Organizations

National organizations may be composed of older people themselves who are a part of a chapter or a unit. They may also have interested members who do not belong to such a unit. Further, there are national associations composed exclusively of professionals, scientists or others who relate exclusively or partially to the elderly.

National Organizations of the Elderly. The American Association of Retired Persons, founded by Dr. Ethel Percy Andrus in 1958, is the most successful voluntary organization of its type in the United States. It is divided into 450 active chapters with 1,000,000 members. It is incorporated as "a nonprofit, nonpartisan, nonpolitical, educational, philanthropic, scientific organization, serving all men and women, 55 years and older irrespective of their race, color, religion or National origin, of the nation." [40] Its activities include research, counseling, correspondence, the magazine *Modern Maturity,* a hospital and nursing home and drug insurance plan, drug service and travel service as well as a bimonthly news bulletin. It sponsors a nursing home and hospitality lounges.

In 1934, the Old Age Revolving Pension Ltd., better known as the Townsend Movement, was formed. Organized by an elderly physician it became one of the largest mass movements the United States has ever known within a year, but declined after 1936. As such the "Townsend Movement was the first old-age movement in the United States. It grew rapidly and wielded so much force for a time that the country was forced to recognize the great potential and political influence of organized old people. The Townsend Movement appealed to the lower social and economic groups of old people in America." [41] The great bulk of the members were over 60 years of age. The ostensible aim of the organization was to get Congress to pass a law giving every citizen over the age of 60 a pension of $200 a month with funds to be obtained by levying a 2 per cent transactions tax. Its downfall began when economists adjudged the plan to be unfeasible and destructive followed by a 1936 congressional investigating committee which showed that the movement yielded considerable income for its promoters. Even so, the thousands of local clubs did affect members in various ways. The Townsend clubs perhaps created the first insights in the modern era by older people as being a social group with common problems.

SCIENTIFIC NATIONAL ORGANIZATIONS. The most significant contributor on the national scene is the Gerontological Society, Inc., which is a society devoted to research on aging. This is a nonprofit national organization, founded in 1945, to improve the well-being of older people by promoting scientific study of the aging process, by publishing information about aging, and by bringing together groups that are interested in research, training and evaluation of services for older people. The professional sections are Biological Sciences, Clinical Medicine, Psychological and Social Sciences, and Social Welfare. There is also a section for Members-at-Large. There are approximately seventeen hundred members.

The *Journal of Gerontology* publishes quarterly reports of original research in the four professional fields listed above. The Journal also includes reviews of recent books and an extensive index of current literature.

*The Gerontologist* is published quarterly and carries articles of general interest in the field of aging—medical care, recreation, housing, social welfare, employment, and other articles designed to keep the readers abreast of new developments in gerontology. In addition, invited contributors review the current status and new developments in research in biological, medical, and behavioral sciences.

To be eligible for membership in the society, an applicant must be interested in and sympathetic with its purposes. All members are entitled to attend and vote at annual meetings and to representation on the council. The society holds annual meetings in various cities. Members are invited to submit papers for presentation before the appropriate professional sections.[42]

PROFESSIONAL NATIONAL ORGANIZATIONS. A recent, yet highly

valuable organization is the American Association of Homes for the Aging. It is the national membership organization of nonprofit, voluntary and governmental Homes for the Aging across the country. The association, originally sponsored by the National Council on the Aging but now an independent body, was founded with a grant from the Ford Foundation. Since its inception in 1961, the American Association of Homes for the Aging has been dedicated to improving programs and standards of institutions serving older people and has been a prime mover in identifying and solving problems of common concern to its membership of approximately nine hundred. The association's program emphasizes (a) practical assistance to administrators through technical aid, (b) close liaison with governmental agencies and legislators on vital issues, (c) promotion of the goals of nonprofit facilities in the accreditation program of the Joint Commission on Accreditation of Hospitals, (d) education and guidance through publication and public relations programs and (e) the strengthening of bonds with state and regional groups. Its home office is in New York City.[43]

A somewhat related national voluntary organization which represents primarily the commercial nursing home is the American Nursing Home Association, in operation for many years. It is divided into seven regions and has more than 7,000 interested members. The American Nursing Home Association sponsors educational meetings and seminars, a National Nursing Home Week, conventions and exhibitions among other vital services for its membership. Its official magazine is *Nursing Homes,* published in Minneapolis, and its home office is in Washington, D.C.

The National Council on the Aging is the leading national, voluntary agency providing professional services for organizations and individuals concerned with the field of aging. It is nongovernmental, nonprofit, and tax-exempt. It has developed standards and materials to help people do a better job for the elderly in the areas of employment, preparation for retirement, health, housing, institutional care, community services, education, leisure time activities, and community planning and development. It offers information and consultation resources including the most comprehensive library in the field of aging; it provides field service when requested; it offers its members a regular library bulletin and the *NCOA Journal;* it undertakes research and studies; it sponsors and cooperates in symposia; and, it has published extensively, among other services.[44]

First organized at the request of community leaders, civic groups, government agencies and others as a result of the great need for professional advice and information in the field of aging, it has provided services on a continuing basis since 1950. The National Council on the Aging has been a meaningful contributor to the achievement of better housing for the aging, more significant leisure-time activities, better family relationships, more community services, and a life of dignity and self-respect.

NATIONAL SCIENTIFIC AND PROFESSIONAL ORGANIZATIONS WHICH INCLUDE AN INTEREST IN AGING. The American Public Welfare Association, consisting of directors of all public welfare agencies and having its headquarters in Chicago, has a permanent section devoted primarily to those problems of the aged which are the professional concern of its members. Its original development grew out of a Doris Duke Foundation grant in the early 1950's.

The National Council for Homemaker Services was incorporated in 1962 to stimulate the expansion and promote the improvement of homemaker services throughout the country. Membership is open to agencies providing homemaker services and to organizations and individuals interested in supporting the council's purposes. Working cooperatively with other national health and welfare organizations and with public and voluntary agencies, the council:

1. Promotes understanding of the values of homemaker services,
2. Provides a central source of information and medium through which knowledge and experience can be pooled and made available,
3. Encourages and guides communities in organizing and extending homemaker programs,
4. Promotes development of standards
5. Publishes reports and distributes educational and promotional materials, and
6. Sponsors conferences and seminars.[45]

Homemaker services to the aged, while not the prime focus of the National Council, is of growing interest.

The American Medical Association, the Group for the Advancement of Psychiatry, and the Adult Education Association also have special permanent divisions for work in aging. Scientific societies tend to follow the pattern of sections devoted to papers on the aging at annual meetings. The American Sociological Society contributes sessions of its annual meetings to research on social aspects of aging. Sociologists and others conducting research on social problems of the aged usually publish their findings in the professional sociological journals. The American Psychological Association created a Division of Later Maturity in 1946 to provide a forum for those interested in research on aging. Sessions are held in connection with the annual meetings of the association and papers appear in the professional journals of psychologists. The American Hospital Association has, since the advent of Medicare, become increasingly interested in the health planning and service aspects of the elderly, especially in extended care. While the American Geriatrics Society, composed primarily of physicians, concentrates on the aged, others of the national physician bodies invariably discuss some aspects of the older aging process. Other scientific and professional groups include select members who devote at least occasional attention to some aspects of the problems of the aged—among them are anthropologists, architects and economists. Some of the professional and scientific groups carry on activities on a local and state level as well as on a national level and statewide gerontological societies have also been organized in a few states.

Most of the organizational scientific and professional interest in older people is of recent origin. This reflects the newer public recognition of the elderly as a special social category. It can be anticipated there will be an increasing expression of interest in older people in the future by voluntary professional and scientific bodies.

## REFERENCES


1. Fox, Sherwood D.: Voluntary Associations and Social Structure. Unpublished Ph.D. thesis, Harvard University, 1953, p. 59-68.
2. Barnard, Chester I.: *The Functions of the Executive.* Cambridge. Harvard, 1938, p. 79.
3. Sills, David L.: *The Volunteers.* Glencoe, Free Press, 1957, p. 1-2.

4. SELZNICK, P.: *TVA and the Grass Roots.* Berkeley, U. of Calif., 1949, p. 251.
5. WEBER, MAX: *The Theory of Social and Economic Organization.* Henderson, A.M. and Parsons, T. (transl.), Parsons, T. (Ed.), New York, Oxford U.P., 1947, p. 329-341.
6. GUSFIELD, J.R.: Social structure and moral reform: a study of the Women's Christian Temperance Union. *Amer J Sociol, LXI*:221-232, 1955. Also, Messinger, S.L.: Organizational transformation: a case study of a declining social movement. *Amer Sociol Rev, 20*:3-10, 1955.
7. MCMILLEN, WAYNE: *Community Organization for Social Welfare.* Chicago, U. of Chicago, 1945, p. 587-591.
8. GARCEAU, OLIVER: *The Political Life of the American Medical Association.* Cambridge, Harvard, 1941.
9. LIPSET, S.M.: The political process in the trade union: A theoretical statement. In *Freedom and Control in Modern Society.* Berger, M.; Abel, T., and Page, C.H. (Eds.), New York, Van Nostrand, 1954, p. 105.
10. *Ibid.,* p. 106.
11. JOHNS, R.E.: *The Co-operative Process Among National Social Agencies.* New York, Assn. Pr., 1946, p. 199.
12. TRUMAN, D.B.: *The Governmental Process.* New York, Knopf, 1951, p. 118.
13. *Ibid.*, p. 116-117.
14. MCMILLEN, *op. cit.,* p. 587.
15. Editorial. *Adult Leadership, 2*(8):11, 1954.
16. JOHNS, *op. cit.,* p. 193.
17. TRUMAN, *op. cit.,* p. 120.
18. LIPSET, *op. cit.,* p. 105.
19. EMBREE, J.F.: *Suye Mura: A Japanese Village.* Chicago, U. of Chicago, 1939, p. 163-170.
20. ROSE, A.M.:*Theory and Method in the Social Sciences.* Minneapolis: U. of Minn., 1954, p. 72-115.
21. ROSE, A.M.: *Sociology.* New York, Knopf, 1956, p. 312.
22. BRYCE, J.: *Modern Democracies.* New York, Macmillan, 1921, Vol. II, p. 542.
23. SELZNICK, P.: *The Organizational Weapon.* New York, McGraw, 1952, p. 96.
24. BARBER, B.: Participation and mass apathy in association. In *Studies in Leadership.* Gouldner, A.W. (Ed.), New York, Harper, 1950, p. 484-486.
25. BROOM, L., and SELZNICK, P.: *Sociology.* Evanston, Row, 1955, p. 440-441.
26. RIESMAN, D., and GLACER, N.: Criteria for political apathy. In Gouldner, (Ed.), *Op. cit.*, p. 505.
27. Editorial. *New York Times*, Dec. 22, 1955, p. 22.
28. KAPLAN, J.: Observations on the somatic and psychosomatic significance of group activity on older people. *Ment Hyg, 38*:640-646, 1954.

29. Glick, P.C.: The life cycle of the family. *Marriage and Family Living, 17*: 3-9, 1955.
30. Kaplan, J.: *How to Organize a Golden Age Club in Your Community.* "How To" Leaflet Number 1. Columbus, Ohio Department of Mental Hygiene and Correction, 1968, p. 1.
31. Kaplan, J.: *A Social Program for Older People.* Minneapolis, U. of Minn., 1953.
32. Williams, A.: *Recreation for the Aging.* New York, Assn. Pr., 1953.
33. North Carolina Recreation Commission: *A Manual of Organization of Clubs for Older Citizens.* Chapel Hill, North Carolina Recreation Commission Institute for Research in Social Sciences, 1956.
34. Maxwell, J.A.: *Centers for Older People: Guide for Program and Facilities.* New York, The National Council on the Aging, 1956, p. 5.
35. *Ibid,* p. 7.
36. Maxwell, *op. cit.,* especially p. 84-117.
37. Kaplan, J.: *How to Develop a Senior Citizen Center in Your Community.* Columbus, Ohio Department of Mental Hygiene and Correction, 1968.
38. Kaplan, J.: *Mister Chairman.* Columbus, Ohio Department of Mental Hygiene and Correction, 1968.
39. Kaplan, J.: *Officer's Hand Book.* Columbus, Ohio Department of Mental Hygiene and Correction, 1968.
40. *Modern Maturity,* Feb.-March, 1967, vol. 10.
41. Landis, J.T.: Old age movements in the United States. In *Social Adjustment in Old Age.* Havighurst, R.J. (Ed.), New York, Social Science Research Council, 1946.
42. *Invitation to Membership.* St. Louis, Gerontological Society, 1968.
43. *Sixth Annual Meeting and Conference Program.* New York, American Association of Homes for the Aging, 1967, p. 2.
44. *An Invitation to Membership.* New York, The National Council on the Aging, 1968.
45. *Report of the 1964 National Conference on Homemaker Services.* New York, National Council for Homemaker Services, 1964, p. 3.

## ADDITIONAL READINGS

Abrams, A.J.: Golden Age Clubs and Centers in New York State. In *Brightening the Senior Years.* Newburgh, New York State Joint Legislative Committee on Problems of the Aging, 1957, p. 12-129.

Hare, P.; Borgatta, E.F., and Bales, R.F.: *Small Groups: Studies in Social Interaction.* New York, Knopf, 1955.

Kaplan, J.: Evaluation techniques for older groups. *Amer J Occup Ther, XIII* (5):221-226, Sept.-Oct., 1959.

Kaplan, J.: Planning the bonus years. *Modern Maturity, 2*(4):12-14, August-Sept., 1959.

KAPLAN, J.: Functions and objectives of a senior citizens center. *Geriatrics, 17*: 771-777, Nov. 1962.

KUBIE, S. H., and LANDAU, G.: *Group Work with the Aged.* New York, Int Univs., 1953.

MATHIASEN, G.: Assessment of services in the voluntary agency as seen by a na-national committee. *J Geront, XIII*(suppl. 2):58-61, July 1958.

MEYER, H.: *Recreation for Later Maturity.* Raleigh, North Carolina Recreation Commission, 1956.

The Ohio Citizen. *Recreational Activities of Ohio's Older People.* Columbus, The Ohio Citizen's Council for Health and Welfare, 1952.

ROSE, A. M.: The impact of aging on voluntary organization. In *Handbook of Social Gerontology.* Tibbitts, C. (Ed.), Chicago, U. of Chicago, 1960, p. 666-697.

SCOTT, J. C.: Membership and participation in voluntary associations. *Amer Sociol Rev, 22*:315-326, 1957.

SWITZER, M., and RUSK, H. A.: Keeping older people fit for participation. *Ann Amer Acad Political Soc Sci,* 1952, pp. 146-153.

*Chapter 17*

# THE RESPONSIBILITY OF THE FEDERAL GOVERNMENT

ADA BARNETT STOUGH

*We shall judge ourselves as we will be judged in the eyes of others, not only by what we do in outer space, but what we do here and now for our senior citizens.*

PRESIDENT JOHN F. KENNEDY

*A basic goal of an enlightened society must be to provide opportunities which enable older people to keep and strengthen their independence and dignity. . . . We have the power to enrich the lives of older Americans and to benefit from their skills, their wisdom and their experience.*

PRESIDENT LYNDON B. JOHNSON

EARLY IN THE 1930s, the United States Government became aware of the rapidly increasing number of older people in the population caused by natural population growth, discovery of antibiotics, and improved living conditions. Aging began to be identified as a problem because of certain characteristics and needs associated with it, the ingredients of which were as follows: health, chronic illness, income security, payment for medical services, employment of older workers, living arrangements, housing, and changing family and social responsibilities. Recognition of the responsibility of Government for helping to meet the needs of persons in their later years followed, and the move toward Government programs began.

The first and most significant step was the enactment of the Social Security Act in 1935 which provided direct money grants to the needy aged and a social security system to build a foundation of economic security for the retired worker.

The First National Conference on Aging was held in 1950, followed shortly after by a Committee on Aging and Geriatrics in the Federal Security Agency. When the new Department of Health, Education, and Welfare was created in 1953, a Special Staff on Aging was established in the Office of the Secretary. This arrangement gave way to an Office of Aging in the new Welfare Administration in 1962. In 1965, the passage of the Older Americans Act established the Administration on Aging as one of the major agencies within the Department.

In the period between 1950 to 1965, significant improvements were made in the social security system, particularly by raising the level of benefits, adding disability insurance, and liberalizing the retirement tests. Federal financial participation in old-age assistance payments and vendor payments for medical care were increased, and a new category of public assistance, medical assistance for the aged was established. Late in 1965, Congress passed the so-called Medicare Bill, which established a long-awaited program of hospital and health insurance.

Government-supported research during this time brought recognition in the health field that diseases are not inevitably associated with advancing age beyond 60. There was a rapid development of government programs for health promotion, prevention of illness, screening and rehabilitation. Increased attention was given by both Federal and State Governments to providing home care and other services to help the elderly remain in their own homes. Great strides were also made in government programs to provide needed housing for older people.

## White House Conference on Aging

The awakening of State governments to their responsibilities for older people came in 1960, when the Congress authorized a White House Conference on Aging and appropriated Federal funds to assist states in assessing the needs of its people and reporting all these facts to the conference. State committees on aging were organized to conduct the studies. The great amount of interest and concern aroused was reflected in the attendance of 3,300 persons at the conference held in 1961. The conference produced a large and comprehensive set of recommendations for action to meet the needs of the elderly, and the skeleton organizations of the states formed at that time became the nucleus of the state organizations subsequently created to administer the Older Americans Act.

## THE OLDER AMERICANS ACT

In 1965, the Congress passed the Older Americans Act which spelled out specific Government responsibility and objectives for older people. The law established an Administration on Aging as one of the principal agencies of the Department of Health, Education, and Welfare, with a commissioner appointed by the President, and authorized financial grants to states to stimulate and aid communities in developing and improving programs and services for older people.

The grants are administered by a legally designated agency, which in most states is a State Commission on Aging. Combined with the leadership and resources of local communities, they are making possible better community planning for older people, establishment of multipurpose centers for recreational, educational, and social pursuits, training and use of older people in volunteer community service and improved social services of many kinds.

The offices of the Administration on Aging in Washington and in the nine regions serve as a clearing house on information on aging and provide technical assistance and consultation to states and communities.

Funds are also available to finance demonstration, research, and training projects to evaluate methods and develop new techniques which will contribute to wholesome, meaningful living for older people.

While the Older Americans Act is one of the most recent laws affecting older people, it provides only a small fraction of the assistance and services made possible by the many older established and well-financed programs of the Federal Government which will be described in the succeeding paragraphs.

## INCOME MAINTENANCE AND HOSPITAL INSURANCE

The great depression of the thirties awakened the country to the inevitability of retirement in an increasingly mechanized society, and the need to set up some system to insure at least a minimum amount of financial security to retired workers. The passage of the Social Security Act in 1935 established an old-age insurance system, financed by a payroll tax of employers and employees. It also authorized a public assistance program of direct money grants to the needy aged, to be financed by funds from the Federal Treasury.

Subsequent amendments to the act have added benefits for the disabled worker, lowered the eligibility age for benefits to 62 years, and increased the monthly payments. In 1966, 85 per cent of persons 65 years of age and over were receiving OASDI payments. The average amounts were eighty dollars for a retired worker without dependents, $142 for a retired worker and aged wife, and seventy-four dollars for an aged widow.

The 1965 amendments to the Social Security Act provided two types of health insurance benefits. The first is a basic *hospital insurance* plan financed jointly by employers and employees under the social security payroll tax. It provides the following:

1. Sixty days in a hospital (except first $40) and all but ten dollars a day for additional thirty days for each period of illness;
2. Up to one-hundred home health visits in a year following hospitalization; and
3. 80 per cent of outpatient diagnostic tests.

The *voluntary medical plan,* financed by monthly payments of three dollars by the enrollee matched by an equal amount from Federal revenues, covers physician's fees and other medical services not covered by the basic plan.

Both the social security and health insurance programs are administered by the Social Security Administration in the U. S. Department of Health, Education, and Welfare.

The old-age assistance program, administered by the Assistance Payments Administration of the Social and Rehabilitation Service of the same Department, provides each state with funds (allotted under a specific formula) to pay part of the cost of financial assistance to aged people unable to meet the minimum cost of food, shelter, and clothing. Payments are made through county welfare departments to those individuals who have been certified as eligible under the laws of that specific state. The Federal Government pays half of the total monthly payment to each individual, the amount of which is determined by legislative action of each state. For that reason, the payments range from a low of nine dollars a month in Puerto Rico to $122 a month in Wisconsin. The average is seventy-nine dollars a month.

There are many persons 65 years of age and over who do not need help for daily living expenses but who cannot meet their medical bills. They are termed "medically needy." Medical assistance for these people is available through direct payments to the suppliers of medical services. Laws determining eligibility and the amount of assistance also vary with each state law.

The Federal Government provides grants-in-aid to states for the financing of a broad spectrum of social welfare services to the aged and disabled. They are administered through county welfare departments. Under certain conditions, matching funds are also available to county welfare departments for projects such as homemaker services, foster homes for the elderly, self-care programs, portable meals, and protective services.

## Health Needs

As early as 1948, the National Health Assembly stated that aging is not a disease and issued the challenge that many people could enjoy health and vigor in their older years. The gradual abandonment of the position that age and disease are inevitably associated in the years beyond 60 has led to an increased interest in medical research and a rapid development of programs and services to promote health, prevent illness, and rehabilitate the afflicted.

### REGULAR PUBLIC HEALTH GRANTS TO STATES

Every year, each state receives financial assistance from the Federal Government for many kinds of health services authorized by the Public Health Service Act and its many amendments. These grants are of two types: (1) the regular formula grants apportioned according to statutory formula; and (2) special project grants for the financing of research, demonstration, studies and services in many different areas prescribed by law.

The one formula grant most closely related to older people is for developing and demonstrating improved methods of providing out-of-hospital services for the chronically ill and aged. The other formula grants for the control of cancer, heart disease, tuberculosis, and water pollution, and for mental and general health services benefit the elderly along with all other age groups.

Numerous project grants are financed to provide support for specific activity to be carried out during a fixed period of time. Those relating specifically to older people cover a wide area ranging from preventive and protective health services, to health maintenance, counseling, comprehensive disease detection, referral for diagnosis and treatment, home health, home nursing and homemaker services, portable meals, coordination of community activities for the chronically ill, training of medical and paramedical personnel, and many others.

### Facilities

The Public Health Service administers a large comprehensive program to stimulate and assist communities to build up an efficient, well-coordinated network of facilities for the acute care, long-term care, and rehabilitation of all persons, including the aged. Thousands of long-term care beds in chronic disease and nursing home facilities are predominantly occupied by older people. They also benefit from the extensive building of regular hospitals and public health diagnostic and treatment centers.

## RESEARCH

Millions of dollars are spent by the Federal Government in research related to aging and the aged. Programs of basic research to increase understanding of the biological, behavioral and social processes that account for the lessening of vigor in advanced years is carried on in the various National Institutes of Health—particularly the Institute for Child Health and Human Development. Basic and applied research in many other related fields are financed by many divisions of the Public Health Service. They include studies of patterns of health services, drug utilization, methods of care for the elderly ambulatory patient, studies of the well-being of noninstitutionalized older people, and many others.

### Other Health Services

Older people benefit also from the accident prevention activities of the Public Health Service, the dental health program, air pollution control, and the many programs looking toward the increase of trained personnel in health and health-related fields.

## HOUSING

Housing became identified as one of the critical needs of older people following the recession in home building brought on by World War II. In recognition of the need, the Housing Act of 1956 was passed authorizing FHA mortgage insurance for housing designed especially for the elderly, and for the first time defined a "family" as one person over 65. Successive legislative action by the Congress added other incentives so there are now four categories of assistance designed to provide good housing for elderly persons from low to moderate income level.

### Low-Rent Public Housing

Low-rent public housing, owned and operated by local housing authorities, can be built through Federal financial assistance. Temporary loans are made to the authorities to build the projects and annual contributions are made to them to amortize bond issues sold on the market by the authorities for permanent financing. Existing private housing can also be leased or purchased by local authorities.

*Housing for moderate income elderly* is assisted through direct loans made at a 3 per cent interest rate for fifty years to nonprofit sponsors. This housing is for older people with incomes too high for public housing but too low for the private housing market; church and professional groups, labor unions, fraternal and civic clubs are eligible for these loans.

*Housing for elderly in a wilder income range* is stimulated by mortgage insurance. The Federal Housing Authority insures private lenders against losses on loans to nonprofit or profit-motivated sponsors. More facilities and services may be included in building under this program than under direct loan projects.

*Rent supplements for the low income elderly* provides for Federal payments to certain new or rehabilitated housing to enable elderly with incomes no higher than those permitted for tenants of public housing to obtain a decent place to live. The rent supplement cannot exceed the amount by which the fair market rental exceeds one-fourth of the tenant's income.

## OTHER GOVERNMENT PROGRAMS

### Rehabilitation

Every year many hundreds of handicapped older persons are rehabilitated enough to resume employment and many others are restored to self-care and independence through programs of the Rehabilitation Services Administration of the Social and Rehabilitation Service, U. S. Department of Health, Education, and Welfare. Rehabilitation personnel is being trained to do proficient work with older people through VRA institutes, projects, and special university long and short term programs. Research is also being carried on to discover and distribute data to show the possible productivity of the older disabled worker.

## Employment

Employment for older workers becomes an increasing problem as the pace of industrial technology is accelerated. Although the U. S. Department of Labor defines the "older worker" as one over 45 years of age, the concern of Government extends (although to a lesser extent) to workers above retirement age who need employment for income and other reasons. Discrimination in employment because of age has been a subject for extensive consideration by the Congress over a number of years, and one on which more definite legislative action can be expected in the years ahead.

The Bureau of Employment Security in the U. S. Department of Labor administers an older worker program by providing older worker specialists in state employment offices and in the employment offices of major metropolitan areas. These specialists spearhead and supervise activities in behalf of older job seekers and informational materials to stimulate the hiring of older workers. In many cases, retraining to keep abreast of job requirements is necessary before a worker can obtain a job. The passage of the Manpower Development and Training Act of 1962 was designed to help meet this need. Most of the programs under this act, administered by the U. S. Department of Labor, are appropriately focused on the worker of preretirement age. However, a few projects are financed to demonstrate the feasibility of retraining workers 62 and over to reenter the labor market.

## Taxes

Tax savings to older Americans are provided under the Revenue

Act of 1964 and other tax laws. The major savings are made possible by the following:

1. A double exemption in computing yearly income tax;
2. A minimum standard deduction as an alternative to the 10 per cent standard deduction or itemized deductions;
3. Increased deduction for medical expenses;
4. A credit on retirement income; and
5. (Under certain conditions) exemption from a capital gains tax on the sale price of a home.

In addition to these tax savings, the tax laws also contain certain provisions that encourage the growth of nondiscriminatory pension plans which will enable individuals to meet retirement needs.

## COST AND UNMET NEEDS

In 1965, the major Federal programs of benefits and services to older people described in this chapter required the expenditure of $26 billion by the Government even though there are still needs which are not being met.

In the everchanging picture of the older person in today's society, problems previously less noticeable, come to the fore. Thus new areas emerge calling for Government action. Legislation must often wait, however, until lines of responsibility become defined and public opinion creates a climate of support.

For this reason, there are as yet no special Federal or state financed programs to assist in preparation for retirement, or for education for leisure-centered living in post-retirement years. Some organizations and agencies and local communities are pioneering in these fields through multipurpose centers, recreation programs, and preretirement courses. A number of projects for these purposes are being funded by state agencies through the Older Americans Act. These may or may not be forerunners of Government sponsored programs of the future.

There are no tax supported programs to help meet the nutritional needs of the elderly, or to create opportunities for useful work by older people in public service.

If developments of the past four decades indicate future trends, it may be safe to assume that the Government will assume responsibility for meeting these and other needs when it becomes apparent it should do so.

## REFERENCES

President John F. Kennedy, Message to Congress, February 21, 1963, 88th Congress, House Document No. 72.

President Lyndon B. Johnson, Message to Congress, January 23, 1967, 90th Congress, House Document No. 40.

1965—Year of Legislative Achievements. In *Indicators.* Department of Health Education and Welfare, Superintendent of Documents, Washington, D.C., U.S. Government Printing Office, 1966.

*The Nation and Its People—Report of the White House Conference on Aging—1961,* Superintendent of Documents, Washington, D.C., U.S. Government Printing Office.

*Older Americans Act.* Public Law 89-73.

*Grants in Aid and Other Financial Assistance Programs.* Department of Health, Education, and Welfare, Superintendent of Documents, Washington, D.C., U.S. Government Printing Office, Jan. 1966.

*Senior Citizens Housing Loan Program.* Washington, D.C., Department of Housing and Urban Development.

*The Older American Worker—Age Discrimination in Employment, 1965.* Washington, D.C., U.S. Department of Labor.

*Tax Benefits for Older Americans, 1965.* Washington, D.C., Internal Revenue Service, U.S. Treasury Department.

*A Time of Progress for Older Americans, 1965-1967.* Report of the President's Council on Aging, Superintendent of Documents, Washington, D.C., U.S. Government Printing Office.

*Working With Older People—A Guide to Practice.* Public Health Publication No. 1459, Superintendent of Documents, Washington, D.C., U.S. Government Printing Office, 1966, vol. 1.

*Chapter 18*

# COMMUNITY HEALTH SERVICES

JOE BALES GRABER

COMMUNITY HEALTH SERVICES are of vital importance to the health and well-being of the aging and aged, and in order to provide adequate health protection for those persons over 45 years of age, generally referred to as aging, a variety of community health services are required. These are services pertaining to both an individual's personal health and his immediate physical and community environment.[1] In the area of personal health, services must be available for the apparently well and the sick adult.[2] Included are services for the ambulatory, the homebound, and the institutionalized person. The apparently well adult should have access to community services which provide for periodic health appraisal, early disease detection, and immunization for certain infectious diseases.

For those who are homebound because of their illnesses or disabilities, there must be an array of care services that can be provided in the home setting; and there must be means, such as ambulance services, for transferring these people to other settings when care is required that cannot be administered adequately in the home. These settings include a variety of public and private facilities: general hospitals for acute care, extended care facilities such as nursing homes for convalescence, personal-care homes primarily for custodial care, health centers and other diagnostic facilities, mental hospitals and clinics, and rehabilitation centers.

In addition to these personal health services and facilities, there must be environmental health programs to protect the individual in his home and in the community. Included would be programs for injury control, air pollution control, protection from radiation hazards, and for the provision of safe food and water. Additionally, the trend toward urbanization and industrialization requires community health activities related to provision of adequate housing and protection from excessive noises; for disposal of domestic and industrial wastes; and for protection of workers and their families from occupational hazards.

## PERSONAL HEALTH SERVICES

An evaluation of systems for health facilities is presently being undertaken in the public health field. There are indications that increased emphasis will be placed on renovation of medical facilities in urban areas and construction of much larger hospitals in metropolitan areas requiring new facilities; increased and more effective utilization of existing facilities by operating various departments on a seven-day-a-week basis rather than the current five-day schedule, by joint management and use of special services and equipment by several institutions in a given community. Emphasis will also be placed on the sharing of personnel in short supply to provide consultation to smaller institutions where professional services are limited by lack of trained manpower; encouraging physicians to participate in the group practice of medicine to take advantage of the trend toward medical specialization; and master planning to determine alternatives to present care patterns. The latter activity may be expected to result in the development of large medical complexes with facilities to provide for comprehensive health care—preventive, diagnostic, therapeutic and restorative on an inpatient and outpatient basis.

Other factors influencing the arrangements for the delivery of services include methods of payments. Titles 18 and 19 of the Social Security Act have made possible payments for health and medical services outside the hospital; and more and more frequently, insurance companies are making provisions for payment for out-of-hospital services and for payment of services by health professionals other than the physicians. In the search for new ways to provide personal health services, some health departments have been experimenting with contractual arrangements in which private practitioners are paid by the hour to staff clinics and with charging fees for service rendered by staff members. Included in the latter demonstrations are diet-counseling services for the homebound patient.[3]

Because services for the homebound and institutionalized older person are so important, it should be recognized that a great majority of the aging population are well and that many of the older people who experience chronic conditions are able to live independently. For the former, there should be public health oriented programs to prevent or to detect diseases before symptoms appear. There should also be supportive services to aid persons in the latter group to continue functioning at their maximum level and to prevent further disability from developing. Services for these groups of persons are provided on an outpatient basis in a setting to which they normally turn for medical advice and care, including the private physician's office, the health department, or the outpatient department of a community hospital.[4]

The importance of planning for a range of services and the more efficient provision of these services can be readily recognized when one considers the fact that the health industry is rapidly becoming a $50 billion a year enterprise. Among other things, planners must consider factors relating to the health status of the older population, such as increased longevity; later onset of final, debilitating illnesses, and the nature of the diseases most likely to affect them; and the potential impact of the availability or nonavailability of health protection, maintenance, and care services on the socioeconomic status of an individual, his family, and his community.

Within the past five years, programs in the Public Health Service in the U. S. Department of Health, Education and Welfare have focused increased attention on identifying and describing community health services which relate to the aging individual's physical, social, and emotional health and on developing materials for use by professionals and others who serve the aging population.[5]

Through these and other efforts, it has been found that the patterns for providing community health services for the ambulatory, the apparently well adult, and the homebound person are changing as much as those for institutional care. As a result, health protection and maintenance services are found more and more frequently in locations convenient to where the older person lives, works, or goes for social and recreational purposes.[6, 7] Organized home care programs which take advantage of the capabilities of many health and allied health professionals, including the physician, nurse, nutritionist, social worker, health educator, are increasing rapidly. Of particular importance to the apparently well adult are the programs providing for periodic health examinations or appraisals — adult health conferences — and screening for hidden diseases.[8]

## Adult Health Conferences

The adult health conference—sometimes called Well Aging Clinics or Health Maintenance Clinics—provides a health appraisal through clinical laboratory tests and procedures; a physical examination performed by a physician; and/or a physician's evaluation based on clinical tests, a dental examination, and health education and counseling services. Diagnoses are made in these conferences and the participants with deviations from normal health are referred to their regular medical resources, usually a private physician or health department, for treatment and followup. Often available are preventive services such as dietary counseling for the obese person, and instruction on proper foot care for the suspected diabetic or person with circulatory problems. For those persons who may be traveling abroad, in particular, the following immunizations are recommended: smallpox, diphtheria, tetanus, poliomyelitis, influenza and gamma globulin for the prevention of infectious hepatitis.

The socioeconomic advantages of health maintenance programs are apparent. However, at the present time, few services of this kind are available, and then mostly to a limited clientele. The major disadvantages of this kind of program are the amount of time the professional staff must use for interpreting the laboratory tests and reports and subsequently, the few people to whom such extensive, time-consuming services may be offered. As a result, the adult health conference is being used more frequently as a referral source for persons needing further examinations following a screening program.

## Screening Programs

Larger numbers of persons may be reached through less costly screening programs. Through these a single test or many tests are offered. The tests, however, are not intended to be diagnostic, but to sort out the apparently well adult who probably has a disease from those who do not. Those persons with positive or suspicious findings are referred to their private physicians or health departments for diagnosis, treatment, and followup. Automated procedures for testing as well as for interpretation of results, with considerable reliance for both being placed on technicians, have contributed to the proliferation of screening programs. And these are being offered by many groups, often as jointly sponsored community services. A number of state health departments and voluntary health organizations utilize mobile equipment for these programs and, as a result, are able to provide statewide coverage on a regularly scheduled basis. Again, working in this area, the Public Health Service has identified a core of tests that could lead to the prevention and control of a number of diseases now among the leading causes of death or disability for persons over 45 years of age, namely, cancer, heart disease, stroke, glaucoma, emphysema, and tuberculosis.

## Laboratory Services

These services are essential to groups providing either personal or environmental health services. Generally, health laboratories provide early case-finding and diagnostic tests and supportive services. They analyze water for sodium content, as well as consult with local and private laboratories. They standardize services and provide reference standards; accredit local and private laboratories as deemed necessary by state and local authorities; and validate certain screening and diagnostic procedures. To accommodate the increased workload imposed by large screening programs, groups are engaged in research and demonstration projects to develop or to improve automated and computerized laboratory procedures.

Of particular importance also is legislation now before the 90th Congress which would provide for the improvement, through licensure, of laboratories engaged in interstate commerce. These laboratories perform millions of tests annually; yet, according to the testimony presented at hearings on this legislation, surveys have shown a 25 per cent error in determinations. To the aging and aged who are large consumers of medical services such as these, the economic and health implications are of considerable significance.

## Health Education and Public Information

These are essential community services for all population groups, including the aging and aged. They are designed to create an awareness of and concern about local health problems in general, as well as to provide information about specific diseases and conditions, and to encourage utilization of local community services such as a screening program, an immunization clinic, or classes on meal planning and preparation. The latter might be especially designed for those persons with reduced incomes following retirement or for those with dietary problems related to a particular disease. Health protection of the older consumer is emphasized also through lectures and news releases on frauds, quackery, and food fads. Though not a part of health education or public information per se, efforts to detect and eliminate fake medical devices and products are equally important and eventually provide the information necessary for consumer protection.

## Social Services

Social services, including individual casework and the organization and conduct of information and referral services, aid many older individuals. Through social service programs in hospitals and in public and voluntary health, mental health, and welfare agencies, an older person—through casework—may be placed in the proper care facility and provided protective services, including legal help to assist those who are mentally or physically incapable of managing their own affairs.[9] He may also be helped to secure financial assistance, especially for medical and dental care; or counseled on marital and other family problems, including those engendered by dependency on children for financial support or housing or both.

## The Information and Referral Service

The information and referral service, on the other hand, is a professionally staffed community service operated for the purpose of contributing to the effective utilization of resources and to the improvement of their quality and quantity.[10] Most of the information and referral services provide assistance in locating community resources needed by other professionals for their clientele, and some provide direct counseling and limited casework services to older individuals if these services are not available elsewhere.

Central files are maintained on all community health facilities; hospitals, clinics, nursing homes, family service agencies, and health and welfare departments. Information is also available on public housing projects, sources of equipment that can be borrowed by the homebound patient, recreational programs, vocational rehabilitation programs, travelers' services, legal services, and employment agencies. It has been demonstrated that such services are excellent administrative tools for identifying gaps in a community's resources, and some information and referral services have frequently provided data to groups planning for additional facilities and services or for the elimination or combining of existing resources.

## Dental Health

Dental health programs are of importance to all persons, particularly adults, and should be available for the ambulatory, homebound, and institutionalized person. Unfortunately, at this time, adequate funds are not available to support sufficient public health dental programs for the aging and aged. However, funds for developing demonstrations of new ways of bringing dental services to older persons, particularly the nonambulatory chronically ill, have been made available by the Federal Government.[11] This has resulted in the development of portable dental equipment for bedside care which some health departments are now making available to private dental practitioners for their use in nursing homes or in private residences.

## Mental Health

In the area of mental health, many new approaches for providing services are being tried. Much emphasis has been placed recently on returning the older mental patient to the community, both to nursing homes and to private homes depending on the amount of care required. This has been made possible, in part, by great strides in drug therapy. Also, community mental health centers are being developed extensively to provide supportive programs for persons with many kinds of mental illnesses, including suicidal tendencies and alcoholism, a growing problem among older individuals.

For the institutionalized psychiatric patients, there are periodic health examinations for the chronically ill, and there are experimental programs to reestablish social relationships between the older patient and his family and between the older patient and the community. Of considerable importance are the pastoral counseling services for the emotionally disturbed.

## Preretirement Counseling

This area of service has been found to be one of the least well-developed of all for the aging and aged. It is, however, one of the most important and should be available to all persons in the work force at least ten years, if not more, in advance of retirement. Such a program should include individual and group counseling activities to cover the following subject areas: health maintenance, nutrition, psychological changes and emotional adjustments, income, investments and retirement systems, legal problems including information on special tax privileges for persons over 65, and use of leisure time. Many groups may participate, such as private industry, unions, universities, and state agencies.

## Recreational Programs and Volunteer Services

Grief over the death and separation from loved ones and friends, loss of social status following retirement, and threats of ill health and dependency are among the problems faced by many persons in the upper age groups. Recreational programs for both the ambulatory and homebound aimed at alleviating these problems are considered health related, and these programs are designed to help the older person find new and interesting ways of occupying his leisure time, new friendships, and pleasure and fulfillment in being needed by others.

In this latter regard, older persons are most effective volunteer visitors to the sick. Not only do they listen to the homebound or institutionalized person, but they may provide a number of other valuable services, such as shopping for or even chauffeuring a disabled person. Older, more mature volunteers are most effective health education aides; and in screening programs, for instance, they are often used to interpret the screening procedures to their peers. In neighborhood health-center programs, these volunteers visit neighbors and encourage their participation in available health programs; and they sometimes make the arrangements for getting their neighbors to the health center.

## Rehabilitation and Nutrition Counseling Services

These two services should be available in institutional settings on an inpatient and outpatient basis, and they should be part of all home care programs. Rehabilitation programs should be directed towards helping older persons maintain their highest level of functional capacity. Therefore, such programs are important components of all medical care: prevention, diagnosis, and restoration. Participating in such programs are many health professionals, including physicians, nurses, therapists, social workers and nutritionists. It should be understood that rehabilitation does not always relate to returning a person to employment. For some, it may mean relearning to feed one's self without help.

The majority of dietitians and nutritionists employed in health departments concentrate on consulting with persons responsible for food services in institutions or with other health workers who have direct contact with individuals in need of such counseling. Much emphasis is placed, therefore, on preparation and distribution of newsletters, cycle menus, and diet and food service manuals. However, as home-care programs continue to increase, nutritionists and dietitians are more frequently being used as a member of the health team to provide direct counseling on normal and therapeutic diets to the homebound patient. The role of home economists with special training in food and nutrition and institutional management is most important in the health field.

## Home Delivered Meals

This is an important supportive service for the convalescent, disabled and homebound, and there is general agreement among health professionals that this service should be provided in conjunction with other home health services. But the provision of home delivered meals should not encourage a person to stay in an environment not conducive to his recovery and well-being. There is agreement also that meals should be provided on a seven-day-a-week basis so as not to encourage poor dietary and food storage habits. Ideally, a nurse, social worker, or other health professional should approve the admission of a person to this service.

## Nursing Services and Home Health Services

A wide range of community health nursing services is needed by the aging and the aged. This includes the services rendered by the nurse in public health clinics and in the patient's home.[13] In some cases, this service will provide direct patient care; in others, it will teach the patient or his family how to provide the care.

Bedside care is the focus of most home health services and since the passage of the Medicare Act, there has been considerable growth in the number of agencies and programs which provide this kind of care. To participate in the Medicare program, these agencies must be certified to receive payments for services rendered to persons covered by the act. To qualify, the agency must provide nursing services plus one other therapeutic service such as physical therapy, occupational therapy, speech therapy, medical social work or home health aides. Whenever home health aides or other nonprofessional personnel are involved in providing personal services to a patient, nursing supervision should be available.

At the present time, 84 per cent of the agencies certified to provide home health services are either health departments or visiting nurses associations. Most of the remaining 16 per cent are hospital-based programs.

## Homemakers and Home Health Aides

A homemaker program is defined as a housekeeping service in the field of public health; and a homemaker used in this program renders no personal services to the patient but fills the very important role of helping a family stay together, especially when the ill person is the mother. On the other hand, a home health aide is trained to provide some personal services under the supervision of a public health nurse.

## Summary

The areas discussed in this section, beginning with adult health conferences, comprise a community checklist of services that should be available to meet the personal health needs of the aging and aged. As yet, all of these services are substantially underdeveloped. This is due in part to limited manpower, inadequate local tax support to finance these programs, and public and professional apathy.

However, many activities of significance to future developments are in progress. Before the 90th Congress is a bill which would establish a number of regional and community centers throughout the country to provide health appraisal and disease detection to any person over 50 years of age residing within the geographic area served by the centers.

In addition, the Secretary of the Department of Health, Education and Welfare and delegates to a recent National Conference on Medical Care Costs convened by the President have endorsed the establishment of a health services research center in the Public Health Service. The center is now being organized and will serve as the Federal focus for health services research and development. It will address its program to research on major problems affecting the availability, organization, distribution, quality and financing of health services and health care facilities and to the training of persons needed to conduct this kind of research.

## ENVIRONMENTAL HEALTH SERVICES

The history of our exploitation of the environment since early in the last century reveals many examples of misuse and abuse and unsuccessful attempts to control the environment. From an agrarian economy concentrated along the East Coast, the country grew into the breadbasket of the world; from a handful of mills along tumbling New England rivers sprang an industrial giant that has no equal in all the world. To serve this industrial revolution came the skilled and unskilled from far and near to cluster into the growing cities. Through the wonders of research and the marvel of mass production came new products and new processes—all adding up to a higher standard of living than the world has ever known.

Today's world is profoundly different from that of even a few decades ago. But progress has been purchased at a price: a million traffic fatalities since World War II, crowded cities bathed in a sea of pollution and filled with noise and squalor. We stand at a point in history when our capacity to enhance or degrade the environment is literally beyond reckoning, but we do not now fully understand how to use this capacity for the benefit, rather than the harm, of our own and future generations.

The effects of environmental change are not manifested solely in threats to man's physical well-being. The pressures of our industrial culture threaten social and psychological well-being. These psychosocial effects of environmental hazards are nonetheless cause for concern in a nation where mental and social ills are recognized as major problems.[14, 15]

Fortunately, as in the case of personal health services, programs have been identified which can lead to the prevention and control of current hazards and potential future threats. However, much depends on public demand for proper and sufficient action to take place at every level—federal, state and local. Effectiveness is dependent also, just as with personal health services, on the involvement of the total community: government, labor and industry, communications media, professional and educational groups, social organizations, and the general public.

## Injury Control

Older people are at high risk for traffic accidents, particularly those in which they are involved as pedestrians, and for home accidents, such as falls, burns, and explosions.[16] Accidental poisoning from the improper use of drugs is another hazard of increasing concern. Presently, the accidental death rate for persons over age 65 is three times the rate for all ages, with older women experiencing an injury rate 20 per cent higher than men. Health departments and other organizations engage in educational programs aimed at reducing the resulting fatalities and disabilities caused by these traffic and home accidents.

To protect those confined to institutions, there are special locally enforced standards relating to the physical environment of hospitals, nursing homes and other care facilities. These standards concern things such as the widths of doors, corridors and other exits to permit ease of access by patients in wheelchairs or by walkers and to assure quick removal of patients in case of emergencies; rules for the handling and use of oxygen; and special equipment such as grab bars and handrails in bathroom and other rooms used by the older or handicapped patient. Also, part of institutional management is concerned with preventing contamination of the air and with control of heat, cold, and noise.

Improper handling of bedridden patients can result in injuries, especially bone fractures in older patients. Thus, many institutions require nursing staffs, aides and orderlies to take refresher courses on the handling and lifting of patients—in bed and into and out of bed. The safeguards used to prevent food contamination may be considered a part of an institution's program of injury and disability control, as well. This includes the preparation and handling of food in the kitchen and dining room and on the wards.

In recognition of the hazard of fires in nursing homes and other institutions, particularly those caring for the elderly, research is being directed toward the development of flame retardant fabrics used for bedding, clothing and decorations and for the development of more fire resistant construction materials, such as slow-burning paint. It has been recommended that Medicare standards for participating institutions require the use of flame retardant fabrics.

New housing designed for the apparently well older person and for certain handicapped persons should utilize many features to prevent or reduce injuries. For example, some of these features are the following: kitchen equipment placed at comfortable working levels to eliminate frequent bending or use of stools to reach cabinets, larger windows to admit more daylight, and nonskid flooring to prevent falls. Home economists and others who assist the older homemaker in safely using equipment that may differ from that used in her former residence, should include safety information as part of their instructions and counseling on home furnishing and management.

The increased use of mobile trailers for both recreation and permanent housing, particularly by older persons, has resulted in the development of a number of special safety education programs for both the operators of the trailer park sites and the trailer owners. Such programs include the importance of a safe water supply; the proper disposal of waste to prevent contamination of the drinking water, especially if supplied by wells; the proper storage and disposal of garbage that would attract flies and rodents; and proper handling of bottled gas to prevent leakage and explosion and to prevent asphyxiation. The latter is particularly important for the elderly because frequently both their sense of smell and hearing are impaired.

New state standards for highway safety programs should help the aging person, both as a motor vehicle operator and as a pedestrian. The most important feature concerns compulsory periodic renewal of vehicle operators' licenses. The exact requirements for licensure renewal will be established by each state; however, it has been suggested that a minimum program should include a check for visual acuity, knowledge of traffic laws, ability to read and comprehend traffic signs and symbols, and ability to operate a vehicle. It is recommended that drivers be reexamined every four years for at least visual acuity and knowledge of rules of the road.

Special education programs have been developed on poison control. People are warned against using old drugs or prescribing for themselves, and suggestions have been made for clearly marking different drugs to prevent mistaking one drug for another or to prevent overuse. Similarly, in care institutions, nursing homes in particular, special efforts have been made to set up drug trays for the older patients with each dose to be administered clearly identified. This is particularly important in those institutions where patient self-help is encouraged.

All of these safety programs are participated in by a variety of organizations and groups, such as official and voluntary health and safety agencies, trade associations and manufacturers. But until the public demands the development and enforcement of stricter safety standards, death and injury rates will continue to be a national disgrace.

## Air Pollution Control

As air pollution increases, so does the incidence of diseases caused by or aggravated by its presence. These include such threats to human health as emphysema, chronic bronchitis, bronchial asthma, and lung cancer. The largest number of victims, the majority of whom are over 45 years of age, are urban dwellers. Under adverse atmospheric conditions, air pollution may affect the entire community. Under other circumstances, it may result from a localized source and affect only those immediately exposed.

In addition to its costly toll on human health, it is estimated that air pollution results annually in a half billion dollar loss in animals and plants and that all property damage due to air pollution is in excess of $12 billion. Property damage includes deterioration of metals, structures, and machines of all kinds; corrosion of metals; weakening and fading of fabrics; weakening of leather; the cracking of rubber; the discoloring of paints; the erosion of concrete and stone; the etching of glass; and the embrittlement of paper. And the cost of such damage is borne to a great extent by the consumer, including the older person.

The sources of air pollution are numerous and varied and include motor vehicle exhausts, the burning of coal and oil, emissions from industrial plants and the burning of rubbish and leaves. Thus, every segment of society contributes in varying degree to the problem.

When large amounts of pollution accumulate, particularly during periods of air stagnation, air pollution episodes often occur. In these comparatively rare but tragic episodes, suffering and even fatalities can occur predominantly among the elderly and others with preexisting cardiac or pulmonary disease. The costs of preventing and controling air pollution may be high and must be borne by government, industry, and the general public. But these costs are nominal when one considers the economic losses caused by air pollution and the real and potential hazards to human health.

Vigorous action is needed at all levels of government, and by industry, to reduce the levels of pollutants in the limited air resources of our country. Public support is imperative if the national prevention and control effort is to succeed. Adequate technology exists to control most sources of pollution, but additional research is needed to provide less costly, more efficient control methods.

Information gained from engineering and biological research, and from surveillance and monitoring activities is being utilized for the protection of the health and well-being of all persons, including the aging and aged. Though not usually thought of as air pollution in the same sense as dust, vapors, and smoke it should be noted that airborne microorganisms cause allergies and communicable diseases, such as tuberculosis, the common cold, and influenza. And, again the aging and aged are those most noticeably affected.

## Radiation Control

The increased use of atomic energy to generate power, the advances in the use of nuclear medicine, and the increased use of x-rays in diagnosis and treatment, are all major trends with a great potential for benefiting many people. At the same time, these mounting uses of radiation augment the risks of deleterious effects on health. Private and governmental programs have been and continue to be instrumental in fostering uses of these and other sources of ionizing radiation to obtain the greatest possible benefits at the lowest possible risk from needless exposure.

Measurement and surveillance networks operate throughout the country. They collect information on sources, levels and trends of radiation, on the nature of radioactive materials in the environment, and on the exposures and doses received by people from all radiation sources including radionuclides, such as strontium 90, cesium 137, and iodine 131, present at times in pasteurized milk and other food products.

Unnecessary exposure to radiation from improper use of x-ray equipment or from defective equipment is of vast importance to the general public. Annually, 148 million medical and dental x-ray visits are made for diagnostic and therapeutic purposes. In order to protect the people involved, standards have been developed and recommended on the use of x-rays and x-ray equipment in hospitals and extended care facilities participating in the Medicaire program for the aged. There is sufficient evidence to indicate that persons working with radium, x-rays and other radiation sources are at high risk for various kinds of radiation-induced malignancies. Depending on their age at initial exposure, of course, many of the victims are likely to be among the over 45 years of age group.

Many unsuspected sources of x-rays are being found. For example, it was recently discovered that color television sets of a certain manufacturer were emitting x-rays above acceptable standards. Warnings that a potential health hazard exists because of this unique situation were widely circulated by the news media, and the manufacturer has pursued a vigorous program to locate and adjust the defective sets that had been distributed. Efforts must be continued to prevent undue radiation exposures such as this to the general public and to workers in high-risk occupations, such as uranium mining. At the same time, technological research into the rapidly growing medical and industrial applications of both x-rays and atomic energy must be carried out.

## Water and Food Quality

Public health workers are concerned with water pollution in relation to the quality of drinking water; the use of water in recreation; the contamination of food sources, particularly shellfish; and the breeding of specific insect vectors of disease. The health threat is of three types: (a) chemical, both organic and inorganic contaminants, which can result in acute toxic or long-term chronic effects on humans; (b) biological and microbiological contaminants and insect vectors associated with communicable diseases, such as infectious hepatitis and salmonellosis; and (c) radiological and radioactive contaminants which in very low concentrations may produce radiation damage in humans.

Of particular interest are the chemical constitutents of drinking water; particularly sodium. The amount of sodium naturally present in water is important especially for those persons on low salt diets. Where such a situation exists, physicians should arrange for dietary consultation for their patients who may need to adjust their diets or use sources other than the water supply normally used.

The protection of water resources for recreational purposes has become more important to the aging and aged because of their increased leisure time in which to enjoy fishing, boating, and swimming. Protection of drinking water supplies used on planes, ships, trains, and buses is another public health function and of growing importance to older persons as their free time permits more travel.

As secure as we may feel about the water we drink, it should be noted that only slightly more than half the population of this country—about 105 million persons—consumes water that meets Federal quality standards, and that some thirty thousand rural communities in the United States are without water systems or have inadequate facilities. The latter could be of critical importance to the elderly, who comprise a large portion of the population of these rural communities. Total water use has increased eightfold since 1900, from 40 billion to 325 billion gallons a day. In our homes are multiple baths, garbage disposals, home laundry units and dishwashers, and more people using more water in more ways than ever before.

A fantastic growth in industry has increased the amount and complexity of wastes going into our streams. In some instances, treated effluents today have polluting effects greater than the raw sewage discharges of thirty years ago. By using synthetic fertilizers and pesticides, the farmer also contributes greatly to the complexity of our water pollution problem, and the net result is that nearly six times as much wastes are contributed to our rivers, streams, lakes, and bays as sixty years ago. Even if, by some miracle, all communities and industries installed, tomorrow, the best treatment we have, so-called secondary treatment, we would still need to develop revolutionary new processes to cope with the amounts and kinds of wastes that are the inevitable result of continuing industrialization, urbanization and population growth.

Environmental health programs must be concerned also with protecting the public from foodborne illnesses that accompany poor sanitation practices. There must be enforcement of sanitary standards concerned with sources of milk supply, processing of milk, and certification of analytical laboratories. There must be enforcement of standards related to raw foods and food products during processing and packaging, and to the preparation and serving of food. The health of food handlers is important also. The benefits are obvious and accrue to all people, including the aging and aged.

## Health in Urban Areas

The concentration of urban life is evidenced by the fact that approximately 70 per cent of our population is crowding into urban areas, which is 10 per cent of our total land. On 35,000 square miles of land area 140,000,000 people are living. Demographers predict that by the year 2000, 80 per cent of an even greater population will occupy this same limited land area. The environmental health hazards already discussed are to be found in great numbers in urban areas. To these must be added problems related to overcrowding; odors, noises, and other stresses which require broadened protection.

From this milieu come many interrelated physical and mental health problems, many of which need additional study. Yet, many of the answers are already at hand and are not being applied. For example, a lack of familiarity with current scientific knowledge has resulted in serious physical health and mental health problems among members of our older population groups which have been uprooted unwillingly from their familiar surroundings because of urban renewal programs or construction of superhighways and freeways. Hopefully, planners of the future will have this information available, and more efforts will be directed toward restoration of one of the older person's most important sources of security—his home. When older persons have to move because of any of these circumstances, they should be helped in planning for their relocation; and they should be informed of available health and social services within the area to which they are transferring.

Also, cities throughout this country have substandard housing near the business districts which older persons prefer to rent because of the convenience to shopping, banking, and health services. For this they are sometimes charged rents far in excess of their ability to pay, since many have incomes below the poverty level set for couples and single persons. Those responsible—slum landlords, primarily—must be held accountable if these environmental conditions which have such an important bearing on the older person's physical and mental health are to be corrected.

Odors, noise, and other factors which cause physical and mental stress are problems about which we need to know more and do more. With regard to noise, for example, we must know more about the subtle effects of noise on health, not the excessive noise that we know can impair hearing or cause deafness, but noise that interrupts sleep, conversation, and work. Pesticides and other chemicals used in the home, garden, and field and in manufacturing processes, add heavily to official responsibilities for safeguarding health. This calls for constant monitoring of environmental levels and for toxicologic investigation of new chemicals, new mixtures, and new additives.

## Disposal of Solid Wastes

Disposal of solid wastes, domestic and industrial, is a major problem in environmental health.[17] Daily, more than 800 million pounds of garbage and household trash, industrial and agricultural waste and abandoned cars must be disposed of somehow. If refuse is burned, it may contribute to air pollution; yet, urban space for burying it is become more scarce. If the refuse is buried, the possibility of contaminating ground and surface waters must be taken into account. These problems of waste disposal are compounded by new kinds of wastes which pose new problems and threats, for example, wastes from nuclear power plants and from hospitals and industries using radioactive materials.

Closely associated with urbanization is industrialization and this, too, is demanding increased attention. There is evidence that many chronic diseases often have a direct relationship to the victim's occupation; and it is known that at least 4 million workers are employed at processes immediately dangerous to their health or in need of continual inspection.

Industrial health programs should provide health services, both preventive and maintenance, and emergency services in case of illness or injury. While most industries employing five hundred persons or more provide these services, only about 16.3 per cent of all workers are employed in companies of this size. For this reason, more efforts are being made to combine the needs of small industries with those of other community health programs.

Studies are being made on the effects of exposure to heat, cold, vibrations, and noise on the physical and mental health of workers; and age is one of the important variables. In addition, we still need to know more about the effects of chemical and other contaminants to which many workers are exposed and to know more about means of disposing of wastes containing these hazardous elements.

## GETTING THE JOB DONE

More than 150 health careers have been identified as essential to the development and delivery of the personal and environmental health services and programs cited in this chapter. Most home economics curricula provide appropriate coursework for persons interested in pursuing a number of these careers. Many of the positions filled by persons with home economics backgrounds are with agencies giving direct services to older people. Others are in organizations or groups—

universities, research laboratories, industries—having a supportive role. These include the design and development of new hospital equipment and furnishings, testing of fabrics and food products, design and development of household equipment and clothing for the apparently well or the handicapped older person, and economic and consumer research and education.

At the Federal level, the Public Health Service in the Department of Health, Education, and Welfare has primary responsibility for health protection of all persons. However, all other agencies of this department support some health activities related to their immediate programs, as do agencies in many other departments, including Labor, Interior, Housing and Urban Development, Office of Economic Opportunity, Veterans Administration, Commerce, and Agriculture. These efforts are augmented at the state and local levels by public, voluntary, and private resources.

## SUMMARY

The lists of personal and environmental health services and programs cited in this chapter are not inclusive. They are provided mainly to call attention to the more basic services that should be available and as such may serve as a checklist for communities wishing to expand or strengthen existing programs or to establish priorities for the development of additional programs. It is quite possible, however, that some of the services might not be of the highest priority in all areas. This is particularly true, for example, in some smaller communities and neighborhoods where strong family and social ties still exist; and a family member responds to an ill person's needs for meals, housekeeping, and shopping.

It is well for all persons working with the aging and aged to keep in mind the socioeconomic impact the availability or nonavailability of personal and environmental health services may have on an individual, his family, and his community. It should be remembered that the total community should participate in planning and developing these services: government, labor and industry, professional and educational groups, communications media, and social organizations. Support for training, research, services and construction related to these programs comes from many resources—public and private—at all levels, Federal, State, and local and persons of many backgrounds must be involved directly or indirectly.

Comprehensive health services—preventive, diagnostic, therapeutic, and restorative—should be available as needed for the apparently well and for the sick adult. Services for the ambulatory person should be located in settings most convenient for those to be served. And there should be a range of institutional facilities to cover periods of acute illness, convalescence, or long-term care, as well as home care programs for the sick at home. Environmental programs must provide for health protection related to the use of all natural resources, such as land, water and air; and for the health protection of the aging and aged person in his immediate environment.

The primary Federal responsibility for health protection of all persons, including the aging and aged, is vested in the Public Health Service of the Department of Health, Education, and Welfare. Two Administrations within the service—the Health Services and Mental Health Administration and the Consumer Protection and Environmental Health Administration—direct the major operating programs designed to meet this goal.[18] In addition, the National Institutes of Health, the other administrative unit of the service, fulfills a basic research mission. Extensive future development of all community health services depends in large measure on a concerted effort participated in by both public and private organizations. Priorities include filling manpower needs, seeking additional financial support for new or expanded services, especially at the state and local levels; and overcoming public and professional apathy.

## REFERENCES

1. National Health Council: *Health is a Community Affair.* Cambridge, Harvard U.P., 1966, 262 pp.
2. Graber, Joe Bales: Findings and implications of a nationwide program review of resources available to meet the health needs of the aging and aged. *Gerontologist, 6*(4):189-200, Dec. 1966.
3. Brunini, Nadeene: Diet counselors serve community in three New Jersey hospitals. *Hospitals, 39*:94, 96-98, Nov. 16, 1965.
4. Public Health Service: *Portraits in Community Health: Aging Center in Sinai Hospital.* Public Health Service Publication No. 1344-2, Washington, D.C., U.S. Government Printing Office, 1965, 31 pp.
5. Public Health Service: *Working With Older People, A Guide to Practice. Vol. 1, The Practitioner and the Elderly.* Public Health Service Publica-

tion No. 1459, Washington, D.C., U.S. Government Printing Office, August 1966, 52 pp.

6. Public Health Service: *Portraits in Community Health: The Dexter Manor Story: Health Services in Housing for the Elderly.* Public Health Service Publication No. 1344-3, Washington, D.C., U.S. Government Printing Office, Oct. 1966, 25 pp.
7. Starin, I., and Kuo, N.: The Queensbridge Health Maintenance Service for the Elderly, 1961-1965. *Public Health Rep, 81*:75-82, Jan. 1966.
8. Public Health Service: *Evaluation of the Aging Patient.* Public Health Service Publication No. 1513, Washington, D.C., U.S. Government Printing Office, 1966, 20 pp.
9. Welfare Administration: *Protective Services for Older People.* P.A. Report No. 54, Washington, D.C., U.S. Government Printing Office, 1965, 36 pp.
10. U.S. Department of Health, Education and Welfare, Public Health Service: *Comprehensive Care Services in the Community.* Washington, D.C., U.S. Government Printing Office, 1967, pp. 25-27.
11. Public Health Service: *Dental Care for the Chronically Ill and Aged: A Community Experiment.* Public Health Service Publication No. 899, Washington, D.C., U.S. Government Printing Office, 1961, 54 pp.
12. The National Council on Aging: Home delivered meals for the ill, handicapped and elderly. *J Amer Public Health* (Supplement), May 1965, vol. 5515, 85 pp.
13. Public Health Service: *Portraits in Community Health, Rural Home Nursing Care for Long Term Illness.* Public Health Service Publication No. 1344-1, Washington, D.C., U.S. Government Printing Office, 1965, 31 pp.
14. Department of Health, Education and Welfare: The task force on environmental health and related programs. *Strategy for a Liveable Environment.* Washington, D.C., U.S. Government Printing Office, June 1967, 90 pp.
15. President's Science Advisory Committee. *Restoration of the Quality of our Environment.* Washington, D.C., U.S. Government Printing Office, Nov. 1965, 257 pp.
16. Rodstein, Manual: Accidents among the aging. *Safety.* New York, Greater New York Safety Council, Reprint, Summer 1963.
17. National Academy of Science-National Research Council: *Waste Management and Control.* NAS-NCR Publication 1400, Washington, D.C., 1966, 257 pp.
18. Public Health Service: *Health Protection: The Target of the Bureau of Disease Prevention and Environmental Control.* Public Health Service Publication No. 1637, Washington, D.C., U.S. Government Printing Office, 1967, 30 pp.

## ADDITIONAL READINGS

Department of Health, Education and Welfare: *Aging in the Modern World: Annotated Bibliography.* OA Publication No. 216, Washington, D.C., U.S. Government Printing Office, 1963, 194 pp.

*Chapter 19*

# EDUCATION FOR AGING

H. LEE JACOBS

EDUCATION FOR AGING in the United States has been fragmentary and uncoordinated, with a history reaching back less than two decades. Nevertheless, one of the most important educational insights turned up by the restless tides of social change in our generation has to do with the capacity of adults for continued mental growth and personal development.

The old idea that education must be concerned solely with the socialization and mental development of children and youth, with only minimal interest in the expansive period of adulthood and virtually no consideration for the older years, is rapidly becoming obsolete.[1, 2, 3, 4]

From about 1909, when the first Child Guidance Clinic was founded in Chicago, down to mid-century, the spotlight of public attention and educational interest was on children and youth. But beginning around 1950, a growing amount of this light has been focused on the middle and later years, and this without any noticeable lessening of interest in children and youth. This is as it should be, and it is also one of the most hopeful signs of the times.

Contemporary society expects older adults to display greater capacity for learning than has any previous generation of oldsters, and older individuals expect more of themselves. Moreover, the conviction is growing among us that education for aging is not simply a humanitarian gesture toward older people on the part of our educational institutions, church groups and sundry other organizations; it is, above all, a matter of enlightened self-interest. In view of the rapidly changing and dynamic world in which we live, all ages, including senior citizens, must keep mentally alert, or, as one educator has phrased it, "study or perish."

A major weakness of the educational system in this country is that it was founded upon, and, to an uncomfortable degree, continues to reflect a terminal philosophy of education, namely, that the educative process should end somewhere in the early years. There is certainly no question in the minds of most educational leaders today that this is false thinking, for two reasons: (1) because it presupposes that individuals can be taught enough in childhood and youth to last them a lifetime, and (2) that older adults cannot learn.

### Research and Learning

From studies on adult learning conducted by Edward L. Thorndike and associates at Columbia University in the late 1920's; the longitudinal studies of William Owens at Iowa State University in 1949, with a follow-up in 1963; the continuing studies of Nancy Bayley and associates at Sanford University before and at mid-century; and the study completed by Mir Zaman at the University of Iowa, ample evidence has been amassed to show that persons do not lose their ability to learn as they grow older; and that they can learn anything that it is necessary for them to learn, if they want to do so.[5, 6]

In response to this more hopeful outlook on the later years, an increasing number of older adults are embarking on new adventures in learning, with many actually returning to school. The truth is that without the benefit of continuous learning, including some education for aging, modern man tends to become progressively obsolete and his later years a burden. For this reason we may well focus our attention on four aspects of education for aging and consider their relevance for educational programming today. Since these overlap at many points, it should be understood that they are being treated as separate items only for the sake of emphasis and the clarification of issues.

## THE INFORMAL APPROACH TO EDUCATION FOR AGING, THROUGH EXPANDING LITERARY AND MASS MEDIA, AND ORGANIZATIONAL DEVELOPMENTS

The preponderance of pioneer effort in any field is apt to begin at the informal level—in communities, groups, families, the press and other mass media. This has been especially true in the matter of the dissemination of information about aging via television, wherein we observe a far more extensive and effective development than most people realize. In fact, it has been estimated that 75 per cent of our leisure today is spent in using mass media, especially television. And it is believed that such extensive passive participation can have important adverse effects on the physical and mental health of all ages, including the elderly.

## Aging and the Press

In addition to the newspapers, which have devoted an increasing amount of space to "aging news" for more than a decade, the phenomenal sale of paperbacks in this area shows that people of all ages today are reading more extensively about matters pertaining to aging than ever before. One of these books which is still enjoying a brisk sale, though published some years ago, is *The Older People in Your Life,* by Justus J. Schifferes. All indications are that the market for such objective, scientifically based reporting will be increasingly favorable.[7]

The first bibliography on gerontology appeared in 1951 and contained 599 pages. This book listed and categorized writings in the field of aging over the first half of the twentieth century. Six years later (1957) a second edition required 525 pages to cover the writings of the six-year period, 1951 to 1957. This represents approximately a tenfold increase. The latest Shock's bibliography (1963) contains 624 pages, hence indicating an even greater enlargement in the scope of the literature on aging in recent years. In fact, it is safe to say that more literary effort in the field of aging has been expended since 1955 than in all preceding generations put together.[8]

While a great spurt of writing of all kinds in the field of aging has taken place since about 1950, some literary effort in the field of aging dates back to 1835. In that year, the Belgian mathematician and social scientist, Adolph Quetelet (1796-1874), published a book, *On Man and the Development of His Faculties.* In this book, he reported data on the growth of individuals from birth to 60 years of age. He is considered the first formulator of the quantitative method in the study of social sciences, including the area of aging. His younger contemporaries, the English anthropologist, Francis Galton (1822-1911); the German experimental psychologist, Wilhelm Wundt (1832-1920);

and the Russian physiologist, Ivan Pavlov (1849-1936), enlarged upon his work, and they, together with an American psychologist and educator, G. Stanley Hall (1846-1924), may be said to have opened up the whole area of human aging to scientific study.[3, 9]

## Aging Tomorrow

The man who built most solidly upon what these men had accomplished, and who added much that was original, was the Russian medical scientist, Vladimir Korenchevsky (1880-1959), who became a naturalized British subject in 1920. Near the end of his life he was called by one of his American contemporaries, Dr. E. V. Cowdry, himself a distinguished leader in the field of aging research, "the father of gerontology, not simply in Britain, but in the whole world." The significance of research into aging tissues, which has become dramatically apparent in the last few years, received its original impetus from the efforts of Korenchevsky. He was the first to present the view, based on extensive biochemical research, that, as yet, human beings do not die a "natural" death (i.e. from physiological old age), but, barring accidents, expire as the result of "pathological interference" in the physiological process. He believed that eventually "degenerative abnormalities and disorders of present day pathological aging will be eliminated and aging will become truly a physiological process." [10]

## Publications

A monumental literary and academic achievement in the field of aging was realized with the publication of the three major handbooks on aging.*

Even a casual glance through professional journals and other publications of almost every description to be found in a large university or public library is enough to convince one that writing on aging has suddenly become extensive. Few publications today go through even six months without including one or more articles on

* These consist of (1) Birren, James E. (ed.): *Handbook on Aging and the Individual: Psychological and Biological Aspects,* 1959; (2) Tibbits, Clark (ed.): *Handbook of Social Gerontology: Societal Aspects of Aging,* 1960; and (3) Burgess, Ernest W. (ed.): *Aging in Western Societies: A Comparative Survey,* 1960.

the subject. Such articles, stories, pamphlets and popularly written books are finding their way in a growing stream into educational channels, supermarkets, newsstands, and paperback sections of book and department stores. While it would seem that this is a good sign of the times, a word of caution is probably in order lest we may be subscribing to a fad, lacking in educational substance.

## Needs of the Elderly

The needs of an aging population differ mainly in degree, extent, and ways in which they are being met. As workers in the area of aging, we are dealing with big problems. From the standpoint of the later years, these include such matters as the following: inequality of opportunity for employment, inadequate income for dignified living, substandard housing, unmet needs in the area of special services, penurious provisions for physical and mental health, the impact on the elderly of changing family life, generally inadequate preparation for and activities in retirement, and, as yet, insufficient investigation of social and psychological aspects of aging.

Popular magazines and other publications, such as *Harvest Years, Fifty-Plus, Retirement Planning News, Senior Citizen, Retirement Life, Modern Maturity, Senior Citizen News, Inc.,* our own University of Iowa monthly, *Adding Life to Years,* and the government publication, *Aging,* have done much to pique the interest of the public, relative to issues concerning the second half of life. Added to this list of purveyors of aging news and views are many excellent publications and professional journals, such as *Geriatrics, Geriatric Focus,* the *Journal of Gerontology,* and The *Gerontologist,* the latter two being official organs of the Gerontological Society. All of these publications emphasize in one way or another a belief in which most educators concur, namely, that persons of all ages, including the very old, can learn, change and adapt to new circumstances. A mighty ally in this informal educational process is the television industry, with its telstar outreach and its growing sensitivity to and objective portrayal of the needs and interests of minority groups, including the elderly.

Among the sizeable and more influential organizations today providing informal education, both about and for aging, are The American Association of Retired Persons (AARP), claiming one and a half million members, and The National Council of Senior Citizens, Inc. (NCSC), which reports two million members. While the announced objectives of both of these national organizations include a wide range of educational and political concerns which impinge upon the lives of older people, the former seems to be more educationally oriented. The AARP is, for example, now emphasizing informal learning opportunities for older adults in two major pilot projects (in Washington, D. C., and Long Beach, California) known as Institutes of Lifetime Learning, while the NCSC is stressing the organization of clubs for senior citizens across the country, with its major purpose being probably equally political and social. Both organizations, at least at the national level, have well-trained and effective leadership and their grass roots educational accomplishments are contributing significantly toward a better public image of aging and the aged.

## LEGITIMIZATION OF RETIREMENT EDUCATION

The concept of retirement is a fairly new thing under the sun. In fact, prior to the passage of the Social Security Act in 1935, the word meant little, if anything, to most people. And as recently as 1956, the head of one large industry remarked to a government spokesman that neither he nor his employees wished to discuss the matter; that the word "retirement," like the term "bereavement," should never be mentioned.[11] However, a host of studies over the past few years have made it abundantly clear how tragically wrong this outlook on two crucial experiences of our human journey really is.

### Retirement Problems

We are convinced now that people should talk about their problems and seek whatever solutions possible. In this way, problems often become opportunities for continued growth. The matter of thinking about and planning for retirement is no exception. In a very real sense, retirement should be looked upon as something that has been happening to us throughout life—not just at the end of the usual work experience. Actually, we retire from one experience to another —preschool to school, bachelorhood to marriage, childless status to parenthood, empty nest to grandparenthood, etc. But retirement from work is a big step for most people, hence it needs special attention.[12]

Technological changes over the past one hundred years have revolutionized our society in many ways, not the least of which is to be seen in how people make a living and what the process has done to many segments of our population, especially to older people. Within the memory of many older persons up to 86 per cent of all males over 65 in this country were still in the labor force, whereas today only 25 per cent are so involved. Over about the same period of time, there was a tenfold increase in the per capita output of energy, which, in turn, resulted in more than quadrupling per capita output, while, at the same time, shortening the work-week about four hours for every decade since the turn of the century. As a result of these developments many erstwhile household activities were transferred to the community, the work-life expectancy was shortened, the amount of leisure time increased, and the practice of retirement came more into vogue.

As our society moves from a work-centered to a leisure-oriented society there is, for the first time, serious consideration being given to retirement not only as a point on the calendar, but as a way of life for millions of adults. In fact, many retirees will spend more time separated from their usual occupations than the length of work-life which their grandparents knew. Senator Walter F. Mondale of Minnesota, Chairman of the Subcommittee on Retirement and the Individual of the Senate Special Committee on Aging, has stated the matter in this way: "It is not unreasonable to assume that the average person soon will be spending from twenty to twenty-five years or more in retirement. We are going to have to start looking on retirement as a distinct and separate phase of life—not as the end of it. We have to stop equating retirement with old age." [13]

These added years will prove a boon to the individuals involved, as well as to our common life, only to the extent that they are filled with meaningful activity and useful living. George Bernard Shaw once put the matter more colorfully when he remarked, "A perpetual holiday is a good working definition of hell." Paraphrasing this, we might say, "Perpetual leisure, without being hooked up to the main procession of life, is a good working definition of hell." Or, to state the axiom in still another way, we might conclude, with Oliver Wendell Holmes, "To live is to function; to stop functioning is to stop living."

People at any age do not surrender their dignity without possible tragic consequences. So why should we expect millions of able-bodied, still functional older adults to be an exception in the matter of retirement, which can mean, especially where adequate preparation is not made, capitulation to hopelessness and disintegration of personal life? A variety of attacks on this problem, referred to by the former Secretary of Health, Education, and Welfare, John W. Gardner, as the "retirement revolution" are being pressed today on numerous fronts—federal, industrial, and educational.

Mr. William D. Bechill, Commissioner on Aging, reporting on hundreds of projects already under way throughout the country with aid from the Administration on Aging, under the Older Americans Act, says: "We will continue to foster the stimulation of both new retirement careers and constructive free-time activities that afford status, dignity, and personal independence to the older person, his family, and his community." [13] This is obviously a many faceted program, at the center of which must be preparation for retirement.

## Pre-retirement Education

One of the finest examples of what can be done in a community to provide short-term, yet high quality, pre-retirement training on a widely representative base is to be seen in a cooperative venture of the University of Rhode Island Extension Division and the Adult Education Division of the Providence Rhode Island Public Schools. This project, a ten-week course, called "Preparation for Retirement," for persons 60 years of age and over, is described in detail by Dr. Mary C. Mulvey in the September, 1967 issue of *Adult Leadership,* one of the two official organs of the Adult Education Association of the U.S.A.[14] She states that the "common characteristic" which unified most of the participants in this course, initiated in 1963, has been mutual interest in preparing for, and/or planning in, retirement. The age range of enrollees extended from 38 to 78 years, with 73 per cent from 60 to 65 years of age, the average 62.5, and the modal age 64. In educational background they ranged all the way from less than a high school education to master's degrees. Likewise, they represented a wide range of employment—unskilled to professional.

The instructional techniques involved in this educational adventure are flexible and are tailored to meet the needs of individuals from a variety of backgrounds. Undergirding this informality, however, is a thorough testing program of interests, aptitudes, and personality characteristics, the vital significance of which in preparing persons for retirement cannot be overestimated.

The course of study, as outlined by Dr. Mulvey, is comprehensive but within reach of realization by most communities. It includes such matters as changes which come with age and how to meet them, housing and living arrangements for the later years, finances and budgeting, family relationships, physical and mental health problems, foods and nutrition, health-providing measures, such as care of teeth, vision, hearing, etc., legal problems, employment, meaningful leisure time, community services and how to utilize them, adult education programs, resources at both state and national levels, second-career opportunities, types of activities in retirement which may be substituted for the accustomed work-roles, and the meaning of new legislation and new programs which have been established for older people. Here is a much needed type of short-term program which, with variations, can be carried out in most communities and which meets the qualifications for assistance under Title V of the Older Americans Act.

These, then, are some of the reasons why, quite aside from the arguments pro and con as to whether the retirement age should be raised or lowered, retirement education is at long last becoming legitimized generally across the country. For example, few industries today make no provision for some kind of retirement education for their employees. Many have extensive programs running over some ten or fifteen years, with the laudable objective of helping their employees look forward to retirement as an expectant and abundant period of life, rather than as a time of great catastrophe and loss. And they reinforce this objective with frequent reference to studies which have shown that retired people, contrary to what was formerly believed, tend to live longer and remain healthier than their cohorts who have not retired.[15]

It is encouraging to note that one of the top ten best-selling novels of a few years ago was *Chairman of the Bored,* by Edward Streeter. Though highly humorous and entertaining, it is centered on the retirement issue. The almost instant success of this novel is an indication of the widespread need for insight in this area of life. When Graham

Crombie, approaching the magic age of 65 and by his own acknowledgment "president of the best investment counsel company in the country" suddenly realizes that he is being "directed" by the retirement clause—"to run away and play"—which he had earlier insisted should be incorporated in his company's pension plan as the basic objective in "retirement," he is panic-stricken. He has not the ghost of an idea what he should do with his time, but more especially with himself, in retirement. The soaring flights of fancy in which he repeatedly indulges, his narrow brushes with personal disaster, as the comfortable old ruts of a business-filled life disappear over night, and what he finally does about his predicament makes a delightfully amusing and, at the same time, insightful and instructive story for all ages, but especially for persons planning their own retirement.[16]

## Unfinished Business in Living

Whether we, as a nation with an ever shrinking work-week, are to be leisure enriched or "leisure stricken," as some predict, depends upon the degree to which we embrace the idea of "productive activity" — that is, activity that is productive of both personal and social good. The best insurance that such an expression of one's life resources will be realized is what might be called a philosophy of unfinished business in living. By this, we mean the establishment, as early in life as possible, of a list of activities, interests, projects and goals, including educational objectives, which, though subject to continuous scrutiny and revision under the lash of change, carry on into the retirement years, bringing deep satisfaction to the end of life.

## EDUCATION FOR AGING IN THE ACADEMIC SETTING

From the standpoint of offerings in educational institutions, the main emphasis until recently has been on discrete, unrelated courses, with a few recreational novelties interspersed, for middle-aged and older adults.

As recently as 1961, this writer completed a survey of education for aging in public school adult education programs in a representative sample of 813 public school systems in the United States. Of the 523 school systems supplying usable data, only eighty-six reported a variety of courses for middle-aged and older adults. Morever, the majority of these courses had been launched less than a decade before, and about 50 per cent within the previous six years. The content of such courses had to do primarily with arts and crafts, current events and some study of languages. No serious consideration of aging as a developmental process was included.[17]

It can be said now, however, that this situation has changed, in that there is a growing insistence in educational circles that the development, conservation, and use of the intellectual and creative potentials of the older members of our society should be one of our major educational objectives. At the same time, we encounter the anachronistic situation of great numbers of older people who still cling to the traditional underestimation of the potentials of persons in the later years, and consequently do not have confidence in themselves as learners and contributors to society. They must be helped to see that this skepticism has no basis in fact; that failure to continue to learn can affect their learning more than their ability to learn. More adequate exposure of this age level, through mass media and group involvement, to the hopeful information now available will be needed to get the job done.

## Educational Offerings

Assuming that educational institutions needed help in learning what activities would attract older adults, if offered, two adult educators, Andrew Hendrickson and Robert E. Barnes, at the Ohio State University completed a study entitled, "The Role of Colleges and Universities in the Education of the Aged," based on an area random sample of persons 65 and over in the population of the Columbus, Ohio community. They were interested in finding out for what activities older persons would make a trip to a campus, which ones they would attend only if offered at a neighborhood center, and which ones they would prefer to participate in by radio or television.

On the basis of their findings, they concluded that not only colleges and universities should take seriously their responsibilities to serve the educational needs of older persons along with those of other age groups, but that public schools should examine the data in this study to see what they can appropriately offer to older citizens, both in activities combining all age groups and those designed for older adults alone.[18, 19] The public schools in this country belong to all the people and, as such, these institutions have a responsibility for meeting the educational needs and interests of all age levels.

Full courses on the subject of aging are feasible at the junior college and college levels, and I am happy to report that these are already multiplying across the country. At least one college, Mt. Angel, in Oregon, has established a bachelor's degree program in gerontology. One college in Missouri, Culver-Stockton, has had a three-hour course in gerontology for about five years. Several other colleges have informed us within the past year that they are offering for the first time courses in aging and would like help with content building. Moreover, a large number of universities now offer a variety of courses in aging. Some, such as Duke, UCLA, Western Reserve, Penn State, Minnesota, Pennsylvania, the Universities of Michigan, Chicago, and Washington University, St. Louis, have Ph. D. programs emphasizing aging.[20]

At the University of Iowa, we now offer, through the Institute of Gerontology, three graduate level courses—"Biological and Psychological Aspects of Aging," "Societal Aspects of Aging," and a seminar "Selected Problems in Aging," or a total of eight credit hours. An increasing number of middle-aged and older adults are enrolling in these courses, along with younger students, in order to improve themselves or to prepare for a second career, or both. Still other courses, related to the subject of aging are being offered in other departments of the same university. There is also some planning now under way in several states to provide more educational opportunities for older adults at various college centers. Special conferences dealing with this matter have been held recently in Iowa and Michigan.

In at least two state institutions, the University of Kentucky and Wayne State University, persons over 65 years of age are offered free tuition for academic work of their choice. These developments chart the course which education for aging, in the framework of public school adult education, colleges and university programs, is apt to take in the immediate future.

In addition to these general academic developments in education about and for aging, there are hopeful indications of closer cooperation in this area between a variety of community organizations and our educational institutions. Perhaps the most outstanding example of this is to be seen in the cooperative educational program for older adults established by the First Baptist Church of Los Angeles, in cooperation with the Cambria Adult School of the public school system in that city. Dr. Oliver W. Cummings, full-time minister for the 2,700 member Senior Citizens Fellowship in this church, is coordinator for the many-faceted program and all courses are taught by instructors from the city school system.[21] Such successful programs of continuing education for older adults operated jointly by schools and voluntary community organizations are demonstrating that education can be a revitalizing force for our older people.

## EDUCATION OF OUR CHILDREN AND YOUTH FOR THE NEW ERA OF AGING

A very important development in the field of aging today has to do with the education of children and youth concerning the aging process and what its implications are for both the young and the old.[1] I say this despite the fact that the National Institute of Child Health and Human Development has recently gone on record as favoring what appears to be the abandonment of the total life-span (conception-to-death) approach to teaching about aging, since it tends, in their words, "to distort and dilute effort directed toward unambiguous study of the aging process." [20] In other words, they seem to imply that there should be, for purposes of curriculum-making at the professional training level, at least, "a clear cut program separation of growth and development from aging," here narrowly defined as the point at which the catabolic (tearing down) exceeds the anabolic (or building up) process in cell metabolism, probably around the fortieth year of life.

### Negative Attitudes

Several studies, such as those carried on at the Age Center of New England (in Boston) and Columbia University (New York), have shown that children begin forming concepts about age very early, possibly by age 3 or 4. By age 6, according to the findings of the New England research, the majority of children have developed a definite bias against old people. The research at Columbia showed that by beginning junior high school age, the average child possesses all the negative attitudes about aging and old people that are to be found among adults. And even at the graduate school level, a semester "psychology of aging" course, as measured by "before" and "after" testing, resulted in little change in the basic negative attitudes about the second half of life.[1, 22, 23] I think it should be said, therefore, that while, as most educators now agree, persons of all ages including the very old, can learn, change and adapt to new circumstances, the sooner education for aging is initiated the more effective our efforts will be. This is why, as I pointed out in a government publication in 1965, I am heartily in favor of including some emphasis on education for aging at all age levels of the public school system.[1]

From many sources today, it is being emphasized that the only corrective for the poor image of aging and the aged which characterizes our culture is a life-span, cradle-to-the-grave perspective in living, wherein the later years are not seen as an inevitable period of incompetency, but as an authentic, integral part of a developmental continuum, with no sharp lines of demarcation separating needs and interests of various age levels.[24]

Unless we work more assiduously at this job of building a positive conception of aging, especially of the later years, in the rising generation we may eventually drift into the extreme and ridiculous situation described in the satirical novel, *Not A Cloud in the Sky,* by Josephine Lawrence.[25] She pictures all persons, 65 and over—sometime in the not-too-distant future—as having been "confined" in a specially prepared city, euphemistically called "Tranquil Acres," a kind of benevolent concentration camp for "senior citizens," supported by the Federal Government and served by the magic wand of youth, in depersonalized, meaningless, carefree nonentity.

It has been well established in anthropological, sociological and psychological research, that culture is prior to human nature; that individuals during the so-called "formative years" tend to absorb ways of looking at life and its values, much as in the case of the osmotic process, whereby plants take on nourishment from the soil. In a culture such as ours, in which older persons are devalued, and in a very real sense rejected, the negative effect on attitudes of children and youth can scarcely be overemphasized.[26]

A rather impressive number of studies on attitudes toward aging and the aged have been reported in the literature over the past decade.

Beginning with the investigations of Lorge, Tuckman and Associates at Columbia University in the early 1950's, dealing with junior and senior high school youth and young adult age subjects,[22, 27, 28] and including the more recent studies with freshmen college students, middle-aged and older adults, done by Kogan, Shelton and Wallach at the Age Center of New England,[29, 30, 31, 32] the study of four-hundred high school and college youth conducted by Betty Lane at Florida State University,[33] and the study of 335 children and teen-agers in Los Angeles, done by Tom Hickey,[34] the insidious nature of the interiorization process, as regards a negative image of aging, has been clearly shown. This apparent attitude impasse tends to become what I have called the "hurdle of the generations," traditionally thought to be insurmountable—something to be stoically accepted and "lived with." However, a more hopeful view is now emerging. It holds that corroding conflict between youth and age is not inevitable; that the real bond between the generations is not blood, but the understandings which they share, the appreciations which they have in common, and those moments of reflection in which they meet.

These qualities, I believe, can best be developed through educational procedures involving cooperative effort between the family, the church, and the school system. Such a program as I here envision was not even mentioned among the summary of eighteen "trends" and "suggestions" presented in the official *Background Paper on Education for Aging* presented at the White House Conference on Aging in 1961. During the intervening years, however, some progress has been made in this direction. But, for one reason or another, such as (a) already overcrowded curricula, (b) inadequate teacher education in the field of aging, or (c) the charge of "irrelevance of academic substance," so far as education for aging is concerned, the utilization of the various levels of the public school system in developing a positive conception of aging in our children and youth will be slow.

## Promising Beginnings

Nevertheless, some promising beginnings on such a program are already in evidence around the country. Thus far, these appear to be largely confined to the secondary school level, but at least two mid-western states, North Dakota and Minnesota, have had both elementary and secondary curricula committees working on education for aging materials for experimental teaching purposes in their schools. In line with this development, I was invited, in the summer of 1962, to serve as guest lecturer and resource person for the annual North Dakota Vocational Homemaking Teachers Conference and Workshop, held at North Dakota State University, Fargo. As part of my assignment there, I presented the first draft of a unit of study on aging for high school youth, titled "Youth Looks At Aging." Since that time, reports indicate this material has been widely utilized in that and other states, by home economists, teachers of social studies, and church groups. In the fall of 1964, the unit was published in the form of a monograph by the University of Iowa.[35]

The purpose of this unit, as I have stated it in the published form, is "to investigate aging in the human area, in relation to its nature, personal implications, human relationship problems involved, and the challenges for life enrichment which it presents." This stresses a positive concept of human aging and places the subject in a scientific frame of reference. Reports which have come to me indicate that youth likes this approach.

The unit, built around eighteen major questions which youth have asked concerning various aspects of aging, was designed as a teacher's guide, and is intended as a three-or-four-week learning venture, to be used in connection with such courses as family living, homemaking, home economics, or American social problems. Among the reports on the use of this material is one from Mrs. Louise L. Campbell, Secretary of the Vigo County Council on Aging and the Aged, Terre Haute, Indiana. She says,

> One of the areas of promotion in which our Education Committee is interested is the use of your unit on aging in the tenth year Home Economics course in our Terre Haute High School curriculum. We are also recommending that this unit on aging be included in required social studies courses, rather than being limited to an elective course which ordinarily reaches only a few girls in the community.

Perhaps the most ambitious utilization of this program to date, especially in a large school system, is being carried out at Des Moines, Iowa, where all five of their high schools are using "Youth Looks at

Aging" in their family living courses. A committee, made up of students and teachers involved, will evaluate the results after the conclusion of the unit and make recommendations for changes and/or improvements which they deem desirable.

This unit may also be adapted for use with church youth groups, or even in formal adult education courses. In fact, reports indicate that churches of various sizes, including some large congregations, are already making use of this material. The Minister of Education in a church of 3,500 members in Kansas City wrote that an all-ages education for aging emphasis was being instituted in his congregation and that the unit "Youth Looks at Aging" was being utilized.

Education for aging to be most effective, of course, should be started at the early elementary level. And this area is receiving some attention from educators. One of this writer's students who recently received her B. S. degree in education developed a sample daily lesson plan for second grade children as a class assignment. It is anticipated that others will develop materials for other grade levels. Several public school teachers have expressed a willingness to experiment with and revise these materials as they are made available. And the chairman of the curriculum committee of one sizeable public school system has expressed a strong interest in seeing education for aging incorporated as an integral part of the educational program from kindergarten through high school in his community.

## CONCLUSION

What we have really been discussing in this chapter is a developmental process, looked at from the angle of mind and spirit and embracing all age levels. While we can legitimately concern ourselves with any specific level, as with the later years, for example, we need to see the process as a whole—how needs and potentialities are linked together in one unbroken line, from the beginning to the end of the human journey. And, as we approach maturity, we will see that it, no less than youth, has its growing pains, its opportunities, which, if recognized and faced with courage and resolution, may be transmuted into satisfying personal growth and enriched common life.

## REFERENCES

1. JACOBS, H. LEE: Developing a more positive conception of aging during the formative years. *Selected Papers: Fifth Annual National Conference of*

*State Executives on Aging,* Washington, D.C.: Administration on Aging, Department of Health, Education, and Welfare, 1965, pp. 59-64.

2. Jacobs, H. Lee: Education for Aging in the Academic Setting. Unpublished MS. of an address given at the Sixteenth Annual National Conference of the Adult Education Association of the U.S.A., Chicago, Illinois, Nov. 12-16, 1966.
3. Birren, James E.: *The Psychology of Aging.* Englewood Cliffs, Prentice-Hall, 1964.
4. *Proceedings: Conference on the Role of Education for Aging and the Aged.* Minneapolis, U. of Minn., Nov. 30-Dec. 2, 1961.
5. Cohen, Charles S.: Research on mental abilities and aging. *Adult Education, 12*(3):165-172, 1962.
6. Zaman, Mir F.: Factors Related to Test Performance: A Longitudinal Analysis. Unpublished Ph. D. dissertation, Iowa City, University of Iowa, 1964.
7. Schifferes, Justus J.: *The Older People in Your Life.* New York, Pocket Books, 1962.
8. Shock, Nathan W.: *A Classified Bibliography of Gerontology and Geriatrics, 1956-1961.* Stanford, Stanford U.P., 1963.
9. Hall, G. Stanley: *Senescence: The Last Half of Life.* New York, Appleton, 1922.
10. Korenchevsky, Vladimir: *Physiological and Pathological Aging.* Bourne, G. H. (Ed.), New York, Hafner, 1961.
11. U.S. Senate Committee on Labor and Public Welfare: *Studies of the Aged and Aging: Employment.* Nov. 1956, p. 167.
12. Johnston, Alberta B.: *Planning for Retirement,* Bulletin No. 60. Corvallis, U. of Ore., 1964.
13. *Aging,* July 1967, No. 153, p. 8.
14. Mulvey, Mary C.: A university helps in preparing for retirement. *Adult Leadership, 16*(3):103-104, 116, 124, Sept. 1967.
15. Tibbitts, Clark (Ed.): *Handbook of Social Gerontology: Societal Aspects of Aging.* Chicago, U. of Chicago, 1960.
16. Streeter, Edward: *Chairman of the Bored.* New York, Pocket Books, 1961.
17. Jacobs, H. Lee: A Study of Education for Aging in Selected Public School Adult Education Programs in the United States. Unpublished Ph. D. dissertation, Iowa City U. of Iowa, 1961.
18. Hendrickson, Andrew, and Barnes, Robert F.: *The Role of Colleges and Universities in the Education of the Aged.* Columbus, Ohio State, 1964.
19. Hendrickson, Andrew, and Barnes, Robert F.: A great university studies educational needs of older people. *Adult Leadership, 16*(1):2-4, 32, May 1967.
20. Donahue, Wilma: Development and current status of university instruction in social gerontology. In *Graduate Education in Aging Within the Social Sciences.* Kushner, Rose E., and Bunch, E. Marion (Eds.), Ann Arbor, Michigan, Division of Gerontology, 1967.

21. STOUGH, ADA BARNETT: *Brighter Vistas: The Story of Four Church Programs for Older Adults.* Washington, D.C., Administration on Aging, U.S. Department of Health, Education, and Welfare, 1965.
22. LORGE, IRVING, and TUCKMAN, JACOB: Attitudes of junior and senior high school students toward aging. In *Growing with the Years.* Senator Desmond (Ed.), New York, 1954.
23. DAVIS, GEORGE (Ed.): *Background Paper on Education for Aging.* Washington, D.C., Administration on Aging, Department of Health, Education, and Welfare, 1960.
24. PRESSEY, SYDNEY L., and KUHLEN, R. G.: *Psychological Development Through the Life Span.* New York, Harpers, 1957.
25. LAWRENCE, JOSEPHINE A.: *Not A Cloud in the Sky.* New York, Harcourt, 1964.
26. WASHBURN, ALFRED H.: Influences of early development upon later life. *Relations of Development and Aging.* Birren, James E. (Ed.). Springfield, Thomas, 1964.
27. TUCKMAN, J., and LORGE, IRVING: Attitudes toward old people. *J Soc Psychol, 37*:249-260, 1953.
28. TUCKMAN, J., and LORGE, IRVING: Attitudes toward aging of individuals with experiences with the aged. *J Genet Psychol, 92*:199-204, 1958.
29. GOLDE, P., and KOGAN, N. A.: A sentence completion procedure for assessing attitudes toward old people. *Journal of Geront, 14*(3):355-363, July 1959.
30. KOGAN, NATHAN, and SHELTON, FLORENCE C.: Images of "older people" and "people in general" in an older sample. *J Genet Psychol, 100*:3-21, 1962.
31. KOGAN, NATHAN, and SHELTON, FLORENCE C.: Beliefs about "old people": a comparative study of older and younger samples. *J Genet Psychol, 100*:93-111, 1962.
32. KOGAN, NATHAN, and WALLACH, M. A.: Age changes in values and attitudes. *J Geront, 16*(3):272-280, 1961.
33. LANE, BETTY: Attitudes of youth toward the aged. *Journal of Marriage and the Family, 26*(2):29-31, May 1964.
34. HICKEY, TOM: The Attitudes of Young People and Children Toward Adults and the Elderly. Unpublished M.A. Thesis, Los Angeles, California State College, 1967.
35. JACOBS, H. LEE: *Youth Looks at Aging: A Unit of Study on Aging at the Secondary Level.* Iowa City, U. of Iowa, Extension Bulletin, No. 819, Oct. 1964.
36. JACOBS, H. LEE: An approach to education for aging for children and youth. *A Symposium on the Aging and Aged—Education for a Whole Life: Proceedings of the Fifth Governor's Conference on Aging,* Indianapolis, Indiana: Indiana Commission on Aging, 1968, pp. 23-44.

# PART VII

# FUTURE DEVELOPMENT IN AGING

*Chapter 20*

# RESEARCH IN AGING–BIOLOGICAL, SOCIAL, AND PSYCHOLOGICAL APPROACHES

CARL EISDORFER
FRANCES WILKIE

THE TERMS *science* and *research* have recently come to be regarded with an almost mystical respect by the layman. In simple terms, *science* is any knowledge that is arrived at by the scientific method of observation, prediction, control, and communication. *Research* is a descriptor for the process of investigation involved.

This chapter on research in aging will describe approaches to gerontological research over the spectrum of disciplines. The emphasis will be upon methods of scientific study in general, and upon approaches and problems involved in investigation of the aging process rather than upon the findings of such studies.

The scientist accepts the assumption that the world is orderly and that events in the world are understandable and lawful. This was exemplified in the study of aging as early as 1835, when Quetelet (1835) in his book *Sur l'homme et le developpement de ses facultes* opened with the sentence, "Man is born, grows up and dies, according to certain laws which have never been properly investigated either as a whole or in the mode of their mutual reactions." [1] Gerontology, or the scientific study of aging, can be thought of as systematic investigation into the regularities of the structure and functions of the living organism during the life cycle, and the organization of such information with particular emphasis upon the events occurring after maturity. The role of the scientist in studying this orderly and lawful process is identical with that in other scientific fields of investigation.

The remainder of this chapter will be divided into two sections. The first section will include a discussion of some of the basic principles of research methodology, followed by a section on some specific approaches and problems involved in the study of aging.

## BASIC RESEARCH METHODOLOGY

It is not too difficult to develop an ideal for research methodology but as Bachrach states "most people don't usually do research the way people who write books about research say that people do research." There are, however, some fundamental methods of research which pertain to any scientific investigation.[2]

### Formal Theoretical Method

This method consists of several stages: (1) observation of events; (2) hypothesis formulation (a statement of prediction based upon the experimenter's observations); (3) experimentation, by which the variables or events are manipulated; (4) testing of results in which the hypothesis is confirmed or refuted; and (5) theory construction, which is a statement of the relationship among the variables.

### Informal Theoretical Method

Designed primarily for those interested in establishing basic information, i.e. "facts" in a relatively unexplored area, this method maintains that hypotheses and theory construction should not interfere with the primary objective of investigation, which is the collection of data.

Regardless of which of the above models is used, the formal or informal, the main goals of science remain that of description, explanation, prediction, and control.

### Definition

Basic to research is data collection, in which the investigator tries to obtain and record his observations with maximum accuracy and minimal interference from irrelevant factors (contaminants). To this end, it is usually advisable for an observer to have specific and clear definitions of what he proposes to observe before he undertakes his task. A major error in research is the use of ambiguous terms or definitions which lead to meaningless observations.

Bachrach points out that there are three levels of definitions: the *daily,* the *poetic*, and the *scientific*. The daily definition is the one universally accepted and for which there is a general (i e. dictionary) understanding. The poetic definition need not be universally accepted or understood, but is treated as belonging within the realm of individual license and aims to create certain images for the recipient. The scientific definition is restricted to a limited group for which the definition has special meaning.[3]

The scientific method in its specificity must employ an operational definition of data in order to approach clarity and certainty. Rapoport states, "An operational definition tells *what to do* to experience the thing defined." [4] According to Quine, "The less a science has advanced the more its terminology tends to rest upon an uncritical assumption of mutual understanding.[5] Only with specific and clear definitions of the actions taken to achieve the observations noted can there be a movement toward relating such observations to the more general body of knowledge. The terms themselves must be so clearly defined in the language specific to a field of study that any qualified person can understand and manipulate the factors described in an experimental setting. Thus, *hot, cold, heavy, light,* and so forth are adjectives which have a limited enough communication value when used in lay terms but virtually no value in attempting to repeat someone's research; however, reports of precise temperature or weights, or of scores on a specific test, allow for confirmation in any facility that can duplicate the conditions of measurement.

## Measurement

Measurement, according to Stevens, "involves the process of linking a formal model called the numbers system to some discriminable aspect of objects or events." [6] A scale is created when numbers are assigned to aspects of objects or events. Stevens also states as follows:

> [T]he type of scale achieved when we deputize the numbers to serve as representatives for a state of affairs in nature depends upon the character of the basic empirical operations performed on nature. These operations are limited ordinarily by the pecularities of the thing being scaled and by our choice of concrete procedures, but once selected, the procedures determine that there will eventuate one or another of four types of scale: *nominal, ordinal, interval,* or *ratio.*[7]

Each scale gives specific information about the events being observed and there are certain mathematical operations which can be applied to the numbers in each scale. The nominal scale implies the attribution of equality and identification of units, such as the numbering of basketball players, or students. The nominal scale gives limited information, such as the number of cases involved or the most frequent occurrence of an event. The ordinal scale implies greater or less than, such as the hardness of minerals or the pleasantness of odors, and allows one to rank the numbers such as in percentiles. The interval scale requires equality of intervals or differences, such as temperatures (fahrenheit and centigrade), calendar dates, "standard scores" on achievement tests. One can work with the numbers in an interval scale to obtain the average occurrence of an event, the variation of other numbers from the average, as well as relating events one to another. The ratio scale is the determination of equality of ratios such as length, weight, density, and pitch and allows for a more complex mathematical analysis of the numbers.

It should be stressed that measurement is never more useful than the observational method by which it is carried out. Any particular measurement scale, whether it be of physical or psychological events, may be questioned on the grounds of bias, low precision, restricted generality, and other factors. One should remember that the usage of a particular scale is a relevant and practical matter. If the data are not amenable to measurement, then some would maintain it should not be considered as scientific data.

The variables, or events, with which the investigator deals must be clearly defined in order to establish some sort of measurement for the phenomenon, and in order that the observations measured may be communicated and replicated by others. (Thus, one could not devise a way of systematically observing the number of angels that can be placed on the head of a pin, since by their nature, angels cannot be seen by mortals. As a consequence, such a question must be considered metaphysical and is meaningless for scientific investigation.) One should not assume, however, that science is concerned only with those observations available at a given point in time. Hypotheses predict to events in which the precision of measurement may not be forthcoming for years or even centuries. Only the nearsighted or pessimistic assume that observations or measurement techniques currently unavailable to us will always remain beyond our reach.

## Control of Variables

In order for an investigator to isolate and study a given event, he must know and recognize other factors which influence the event and attempt to keep these extraneous factors (uncontrolled variables) as much under control as possible. Often repeated eperimentation must be undertaken in order to determine the interrelations of variables in a study. The researcher exercises control over such variables by: selection of his subjects (i.e. age of the subjects, sex, socioeconomic level, intelligence, physical condition, etc.); control over the environment during data collection (i.e. noise level, temperature, etc.); time of measurement; and through a wide variety of other manipulations.

Another problem for the investigator is that the natural course of an event might be distorted by the study itself, with the result that all of the relevant information is not obtainable at the same time. For example, Troyer, Eisdorfer, Wilkie, and Bogdonoff, in a study of the role of anxiety in learning in the aged, demonstrated that the laboratory situation itself generated anxiety; this necessitated the design of another study in which the role of anxiety could be more accurately isolated and measured.[8]

## Prediction and Theories

The prediction of an event as the outcome of a known constellation of other events can be considered a hypothesis and is intimately related to the role of theory construction. Theories, which are statements of the functional relationships among identified and conjectured events, should evolve in any science. In discussing the essentials for a sound scientific theory, Hull says that through observation of the events and experimentation one can determine whether the theory is true or false. A theory should yield testable hypotheses, but there always remains a shadow of doubt because an experiment tomorrow may produce results which flatly contradict it.[9]

Bachrach offers a modified version of Rapoport's rules for testing a theory:

1. *The problem of definition.* The concepts and definitions must be expressed so they can be clearly communicated to others with operational exactness.

2. *The problem of reality.* One should be able to check the effect of the events and show that they do not vary under specific circumstances, that they are, in fact, stable and invariant.
3. *The problem of verification.* The assertions should be verifiable by experience and subject to accurate prediction.
4. *The problem of deduction.* The assertion must be valid.
5. *The problem of causality.* Why did the event occur?
6. *The problem of communication.* The terminology or other formal structure must not be vague; it should be comprehensible and clearly communicated.
7. *The problem of parsimony.* Sometimes called the principle of economy, parsimony calls for the simplest available explanation of a theory.
8. *The problem of relevance.* Can the statements made about particular events be generalized to other events? [10]

A theory must not be so rigid that it applies only to that one set of experimental observations in that particular period of time. The scientist must be sufficiently flexible in his thinking so that he will not make the error of using his data to support the existing theory regardless of what the results show. Whenever the results conflict with a theory, then the theory should be questioned. In general, a theory is not a road map, which should be used for every path you travel, but rather a compass enabling the user to establish the direction in which he wishes to proceed. New theories are not always readily accepted. Great men are often doubted and attacked, yet ultimately their theories, if valid, emerge, since data, not men prevail.

## Accidental Discovery

As Cannon indicates, "serendipity," or accidental discovery, is a major quality of research.[11] The term "serendipity" was taken from Walpole's *Three Princes of Serendip* in which three princes traveled around the world searching for something they could not find. On their journeys, however, they did discover many things which they had not sought. In research, many unexpected events might occur. Even when the investigator has been careful in planning and executing his study, he must be on guard not to become so rigidly bound to his experimental design and preconceptions that he is incapable of seeing accidental discoveries as they appear. Penicillin was accidently discovered after Fleming's observation that green mold was responsible for the destruction of some bacteria he was cultivating. Since his bacteria and experiment were destroyed, he could have ignored the mold and thrown away his cultures as many had previously done under the same circumstances. His initial goal had been interfered with by this new problem, but in order to control this contaminant and because of the unexplained activity of this mold, he took the time to establish a relationship between the two observed events in his study. A most important facet of serendipity is the alert scientific mind, which combines basic knowledge with a readiness to perceive the unusual. These accidental discoveries or observations may not lend themselves to the investigator's current design, but they can serve as potential stimuli for further research.

## Communication

Another important area of science is the communication of research information. The investigator has a responsibility to communicate the methods and findings of his studies to his colleagues. It is regrettable that scientific papers are usually astringent and formal but they generally follow the predetermined and formal outline of journals, which generally require operationally defined terms and observations as well as the presentation of relevant data and their analysis. The final published paper is usually a dehydrated form of the study itself and the training of the reader is often an essential factor in amplifying such reports.

The manner in which a scientist's ideas and results are presented to the public can present a different type of problem. For their own purposes, the news media frequently present such material as entertainment or news described in such terms as "miracle," "wonder," or a "major breakthrough in science," when indeed the research may be in its preliminary stages and not yet proven.

## Statistics

Statistics is an important *tool* of research, but no more than a technique for handling some (but not all) research data. Many students do not attempt serious research because they equate it with tedium and involved mathematical procedures—many books presuming to cover research methods are merely concerned with statistics in research. Actually, the proper use of statistics in scientific research is primarily a matter of sound judgment coupled with a knowledge of some simple statistical techniques. In general, such techniques have been developed to facilitate proper study design, description, and inference with regard to quantitative phenomena, but they in no way substitute for sound logic and good "horse sense" in the planning and conduct of research. Every investigator has the responsibility of reviewing his material to see if it is worthy of publication. He should make available all of his results, including any findings which are anomalous or inconsistent with viewpoints currently accepted. He is also obligated to elaborate on the implications of his principle findings to suggest directions for future research.

### Bias

According to Ungerleider and Smith, bias may occur where decisions or choices are made by either the investigator or the subject.[12] These points need special attention in evaluating a research study: (1) Cases studied. What kind of people were used in the study and how representative were they of the population? Did the people volunteer for the study? What kind of people were not used in the study? (2) Variables or events studied. What variables were studied, which neglected and how were they measured? What summarizing statistics were used? (3) Differences or relationships studied. (4) Theoretical viewpoints. (5) Material that was published. At each of these points decisions were made to focus on certain points in preference to others and any unconscious bias in these directions may vitiate an otherwise satisfactory piece of research.

## Ethical Considerations in Research

Another very real problem in research is that ethical considerations must be dealt with in using human beings and animals as participants in the research program. Berg lists three basic elements of ethical research where humans are involved: *consent, confidence,* and *standard* or *accepted procedure*. First, the consent of the person or responsible guardian must always be obtained. "Where the information requested is highly personal or where the experiment involved some pain, discomfort, or risk, the person should be made aware of what he is consenting to, at least in a general way.[13] If hospital records are used, patients' identities must not be publicly revealed. The investigator is bound to the principle of confidence in his work, because no person would be pleased in having his performance scores, attitudes, or medical history made public. Thus, in order to insure trust and respect between the scientist and the public, the strictest confidence must be maintained in the handling of research data. It is important that the investigator make absolutely certain that normal precautions are taken in all of his procedures to avoid either physical or emotional injury to his subjects.

## RESEARCH IN AGING

Although the United States is thought of as being a youth-oriented culture, it is, nevertheless, characterized by increasing numbers of aging citizens; and an increasingly large proportion of the population is aged. As of 1964, the population of those 65 years of age and over numbered 17.9 million and represented 9.3 per cent of the total population in the United States. In addition, the ratio of persons 65 and over as compared to those in the 18 to 64 age group was about 17 per 100, according to Brotman.[14] As a result, the visibility of the aged population and its associated problems has increasingly come to the attention of the scientific community, and research contributions to the field of gerontology have been greatly accelerated for the past two decades.

Research in aging may occur at three different levels, according to Birren: (1) as a basic fiield of inquiry in itself; (2) as a source for testing theories from other areas of science, and; (3) as an applied field for determining and meeting the immediate needs of the aged.[15] The following sections will cover some of the specific approaches and problems involved in these various approaches to research in aging.

### Patterns in Aging

One of the basic questions in aging research is the determination of the sequences of states or patterns of change in the biological, social, and psychological aspects of man.

The aging process, during the post maturity stage, is usually associated with a decline of efficiency and functioning that eventually results in death. Aging in a biological sense can be regarded as basically a matter of disturbed "normal" relations. As Weiss points out,

> Time magnifies the effect of critical disturbances of interactive relations; the study of the aged will favor the discovery of such relations. This will stimulate the backtracking of those relations through their prior life history, when their ever present fluctuations and distortions had not yet become grossly disruptive, hence were accepted as normal.[16]

In a sense, then, through this study of the aging process, we may be able to delve into the earlier life span of the individual in order to discover how a series of body components accumulates its own unique history, which might have been considered a normal variant during youth and middle age but emerges in old age as a contributing factor toward the process of decline and negative change, leading to death.

To talk about the "normal" aging process would seem to be almost an absurdity, since with increasing age there is a greater probability of illness. Much of the research in aging is contaminated by the necessity of defining "sick" old versus "healthy" old. Yet, it is just as important in describing the "normal" aging process to distinguish between the sick and healthy old individuals, as it would be in research into the "normal" growth patterns of children where sickness could interfere with the growth process. In the study of aging, it is an essential, albeit difficult, task to make the distinction between pathological and normal breakdown of a biological system due to age. Thus, while disease is more probable with advanced age, it may not be identical with it.

## The Concept of Age

Chronological age, which is the actual number of years a person has lived, has been widely used for grouping and statistical purposes. However, it is not a reliable basis for making assumptions regarding the functional capacity of an individual, since people decline at different rates.

The concept of "biological age" is used to account for the physical and mental differences observed when one 60-year-old person functions like a much younger person, while another 60 year old may function at a much less effective level, similar to a typical 70 or 80 year old. Thus, the biological age of an individual would be extremely useful, if it could be accurately determined. These biological processes are inevitable changes related to time and to heredity, and to an undefined extent are interactive with stress, trauma, or disease.

Since biological processes seem to be related to heredity, the masking of these genetic factors by environmental variables, poses a special problem to an investigator. It is extremely difficult to make a distinction between heredity and environment; this is true even in carefully controlled laboratory situations involving animals, where there is obviously more control than would be possible in dealing with human beings living in the community. One can see that the age of 40 may have entirely different implications for a jungle tribesman than for the same aged American white or blue collar worker. Such individuals have different probable life spans, and in each culture the concept of their age has different meaning.

Thus, in addition to the "biological age," it could be useful to postulate the concept of "psychological age" which takes into account the organism's physical state and capacity to adapt, as well as, the "social age" of the individual which includes not only survival elements and adaptive capacity but also the social roles of the individual in concert with his culture.

## Methods of Approach in Aging Research

The investigator must decide on some method by which he can best approach and observe the aging process. Two classic strategies have been used: (1) the cross sectional method, and (2) the longitudinal method. In addition to these two approaches, there has more recently emerged a third method, the cross sequential study.

THE CROSS-SECTIONAL METHOD. The cross-sectional method involves the sampling of a reference population across the age dimension at a given point in time. For example, if an investigator was interested in the changes that occur in intelligence with age, he would examine a group of subjects at various age levels, (i.e. a group of 16 year olds, a group of 18 year olds, 20 year olds, etc.) and based upon their scores would then generate a curve for intellectual changes as a function of age, such as that shown in Figure 20-1.[17] This figure

ADULT INTELLIGENCE

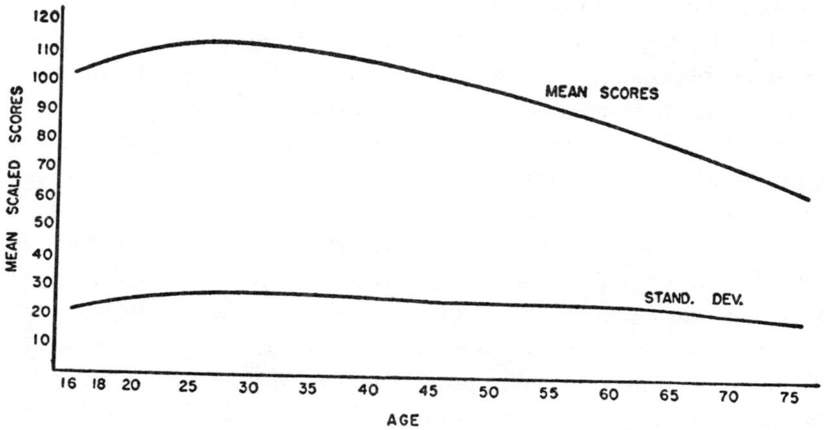


Figure 20-1. Changes with age in Full Scale Scores of Wechsler Adult Intelligence Scale. Ages 16-75 and over.

shows the classic "bow" shaped curve of intellectual improvement and decline that occurs with increasing age.

Much of the research in the behavioral sciences is presented as cross-sectional studies. It is a useful model for comparing the performance of a group of old subjects to a group of young subjects across some dimension such as learning performance, reaction time, etc. Biological investigations involving samples of aged tissues and organs would also employ the cross-sectional design.

The advantages of the cross-sectional method are numerous. The investigator and his team do not have to commit themselves to years of research before obtaining any degree of fruitful and meaningful results. Since the subjects are only seen once in a cross-sectional design, there will be a consistency of measurement with a minimum loss of material. The investigator does not have to concern himself with keeping subjects interested in his research program so that they agree to return for follow-up studies in the future. In addition, there is not the problem of subject loss due to moving, sickness, death, or becoming unsuitable for study due to unpredictable reasons.

The principal negative feature of cross-sectional research involves the necessity of generalization from a cross-sectional pattern to the life span of an individual. In analyzing data from cross-sectional studies, it is also important to recognize the occurrence of a variety of uncontrollable but relevant variables in certain periods of history which might influence a subject's health and functional capacity. For example, in a study of intellectual changes due to age, the subject's educational level should be considered as an important factor. It is difficult, however, to equate the standards and quality of education over a wide span of years.

In a group of 60 year olds, one would find a median education level of eight years and an illiteracy rate of about 7 per cent, while with 25 year olds the median education level would be expected to be about 12 years with an illiteracy rate of about 1 per cent, according to the U.S. Bureau of the Census.[18] If the investigator attempted to control for education by selecting a group of 25 year olds with eight years of education, he would probably find they represented a different segment of the population than would his 70 year olds. The investigator, therefore, has to find other methods for equating his old and young groups, i.e. selecting them from the same socioeconomic level, etc.

Similarly, in studying the emergence of certain disease patterns, the existence of epidemics during some critical point in an individual's life time might result in damage which could emerge as a serious manifestation in later life. For example, it has been suggested by Coleman that the increase in Parkinsonism today may not be a simple function of the increased number of aged people, but rather of the aging of many people who were subjected to the influenza epidemic of 1918.[19] Thus, in a study, it is important to obtain information from the subject on matters relevant to the purpose of the investigation and to control these phenomena as much as possible, since such uncontrolled variables could possibly contaminate any interpretation of the data. When contamination occurs in a study, it becomes difficult, if not impossible, to determine which particular variable is responsible for distorting the end result.

While cross-sectional research is valuable for identifying differences between age groups as well as for generating hypotheses, the changes in child rearing practices, patterns of nutrition, economic conditions, and a host of other events specific to a given age group at a particular calendar time all make it difficult to interpret results from such studies.

The utility of findings from cross-sectional investigations are seriously limited, then, by two main factors: (1) the problem of generalizing from a cross-sectional sample to the *process* of aging, and (2) the difficulty in controlling the host of intervening factors which could influence the main event being measured.

The Longitudinal Method. The longitudinal method is based on repeated observations and measurements of the same subject sample over a period of time, with the observations being made at least three times under approximately the same conditions.

The data from a longitudinal sample can be utilized in several ways. One could use the first set of observations as in a cross-sectional approach and compare differences between subgroups within the sample, such as age differences (i.e. 60 year olds, 70 year olds, etc.), sex differences, socioeconomic groups, and various disease groups such as those having no cardiovascular illness as compared to those with mild or moderate symptoms of the disease. Comparisons can be made between the first, second, or third longitudinal observations from point A to B to C.

Busse points out some of the positive features of the longitudinal method: (1) It provides an opportunity to identify contributing or causative factors which presage the appearance of change, disability, or death; (2) Comparisons can be made between the decline in functioning as a whole and variations found in decline within subunits of the whole group.[20] Thus for the individual, we can examine the interrelations between physical and behavioral changes over time; (3) Observations over time reduce the possibility of retrospective falsification on the part of subjects such as sometimes occurs in the collection of medical or social histories in a single contact interview; (4) The individual serves as his own control and inter-individual differences may be studied more effectively; (5) It permits prediction and is therefore a check on the validity of hypotheses; (6) It provides the opportunity to distinguish between decline in functions which are the result of the passage of time as opposed to those which may be directly related to disease or trauma; (7) It raises the possibility of distinguishing between age differences and age change.

Thus, while the cross-sectional method gives only age differences, the longitudinal method enables us to determine whether indeed there is a change in a function with increasing age; (8) It enables us to study phenomena retrospectively from a denoted end point, i.e. death. Since the investigator has a number of observations on the individual, he could possibly uncover hitherto unsuspected factors leading to the negative change and finally death. Another factor to consider is that in a cross-sectional study, it is obviously impossible to know what a group of 70 year olds were like at age 30, while observations on a group of 30 year olds may be biased because some of the subjects included will die before the group reaches 60 or 70 years of age. The longitudinal method helps to solve this dilemna by having repeated measurements on the same individual as he ages.

The liabilities of the longitudinal method are numerous. It is an extremely expensive approach. A team of investigation must be retained and the training of staff replacements is a serious burden. Subjects must be recruited and contact kept up with them for years. Data for analysis are slow in coming and thus the professional careers of the staff may suffer, although it is true that once the mass of data is available, it can be rapidly processed due to the modern computers which allow for storage of data, as well as rapid retrieval and analysis of the results. Types of tests and methods of observation change during the years, but procedures used in a longitudinal study should remain relatively constant. This becomes a real problem in some cases, since tests used at one age level are sometimes inadequate at a subsequent age level and laboratories must modify their procedures with new sets of "normal" values or a new range of numbers that would be considered "normal" for that age group.

The longitudinal method, then, enables one to determine whether there is a change in a function with increasing age, based upon repeated observations of an individual over a wide span of years. The cross-sectional method tells one that there are age differences based upon findings from different groups of people during a given point in time.

Schaie and Strother have pointed out that the cross-sectional and longitudinal methods may yield different results, even when studying the same phenomena.[21] They suggest that "the cross-sectional method may give results which indicate a difference between age groups which might be a function of differences between cohorts (generations), or due to both age and cohort differences." For example, if an investigator found differences between a group of 20 years olds and a group of 60 year olds on a task, it would be difficult to determine whether the differences were actually due to age or to differences that exist between the generations.

Similarly, Kleemier has stated that there is a rapidly accelerated decline on the performance sections of an intelligence test, within a year to eighteen months preceeding death.[22] If this is the case, then the decline in intelligence that occurs with advancing age (see Fig. 20-1) is an artifact, since it doubtless reflects increased probability of death (i.e. within a given age-group of old subjects where there would be some people declining at a graduate rate while decline in intelligence, with this latter group's scores tending to lower the average score for the group as a whole).

In the longitudinal method where one compares a group of subjects from the same generation, who are examined at periods of time over a span of years, differences if found could be a function of age differences or of effects of the environment upon the sample over time, or due to both age and time differences. Thus, if a group of 60 year olds were examined every two years for a ten-year period, it would still be difficult to determine whether the differences were due to age or to environmental changes in the intervals between testing.

There are obviously some flaws in the traditional cross-sectional and longitudinal approaches to the aging process. Schaie suggests the following:

> Caution is in order at this time lest the premature conclusion be reached that increase in sophistication of our methods has indeed led to a better understanding of how and why organisms age. Thus far, it seems just as likely that all which has been investigated refers to differences among generations and thus in a changing society to differences which may be as transient as any phases of that society. Only when we have been successful in differentiating between age changes (the longitudinal method) and the age differences (the cross-sectional method) can we understand the nature of the aging process.[23]

THE CROSS-SEQUENTIAL METHOD. Schaie's cross-sequential model is offered as an alternative method to the traditional cross-sectional and longitudinal designs.[24] The cross-sequential method involves the repeated measurement of subjects in a cross-sectional sample and is exemplified in a study by Schaie and Strother, where they obtained psychological measures on a group of five hundred people, with the group sub-divided into smaller units of fifty subjects in each five-year-age interval from 20 to 70 years of age.[25] Seven years later, all of the available subjects from the first study were retested. The results indicate that the age changes over time within an individual (the longitudinal method) appeared to be much smaller than differences between generations (cross-sectional method). Thus Schaie's cross-sequential model combines the cross-sectional and the longitudinal methods within the framework of a single design and gives a more valid indication of the aging process.

Schaie and Strother also state that

> since the effect of environmental change will be constant for each age group, it may therefore be argued that differences in such change ought to be due to the effect of maturational variance, and that the composite longitudinal age gradient offers a more proper comparison with the cross-sectional findings than would be given by a conventional longitudinal study.[26]

This cross-sequential approach does seem to correct for some of the flaws which have been found with the more traditional methods of investigation and can be used in studies involving a variety of changes over time in adults.

## Research Teams and Groups

The biologist, behavioral and social scientist, and physician are all concerned with the aging process from their individual orientation. Since the aging process is so complex, it is difficult for an isolated investigator to study it on a short term basis; consequently, numerous instances have developed where teams or groups of scientists study the aging process. The investigators need institutional support for a variety of reasons, including the availability of subject pools, funding of research projects, and the possibility of combining the biological, social, and psychological research into a central data collection program.

Group Research. Group research usually involves two or more persons of the same or different disciplines, working independently, who have some areas of similar interest in their approach to research. This allows for a cross-fertilization of ideas among the investigators in a field like aging.

TEAM RESEARCH. According to Busse, in the team research approach, there are scientists from many different areas working together, with each member of the research team having an assigned task of data collection within his own field with his major efforts centered around the teams' goal and his work timed according to the team's overall plans.[27] There would be cross-correlation of the data such that the medical investigator could relate his findings to the social and psychological findings of other team investigators. Ideally, the team of investigators should all participate in the formulation of the program's hypotheses, questions, and developing of research methods, because if one person changes his method independently, it could possibly invalidate the observations of other team members and consequently could make a segment of the work useless. Although individual members do have a responsibility for collection and organization of segments of the data, generally the data are pooled and would be available for all members of the team to use, according to rules which the team has established.

## Method of Subject Selection

Basic to research in aging is the subject. For each area of special interest in aging, there is a certain type of subject who will be best suited for the investigator's needs. The biologists generally study animals, the botonist would require plants and trees, while the scientists interested in physiology and medicine, as well as those in social and psychological specialities, would be more inclined to work with human beings. As we indicated earlier, much of the early research in the behavioral aspects of aging has been with institutionalized people. There is, however, a growing recognition that to investigate the "normal" aging process there is a need to work with healthy and intellectually intact people who can still function in the community. The selection of subjects for a proposed research project does generally pose problems. There are, however, several possible methods for selecting subjects: the volunteer method and the random sample.

THE VOLUNTEER METHOD. In the volunteer method a person

selects himself for the study. One negative feature of using volunteer subjects is that the data cannot be generalized to people in general, but only to the relationship among factors in the aging process under available conditions. If a large number of subjects could be obtained for a study, one could more accurately attempt to generalize the findings to a locale by selecting from the group of volunteers only a certain percentage of subgroups which would correspond to the percentage of those living in the community of a certain age, sex, ethnic and socioeconomic level based upon census findings for that locale.

Frequently the volunteer method is the only feasible approach an investigator has for obtaining subjects. But as Maddox points out, in a longitudinal study requiring clinical evaluations on subjects, it is diffiicult to get people living in the community into a laboratory for a single evaluation, much less for a number of different examinations; and the problem is increased due to the repeated follow-up studies and the increasing age of the subjects.[28] Thus the investigator may have to be content to make his statements apply only to specific conditions rather than to the elderly in general. In addition to the problem of generalization, Maddox points out that

> volunteers used as "normal controls" in clinical research may in fact neither be normal nor provide controls. In specific instances, it has been demonstrated that volunteer subjects have introduced an uncontrolled but definitely biasing effect in clinical experiments. The fact that an individual is not institutionalized and not a patient does not necessarily make him a normal control within any frame of reference.

There is always the question of what kind of person will volunteer for such studies and how he differs from the population as a whole.

RANDOM SAMPLE. Kish in discussing sample design, describes it as a joint procedure of selection and estimation.[29] In order to obtain the exact value of an event occurring in the population, one would have to make observations on all the elements in the entire population. This can seldom be done due to cost, time, etc. Thus inferences are made about the population values from data based on a sample taken from this population. As an example of the basic random sample, take the instance of an investigator who wanted to study the attitudes of twelve thousand employees of a factory. He might decide to interview only four hundred of the employees in an attempt to generalize his findings to the remainder of the workers. His first task would be to obtain the names of all twelve thousand employees (possibly through payroll lists), and then give each person a number. From a table of random numbers, he would then draw four hundred numbers, each drawing consisting of a five digit number not greater than twelve thousand. These four hundred numbers would designate the four hundred employees to be interviewed. A table of random numbers, composed by experts, is a more accuate method for selection of subjects than would be found by using the lottery method of drawing names from a bowl.

In compiling a list of subjects from which selections will be made, it is important to identify the characteristics of people listed and, if necessary, to modify the list before beginning to examine the sample. Some of the factors which should be known about a sample are as follows: (1) Trends within the list. One should know how the people are listed, i.e. in the example of interviewing factory employees it would be important to know whether the list begins with those employees having the greatest seniority, or by age, sex, etc. (2) Duplications. If several lists are used for obtaining possible subjects, a person might appear on both lists. (3) Group differences. If several different lists are used, one might distinguish between different subgroups, i.e. a list might all be grouped according to age, sex, white or blue collar workers, etc. Thus, it is important to know the characteristics of the people on the list.

There are modifications of the basic random sample design: (1) Stratification, which involves the classification of the population of total elements into subpopulations based upon some criteria of levels and called strata; and each stratum is described separately according to sex, age, work departments, socioeconomic groups, etc.; (2) Systematic sampling, in which the units selected are separated on the listing by the length of an interval, with the first selection based upon a random number. Thus one could decide to interview every thirtieth person on the list, with the starting point based upon the selection of a number from a table of random numbers, i.e. number twenty-nine is selected from a table of random numbers, then one would add thirty to it and so forth. This is a popular method for subject selection, and (3) Clustering, which involves the use of existing groups within the population, i.e. if one wanted to investigate the attitudes of an entire city, he would then divide the city into blocks or sections and select a random sample of these sections and interview all dwelling units located within these areas.

Maddox in discussing random selection indicates that the random selection indicates that the random sample allows one to generalize more from his sample to the total population and in addition it "minimizes the probability of introducing systematic bias from unrecognized or uncontrolled but potentially significant sources into the analysis of relationships among variables." [30] Maddox also indicates that a number of studies involving noninstitutionalized elderly subjects have employed random sampling techniques.

> The nonparticipation rates in such studies have been high, especially when clinical evaluation of subjects has been involved. It is entirely possible that a high refusal rate in such instances produces a sample which is essentially the equivalent of a collection of volunteers.

## Subjects

It might be expected that aged research subjects would be more distressed than would a younger group. However, Shanas indicated that in one national survey, 93 per cent of the elderly cooperated and showed little distress about it.[31] About 44 per cent of a group of experienced interviewers said it was harder to interview the aged while the remainder felt it was about the same or not as hard. In general, the experienced interviewers tended to accept the task as "just another interview." Shanas also indicates that in interviewing within the community, it is sometimes easier to work with the elderly person, since a greater number of them would be at home and could be located. On the other hand, there is the problem of some being "too sick," "hard of hearing," or unable to speak English. Many older people will volunteer for laboratory examinations for a variety of reasons: to help others, boredom, or monetary needs. It has been found that since the aged are usually concerned about their health, an offer of a free physical examination is an excellent incentive for volunteers.

In working with the aged, Shanas indicates that brevity is desirable in an interviewing situation, but an hour or longer is acceptable, particularly when older people are asked about things that interest them.[32] An exception to the limited testing, has been found in the Duke University Center for the Study of Aging, where community volunteers come into the hospital setting for two days of extensive physical, social and psychological examinations. However, when the subjects are in their 80's and 90's there are noticeable signs of fatigue and they should be allowed to rest occasionally. When the aged are physically unable to go to the laboratory for examinations, particularly in longitudinal studies where it is valuable to follow the subject through the post-maturity life span, many institutions are using elaborately equipped electronic mobile units which allow the investigator to examine the individual in his home.

In the actual testing of the aged, Shanas suggests that the content of questions should reflect the purpose of the investigation, i.e. income, leisure time, etc.[33] In many interview situations and particularly in psychological testing, a standard procedure must be used with all subjects; however, whenever possible the interviewer should be free to rephrase questions, if they are not clear to the older adult. In an experimental situation, the older person often withholds answers more frequently than a younger person, but when given additional time they respond significantly more frequently (Eisdorfer, Axelrod, and Wilkie).[34] Thus it is necessary (1) to give the older person more time to answer questions and (2) to try to control for any anxiety the test situation causes. Frequently the procedure of allowing the aged person to familiarize himself with the laboratory situation (such as bringing the subject into the laboratory on two separate days, with the second day being the actual testing day) considerably alleviates anxiety and allows for the more accurate measurement of abilities (Troyer, Eisdorfer, Wilkie, and Bogdonoff).[35] One problem, which requires more study, involves the relationship between the interviewer or examiner and the subject. Such issues as race, according to Jackson,[36] and age, according to Donahue,[37] and affiliation of the experimenter in relation to the subject may be quite important under certain circumstances. This should be a source of future study.

In some studies, the purpose of the investigation may require the examination of older people who are severely physically and mentally impaired, which leads to a number of problems in testing them. Rosenfelt, Kastenbaum, and Kempler in discussing the testing of handicapped older people, say that as they often live in impoverished social environments, their interpersonal skills tend to atrophy, and they withdraw from or do not have the opportunity for meaningful relationships with others which results in many being fearful and suspicious.[38] The testing situation makes a greater impression upon them than it would probably have for younger or the more normal aged person. Thus the examiner must not only look at the handicapped person's performance scores on the tests, but also be aware of the subject's reaction and total behavior pattern during the testing. With the handicapped older person, there may be a reduction in the amount of usable data, due to a slowness in performing, speech handicaps, psychomotor retardation as well as from fear and uncertainty. The more normal aged person as well as the handicapped may be reluctant to reveal the decline in his mental abilities, both to the examiner and to himself.

If there is a minimum output of data, the investigator must use whatever is possible and develop new ways to look at the results. According to Rosenfelt, et al.

> quantification may have to be abandoned in favor of qualitative or other systems of classification. New methods and interpretations must be found for behavior that doesn't fit the standard. It is the continuity and lawfulness to the behavior of the most regressed aged person's behavior that must be found.[39]

The problem of introducing the subject to the testing situation and ending it must be considered. Rosenfelt, et al. also states that "when assumptions are explicit, limitations realized, and the scope of applicability comprehended, there is no need to designate a large group of our fellow human beings as untestable." [40]

## CONCLUSION

We have attempted to set gerontological research within the context of the broad spectrum of science. Scientific methodology involving observation, hypothesis formulation and testing, and the development of theories is as important in gerontology as in any other branch of science.

Some specific problems encountered in the study of aging have been discussed: (1) patterns in aging; (2) the concept of age, including the chronological, biological, social, and psychological ages of an individual; (3) the methods of approach in aging research; (4) the development of research teams and groups; (5) subject recruitment through the volunteer and random sample procedure; and (6) the aged individual as a subject in research. Only an understanding of these variables and their interrelationships in the aging process can lead to intelligent planning for basic research and to the implementation of applied research into programs designed to improve life for the elderly.

Finally, it is well to remember that current hypotheses and theories, as well as research strategies, may change with the passage of time and the development of more refined methods of investigation.

## REFERENCES

1. Quetelet, A.: *Sur l'homme et le developpement de ses facultes.* Paris, Bachelier, 1835.
2. Bachrach, A.: *Psychological Research.* New York, Random, 1962.
3. *Ibid.,* 1962.
4. Rapoport, A.: What is semantics? *Amer Sci, 40*:123-135, 1952.
5. Quine, W.: Truth by convention. In *Philosophical Essays for Alfred North Whitehead.* New York, Longmans, 1946.
6. Stevens, S. S.: Mathematics, Measurement, and Psychophysics. In *Handbook of Experimental Psychology.* Stevens, S. S. (Ed.), New York, Wiley, 1963, pp. 1-49.
7. *Ibid.,* 1963.
8. Eisdorfer, C.; Axelrod, S., and Wilkie, F.: Stimulus exposure time as a factor in serial learning in an aged population. *J Abnorm Soc Psychol, 67*:594-600, 1963.
9. Hull, C. L.: Hypothetico-deductive method of theory construction. In *Readings in Learning.* Stolurow, L. (Ed.), New York, Prentice-Hall, 1953, pp. 9-30.
10. Bachrach, *op. cit.,* 1962.
11. Cannon, W. B.: *The Way of Investigation.* New York, Norton, 1945.
12. Ungerleider, H. E., and Smith, C. C.: Use and abuse of statistice. *Geriatrics,* Feb. 1967, pp. 112-120.
13. Berg, I. A.: The use of human subjects in psychological research. *Amer Psychol, 9*:108-111, 1954.
14. Brotman, H. B.: *Facts on Aging.* Office of Aging, U.S. Department of Health, Education, and Welfare, No. 9, June 1965.
15. Birren, J.: Research on the psychology of aging: concepts and findings. In *Psychopathology of Aging.* Hoch, P., and Zubin, J. (Eds.), New York, Grune, 1961, pp. 203-222.

16. WEISS, P.: Aging: a corollary of development. In *Perspectives in Experimental Gerontology.* Shock, N. (Ed.), Springfield, Thomas, 1966, p. 321.
17. WECHSLER, D.: *The Measurement and Appraisal of Adult Intelligence.* Baltimore, Williams & Wilkins, 1958, p. 96.
18. United States Bureau of the Census: *Educational Attainment of the Population Twenty-Five Years Old and Over for the United States.* Washington, D.C., Series Pc-7, No. 6, 1950.
19. COLEMAN, J. C.: *Abnormal Psychology and Modern Life.* New York, Scott, 1950.
20. BUSSE, E. W.: Administration of the interdisciplinary research team. *J Med Educ, 40*:832-839, 1965.
21. SCHAIE, K. W., and STROTHER, C. R.: A Cross-Sequential Study of Age Changes in Cognitive Behavior. Paper presented at the Meeting of the Midwestern Psychological Association at St. Louis, Missouri, April, 1964.
22. KLEEMIER, R. W.: Intellectual changes in the senium. In *Proceedings: Social Statistics Section of the American Statistical Association.* Washington, D.C.: American Statistical Association, 1962, pp. 290-295.
23. SCHAIE, K. W.: Age Changes and Age Differences. Paper presented at Gerontological Society Meeting at Los Angeles, California, Nov. 13, 1965(b).
24. SCHAIE, K. W.: A general model for the study of developmental problems. *Psychol Bull, 64*:92-107, 1965(a).
25. SCHAIE and STROTHER, *op. cit.,* 1964.
26. *Ibid.,* 1964.
27. BUSSE, *op. cit.,* Vol. 40, pp. 832-839, 1965.
28. MADDOX, G. L.: A longitudinal multidisciplinary study of human aging: selected methodological issues. In *Proceedings: Social Statistics Section of the American Statistical Association.* Washington, D.C., American Statistical Association, 1962, pp. 280-285.
29. KISH, L.: Selection of the sample. In *Research Methods in the Behavior Sciences.* Festing, L., and Katz, D. (Ed.), New York, Dryden, 1953, pp. 175-240.
30. MADDOX, *op. cit.,* pp. 280-285, 1962.
31. SHANAS, ETHEL. National study of older people in the United States. In *Process of Aging: Social and Psychological Perspectives.* Williams, R. H.; Tibbits, C. P., and Donahue, W. (Eds.), New York, Atherton, 1963, pp. 1-29.
32. *Ibid.,* pp. 1-29, 1963.
33. *Ibid.,* pp. 1-29, 1963.
34. EISDORFEF, AXELROD, and WILKIE, *op. cit.,* vol. 67, pp. 594-600, 1963.
35. TROYER, W.; EISDORFER, C.; WILKIE, F., and BOGDONOFF, M.: FFA responses in the aged individual during performance of a learning task. *J Geront, 21*:415-419, 1966.

36. Jackson, J. J.: Social gerontology and the Negro aged: a review. *Gerontologist, 7*:168-178, 1967.
37. Donahue, W.: Relationship of age of perceivers to their social perceptors. *Gerontologist, 5*:241-245, 1965.
38. Rosenfelt, R. H.; Kastenbaum, R., and Kempler, B.: The untestables: methodological problems in drug research with the aged. *Gerontologist, 4*:72-74, 1964.
39. *Ibid.,* pp. 72-74, 1964.
40. *Ibid.,* pp. 72-74, 1964.

*Chapter 21*

# TRAINING IN SOCIAL GERONTOLOGY

Helen M. Flint

The number of community facilities and services designed to serve older people has increased tremendously in recent years. There has been a rapid growth of (a) program planning at the state and community level, (b) housing designed for older people, (c) senior centers, (d) recreational and adult educational programs, and (e) an expansion of a wide range of social and health services for our older population. Yet, programs would have proliferated even more rapidly if trained people had been available to plan and develop them. As Kleemeier and Birren pointed out, attention must be paid to the basic process of aging if services are to be administered intelligently and effectively.[1] Experience has borne out this theory. Agencies, aware that the quality of a program depends on the persons staffing it, have been reluctant to hire untrained persons. Trained persons, on the other hand, have been—and still are—in short supply.

## THE NEED FOR TRAINING

The need for training in aging has long been recognized by leading gerontologists, and early attempts to establish training programs are described in the literature. Various professional organizations, including the American Home Economics Association, participated in these efforts. Donahue's account, "Development and Current Status of University Instruction in Social Gerontology," is both authoritative and comprehensive.[2]

Obstacles to concerted action in the development of training in social gerontology were discussed during the White House Conference on Aging held in 1961. In a background paper on the role and training of professional personnel, the roadblocks to progress were identified as lack of funds, lack of facilities, difficulty in recruiting, lack of public understanding, and absence of national policy.[3] Concluding remarks in this connection were as follows:

> Aging and the social consequences of increasing numbers of older persons in the population are only one among the myriad problems of our generation and our nation. . . . We must therefore insist on its right to be considered, to be weighed along with others, to be financed and given research and training aid and opportunities for recruitment.[4]

Training got underway with grants from the National Institute of Child Health and Human Development and the National Institute of Mental Health. It was expanded with the passage of the Older Americans Act which authorized grants and contracts under Title V of the Act for "the specialized training of persons employed or preparing for employment in carrying out programs related to the purposes of this Act." [5] Training is authorized, also, under Title III of the Act which provides grants to the States for community planning, services, and training.[6]

## CATEGORIES OF PERSONNEL NEEDS

One of the first steps taken by the Administration on Aging with respect to training under Title V of the act was to identify categories of personnel needs. These are set forth in an AoA publication[7] as follows:

1. Professional social gerontologists to plan, administer, and coordinate programs in aging at Federal, State and community levels.
2. Managers of staff for retirement housing, hotels, villages, and homes for older people.
3. Directors and staff for multiservice senior centers.
4. Professional personnel with specialization in aging within such fields as architecture, adult education, home economics, library science, and social work.
5. Faculty with specialization in aging for teaching and research.
6. Leaders for State and community committees in aging and organizations of retired persons.
7. Technical personnel and aides for a variety of programs serving older people.

The Administration on Aging gives highest priority to these principal unmet areas of need and is supporting a number of training programs in an effort to meet them. Some of the programs are described later in this chapter.

## MANPOWER STUDIES

Although categories of personnel need have been identified, there are, as yet, no reliable estimates of the *number* of persons needed. The lack of such information has been a deterrent to the initiation of programs by universities. Without some definitive data giving assurance that students trained in aging would be in demand, universities have been reluctant to commit themselves to such programs. Some efforts have been made to estimate the numbers, on a limited basis, but funds were lacking for a comprehensive survey.[8] The Congress, however, convinced of the need, made provision for such a study through the 1967 amendments to the Older Americans Act.[9]

Section 503 of the Older Americans Act Amendments of 1967, entitled "Study of Need for Trained Personnel," is as follows:

> The Secretary is authorized to undertake, directly or by grant or contract, a study and evaluation of the immediate and foreseeable need for trained personnel to carry out programs related to the objectives of this Act, and of the availability and adequacy of the educational and training resources for persons preparing to work in such programs. On or before March 31, he shall make a report to the President and to the Congress, of his findings and recommendations resulting from such study, including whatever specific proposals, including legislative proposals, he deems will assist in insuring that the need for such trained specialists will be met.

In order to carry out the study required by the Amendments, the Administration on Aging made two grants and one contract, the results of which will be made known probably sometime in 1968. Under one grant, the National Association of Housing and Redevelopment Officials is compiling an inventory of publicly assisted housing for older people who are living independently and making a survey of the staff employed in these housing projects. The National Recreation and Park Association, under the other grant, is studying the supply and demand for trained personnel to serve older people in public and private recreational programs in the United States. The Association's final report will include a summary of activities now being undertaken and suggestions for appropriate training programs.

Surveys and Research Corporation, a private agency, is making a comprehensive study, under an AoA contract. Its purpose is to identify current and emerging needs for personnel in programs serving older people and to make recommendations concerning training programs required to meet the needs. Data are being collected on (1) occupations, such as the health professions, whose personnel work with all age groups including older persons, (2) the proportion of people in these occupations working with older people, (3) future demand for people to work in the field of aging, and (4) existing training programs that prepare personnel for work with older people.

It is expected that specific information emerging from these studies will demonstrate the extent and severity of the current shortage of personnel. Hopefully, then, the necessary support will be forthcoming both for recruitment and for training.

## Job Descriptions

In an effort to describe some positions in aging more fully, the Administration on Aging prepared and published a set of prototype position descriptions.[10] This effort was in response to requests, particularly from state agencies, for assistance in locating persons qualified for positions in aging. Also, it was believed that the specifications would be useful to persons developing training programs in aging and to individuals seeking careers in the field. The position descriptions do not represent federal requirements or standards but serve as guides for persons who are developing position descriptions for specific situations.

Fourteen classes of positions in the field of aging are included, with a breakdown showing duties, knowledge, and abilities required for each. Eleven of these fall into the general category of *planning, administering, and coordinating programs* which, as stated earlier, is a category to which the Administration on Aging gives high priority. Included among the eleven are the following prototype positions, located in a state unit on aging: Executive Director, Deputy Director, Field Representative, and Program Specialist. Other administrative positions described in the publication are located in such state-level agencies as public welfare, health, vocational rehabilitation, and education. Some are located at the county or community level. The three remaining position descriptions relate to senior center direction and housing management—also AoA priority areas.

All fourteen descriptions require, as a minimum, knowledge about aging. The extent of such knowledge varies from position to position. One description, for example, suggests as a requirement "a *thorough* knowledge of the social, emotional, economic, and health needs . . . and techniques for involving older persons in worthwhile activities."[11] Others call for "*considerable* knowledge of the problems of the aging and methods of attacking the problems" and "*considerable* knowledge of community organization and resources for older people."[12] Still others suggest a need for knowledge of a rather specific aspect of aging such as "*some* knowledge of current research in the field of health of older persons," or "*some* knowledge of the current position of government management, and labor concerning employment of older persons and of handicapped persons."[13]

Although no description is given for a position requiring a home economist, several might readily be adapted for this professional field. One of these is Program Specialist, State Commission on Aging.[14] The Specialist's primary function is to serve as consultant to the executive director of the state agency on aging and to provide leadership in the development of a specialized state-wide program of services for older persons. If these programs were concerned with services such as food and nutrition or home care services for the elderly, the position might well require a Master's degree in home economics. This person might have such duties as (1) compiling and maintaining information on existing resources for food and nutrition programs, (2) identifying gaps in the state's program, (3) planning and developing a state-wide food and nutrition program and/or home care services, (4) creating public understanding of the program, providing consultation to communities, organizations, or groups, (5) providing consultation on training programs for paid staff and volunteers working with the specialized home economics program, (6) stimulating research and demonstration projects, and (7) providing consultation in the planning and conducting of conferences, workshops, and seminars concerned with the specialized state-wide program.

Knowledge required for fulfilling these duties would include a thorough knowledge of the specialized area, such as food and nutrition, and its application to the needs of older persons including those who are in good health and those who are confined to institutions or homes. Basic to this would be an intimate understanding of the characteristics differentiating older people from younger ones and of the underlying forces creating the characteristics.

## A Body of Knowledge

It should be evident from the foregoing that there are many aspects of aging which need to be understood by persons working in this field. A body of knowledge covering the many aspects of aging exists and is being systematized. Although there is some difference of opinion as to how it should be taught—that is, within existing curricula or as social gerontology per se—there is general agreement as to the basic content needed by persons working in the field of aging.

A proposal for a two-year curriculum was published by the U.S. Office on Aging (now the Administration on Aging) early in 1965.[15] In the introduction, Donald P. Kent, then the Director of the Office of Aging, pointed out that it "drew heavily upon curriculum content proposed by the Division of Gerontology of the University of Michigan and upon the experience of several other universities offering courses in gerontology." He concluded by saying, "It is the hope of the Office of Aging that this proposal, the first of its kind, will stimulate universities in all parts of the country to develop and experiment with programs in gerontology." The publication outlined a curriculum consisting of (1) Basic Courses in Social Gerontology, (2) Courses in Applied Social Gerontology, and (3) Courses from Related Fields.

More recently, a four-semester curriculum in social gerontology for professionals, developed by Tibbitts, appeared in *Graduate Education in Aging Within the Social Sciences*.[16] He also outlined a single course in social gerontology capable of giving an overview of the field.[17] Three basic texts for the course are suggested.[18, 19, 20] Tibbitts explains that the course, covering the salient features of aging of the individual and of societal involvement in aging, can serve several purposes. It can, for example, be presented at the advanced undergraduate level in the context of liberal education; in the first year of graduate study in the behavioral and social sciences; or within the curriculum of a professional field such as home economics, social work, or public health.

The single course outlined by Tibbitts is divided into four parts: (1) *Demographic and Sociocultural Factors in Aging* which covers older people in American society and older people in other high-energy societies, aging and old age in low-energy societies; growth of older populations in high-energy societies, aging and technological change, the value system and older people. (2) *The Aging Individual As a Person* which covers sociological changes, biological changes significant for performance and status, physical health and illness, psychological changes with age, changes in personality and organization of behavior, mental health and mental illness, and stages in the later life cycle. (3) *Middle-Aged and Older People as Members of a Social System* which covers nature of the social system, institutions, norms, and roles, socialization and social adjustment, and collective behavior of aging and older people (4). *Aging and the Structure and Functions of Society* which covers society as a system of values, institutions and organizations for the satisfaction of individual, group, and social needs, impact of older people on society, social responsibilities for older people, the economy and aging, aging and the political system, societal programs and provisions for older people, societal organization and structure, and population quality.

A number of universities are incorporating the basic content on aging contained in Tibbitts' outline in the existing curriculum or using it as a pattern for the development of new courses and seminars.

## TYPES OF TRAINING PROGRAMS

To date, no complete catalog of the academic programs having a significant focus on social gerontology exists, although the Administration on Aging is developing such a publication. There are increasing numbers of training programs in aging receiving financial support from federal agencies, particularly those of the U.S. Department of Health, Education, and Welfare. The D/HEW agencies providing primary training support are the Administration on Aging (AoA), the National Institute of Mental Health (NIMH), and the National Institute of Child Health and Human Development (NICHD). Other D/HEW agencies, such as the Bureau of Health Manpower of the Public Health Service and the Rehabilitation Services Administration of the Social and Rehabilitation Service, are making contributions to training in the area of aging through the support of some short term training programs. An example of the latter is a short-term course on the older disabled worker presented by Northeastern University under the sponsorship of the Vocational Rehabilitation Agency (the predecessor of the Rehabilitation Services Administration).

Although the Administration on Aging is a major source of basic information on existing programs, detailed information on such matters as traineeships must be obtained directly from the universities. They, rather than the Federal Government, select individual students for programs in aging and give traineeships or other forms of financial support to them.

For the purposes of this chapter, training programs are classified according to the categories of personnel needs outlined earlier. No attempt is made to cover all existing programs but to suggest, through examples, the kinds of training now available. The program descriptions are followed by a discussion of an institute of gerontology—the pattern now emerging as a highly effective organizational arrangement for meeting priority training needs.

## Professional Training for Program Planning, Administration, and Coordination

Professional social gerontologists are critically needed to plan programs at all levels, to administer them, and to coordinate the efforts of the many agencies—both public and private—that recognize the need to serve an aging population. Needed by this group is career education at the master's and doctoral level and short-term training for those who are currently employed.

An example of this kind of *long-term* training is that offered by the Florence Heller School for Advanced Studies in Social Welfare of Brandeis University. Its objective is to train doctoral students for positions of the highest responsibility in planning, administration, teaching, and research in social gerontology and its application. The program combines social theory, professional techniques, and research data from the clinical, biological, and social sciences in an effort to develop skills needed for the performance of such tasks as conducting analysis and research in gerontology, translating research findings into concrete policy and program proposals, planning and implementing administrative and interorganizational policies and programs, and blending and coordinating specialized gerontological programs with more broadly focused programs. Successful trainees receive either the Ph.D. or D.S.W. degrees and are expected to be ready to occupy high-level positions within three years of their entry into the training program.

Brandeis University also offers *short-term* training in social gerontology. In 1967, for example, it offered a six-day Institute for State Executives in Aging to assist them in developing greater skill in policy analysis, translation of research findings into concrete policy proposals, and in dealing with the complexities of local, regional, statewide, and national organizations involved in aging. The institute called "Creative Administration in Social Gerontology," was held at the conference headquarters of Brandeis University for twenty-eight state executives in aging. All the participants were selected and invited by the National Association of State Units in Aging. The program was given by Brandeis staff members and special lecturers, all leading authorities on various facets of aging or public administration.

## Training for Managers and Staff of Senior Housing and Homes

In recent years, housing designed specifically for middle-aged and older people has been developing rapidly in quantity, variety, and concept. High-rise apartments, clustered garden apartments and row housing, retirement villages, and retirement hotels are now relatively common. Paralleling the wide variety of housing facilities are the many skills and job components essential to their management. Only within the last several years have universities committed themselves to training people to administer these facilities and programs. Career education and training at the master's level is needed to meet this high-priority need. Also, short-term training programs are required to train those persons already employed in this area of service to older people.

A program offered by North Texas State University is an example of *long-term* training in the area of housing management. The university has established a Center for Studies in Aging where candidates for the master's degree prepare for careers as administrators of homes for the elderly and as directors of community and voluntary agency programs for older people. The major components of the program are (1) behavioral and social science content with primary emphasis on aging, (2) seminars on programs for the aged and administration of the programs, (3) business administration or public administration courses, (4) an internship, and (5) a thesis or equivalent.

Other universities offer *short-term* training programs from time to time. An example of such a course is one developed by the National Association of Housing and Redevelopment Officials in cooperation with the University of Michigan. The University conducted this six-day program on its campus; NAHRO provided administrative support. Special emphasis in this six-day course was on management of housing for older persons who live independently. Training content focused on the human aging process; social and economic factors affecting older people; federal, state, and local resources for helping to meet the needs of older persons; and the policies and practices of management that are peculiar to senior citizen housing.

## Training for Directors and Staff of Multiservice Senior Centers

Senior centers are emerging rapidly throughout the country as multi-purpose facilities designed to meet varied needs of older people. Initiated as activity centers providing opportunity for socialization, recreation, and participation in creative pursuits, the more complex centers now offer a wide variety of opportunities and have added counseling and referral service, health examinations, and services leading to paid or voluntary employment. This concept was stressed by Commissioner on Aging, William D. Bechill, who said,

> We in the Administration on Aging feel that the proper direction is for these centers to become multipurpose in character. By multipurpose, we mean providing many different kinds of services, activities, and opportunities for older people, including the objective of having a good time. The multipurpose senior center provides a wide and varied program, aimed towards specific and relevant objectives, and under the coordinated direction of trained personnel and volunteer leadership. Among its purposes are the development of meaningful and creative services and activities for individuals and groups, the discovery of opportunities for older people to perform community service, and the availability of information about community resources and plans relating to older people.[21]

The number of senior centers has been increasing. With regard to the number of centers, Wilbur J. Cohen, Secretary of the Department of Health, Education, and Welfare, stated,

> The department, through the Administration on Aging, will soon be conducting a second national survey of senior centers. In 1965, when the first survey was conducted, we identified some three hundred centers. Now we know of nearly three thousand centers open three or more days a week.[22]

Persons qualified to serve as directors of multipurpose senior centers and other facilities are in extremely short supply. In response to this need, several universities are now offering long-term training to prepare persons for careers in this field. Short-term training programs are also being developed for persons currently employed.

The program offered by Teachers College, Columbia University is a good example of the *long-term* training which prepares master's level students for senior center direction and recreation leadership. Required course work is drawn from a variety of disciplines and includes such courses as psychology of maturity and aging, biological aspects of the aging process, and community service and the older population. A number of community agencies are cooperating in the program and providing students an opportunity to observe and gain experience in programs in senior centers, homes for elderly persons, and community centers serving older people.

*Short-term* training is provided through workshops and seminars for senior center directors. A number of them have been held throughout the country, often with financial support provided by a state unit on aging under Title III of the Older Americans Act. Typical of these is a regional workshop held in Charlottesville, Virginia, for senior center directors from the District of Columbia, Kentucky, Maryland, North Carolina, Virginia, and West Virginia. The two-day program included lectures on such topics as "the challenge of senior service centers" and "resources for providing comprehensive services." In addition to the lectures, there was group discussion based on case studies dealing with such problems as racial integration, promoting the involvement of men in senior center activities, and coordination of services in a senior center.

## Gerontological Training Within the Professional Service Fields

Numerous occupational groups serving older people were identified by participants in the 1961 White House Conference on Aging and grouped under four major headings.[23] These were (1) health and medical services, (2) social work, (3) educational, religious, and recreational services, (4) and environmental planning and administration. Since that time, a number of training programs have been developed within the various professions for the purpose of enabling graduates to serve older people within their own areas.

The greatest number of *long-term* programs has occurred within the social work profession. The National Institute of Mental Health is supporting programs in some fourteen different schools of social work, with special emphasis on casework and group work with older people. The Administration on Aging also has made grants to schools of social work for programs in aging with highest priority given to the community organization aspects of aging. An example of an AoA-supported program recently initiated is that of the University of Washington School of Social Work. Students in the program will enroll in the school's regular social work curriculum and specialize in community organization in the second year of their studies leading to the M.S.W. In addition to concentrating on aging in the Human Behavior and Social Environment Sequence and in the Social Welfare Organization Sequence, students will be required to enroll in a three-term seminar on aging. Field work experience in working with and for older people will be gained through placements in a variety of community agencies.

An example of a *short-term* training program for a professional group is one given by the Pennsylvania State University to train ministers in aging. The program, entitled "A Career Enrichment Program in Aging for Ministers" was a nine-day conference attended by thirty-eight ministers. The program was designed to be a genuine learning experience, to bring about attitudinal change, and to motivate individual, community, and denominational efforts in the field of aging.

Another short-term program that might be mentioned is a three-day conference held by the School of Home Economics of the University of Southwestern Louisiana to encourage the development of school and other institutional curricula related to home economics and aging. The conference was planned by a steering committee with representatives not only of the university's school of home economics, but also of the Louisiana Commission on Aging, state education department, and the Louisiana Home Economics Association.

Perhaps the earliest and most consistent effort in the area of short-term programs is that at the University of Iowa, where a variety of training opportunities have been provided, beginning with an annual five-week course for nursing and retirement home administrators in 1963. In its seventh consecutive year (1969), the course was expanded to ten weeks. Approximately 400 administrators had received this training up to that date. Supplementary to this, over the past three years has been a two-day Advanced Training Institute, held each fall, and six regional clinics for administrators of facilities for the care of the aged. These latter programs were initially financed in part from funds under Title I of the Higher Education Act of 1965. In the summer of 1964, the Department of Home Economics and the Institute of Gerontology at the University of Iowa, sponsored a two-week workshop on Social Gerontology for Home Economists.

## Training for Research and Teaching

The need to train persons for research and teaching in social gerontology was stated by Tibbitts as follows:

> The compelling need for service, administrative, and research personnel in aging within the established and emerging professions creates, of course, an equally imperative need for teaching faculty in colleges, universities, and professional schools. It is patent that, without teachers, research and service personnel cannot be produced.[24]

A number of attacks are being made on the problem of increasing the number of college and university teachers equipped to train others in the theoretical and applied aspects of aging. Career education at the master's and doctoral level, as well as seminars and short courses for employed faculty members, is needed.

Although nomenclature varies, a growing number of programs to meet this need can be identified. A good example of a *long-term* program is the one in adult development and aging being offered by the University of Chicago's Committee on Human Development. Its objective is to train doctoral students for research and teaching in gerontology within any one of the following fields: anthropology, education, health administration, human development, psychology, sociology, or social service administration. A student registers in the school, department, or committee from which he is seeking a degree. He must meet the departmental requirements for the Ph.D. degree and also participate in an ongoing seminar in adulthood and old age, take courses in research methods and research design, and participate in ongoing research projects. Post-doctoral research training is offered for psychiatrists.

An example of a short-term training program for faculty members is one initiated by the University of Georgia in 1966. The program consisted of a series of seminars for faculty members of state universities and small private colleges from six nearby states. The training sessions were held on ten weekends, over a period of eleven months. Faculty members from such schools and departments as home economics, psychology, business administration, sociology, social work, and pharmacy participated. The seminars focused on such topics as (1) psychological aspects of aging, (2) personality development and age, (3) biological and physiological aspects of aging, (4) mental health needs and programs for older adults, (5) income maintenance, (6) housing and living arrangements for older adults, and (7) community service programs for older adults.

## Leadership Training

It is generally recognized that effective leadership is the most important single factor in conducting successful community programs. A combination of both professional and volunteer leadership is needed. As states and communities develop programs *for* older people, they are giving increasing emphasis to the involvement of older people themselves in these leadership activities.

Training is being offered under the sponsorship of educational institutions and a variety of public and voluntary agencies in aging. Some are receiving support under Title V of the Older Americans Act. An example of a *long-term* training program with AoA support is that of the University of California (Davis) for the regional training of leaders to work with older people. Many older people themselves are among the trainees. Through the project, regional and local training conferences are being held and the university is beginning the planning and inauguration of a curriculum to train adult education specialists in aging. The training conferences, held as part of the total project, focus on extending knowledge of the aging process; providing information on federal, state, and local programs and resources for older persons; and furnishing information on the community organization process.

Many projects supported under Title III of the Older Americans Act have a training component. Sometimes the training is incidental to other functions, but in a number of projects, training is the sole component. One of the general training categories is that of community leadership. Most frequently, training is conducted under the auspices of a university or a senior center. Some examples are (1) a five-day training program given by the University of Kansas focusing on techniques and guidelines to meet community needs on aging, (2) a short-term program to train community leaders to raise the quality of their leadership and identify needs of older people, provided by the Cooperative Extension Service of the University of Maine, and (3) a short-term program for professionals and lay leaders to train them for leadership in programs for the aging presented by Washington State University.

## Training for Technical Personnel and Aides

If older people are to be served, large numbers of technical personnel and aides are needed to augment the limited supply of professional persons trained in aging.

An example of a program for training aides is the federally sponsored series of pilot projects for training home health aides. The purpose of this national program was to recruit, select, and train older, poor people for employment as home health aides. (For purposes of employment programs, persons aged 45 and over are considered "older workers.") The Office of Economic Opportunity, the Public Health Service, and the Administration on Aging cooperated in the sponsorship of the program. Projects varied from state to state. The program in Oklahoma, for example, was statewide, with funds provided to the state department of health for training home health aides. The program was launched in forty of the state's seventy-seven counties and, in cooperation with the state department of education and other agencies, a training manual and trainee handbook were developed.

Trainees were recruited by community action agencies, state and county health and welfare departments, the state employment service, senior citizen organizations, district social security offices, and voluntary health and educational organizations. The State Vocational Home Economics Department worked with the health department in providing the training course.

Another approach to training persons to serve older people is that taken by the U.S. Office of Education under the Vocational Education Act. Whereas these programs once focused on preparing people for homemaking; they now have the added goal of preparing people for employment. In this connection, the Office of Education has identified a number of occupations falling within the field of home economics and offering employment opportunities. One of these is "Companion to an Elderly Person." A curriculum guide has been prepared to serve as resource material for the development of programs at the local level.[25] The guide suggests four course units: (1) orientation to the nature of the work and interpersonal relations, (2) some common physical, mental, and emotional needs of older persons and implications of these needs for giving satisfactory service, (3) assisting with personal, social, and business matters, (4) and handling emergencies.

Another technical area in which people are being trained to serve older people is in the health occupations. Special efforts are being made to meet the ever-increasing need and demand for licensed practical nurses. The U.S. Office of Education is encouraging states to use allotted funds to provide for training of practical nurses and to upgrade others who were trained some time ago and under circumstances which would not meet today's licensing requirements. In connection with upgrading, the Office of Education is cooperating with the Public Health Service to stimulate the development of vocational training programs for personnel serving in nursing homes, extended care facilities, and hospitals participating under Medicare and Medicaid.

## INSTITUTES OF GERONTOLOGY

It should be clear from the preceding descriptions of programs that administrative arrangements for training in aging vary. One of the most effective approaches, however, appears to be the establishment of a multidisciplinary institute of gerontology as an identifiable unit with a university. It may be located administratively in the office of the president, in the graduate school, or in some other organizational unit that is not dominated by a single discipline.

Institutes perform a number of general functions:

1. *Recruiting and training needed professional and para-professional* personnel for the field of aging;
2. Providing an opportunity for teams of scientific and professional personnel to *conduct research* that extends our knowledge about older people and to make studies and evaluations of programs for them;
3. *Providing consultation and assistance* to public and voluntary agencies, to states, and to communities in their efforts to meet the needs of older people.

Historically, research was given major emphasis. At least this was true in the multidisciplinary centers established by universities with support from the National Institutes of Health. In 1964, however, the National Advisory Council for that Institute under the stimulation of Dr. James E. Birren, then head of the Aging Program of the National Institute of Child Health and Human Development, recommended that training should constitute a part of any major university research program in gerontology.[26]

An example of such a program supported by the National Institute of Child Health and Human Development is *Duke University's Center for the Study of Aging and Human Development.* This training program enables interested predoctoral and postdoctoral students to undertake research training in selected aspects of aging and human development with a specific focus on individual and group behavior and behavioral physiology. Each trainee is provided with specific investigative skills in one of the specialized areas of aging and human development that is available at the university, in order that he may eventually achieve independent status as an investigator. The program stresses methodology and acquisition of specialized skills, which are acquired by working in a laboratory or in field research under the personal supervision of an experienced investigator. Course work supplements laboratory and training seminars. This multidisciplinary training program is located in the university's medical school and is under the direction of a steering committee representing various medical specialities including medical psychology and medical sociology.

Another example is the *University of Michigan-Wayne State University Institute of Gerontology.* This unit was established by statute of the Michigan Legislature in May 1965 and is the first Institute of Gerontology so created in a university setting. Its purpose, as stated in the bill is

> developing new and improved programs for helping older people . . . for the training of persons skilled in working with the problems of the aged, for research related to the needs of our aging population, and for conducting community service programs in the field of aging.[27]

In the areas of training, the institute is mandated to (1) stimulate and contribute to training in gerontology in the various schools and departments of the universities, and (2) offer specialized interdisciplinary training in gerontology at the graduate and postgraduate levels for those entering or already working in the field.

Although jointly sponsored by two universities, the institute operates as a single unit. It is administered by an executive board made up of five members from each of the two universities responsible to the presidents of the two institutions. Eventually the institute will have two co-directors, but to date the co-director for the University of Michigan, Dr. Wilma Donahue, is also serving as acting co-director for Wayne State University. The institute has a threefold focus covering research, training, and community service. In March 1967, with support from the Administration on Aging, the institute launched a training project consisting of five phases. Accomplishments up to March 1968 are summarized below:

1. *Long-term career training.* This program leads to a master's degree in public administration and specialist certificate in aging. Both the University of Michigan and Wayne State University introduced two-year MPA/Gerontology programs offering specialization in aging. In addition to required courses in public administration, students take two courses in gerontology (3 hours credit), one course in income maintenance programs for older people (2 hours credit), and two semesters of a noncredit proseminar in aging. In addition, Wayne State University students are enrolled in a course in directed research

(4 hours credit) and some University of Michigan students take an architecture course in housing the elderly.

Since the goal of the Institute is to see that the two universities become a center for training professional personnel in aging, the strategy has been to interest the faculties of various teaching units in offering curricula providing specialization in aging within specific fields. As a result, three new teachng units will offer their students opportunities to specialize in aging at the master's level. These are (1) Housing the Elderly in the University of Michigan's School of Architecture, (2) Community Organization in the Schools of Social Work at Wayne State and at the University of Michigan, and (3) Recreation Multiservice Senior Centers in the School of Education at the University of Michigan. Some effort will be made to stimulate various departments to extend their program to include training at the doctoral level.

2. *Short-term (14-week) training.* Residential institutes are held to train persons in retirement housing management, multiservice senior centers, or milieu programs. The curriculum consists of a set of five core courses and certain specialized courses. Core courses include social gerontology, community organization and social services, adult health and health services, theory of milieu intervention, and proseminar in aging. The specialized courses are elected in accordance with students' special interests (housing, multiservice centers, or milieu programming).

The Institute plans to continue the residential institutes and also to add a new short-term training program in the form of a series of "technical assistance workshops" aimed primarily at in-service training of mental hospital and nursing personnel in use of the therapeutic community as a treatment agent. Special focus of the workshops will be on the planning and operation of sheltered workshops.

3. *Curriculum consultation conferences.* Two of these conferences—one on retirement housing and one on multiservice senior centers—were held to gain the advice of university personnel, practitioners, and generally knowledgeable persons in the planning of long-term and short-term instructional programs in aging.

4. *Textbooks.* As a means of increasing the amount and availability of instructional materials, the Institute plans to prepare two textbooks, one on retirement housing management and another on

multiservice senior centers. Planning and development of the first of these is well along. It is expected to consist of two parts: Part I—The Behavioral and Environmental Factors Related to Housing the Elderly, and Part II—Organization and Administration of Old Age Homes and Retirement Housing. It is planned to include content on food and dietary management, covering such topics as organization of food service, purchasing, storage, preparation, types of service, cleanup, special diets, special events, scheduling, and concepts of nutrition.

5. *Reference and study center.* The major objective of this part of the training program is to systematize and make readily available to trainees, faculty, other researchers, and community planners the extensive collection of gerontological and related social and biomedical materials already collected.

## CONCLUSION

The growth of the older population and the increasing numbers of programs to serve them have focused attention on the need for trained persons in the field of aging. The supply of persons, qualified by training and experience, for careers in the field is pitifully short, despite the early warnings of leading gerontologists who have been proclaiming the need for two or more decades. Their efforts, however, were not in vain. The body of emerging knowledge has been organized as instructional content by persons knowledgeable in the field. The Congress has increasingly recognized the need for training programs in aging and has supported them through appropriations for Title V of the Older Americans Act. As a result, sound programs are growing in strength and maturity and are using varied approaches as this chapter has suggested.

Although much remains to be done, the total picture is encouraging. As Clark Tibbitts, Director of Training Grants in the Administration on Aging said in a recent speech before the annual scientific meeting of the Gerontological Society, Inc., "Education and training in gerontology is emerging from the foot-in-door stage. It is now beginning to reveal its stature as a commanding presence in some of the most respectable institutions of learning." [28]

## REFERENCES

1. Kleemeier, Robert W., and Birren, James E.: Society and the study of aging. In *Graduate Education in Aging within the Social Sciences.*

Kushner, Rose E., and Bunch, Marion E. (Eds.), Ann Arbor, U. of Mich., Division of Gerontology, 1967, pp. 9-10.

2. DONAHUE, WILMA: Development and current status of university instruction in social gerontology. *Ibid.*, pp. 76-101.
3. White House Conference on Aging: *Background Paper on Role and Training of Professional Personnel.* Washington, D.C., May 1960, pp. 137-140. (Out of print).
4. *Ibid.*, p. 40.
5. *Older Americans Act.* P.L. 89-73, sec. 501-502, 89th Congress, 1st Session, 1965.
6. *Ibid.*, sec. 301-305.
7. Training grants of the administration on aging. *Federal Financial Assistance for Projects in Aging.* Administration on Aging Publication No. 709, Washington, D.C., U.S. Department of Health, Education, and Welfare, 1967.
8. SMYTH, VIRGINIA M., and COLE, W. E.: *A Pilot Survey of Personnel Training Needs in the Field of Aging,* U.S. Department of Health, Education, and Welfare, Office of Aging, Atlanta Regional Office, Atlanta, Georgia, 1963.
9. Older Americans Act Amendments of 1967, P.L. 90-42, 90th Congress, 1st Session, 1967.
10. FLINT, HELEN M.: *Guide Specifications for Positions in Aging at State and Local Levels.* Administration on Aging, U.S. Department of Health, Education, and Welfare, Washington, D.C., U.S. Government Printing Office, 1965.
11. *Ibid.*, pp. 15.
12. *Ibid.*, pp. 47, 58.
13. *Ibid.*, pp. 39, 43.
14. *Ibid.*, pp. 25-27.
15. Anon.: *Training in Social Gerontology and Its Application.* Office of Aging, Washington, D.C., U.S. Department of Health, Education, and Welfare, Welfare Administration, 1965. (Out of print).
16. TIBBITTS, CLARK: Social gerontology in education for the professions. Kushner and Bunch (Eds.), *op. cit.*, pp. 53-64.
17. KLEEMEIER, ROBERT W.; HAVIGHURST, ROBERT J., and TIBBITTS, CLARK: Social gerontology. Kushner and Bunch (Eds.), *op. cit.*, pp. 46-52.
18. TIBBITTS, CLARK (Ed.): *Handbook of Social Gerontology.* Chicago, U. of Chicago, 1960.
19. BIRREN, JAMES E. (Ed.): *Handbook of Aging and the Individual: Psychological and Biological Aspects,* Chicago, U. of Chicago, 1960.
20. BURGESS, ERNEST W. (Ed.): *Aging in Western Societies, A Comparative Survey,* Chicago, U. of Chicago, 1960.
21. BECHILL, WILLIAM D.: The Waxter Center in National Focus. Speech presented at the Public Rally, Waxter Center for Senior Citizens, Baltimore, Maryland, Oct. 22, 1967.

22. Cohen, Wilbur D.: Brighter Horizons for the Aging. Speech presented at the dedication of the Multipurpose Senior Center, Milwaukee, Wisconsin, May 19, 1968.
23. Anon.: The role and training of professional personnel in the field of aging. In *Reports and Guidelines from the White House Conference on Aging.* No. 8, Washington, D.C., U.S. Department of Health, Education, and Welfare, 1961, pp. 8-9.
24. Tibbitts, Clark: Social gerontology in education for the professions. Kushner and Bunch (Eds.), *op. cit.,* p. 57.
25. Anon.: *Companion to An Elderly Person; A Suggested Training Program,* OE-87006, Washington, D.C., U.S. Government Printing Office, 1964.
26. Donahue, Wilma: Development and current status of university instruction in social gerontology. Kushner and Bunch (Eds.), *op. cit.,* p. 96.
27. State of Michigan House Bill 2748, April 13, 1965.
28. Tibbitts, Clark: Main Currents in Training in Aging. Speech prepared for presentation at a Fireside Meeting on Training in Psychological and Social Gerontology, Annual Scientific Meeting of the Gerontological Society, Inc., St. Petersburg, Florida, Nov. 9, 1967.

*Chapter 22*

# FUTURE DEVELOPMENTS IN AGING–PERSPECTIVES

ARNOLD M. ROSE

THE ELDERLY have always been part of society, and debilities and handicaps have always characterized them, but they have only recently been considered a social problem. This recent shift in attitude toward the aging has two sets of causes: (1) Changing objective conditions affecting the aging have made their debilities and handicaps both more severe and more salient. (2) The public has recently come to recognize that it is possible and feasible to alleviate some of the difficulties facing the elderly. These two sets of social changes will be the subject of our analysis, and the basis of our perspectives into the future. Together they make of aging, a contemporary social problem, for the latter is generally defined as

> a situation affecting a significant number of people that is believed by them and/or by a significant number of others in the society to be a source of difficulty or unhappiness, and one that is considered to be capable of amelioration.[1]

While population statistics for earlier periods of history are generally faulty, it is likely that the proportion of the elderly—defined as those over 65 years of age—did not vary significantly from the figure of 4.1 per cent which was found for them in the year 1900 in the United States. But from that year until the present, the elderly have formed a steadily increasing percentage of the population; in 1960 they accounted for 9.3 per cent of the population. Thus, the elderly are relatively more than twice as numerous as they were 60 years ago—twice as salient.

One major reason for this change, of course, is that there has been a major improvement in medical knowledge and preventive medicine. One category of diseases—the acute, infectious illnesses—have been virtually wiped out as a cause of death. This has led to a new problem of medical care for the elderly. They now usually survive the infectious diseases to acquire the chronic diseases—the deadly heart diseases and the cancers, as well as the handicapping arthritis and rheumatism—all of which cost much more in medical care, in nursing care and hospitalization. Whereas one formerly typically died of influenza or pneumonia after only a week or two of illness, and it was relatively inexpensive to die, today there are usually expensive and long-drawn-out medical costs attached to both living and dying as an elderly person. In the National Health Survey of July, 1959 to June, 1960, it was found that 77 per cent of the elderly population had one or more chronic illnesses.[2]

In the short span of years between 1901 and 1955, according to another study, the proportion of persons over 65 years having one or more chronic diseases rose from 46 per cent to over 81 per cent.[3] At about the same time, the costs of medical care rose with extraordinary sharpness: Despite a half-day average reduction in the length of hospital stay, the cost of the average hospital confinement rose from $148.64 to $279.91 between 1952 and 1962, a rate of increase about six times as great as that for all other living costs.[4]

## RISING COST OF ILLNESS AND DEATH

This combination of circumstances have created one major facet of the contemporary social problem of the aging: The high cost of illness and death. It is estimated by the President's Council on Aging that, in 1961, only about 14 per cent of those past 65 years of age have total incomes of more than $3,000 a year,[5] which might reflect the minimum amount of savings large enough to permit them to pay for a year's siege of chronic illness.

Obviously only a minority of the elderly could pay for catastrophic medical care out of savings. While about half the elderly had some form of medical insurance in 1960, very few of those who had private policies found that these took care of their medical costs.[6] The cost of medical insurance rose rapidly: Between 1952 and 1962, it rose 120 per cent, which was eight times as fast as all other living costs and three times as fast as wages.[7] Further, this private insurance was not economic. The high benefits to the elderly subscribers resulted in high insurance rates for middle-aged and younger subscribers.

## Ameliorative Programs

In 1960, Congress passed the Kerr-Mills Act which compensated the states for providing medical care for those of their elderly citizens who were on public assistance, thus expanding to most of the nation what a few states—like Louisiana, Massachusetts, and Minnesota—were already doing for their elderly indigent. Most of the states were laggard, however, in adopting the second major provision of the Kerr-Mills Act—namely, to set up a new category of the "medically indigent," indigent by virtue of medical expenses only, and share with the Federal Government the medical costs for such persons.

For these reasons, there was a great national drive for "medicare" during the period 1960 to 1965: The great middle classes of the American elderly—too well-off to get on the relief rolls and too poor to have saved enough to pay for catastrophic medical costs—were not getting the benefits of modern medical care. The United States dropped to twelfth position among the nations of the world in length of life.

In 1965, after eight years of one of the most spectacular Congressional battles of the decade—in which the American Medical Association, the U. S. Chamber of Commerce, and most of the Republicans and southern Democrats were lined up against associations of the elderly, organized labor, social welfare agencies, and practically all of the northern Democrats—Congress, under the leadership of President Lyndon Johnson, passed a strong Medicare Act. It not only provided for free hospital, nursing, and most drug care for those past 65 years of age, but at the last moment, provided that the elderly could obtain physicians' and surgeons' care by voluntarily joining an insurance program at the cost of $3 a month (and the Social Security Act benefits were simultaneously raised to more than cover this).

While not all the medical care costs of all elderly citizens are yet covered—notably dental care, the cost of eyeglasses, and some periods of hospital care—the Medicare Act of 1965 went a long way to taking care of the catastrophic medical costs of all the elderly. The first year's experience indicates that the act is not being abused (perhaps because of the inclusion of a provision for minor contributory payments by the elderly) and that it has not disrupted medical services for the rest of the population—as was direfully predicted by the organized medical profession. Thus, after a huge political battle, it can be said that the medical care costs' problem has now been solved, and we can expect the aging persons' length of life to increase another half a dozen years or so, to bring it up to the top world level. There remains a need for better diagnostic and preventative health care services before the age of 65 years, and Senator Harrison Williams (Democrat, New Jersey) is leading a Congressional effort to obtain this.

## Health Habits and Life Expectancy

It is hazardous to speculate whether the "span of life" (as distinguished from the current "length of life"—now averaging about 70 years when calculated from birth) will increase in the near future. Biologists are making some spectacular experiments among some of the lower species of animals in lengthening their biological span of life, but there is no sure sign that this knowledge can be extended to man. More likely for the near future is that there will be breakthroughs in knowledge of how to prevent and cure the two great killers of old people: cancer and the heart diseases. While these chronic diseases cannot yet be "cured," they can be partly prevented and "symptom-treated" by better health habits, earlier diagnosis, more use of empirical treatments. It is not unlikely that the year 2000 will see the American length of life rise to 90 years.

Almost as dramatic in changing the lives of older Americans as the increase in their life expectancy has been the increase in compulsory and voluntary retirement from occupations. "Retirement as it is known today was relatively uncommon in 1900 and the difference between life expectancy and work life expectancy was a scant three years." [8]

## Retirement Policies and Practices

Even as recently as 1950, only eighty-three out of every one thousand men 64 years old left the labor force before they were a year older. Today the retirement rate between 64 and 65 is 234 per one thousand—nearly a three fold increase in one decade.[9]

The decline in the number of self-employed men has been a major factor in this shift: Farmers, small storekeepers, and independent artisans are far less numerous, relative to the general growth in the population, than they were just a few generations ago. Further, the industries which hire the great bulk of employed Americans have established compulsory retirement ages, for both blue-collar and white-collar workers. The drive to have a continual accession of more vigorous, more recently trained, and more efficient workers has undoubtedly been a major reason for this, but there has also been the belief that a person in his 60's has worked long enough and should have the privilege of retirement. With the increasing availability of Social Security and pensions, the elderly seem to be more willing to retire.[10] With the simultaneous improvement in the health conditions of the elderly, they are now likely to have a considerable number of years ahead of them upon retirement, during which they will be physically and mentally vigorous. The average length of life for a man who has reached 65 years today is 12.9 years, while for a woman, it is 15.9 years.[11]

While this is the length of life for the average person just retiring from a gainful occupation, the situation for the woman whose chief life roles have been those of mother and homemaker is more complicated. The average woman of today has completed the task of raising her children while she is in her mid-forties. Modern household appliances and the use of manufactured clothing and many semiprepared foods have greatly diminished the tasks of the homemaker. Thus, in a sense, the nonemployed woman reaches retirement at about the age of 45. An increasing number of these women then seek gainful employment, but not all of them find appropriate jobs.

## Social Change and Disengagement

Thus, a combination of social changes has created a situation for the aging which Ernest W. Burgess has called "the roleless role" and which Elaine Cumming calls "disengagement." While Cumming considers disengagement inevitable and desirable, a more appropriate interpretation would be that it is an unintended product of recent social changes which our culture has not yet devised means for which to compensate.[12] The retired of today, healthier and more vigorous than the retired of a generation ago, are seeking new roles, and this is a major challenge to our society. Some resist retirement from their regular occupations, but with the shortage of job opportunities today even for younger workers, they are not likely to be very successful.

## Creative Activities for the Elderly

Some older people do find marginal part-time work—in selling, babysitting, the crafts—which keeps them happily busy while it adds to their usually meager income. Much more needs to be done to develop part-time remunerative jobs, especially in the service occupations, for older people. But most older people now are searching for nonremunerative activities, and the past decade, especially, has seen a tremendous development of such activities. Some take the form of individual hobbies and "do-it-yourself" activities around the home. Still others take the form of increased participation in the regular, non-age-graded voluntary associations through the society, such as the church organizations, the social welfare organizations, political parties, and the fraternal-recreational associations of many types.[13] Younger and middle-aged people are increasingly going to see older people active in the voluntary associations, often putting their juniors to shame with their energy and their activity.

A new type of activity for the elderly is springing up which might become the characteristic solution for the increased leisure-time problem for the retired in our society. This is the association exclusively for the elderly.[14] Some of these are organized by nonelderly social workers or by welfare-minded citizens; still others are organized by the older people themselves. Some grow out of existing social structure—such as churches—while others are formed *de novo* without a parent organization. Most of them have recreational-sociable activities, but some have purposes beyond meeting the needs of the participants themselves—such as visiting the home-bound, sewing for institutions, seeking a reduced bus-fare, propagandizing for medical care for the elderly. Some of these associations have a formal structure, while others are so informal as to be nothing more than a fairly regular coming-together of congenial people. Obviously, these associations have been formed to meet a need among their elderly participants. Whether they are structured enough, or offer enough activity, to meet the need satisfactorily is something almost completely unknown, as there have been practically no evaluative studies of these associations.[15] That they should be successful is a challenge to our society.

In this time of cultural transition for the elderly, it is difficult for them to know what to do. They have to take the initiative and make major decisions for themselves when the culture does not offer clear-cut guide lines for appropriate behavior. Problems of income, employment, housing, medical care and leisure-time activities arise, toward a solution for which the elderly have no guidance in the general standards of our society. In the larger cities, social work agencies exist to provide help in the more severe cases. But the problems of most older people are not severe enough for them to be directed to the welfare agencies, or they feel they would be losing their independence if they were to go to the welfare agencies. What is needed, and now occasionally provided, is a regularly-repeated educational series of lecture-discussions on the typical problems faced by older people. Persons informed of the extensive body of gerontological research conducted during the past decade or so, and who are skilled in leading discussions, are needed to present programs in the existing neighborhood organizations for the elderly and making these programs available also to those who are not members of these organizations. Periods of rapid social change create new needs and new opportunities for adult education.

## Housing Needs and Provisions

While the health and employment changes affecting the aging have resulted from great impersonal forces impinging on the entire society, the changes in housing for the elderly are more a result of deliberate and specific planning. Of course, this is not true of the reduction of the number of farms in our society, but even many of the elderly farmers who have moved into village and town homes have done so out of their own choice. Voluntary choice has also been the major factor in the movement of a significant number of Eastern and Middle-Western retirees into states like Florida, Arizona, and California. After the migration, the dwelling places tend to be smaller than they were before the migration. Some are even trailers, hotel rooms, and small units in settlements specifically designed for the aging.

Throughout the United States, we are copying the Europeans in providing—with both private and public funds,[16] apartments and small homes designed to meet the special needs of older residents. These can be entered without climbing stairs, and, if not on ground level, are serviced with elevators (large enough, usually, to accommodate a movable bed as well as standing passengers). The hallways and rooms of these modern dwelling places are fitted with handrails or grab bars at strategic spots. The doors are opened with levers rather than knobs, to meet the needs of the arthritic. Electric wall outlets are three feet off the floor so they may be reached without bending.

The bathrooms, especially, have equipment which shows they are intended for use by the elderly; shelves and lighting fixtures can be reached without stretching or standing on ladders; faucets can be opened with levers instead of knobs, washbasins are so constructed that a wheel chair can be rolled underneath, handrails are located near the tub and toilet, the toilet is constructed with a seat three to five inches higher than standard so that less bending is required, and sometimes a sitzbath is installed instead of the ordinary tub. While many of the basic furnishings in these dwelling places are as new as the structures themselves, the inhabitants are encouraged to bring in a few items of furniture from their old homes in order to give them a feeling of continuity with their past.

Because the units are small, there are many common rooms in the complex for recreation, for entertaining, for laundry use and sometimes even for everyday eating. The complexes themselves, while inhabited exclusively by older people, are usually located in the midst of family residential areas, unless they are in the so-called retirement towns, like St. Petersburg. Generally, they are located near downtown or other shopping areas. It is evident that a great deal of thoughtful planning has gone into the location and construction of dwellings for the elderly.

But it is still only a minority of the older people who live in this modern kind of private dwelling. About 5 per cent are obliged by poor health to live in nursing homes or other kind of institution; and this proportion has been slowly growing with the increasing availability of nursing homes and the greater need for them to serve the chronically ill. Three-generation dwelling under one roof is almost as common as it ever was. But whereas it previously took the form of a younger family living in the grandfather's large home, now it is likely to be the case of a widowed grandmother added to a young family's limited quarters.[17]

The largest number of older people continue to dwell by themselves in large, old homes, in which they raised their families or could have. Such dwellings are not suited to elderly inhabitants, unless they have been converted into rooming houses and provide both income and a small modern apartment for their aging owners. The old houses are too large and too difficult to maintain for an older person or couple. They often have stairs and shelves which cannot be reached except on a ladder. Even the apartments among the older dwellings do not have equipment for the safety and convenience of elderly inhabitants. If, as usual, they are intermingled with units in which younger families dwell, the younger adults do not associate much with their aging neighbors,[18] and their children often create a nuisance with noise and thoughtless behavior from the standpoint of the older folks. It is an obvious need and challenge to our society to move older people into modern housing units particularly designed to serve their special requirements. This is actually being accomplished steadily, although some would question whether it is being done rapidly enough.

Most of the newer housing units for the elderly (privately and publicly sponsored) are being built in the central cities, which is where the elderly want them, so they may have access to the central business districts, to neighborhood shopping centers, to parks, etc. The old family homes of the elderly are also in the central cities, as are the rooming houses which attract some of the older unattached men. Very few older people move out to the suburbs, as do younger and middle-aged white people. Thus the central cities are increasingly becoming the dwelling places of ethnic minorities, and of the elderly of all groups. This is true of all the established cities, as well as of the few "retirement" cities located in warm-climate states like Florida, California, and Arizona.

The other place of concentration for the older-person dwelling is the smaller town in the farm states: The younger families are moving out of these states, while the retirees move from the farm to the nearby village or town. It is not widely known that of the ten American states with the highest proportion of older people in their populations, six are farming states in the Midwest, and three others are rural states of New England (the tenth state is Florida). These trends will continue, and older people are likely to be increasingly "segregated" in American society.

## Aging and Modified Food Habits

An often ignored problem of the elderly is that of diet. Most people as they grow sedentary do not want as much to eat. What they often do not realize is that, as they reduce the total intake, they must maintain a proper combination, especially of vitamins. Associated with the smaller appetites are lesser motivations to cook. When a woman has to cook only for herself alone, or for herself and husband only, rather than a large and growing family, she is less motivated to cook well and carefully. The older woman tends to cook in a desultory and often careless manner, which further reduces appetite.

Until recently, it was difficult to find packaged goods in grocery stores in small enough packages to make it worthwhile to purchase them for one or two persons. Much of the contents would spoil before they could be used up. Packages, like homes, were made for families. In the last decade or so, wholesalers have become aware of the one and two-person families which abound in our society, especially among the elderly, and are now increasingly producing foods in small packages. We may expect this trend to continue so that all foods will soon be available in small as well as large packages, which may motivate elderly cooks to do a better job with their *cuisines*.

## Income Dilemma of the Aged

Low income has been a chronic dilemma for the elderly, as their energy declines and their skills become outmoded. As noted, this has become accentuated by the decline in self-employment and the increase in compulsory retirement of employees. Our society has met the problem with relative directness: The Social Security retirement insurance program was inaugurated in 1935 and by now has been extended to most segments of the population. As recently as January, 1953, only 3.5 million older Americans and their dependents were collecting Social Security checks. Just ten years later—in January,

1963—12.7 million collected such payments, almost four times as many.[19] This is supplemented by the Old Age Assistance (OAA) program to meet the basic needs of the minority not covered, or insufficiently covered, by Social Security. Of those receiving old-age assistance, 43.8 per cent are also receiving Social Security benefits, but not enough to provide for their minimum cost of living.[20] That OAA does not meet the basic needs of all is shown by the fact that twenty states require a five-year residence, and three more states require between one and five years' residence, before allowing an elderly person to be eligible for OAA.[21] However, the income of the elderly is augmented by the fact that many industries have inaugurated pension programs, usually with contributions from both employers and employees.

There remain two major unsolved problems. One of the problems of the contemporary economy, especially salient since 1945, has been the steady rise in the cost of living. Income from Social Security and from private pension plans thus becomes progressively insufficient to meet even the minimum needs of the retirees. The Old Age Assistance program—based on concepts of "government relief" and the "means test"—is both an inefficient and socially unhealthy means of providing income to the elderly; it has been useful as a stopgap until the Social Security system could come into full operation and it serves as a continuing foundation program for the socially disorganized welfare client.

But the Old Age Assistance program, however, should not be used to supplement the income of a retiree who has earned his own income all of his working life because inflation has decreased the purchasing power of his life savings and his Social Security insurance. Social Security income should be shifted from fixed dollar payments to purchasing-power payments, which would require Federal Government subsidy to the program during periods of inflation. This would not only be psychologically beneficial to the retiree, but would also relieve the pressure on state and local governments now hard pressed to maintain the Old Age Assistance program and not able to benefit from inflation in the way that the Federal Government does.

The second problem of sustaining the income of the elderly also arises out of large-scale impersonal social forces which the individual worker cannot control. This is the effect on jobs of the continuing technological revolution—sometimes called "automation." The worker in manufacturing, construction, and certain clerical occupations frequently finds his employment threatened by technological improvements which increase the economic efficiency and wealth of the society as a whole. If he is past the age of about 45 years, it is seldom economically worthwhile to retrain him for the new positions in automated industries.

In a small way, our Government has embarked on programs to accommodate such displaced workers in service occupations with low skill requirements, and has lowered the age at which Social Security payments may begin. But these efforts fail to meet the employment needs of the older worker displaced by automation and of the retiree who begins his Social Security benefits after a period of unemployment which resulted from no inadequacy on his part. This is a large part of the major challenge to our society to adjust to the disruptions created by technological progress.

## CHANGING PUBLIC IMAGE OF AGING

Thus far, we have examined the many objective social changes affecting the aging which have made their natural debilities and handicaps more severe and more salient, and which provide challenges to a civilized society to make the organized and rational action necessary to alleviate the additional hardships created for the elderly by these changes. We shall now turn to some more speculative observations about the changing public image of the aging in American society, both on the part of the aging themselves and on the part of the less-elderly public. Generally speaking, the culture of the United States has put a very low value on aging. Until very recently, no privileges or titles of honor were conferred on the elderly because of their age, as has been true of many other cultures. The aging have not been assumed to have special wisdom or other admired characteristics, but, on the contrary, are widely considered to be "old-fashioned" and to have other undesirable characteristics.

Ours is a youth-centered society, in which the aged are an anti-model. In addition to the natural debilities and objective deprivations of old age, the elderly have had to suffer neglect and negative regard.

Many have tried to avoid acknowledging their age, at least until they have achieved some remarkable age such as 90 years, and the word "aged" has not been considered a polite appelation.

There are, however, some evidences now that this is changing. Since the 1930's, the Government has been paying attention to the economic needs of the aging, since the 1950's to their housing needs, and since 1960 to their medical needs. Especially since 1950, churches, private voluntary associations, and social welfare agencies have been giving attention to the recreational, educational, and sociable needs of the aging. A great number of conferences, lectures, and discussions are being devoted to the problems of the aging. The private citizen is being urged to pay more attention to the elderly, and to perform little services for them, such as driving them to meetings. Politicians are paying more attention to the large number of elderly voters (estimated at 17 per cent of the national electorate). Thus, there is evidence that the United States is becoming more "aging conscious," and is less inclined to ignore the elderly even if it does not evaluate them highly.

## Emerging Aging Group Consciousness

Among the elderly themselves there seems also to be a change in self-image. Perhaps as a result of all the public attention to their problems, they are beginning to become aware of themselves as a group. They are starting to think of their problems less in individual terms and more in collective terms. Those who are taking advantage of the new opportunities to meet together show some interest in protesting against some of the discriminations under which the elderly have long lived and in taking positive action to reduce their handicaps. They show more of a tendency to share each other's company—to have more age-graded social relations—and to exhibit pride in such achievements as hobbies and performances of skill (for example, the "life begins at 80" activities). There are some among them who are urging the elderly to use their significant voting power to gain political benefits for the elderly as a group. In sum, there is evidence of a nascent "aging group consciousness" among the elderly.

If both these phenomena—the "aging consciousness" in the general public and the "aging group consciousness" among the elderly themselves—should grow to significant proportions, American culture will be significantly changed. Already there is considerable evidence of an "aging subculture" growing among the elderly, regardless of their consciousness of it. New values concerning social status, personal worth, sex, interpersonal relations, and other important aspects of life, are emerging among the elderly. Especially as a result of their growing numbers and salience, this is bound to have some impact on general American life.

It is evident that we are living in a period of great social change for the elderly, and that this will offer new opportunities and new challenges to American society which are not yet clear.

## REFERENCES

1. Rose, Arnold M.: *Sociology: The Study of Human Relations,* 2nd ed., New York, Knopf, 1965, p. 577.
2. U. S. National Health Survey, Series B, No. 31, Table 2.
3. Metropolitan Life Insurance Company. Major aspects of american morbidity. *Statist Bull Metrop Life Ins Co, 41*:1-3, 1960.
4. Martin E. Segal Company: *The Machinist.* Nov. 7, 1963, p. 3.
5. President's Council on Aging: *The Older American.* Washington, D.C., U.S. Government Printing Office, 1963, p. 9.
6. U. S. Senate Special Committee on the Aging: *Annual Reports, 1960.* Washington, D.C., U.S. Government Printing Office, 1961, *et seq.*
7. Segal, *op. cit.*
8. U.S. Department of Labor: *Manpower Report No. 8, The Length of Working Life for Males, 1900-60.* Washington, D.C., July 1963, pp. 7-8.
9. *Ibid.,* pp. 11-12.
10. Ohrbach, Harold: Social and Institutional Aspects of Industrial Workers Retirement Pattern. Unpublished paper presented to the International Gerontological Seminar, August 6-9, 1963.
11. Metropolitan Life Insurance Company. *Statist Bull Metrop Life Ins Co, 44*:2, 1963. (These figures are for whites only. For non-whites in the United States, the expectation of life at 65 years is 12.7 years for males and 15.2 years for females.)
12. Rose, Arnold M.: A current theoretical issue in social gerontology. *Gerontologist, 4*:46-50, 1964.
13. Rose, Arnold M.: The impact of aging on voluntary associations. In *Handbook of Social Gerontology.* Tibbitts, Clark (Ed.), Chicago, U. of Chicago, 1960, pp. 666-697.
14. Rose, Arnold M.: The subculture of the aging: a topic for sociological research. *Gerontologist, 11*:123-127, Sept. 1962.
15. Rose, Arnold M.: Group consciousness among the aging. In *The Aging and their Social World.* Rose, A. M., and Peterson, W. A. (Eds.), Philadelphia, Davis, 1965, chap. 2.

16. President's Council on Aging, *op. cit.,* p. 44. Publicly-aided housing for the elderly got under way after 1956; by 1962, $550 million dollars was spent by the federal government for this purpose.
17. MATHIASEN, GENEVA: A New Look at the Three-Generation Family. Unpublished paper presented at the 87th Annual Forum, National Conference on Social Welfare, June 1960.
18. ROSOW, IRVING: Local Concentration and Social Contacts of Older People. Unpublished paper read at Sixth International Congress of Gerontology, Copenhagen, August 1963.
19. President's Council on Aging, *op. cit.,* p. 43.
20. U.S. Department of Health, Education and Welfare: *Aging,* Jan. 1964, No. 111, p. 28.
21. *Ibid.,* p. 46.

# BIOGRAPHICAL SKETCHES

**Patricia S. Aughenbaugh,** B.A. (College of William and Mary)
Special training in organic chemistry and physiology, Johns Hopkins University and University School of Medicine, Baltimore, Maryland. Research Associate, National Institutes of Health. Areas of research: rat heart-lung preparations and heart function in association with the aging process; aging and nutrition; and obesity. High school valedictorian and college honor student. Co-author of "Aging and the Functional Capacity of the Rat Heart-Lung Preparation," with N. Solomon, R.I. Gregerman, and N.W. Shock, *The Gerontologist, 5*:39, 1965.

**Leonard Z. Breen,** Ph.D. (University of Chicago)
Professor and Head, Department of Sociology, Purdue University. Articles published on various aspects of aging in professional journals including *Sociology and Social Research, Geriatrics, Nursing Homes, Journal of Gerontology, Journal of Social Studies* and *Journal of Home Economics.* Contributed chapter in *Handbook of Social Gerontology* and co-authored "Pre-Retirement Education Among Labor Unions," a monograph published by the National Institute of Labor Education. As visiting Professor of Sociology at the Indian Institute of Technology, Kanpur, U.P. India, was responsible for development of a Division of Social Sciences at the Institute and for conducting research on aging and on urbanization and industrialization in India.

**Austin B. Chinn,** M.D. (University of Virginia)
Director, University of Southern California Rehabilitation Research Center. Medical Consultant, U.S. Senate Special Committee on Aging. Former Chief, Gerontology Branch, Division of Chronic Diseases, U.S. Public Health Service. Associate Editor for *Clinical Medicine, Journal of Gerontology.* Principal investigator: "An Integrated Interdisciplinary Program of Research in Aging." Medical practice in Washington, D.C., and Cleveland. Member of School of Medicine Faculty of George Washington University and Western Reserve University. Chairman, Western Reserve University Commit-

tee on Aging Research, Dirctor of University Teaching Program in Comprehensive Health Services, and Associate Dean of the Medical School. Ohio State Delegate to White House Conference on Aging. Active duty, U.S. Army. EOD, Major; RAD, Lt. Col.

**Donald O. Cowgill,** Ph.D. (University of Pennsylvania)
Professor of Sociology, University of Missouri. Past President, Midwest Sociological Society, Midwest Council for Social Research on Aging and the Kansas Council on Aging. Consultant, Golden Anniversary White House Conference on Children and Youth, 1960. Delegate, First National Conference on Aging, 1950, and the White House Conference on Aging, 1961. Fellow, Midwest Council for Social Research on Aging and the Inter-university Institute on Social Gerontology, University of California. Fulbright lecturer, Chiengmai University, Chiengmai, Thailand, and visiting professor, Mindolo Ecumenical Center, Kitwe, Zambia. Author of over thirty-five articles in professional journals and chapters in two books. Recipient of Distinguished Alumnus Award, Park College.

**Carl Eisdorfer,** Ph.D. (New York University), M.D. (Duke University)
Associate Professor of Medical Psychology and Psychiatry, and Director of Training and Research Coordinator, Center for the Study of Aging and Human Development, Duke University. Fellow, American Psychological Association, Gerontological Society, American Geriatrics Society, and North Carolina Psychological Association. Consultantships include National Institutes of Health, Children's Hospital of Washington, D.C., Peace Corps, North Carolina State Board of Health, and Veterans Administration Hospital. Numerous committee memberships, chairmanships and other services in professional organizations. Recipient of research grants and author of many articles in professional journals. Affiliations include American Federation for Clinical Research, Society for Psychophysiological Research and the Society for Research in Child Development.

**Helen M. Flint,** Ed. D. (George Washington University)
Director, Training and Education Developments Division, U.S. Navy Personnel Research Laboratory. Former Senior Training Project Specialist (or training grants program under Title V, Older Americans

Act), Department of Health, Education and Welfare. Prior appointments in government as educational specialist with Department of Defense involving experience with private industry and universities in planning and administering training programs, writing textbooks in management and personnel administration, and developing curricula, instructors' guides and correspondence courses. Author of a number of publications in the field of aging including "Guide Specifications for Positions in Aging at State and Local Levels: Federal Financial Assistance for Projects in Aging," and "Planning for Retirement: A University-Labor Union Program." Affiliations include Adult Education Association of the U.S.A., Gerontological Society, American Educational Research Association and the American Society for Training Directors.

**Joe Bales Graber,** M.P.H. (Yale University)

Assistant to the Assistant Director for Liaison, National Center for Health Services Research and Development, Health Services and Mental Health Administration, Department of Health, Education and Welfare. Prior appointments in government include Special Assistant to the Director, Bureau of Disease Prevention and Environmental Control; Assistant to the Chief, Office of Aging, Office of the Chief, Bureau of State Services; Liaison Officer, Gerontology Branch, Division of Chronic Diseases, Bureau of State Services; Special Assistant for Heart, Cancer and Stroke, Office of the Chief, Division of Chronic Diseases, Bureau of State Services. Publications include articles in *Public Health Reports, Gerontologist, American Journal of Public Health, Nation's Health* and the Proceedings of the 1966 International Congress of Gerontology. Affiliations include Gerontological Society (Fellow), American Public Health Association, American Public Welfare Association, Society of Public Health Educators and American Medical Writers' Association.

**Robert J. Havighurst,** Ph.D. (Ohio State University)

Professor of Education and Human Development, Department of Education, University of Chicago. Director, General Education Board, Rockefeller Foundation, 1937. Staff member of first UNESCO Seminar on Education in Paris. Participated in Rockefeller Foundation work in education and social rehabilitation of central Europe, 1947. Fulbright Professor of Education, University of New Zealand.

UNESCO assignment as Co-director of Brazilian Government Center for Educational Research. Conducted Research Seminar in Sociology of Adolescence at University of Buenos Aires as Fulbright Professor. Past President, Gerontological Society and Division of Maturity and Old Age, American Psychological Association. Engaged in a variety of advisory, consultative and leadership roles both here and abroad for national organizations in education and the social sciences and for governments in many areas of education including juvenile delinquency and gifted children. Represented the Gerontological Society at hearings on the proposed Institute of Child Health and Human Development. Co-author of twenty-five books in many areas of education, the social sciences and research. Affiliations include leading scientific and educational organizations.

**Adeline M. Hoffman,** Ph.D. (Pennsylvania State University)
Professor, Department of Home Economics and affiliate staff member, Institute of Gerontology, University of Iowa. Clothing specialist, Defense Welfare Services, Department of Health, Education and Welfare, 1956-57, and consultant, 1963. Co-director, Workshop on Social Gerontology for Home Economists, University of Iowa, and lecturer, Workshop on Home Economics Curriculum Development on Aging, University of Southwestern Louisiana. Visiting professor, University of Maryland. Contributor to "Emergency Welfare Services Manual," Department of Health, Education and Welfare. Author and co-author of articles in field of Gerontology in *Journal of Home Economics* and *Adding Life to Years.* Author of chapter on "Social and Therapeutic Values of Clothing" in *Nursing and Retirement Home Administration.* Affiliations include Gerontological Society, Midwest Council for Social Research on Aging, American Home Economics Association and American Dietetic Association. Recipient of Women's Centennial Honor Award, University of Missouri.

**Frank Itzin,** M.A. (University of Chicago)
Professor, Jane Addams Graduate School of Social Work, University of Illinois. Fulbright lecturer, University College of South Wales and Monmouthshire. Appeared on programs of thirteen short courses, institutes, workshops and staff development activities and gave papers and lectures at twelve conferences including five in England and Wales. Held offices and chairmanships in many professional organi-

zations, and served on the Board of Directors, Iowa Welfare Association. Recipient of Award of Distinction for service to public welfare, 1963. Author or co-author of fourteen articles in professional publications including two in the *British Journal of Psychiatric Social Work.*

**H. Lee Jacobs,** Ph.D. (University of Iowa)
Associate Professor, Institute of Gerontology, University of Iowa, Fellow, Gerontological Society. Other affiliations include Adult Education Association of the U.S.A. and National Council on Family Relations. Past President, Iowa Council on Family Relations. Board of Directors and consultant, Iowa Town-Country Community Fellowship. Board of Directors, Chicago Theological Seminary. Coordinator, five-week courses for nursing and retirement home administrators, conference on The Older Person in the Family, and University of Iowa Conference on Gerontology: "Education for Aging, A Necessity for the Middle and Later Years." Special consultant on problems of aging and the aged for educational institutions including University of Minnesota, Culver Stockton College, Iowa Wesleyan College, William Penn College, Iowa State University, North Dakota State University and Gustavus Adolphus College. Other consultantships include Division of Adult Education Programs in Office of Education, American College of Nursing Home Administrators, Senior Adult Camps, and Workshop on Work with Older Adults. Publications include articles in professional journals and monographs. Co-editor of *Nursing and Retirement Home Administration.*

**Jerome Kaplan,** Ph.D., (University of Minnesota)
Executive Director, Mansfield Memorial Homes, Inc., and Senior Member and Resident Sociologist, Department of Sociology, Mansfield Campus, Ohio State University. Publications include three books and seventy-six professional and scientific journal articles. Fellow, Gerontological Society and Royal Society of Health (England). Editorships include Associate Editor for *Social Welfare Research, The Gerontologist;* Consulting Editor, *Nursing Homes;* Editorial Board, *Geriatrics;* Advisory Editor, *International Survey of Gerontology,* and Abstract Writer, *Excerpta Medica.* Designed, developed and completed twenty research projects. Consultant to the U.S. Senate Subcommittee on Problems of the Aged and Aging, and to four state groups. Has held many offices and chairmanships in professional organizations.

**David O. Moberg,** Ph.D. (University of Minnesota)
Professor and Chairman, Department of Sociology, Marquette University. Fulbright Professor of Sociology, State University of Groningen, The Netherlands, and Senior Fulbright Lecturer in Sociology of Religion, Munster University, West Germany. Author of two books, co-author of one, and contributor of many articles to professional journals. Fellow, American Sociological Association, Gerontological Society, Religious Research Association and American Scientific Affiliation. Other memberships include Midwest Sociological Society, Midwest Council for Social Research in Aging, Minnesota Conference on Social Work Education, and the Society for the Scientific Study of Religion.

**Woodrow W. Morris,** Ph.D. (University of Michigan)
Director, Institute of Gerontology and Associate Dean, College of Medicine, University of Iowa. Fellow, Gerontological Society. Member, National Advisory Committee, White House Conference on Aging. Vice-chairman, Iowa Commission on Aging. Vice-chairman, Committee on Aging, Comprehensive Mental Health Plan in Iowa. Board of Trustees, Methwick Manor and Mayflower Home Corporation. Board of Directors, School of Religion, University of Iowa. Chairman, Great Plains Regional Group on Student Affairs, Association of American Medical Colleges. Medical College Administration Test Advisory Committee, Association of American Medical Colleges. Cited by Iowa Nursing Home Association for contributions to the field of aging and as originator of education programs for nursing home administrators, and recipient of "Better Life Award." Author of approximately twenty articles on aging, psychology and medical education and co-editor, *Nursing and Retirement Home Administration.*

**William E. Oriol,** B.A. (New York University)
Staff Director, U.S. Senate Special Committee on Aging. Came to Washington, D.C. in 1959 as assistant to Senator Harrison A. Williams of New Jersey and served on the Committee since 1963. Before coming to Washington, was feature and political reporter for *Bergen Evening Record,* a daily newspaper in northern New Jersey.

**Margaret O. Osborn,** Ph.D. (University of Iowa)
Associate Professor, Department of Home Economics, University of

Iowa. Fellow, Nutrition Section, American Public Health Association; certified as Specialist in Human Nutrition, American Board of Nutrition. Past President, Iowa Dietetic Association. Affiliations include American Association of Dental Schools, American Home Economics Association, American Dietetic Association, and five national honor societies in home economics, science and education. National President, Omicron Nu. Sixteen research reports authored or co-authored.

**Edith G. Robins,** B.A. (Boston University)
Information Officer, Public Health Service with specialty in Adult Health Protection and Aging activities since 1961. Consultant to U.S. Senate Special Committee on Aging, 1959 to 1961. Former Information Officer, National Institutes of Mental Health Service and Division of Hospital and Medical Facilities. Free-lance writer in fields of health and social welfare—articles in *Journal of National Education Association, Look, Parade* and *Good Housekeeping.* Author of book *Social and Medical Aspects of Poliomyelitis* for the Public Health Service and National Foundation for Infantile Paralysis.

**Arnold M. Rose,** Ph.D. (University of Chicago)
Professor of Sociology, University of Minnesota. Devoted himself to the application of sociological theory to race relations, old age, mental health and politics. Past President, Society for the Study of Social Problems, and Midwest Sociological Society. Served a term in Minnesota Legislature, was a member of the National Advisory Committee on Housing for Senior Citizens, and a consultant to the Minnesota Youth Conservation Commission and to the National Institute of Child Health and Human Development. Was Fulbright research scholar in France and Fulbright professor in Italy. At time of his death (January 1968), was President-elect, American Sociological Association. Best known writings include five books, last of which is *The Power Structure,* which was recommended for a Pulitzer Prize.

**John R. Schmidhauser,** Ph.D. (University of Virginia)
Professor of Political Science, University of Iowa. Faculty affiliation from 1954 to date with exception of 1959 to 1960 as Research Fellow,

University of Chicago Law School and 1965 to 1966 as Congressman, First District of Iowa, 89th Congress. Scholastic honors include Phi Beta Kappa and Phi Kappa Phi. Held Du Pont Scholarship at University of Virginia. Author of fifteen articles and three books—*The Role of the Supreme Court in Federal-State Relations 1789-1857, The Supreme Court: Its Politics, Personalities and Procedures, and Constitutional Law in the Political Process.* Professional affiliations include American Political Science Association and American Civil Liberties Union.

**Nathan W. Shock,** Ph.D. (University of Chicago), D.Sc. (Hon.) (Purdue University)
Chief, Gerontology Branch, National Heart Institute, National Institutes of Health, Bethesda, Maryland, and the Baltimore City Hospitals, Baltimore, Maryland. Past President, Gerontological Society and Division 20 of American Psychological Association, and President-elect, International Association of Gerontology. Editor-in-Chief, *Journal of Gerontology.* Chairman, American Division, International Association of Gerontological Societies. Honorary member, Socidad Argentina de Gerontologia y Geriatria and British Society for Research on Aging. Recipient of many awards and citations including First Annual Award for Meritorious Contributions to Research by the Gerontological Society, Willard O. Thompson Award of the American Geriatrics Society, Modern Medicine Award, Superior Service Award of the Department of Health, Education and Welfare, Citation for Service to Research Committee, American Heart Association, and Citation for Service, American Association for Retired Persons. Fellow, Gerontological Society and American Heart Association. Has published widely and held numerous offices, chairmanships and editorships in professional organizations with which he is affiliated.

**Anthony V. Sinicropi,** Ph.D. (University of Iowa)
Associate Professor and Associate Director, Center for Labor and Management, College of Business Administration, University of Iowa. Primary responsibility for the development, administration and instruction in labor education programs, including research and materials development. Consultant to business and labor on personnel and industrial relations. Guest lecturer at five midwest universities.

Publications include monographs and articles in professional journals. Vice-president, University Labor Education Association; panel member, Federal Mediation and Conciliation Service and American Arbitration Association. Other affiliations include Industrial Relations Research Association and American Economic Association.

**Neill Solomon,** M.D. (Western Reserve University), Ph.D. (University of Maryland)

Assistant Professor of Medicine and Associate Professor of Physiology, School of Medicine, University of Maryland. Assistant Chief of Medicine, Baltimore City Hospitals, Baltimore, Maryland. Endocrinology Consultant to Gerontological Branch, National Institutes of Health. Lecturer at medical conferences in United States, Denmark, Scotland, and Russia. Chairman, Committee on Medical Education, Western Research University School of Medicine. Co-author of twenty-two publications in professional journals in the field of medicine and gerontology. Fellow of Arthritis and Rheumatism Foundation. Recipient of the Arron Brown Scholastic Prize (National Phi Delta Epsilon); Lederle Award, American Geriatric Society; and the Schwentker Award, the Johns Hopkins Hospital.

**Ada Barnett Stough**

Program Policy Staff, Administration on Aging. Assists in devolopment of policy and coordination of programs on aging in various government departments and establishes and maintains effective liaison between the Administration and national voluntary and religious organizations. Served for ten years as executive director of the American Parents Committee, Inc., where her special concern was federal legislation affecting the health, education and welfare of children.

**Marvin B. Sussman,** Ph.D.

Professor and Chairman, Department of Sociology, Case Western Reserve University. Past President of Ohio Valley Sociological Society, Society for the Study of Social Problems, Northeast Ohio Rehabilitation Association and Ohio Council on Family Relations. Editor, *Journal of Marriage and the Family,* and *Source Book of Marriage and the Family.* Past editor, *Community Structure Analysis* and

*Sociology and Rehabilitation*. Has published over sixty papers and co-authored three books. Consultant to Rehabilitation Services Administration and member of research grants panels since 1961.

**Walter K. Vivrett,** M.A. (Massachusetts Institute of Technology)
Professor of Architecture and Planning, Project Director, Minnesota Experimental City, and Director of Graduate Studies in Architecture and Planning, University of Minnesota. Consultant, Housing and Home Finance Agency, Washington, D.C. Architect Consultant, Public Housing Administration, Washington, D.C. Co-director, Institute in Residential Rehabilitation, Minneapolis. Director, Planning Study of Housing and Care Facilities for the Aging, St. Paul, Minnesota. Chairman, Council on Aging, State of Minnesota. Publications include "Designing a Retirement Village," chapter in *A Handbook on Retirement Villages;* "Housing and Community Settings for Older People," chapter in *A Handbook for Social Gerontology,* and articles in professional journals.

**Frances L. Wilkis,** M.A. (University of Mississippi)
Research Associate in Medical Psychology, Center for Study of Aging and Human Development, Duke University Medical Center. Member, Southeastern Psychology Association and Gerontological Society. Co-author of seven papers.

# NAME INDEX

# SUBJECT INDEX

## D

## I

## Y

[redacted]